CURIOSITY

Charles Enslen, "What happened to this eight-foot high, fourteen-ounce figure on 12 July 1784 at the Citadelle de la Ville de Strasbourg." By permission of the British Library

CURIOSITY

A CULTURAL HISTORY
OF EARLY MODERN INQUIRY

Barbara M. Benedict

THE UNIVERSITY OF CHICAGO PRESS
CHICAGO AND LONDON

Barbara M. Benedict is professor of English at Trinity College. She is the author of *Making the Modern Reader* and *Framing Feeling*.

The University of Chicago Press, Chicago 60637
The University of Chicago Press, Ltd., London
© 2001 by The University of Chicago
All rights reserved. Published 2001
Printed in the United States of America

10 09 08 07 06 05 04 03 02 01   1 2 3 4 5

ISBN (cloth): 0-226-04263-4

Library of Congress Cataloging-in-Publication Data

Benedict, Barbara M.
    Curiosity : a cultural history of early modern inquiry / Barbara M. Benedict.
        p.   cm.
    Includes bibliographical references and index.
    ISBN 0-226-04263-4 (alk paper)
    1. English literature—18th century—History and criticism.   2. Curiosities and wonders in literature.   3. English literature—Early modern, 1500–1700—History and criticism.   4. English literature—19th century—History and criticism.   5. Literature and science—Great Britain—History.   6. Literature and society—Great Britain—History.   7. Collectors and collecting in literature.   8. Curiosity in literature.   9. Monsters in literature.   10. Museums in literature.   I. Title.
    PR448.C87 B46   2001
    820.9′353—dc21   00-009934

CONTENTS

ILLUSTRATIONS

ACKNOWLEDGMENTS

For assistance in this project, I am very grateful to the National Endowment for the Humanities for a year-long fellowship, to Trinity College for a faculty research grant, and to the American Society for Eighteenth-Century Studies, the Clark Library, and the Harry Ransom Humanities Research Center for research fellowships. Earlier versions of parts of the introduction and chapters 1, 2, and 5 appear in my article "European Monsters through English Eyes: Eighteenth-Century Cultural Icons," in *Symbolism* (forthcoming). A version of part of chapter 3 has been published as "The Curious Genre: Female Inquiry in Amatory Fiction" in *Studies in the Novel* 30, no. 2 (summer 1998), 194–209; and a version of part of chapter 5 has appeared in *Women, Revolution, and the Novels of the 1790s,* edited by Linda Lang-Peralta (Ann Arbor: Michigan State University Press, 1999).

My thanks also go to the library staff at the Clark Library, the British Library, the Harry Ransom Humanities Research Center and the Harry Ransom Center Art Collection, and especially to Pat Bunker and the other research librarians at Trinity College: Rebecca Wondriska, Mary Ann Trendowski, Susan Gilroy, and Janice Arlington, and to David Toole, my energetic copy editor. For inspiration and encouragement, I am also deeply grateful to numerous colleagues, particularly Paul Hunter, Claude Rawson, Kathy King, Todd Gilman, Judith Hawley, Jay Tribby, and Fred Pfeil. My thanks also go to my father, Burton Benedict, and my mother, Marion Steuber Benedict, for encouraging the most exciting kinds of curiosity. My gratitude to my husband Mark Miller for his extraordinary generosity, affection, and help is too great to express. His kindness and support is wonderful indeed.

Inspecting and Spectating: Monsters, Rarities, and Investigators

C uriosity has long been considered a virtue in Western culture. Thomas Hobbes attributes the human institutions of language, science, and religion to it, and David Hume identifies it directly as "that love of truth, which [is] the first source of all our enquiries."[1] Yet for even longer, curiosity has also been depicted as the cause of mankind's errors.[2] While much literature praises curiosity as the sign of a free intellect and society, much also, even simultaneously, despises it as the stigma of original or cultural corruption. Eve and Oedipus, Faust and Frankenstein, Lemuel Gulliver and Sherlock Holmes all pursue knowledge by empirical means: observation, experimentation, exploration. In literature, empirical investigation may define the bold explorer, the private eye, or the medical genius, but it frequently denotes naiveté, corruption, vice, or debility: the monster-seeker and the monster himself. Often, curious people also become or produce objects of curiosity.

Why? What is it that curiosity promises or threatens? Why are curious people sometimes heroized, sometimes derided, and sometimes both within the same moment of culture and within the same imaginative work? When, how, and why does the curious person become a curiosity to others? This book seeks to answer these questions by exploring the representation of curiosity, of curiosities, and of curious people in England during the era when curiosity became the trademark of progress itself.

This book, however, is not a history of science. I do not attempt here to narrate the experimental procedures of scientists in the manner of such fine studies as those by Michael Hunter, Peter Dear, Steven Shapin, and Simon Schaffer, among others. Rather, this is a broad study of questioning in the early modern period. I analyze literary representations of the way curious people, including scientists, authors, performers, and readers, were engaged in practicing and producing curiosity itself.

By asking how a curious person becomes a curious object, this book maps the fluid exchange between agency and objectivity, curiosity and curiousness. I argue that English culture portrays curiosity as the mark of a threatening ambition, an ambition that takes the form of a perceptible violation of species and categories: an ontological transgression that is registered empirically. Curiosity is seeing your way out of your place. It is looking beyond.

In the early modern period, when curiosity rose to a peak of frenzied attention, it took on distinct historical shapes. From 1660 to 1820, scientists, journalists, women, critics, collectors, parvenu middle-class consumers, and social reformers asked questions that challenged the status quo. They inquired into forbidden topics: for example, physical generation and sex, the motion of the spheres and religion, social customs and human nature, the sources and uses of wealth, history and hierarchy. In reaction, conservative literary culture represented these queries as social or intellectual transgressions that were parallel to the physical transgressions of oddly formed people. Curious people thus appeared as monsters, "queers," and curiosities. Their violation of social roles was depicted as a physical violation of the order of being: their ambition to know, to know the hidden, and/or to know more than they were told condemned them as traitors to their own species. The curiosity of these social challengers made them curiosities themselves.

Several social practices thread through the early modern cultural history of questioning. These practices enact the social ambition behind curiosity by manifesting the interrelationship between inquiry and accumulation or collecting, known in the Renaissance as the "habit" of curiosity. Among the most prominent of these practices are gossip, an unregulated exchange of an unverified information that commodifies others; hoarding, usury, and idleness, conceived as vicious kinds of acquisition that feed off society for personal gain; occult investigation, the pursuit of prohibited information about life beyond, before, or after death; and the public assertion of a professional identity, the colonization of values by self-defined experts. As they are represented in literary culture, all of these practices become focal points for the interrogation of the social uses of inquiry and of the relationship between private profit and public gain. And historically, all of these practices stimulate the contrary reactions of applause and horror. These representations and reactions reveal, in turn, the contemporary awareness of the way these practices embody the threatening and unstable essence of inquiry itself. That essence is ambition.

Curiosity is the mark of discontent, the sign of a pursuit of something beyond what you have. In ancient literary culture, curiosity betrays the desire to know and therefore to be more than you are. Augustine associates it with a pride that turns the mind from God.[3] Early modern texts represent this desire as a passion that turns the inquirer into either a savior or a monster, for both trample the conventions of nature, culture, and society. The difference between the two possibilities relies on both the perspective of the writer and the pervious relationship between curiosity as an activity and as an identity. Are inquirers masters of their curiosity, or does their curiosity master them?

In the early modern period, the violation of what was conceived of as humanity's rightly subordinate role is registered empirically: curiosity is a transgression visually received. This ocular association reflects the interlocked meanings of the term as both an elite and intellectual "inclination to enquiry," and a mechanical carefulness associated with intricacy, novelty, and elegant workmanship.[4] Early modern literature interlaces these meanings: both the peeping Pandora and the cunning Penelope are curious maids; both the speculative scientist and the skilled watchmaker are curious men. According to such definitions, curious things or people have a great but hazardous value; their value is hazardous because they confuse distinctions between the abstract and material and they have the potential to usurp common culture with idiosyncratic concerns.

This paradoxical quality by which curiosity represents both value and valuelessness demarcates curiosities as objects without a clear use. They are ornaments selected because they look too strange to be ornamental; broken tools or implements immobilized in cabinets so that they can never be used; coins in cases or framed paper money that serve as icons outside economic circulation: things that have no function but to be looked at. People can be deemed "curious" in this sense not because they inquire but because they have socially irregular aspects: behavioral or physical traits that seem to violate accepted norms of use. Human curiosities exhibited in newspapers, ethnographical writings, and fairs, and artful or natural wonders displayed in cabinets and museums escape both the taxonomies of the spectator and the ontologies of the subject. This escape is translated as the desire to violate cultural boundaries, the ambition to replace public values with idiosyncratic meanings.

Ambiguity characterizes curiosity in all its manifestations throughout the early modern period. The expansion of curiosity from a passion to a product reflects the revolutionary shift in English society as wealth flooded in from colonies and new inventions and as all aspects of culture became subject to reification. For conservatives, curiosity retained its moral taint:

as curious people showed a perverse desire—the desire to know the forbidden—so curiosities commodified a perverse pursuit. For progressives, curiosity promised improvement. Both kinds of thinkers, however, recognized that as humanity's traditionally insatiable appetite, curiosity is always transgressive, always a sign of the rejection of the known as inadequate, incorrect, even uninteresting. Whether scientists or performers, curious people seek and manifest new realities and reshape their own identities, and their products—curiosities—incarnate these new realities and identities as examples of ontological transgression. As they acquired these new identities, curious people and curious things destabilized the categories and identities of others. These others, in reaction, excoriated curious spectators and curious spectacles as "monsters" who had crossed the conventional boundaries. Inquiring people and new products were put on the same spectrum as such traditional "monsters" as the Monk-Calf, who by apparently combining two species or bodies in one slipped out of comfortable categories. Like explorers and scientists who crossed the borders of new lands and ideas, these "monsters" crossed the borders between art and nature, animate and inanimate forms, male and female, animal and human.

This violation of convention prompted attacks on curiosity as a chase for novelty, an endorsement of meaningless innovation over tradition. In many texts and contexts, curiosity was defined as useless. Here, the individual, empirical pursuit of information was seen to challenge the social use or organization of knowledge, just as the proliferation of intricate artistry in "curious" works frittered away valuable labor. This criticism of curiosity rests upon ideals of knowledge as the means for social good and of labor as a social value.

Both proponents and denigrators of curiosity recognized it is a powerful tool for propaganda, especially through print. Religious polemicists and proponents of the New Science used it to promote piety and denigrate heresy or criticism, while to reformists, curiosity garnered a radical new valuableness precisely because of its valuelessness in a world of corrupt values. Curiosity thus signified transcendental value, a nonmaterial power whose value was proved by the very ambiguity of its social status and of its power to make the aberrant valuable.

In this capacious power to usurp meanings, co-opt categories, and overturn conventions, curiosity is imperialistic and aggressive. A product of the age of discovery, it vibrates between the spectator and the spectacle, the possessor and the possession, struggling to subsume one or the other. This mirroring quality links the inquiring or curious person with the sight or question in a way that pits them against each other. Stephen Greenblatt notes a related process in regard to the marvelous: "The marvelous functions for Columbus as the agent of conversion: a fluid mediator between outside and inside, spiritual and carnal, the realm of objects and the subjective impressions made by those objects, the recalcitrant otherness of a new world and the emotional effect aroused by that otherness. More precisely it registers the presence of Columbus's fears and desires in the very objects he perceives and conversely the presence in his discourse of a world of objects that exceed his understanding of the probable and the familiar."[5] This experience of the marvelous makes otherness a sign of God. Pious, passive, and aesthetic, wonder, like awe, reveres the novelty it encounters. Early modern curiosity, however, seeks to explain it.

Whereas wonder reciprocally compliments both the observer and the observed as spiritual vessels, curiosity arrogates the power to determine value and subordinates the observer as object. It is irreligious and proactive. In *Wonders and the Order of Nature*, Lorraine Daston and Katharine Park suggest that in the eighteenth century, curiosity moved from proximity to the passion of lust to that of greed, and they trace the class distinction between noble, hard-working curiosity and popular excitement in ignorance.[6] These distinctions illuminate part of the social context that surrounds curiosity but underrate the links between elite and ignorant curiosity: both threaten the status quo. Curiosity resists control, both as an appetite and as a material object.

Early modern literature depicts the aggression of curiosity as ambition, the desire for power over others. This desire manifests itself as an ontological transgression that usurps public space, institutions, materials, bodies, and meanings for private use. Such private use may, however, indict the public world. Sentimental heroes like the physically oversensitive Matthew Bramble are curiosities to cynical society because they possess a moral trait that condemns the unfeeling world about them. By their ontological criticism of society, such heroes become "monstrous," a term itself coined only in the eighteenth century as a colloquial intensive to mean excessive or iniquitous.[7] Like teratologically classified monsters, part of the human nature of these men of feeling has violated its boundaries and become something that conventional society deems useless, excessive, even dangerous to humanity itself.[8] Literature expresses this ontological criticism as deformity, ugliness, foreignness, or monstrosity, in that it distorts the classical symmetry that traditional early modern aesthetes, before the passion for sublime contrast, often believed defined ideal beauty.[9]

He who is deemed a monster by a monstrous society, however, may be a hero in a moral one; the power to reverse curiosity lies in the spectator.

Figure 1. George Cruikshank, "Monster discovered by the Ourang Outangs." ca. 1810. This colored engraving depicts an exhausted explorer captured and surveyed by a society of apes. By reversing the identification of monster and man, this satire suggests that context alone defines monstrosity. Courtesy of the Art Collection, the Harry Ransom Humanities Research Center, University of Texas at Austin

While conservative literature turns the inquirer into the object of inquiry, radical literature transforms curiosity into the norm. In the competition for cultural dominance, objects and subjects of curiosity wrestle to create one another (fig. 1).

The peculiar aggression of curiosity can be discerned by contrasting it with similar ideas. Notably, the term "monster," whether derived from *monstrare*, "to show," or from *monere*, "to warn," nevertheless demonstrates a passive exhibition.[10] Early modern apologists collapsed these derivations to point to monsters as evidence of God's omnipotence, since by violating the natural law of species reproduction, they demonstrated God's power over nature itself. Hence monsters were "freaks" or "sports" of nature, simultaneously metaphorical and scientific.[11] However, when disproportionate creatures were "shown" or demonstrated to an audience, they became the early modern phenomenon of a curiosity. Their strangeness existed through their impact on spectators, so that it is only in proximity to normality that a monster exists. Showmen knew this; they frequently posed

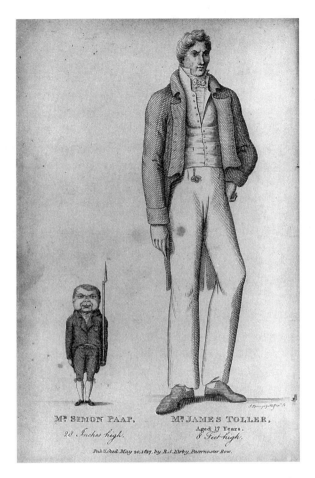

Mᴿ SIMON PAAP,   Mᴿ JAMES TOLLER,
                            Aged 17 Years.
28 Inches high.   8 Feet high.

Published May 20.1817, by R.S.Kirby, Paternoster Row.

Figure 2. Mr. Simon Paap and Mr. James Toller side by side. The contrast between an abnormally small and an abnormally large person usually implies the spectator's normality. From *Kirby's Wonderful and Eccentric Museum*, vol. 2 (20 May 1817), following p. 144. Courtesy of the Harry Ransom Humanities Research Center Library, University of Texas at Austin

giants beside dwarves to dramatize physical extremes—a practice continued by P. T. Barnum's exhibition of Tom Thumb (fig. 2).

Much of this classification of monstrosity works within the matrix of the wonderful. Early modern England was fascinated by marvels because, fusing empiricism and allegory, they seemed to reveal the secrets of the universe, particularly the source of life, the relations between species, and the logic of physical development—the subject of what we now call biological science.[12] Whether used as part of scientific reasoning or as a demonstration of God's power and mystery, these wonders offered visible clues of God or of the nature of mankind. If, however, these demonstrations of inexplicable nature were designed by entrepreneurs to promote awe, they also presented the possibility of the opposite perspective: satire. Physical deformities suggested moral degeneration; unnatural features hinted at humanity's perversion of nature. Moreover, the ancient tradition of allegorical monstrosity, strengthened by the dissemination of literary and printed information in the late seventeenth century, was persistently combating the New Science. As Barbara Maria Stafford has pointed out, no matter what the observer's specialty, "the appearance of abnormality was still described according to the hallowed Aristotelian terms of excess or defect."[13] Thus, monsters and wonders moralized science, objectified satire, and seemed to prove religion through empiricism, prompting a rich interfusion of ostensibly contradictory structures.

Curiosity, however, even while absorbing much of the discourse around monstrosity, clears out a new space. Curiosity is a historical phenomenon that crests when opportunities and commodities that encourage and manifest it crest: the late seventeenth and eighteenth centuries. These opportunities and commodities stimulate a distinctly modern pleasure in novelty and consumption that extends to a panoply of curious subjects, topics freshly open to semi-licit inquiry: nature, the supernatural, the occult, sexuality. By investigating these previously taboo topics, the modern subject walks over conventional restrictions and into a new identity in which knowledge is available and can bring the individual power. Rather than sexual discovery motivating the pleasure of curiosity, as Freudian thought suggests, it is the historical phenomenon of curiosity that sexualizes discovery. Curiosities are not considered manifestations of morality but items for pleasure and personal prestige; curiosity itself is the search for personal advancement, not for a wonderful God. Whereas ominous monsters end their long march from the distant past in early modern England, curiosity is born at this moment as the mark of the peculiarly modern identity of the solitary searcher, the inquiring everyman, the democratic detective. The curious perspective makes monsters private entertainment, not a public warning.

The selfishness of curiosity remained a sore point in the early modern period. Although writers pointed out that despite claims of disinterest someone always profits from the staging of curiosity in public spaces, whether Bartholomew Fair or the *Philosophical Transactions*, scientists averred their high motives, and many performers echoed their rhetoric. Indeed, the categories of scientist and showman blurred as many inquirers were figured as performers—like the armless and legless dwarf, Miss Sarah Beffin—who exhibited their body or mind as art or spectacle.[14] Although carnivals, shows, and fairs promised only to amuse, museums and certain public stagings of "scientific" experiments like balloon launchings claimed a didactic function. The justification for these exhibitions and experiments, however, continued to waver. Particularly in the late seventeenth century, when science was still fighting for legitimacy, and in the late eighteenth century, when it appeared to many people to have lost it, the connections between popular exhibitions and scientific experiments seemed to many satirists far closer than their differences. The claim of curiosity as disinterested science wrestled with the popular conception of it as self-indulgence throughout eighteenth-century culture.

Resonating both as an objective and a subjective characteristic, curiosity even today has a double role for questing humans. Curious spectators become simultaneously subjects and objects of inquiry. In *The Order of Things*, Michel Foucault examines this "empirico-transcendental doublet" in relation to the growth of the human sciences, one of the primary arenas in which curiosities were historically reconceived as scientific data. Foucault points out that with the rise of disciplines like biology, anthropology, economics, and the like, "man appears in his ambiguous position as an object of knowledge and as a subject that knows." Using Foucault's insight, Tony Bennett argues that man also functions both as object and subject in museum ethnography, the offspring of Renaissance curiosity cabinets.[15] As both the social scientific disciplines and museums exploit this ambiguity for purposes of social regulation, so, too, does early modern English literature. In literary and visual representations of curiosity, this doubleness of representation works to make readers both curious consumers and consumers of curiosity. Like images in a hall of mirrors replicating their reflections, curious spectators inhabit simultaneously the roles of inquirer and object of inquiry, watching themselves watching, and creating ever more curious consumers. This solipsistic aspect makes curiosity vulnerable to the host of moral charges traditionally associated with narcissism.

The charge of self-indulgence reflects resistance to the new wealth of the eighteenth century. From the late Renaissance to the nineteenth century, and particularly in the eighteenth century, the practices and objects associated with precious courtly culture became increasingly available to the middle and even laboring classes.[16] This cultural commodification made rarities common and thus emptied out much of the justificatory rationale for art. As Jürgen Habermas has argued, the commodification of art—including literature, drama, exhibitions, rare discoveries, and finely made objects—freed culture from serving as a means to stage and enforce state power and opened it as a space to be filled with individual meaning by a consuming bourgeoisie.[17] While the severance of art from court or state power legitimized individual interpretations, it also undermined the essential rationale for culture. As Tony Bennett explains, it "allowed cultural products to be made generally available . . . only by simultaneously detaching those products from their anchorage in a tradition which had previously vouchsafed their meaning."[18]

Much of the hostility that curiosity and curiosities garner in the period reflects this fundamental crack in art's meaning. Curious people—virtuosi, collectors, people with private cabinets—take valuable objects out of the sphere of public meaning and use them in their individual construction of a mirroring but independent field of power. Like the cabinets of kings, these private cabinets proclaim their owners' power to reserve objects from circulatory exchange.[19] Amateur collectors use items that publicly signify power as tokens of bourgeois leisure, thus challenging first the authority of the state and, later in history, that of professional institutions in regulating consumption and inquiry.[20] The traditional opposition between free inquiry and self-assertion, and social conformity colors the history of inquiry. Peeping Toms, human curiosities, witches, virtuosi, and curious commentators all challenge the status quo by ignoring authority and asserting their independent identity.

As the relationship of the inner elite to the outer margin of society shifts during the period, curiosity as a liminal marker shapes the creation of new literary forms. Conservative writers, in order to castigate collecting merchants, amateur scientists, would-be poets and critics, and other social upstarts for their efforts to enter elite culture, portray their acquisitions, their productions, and even their bodies as parodic wonders: grotesque phenomena outside the natural order. These attacks objectify curious people in order to enforce the otherness of what the conservatives desire to exclude. Of course, such a technique could be co-opted by the ambitious. Sentimental fictions and the early Gothic, among other genres, employ curious heroes, nonteleological cataloguing techniques, and occult or marginal topics that challenge literary convention. These genres contrive a status as secular relics that colonize the occult and validate unconventional inquiry.

The ambiguity surrounding the uses of curiosity as rebellion, revelation, and freedom partakes of the tension surrounding the larger shift in the uses of culture during the early modern period. The power of curiosities to represent value paradoxically removed from the public sphere derives from the items of cultural rarity immured in early collectors' cabinets. These items often represent fetishized labor: objects that were once designed for use are reinvented in the cabinet's space as souvenirs, art objects, or artifacts.[21] Moreover, the objects themselves often vaunt wasted work, and this waste becomes part of the power displayed in the virtuoso's collection. Just as a carved cherrystone showing a hundred facets, for example, emblematizes the elite power to command labor for no practical use, so the same object, placed in a collector's cabinet, represents the owner's power to collect labor, or to labor merely to collect, without reference to social use. This conversion of labor to entertaining display is corporealized in the carnivalesque exhibition of human curiosities. Oddly formed people whose labor was so difficult that it constituted a rarity itself, like legless dancers and armless artists, formed the basis of public circuses, where, as Robert Bogdan points out, observers could enjoy the sensation of superiority.[22]

This tradition of commodifying the body as a rarity of complicated labor drew increasing criticism. The public delight in odd sights seemed to treasure curiosity at the expense of beauty and reward laborless leisure at the expense of original work (fig. 3).[23] Being seemed to replace doing as the source of fame and fortune. To cultural critics, curiosity manifested the rejection of conventional public values, the mass taste for self-pleasing triviality and idleness, the impertinent delight in watching.

Writers exploited the equation of irregularity or unfamiliarity with uselessness, particularly in travel tales written for profit. Pilgrims, adventurers, and cultural spectators like Sir John Mandeville, Thomas Coryate, and Samuel Johnson deemed foreign customs "curious" because they violated conventions and even appeared to violate nature. These curious customs seemed at best to serve no practical, social purpose, at least none that the spectator could recognize. In order to astonish readers and increase profits, travelers manufactured curiosity by concealing the purpose and context of the wonders they reported, thus making their information strange.[24] Often, the apparent uselessness of foreign customs served to confirm the benightedness of others. For example, to intensify xenophobic curiosity, Henry Iliff energetically stirred up his readers' horrified wonder by intoning, after his description of the Sardinian penal practice of fastening the criminal to a mill wheel so that he is sliced to ribbons, "We know no such punishments in England."[25] Curiosity thus bred consumers and

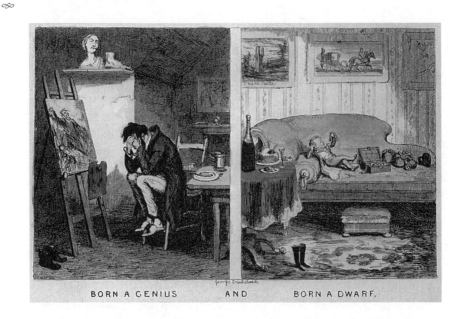

BORN A GENIUS   AND   BORN A DWARF.

Figure 3. George Cruikshank, "Born a Genius, Born a Dwarf." (Colored etching, n.d.)
This figure contrasts the poverty of creation with the luxurious idleness of the
commodified spectacle. Courtesy of the Art Collection, the Harry Ransom
Humanities Research Center, University of Texas at Austin

replicated objects for consumption. Curious tales became themselves curious items, sliding, like curious people, between the function of representing rarities and becoming one of them.[26]

This separation of a datum from any intentional narrative defines the
"facts" of modern evidence, as opposed to the procedures of ancient, Aristotelian science.[27] However, the decontextualized observation of people or
customs liberates information for private, implied narratives: "curious"
tales.[28] Such recontextualizations paradoxically link unregulated and regulated questioning, the disorder of unstructured inquiry manifested in gossip and superstition, and the formal procedures of taxonomy and science.
In early modern England, the institutions of inquiry—the Royal Society,
the press, the judiciary, literature—compete to establish procedures of investigation that guarantee truth. Each attempt to establish such procedures, however, provokes attack by questioners or advocates of other methods, or, indeed, merely provokes other questions. All these queries expose
the self-interest or ignorance in objective empiricism. Gossip, for example,
roots out the personal element that disrupts the disinterestedness of sci-

ence, and thus challenges objective methodology. Correspondingly, the individual principles that organize private eighteenth-century curiosity cabinets in which the collected items—rocks, fossils, birds' eggs, miniature carvings, coins, weapons—are arranged according to the owner's private system of classification undermine the objectivity of formal taxonomy. Thus, in the late seventeenth and eighteenth centuries, taxonomic curiosity and unlicensed questioning or peering conjoin as idiosyncratic and rebellious ways of ordering reality: classification and disorder depend upon and define each other. In the later eighteenth century, in contrast, questioning itself becomes a form of taxonomy by means of printed forms like the periodical that define how and what to ask.

Curious customs may do more than merely elude the spectator's system of use-value or proliferate valueless frivolities; they may actually reverse the rituals that make up the spectator's norm.[29] Similarly, monsters, by outraging the proportionality and order of common nature, challenge the definition of common nature itself. Peter Brooks transfers this notion to the symbolic realm when he suggests that the monstrosity in Mary Shelley's *Frankenstein* lies in the creature's violation through excess of the classification principle of language.[30] Monsters and curiosities present the possibility that no order of value can encompass all phenomena. Andrew Curran and Patrick Graille have shown that despite enlightenment efforts to contain monstrosity by systematization it remained "somewhere between the limits of empirical knowledge and the territory of fantasy." They suggest provocatively that the monster served in the enlightenment as "the anatomical corroboration of the breakdown of objective truth."[31] It is not despised monstrosity, however, but competitive curiosity that challenges objectivity, and curiosity does this by not merely rejecting but replacing conventional limits. Just as curiosity cabinets rearrange items to suit an idiosyncratic system of classification, so curious customs reorder behavior according to the specific ideas of a particular society. Such customs thus reinterpret culture, sociability, and even human nature by relative, not absolute, principles, and those who cultivate watching or admiring these customs seem to prefer disorder.[32] The license for private classification that curiosity endows perpetually undermines state attempts to regulate it as a disciplined methodology.

If wonder designates a response to the unknown, curiosity is conceived throughout English literary culture as an appetite for it. Curiosity makes monsters, or so early modern culture claimed, whether in life, the laboratory, or literature. Bordering mind and body, aggressive and fleshly yet intellectual, curiosity marks the margins between humanity's natural and

unnatural desires.[33] It thus works both to differentiate humans from monsters, and also to link them together as incarnations of forbidden appetite
(fig. 4). Throughout Europe in the early modern period, Eve's taste for the
apple is transformed into the appetite, displayed for a fee, for a host of
forbidden fruits. Even today, cannibals and "geeks," circus exhibitors who
bite off the heads of live chickens, show the natural trait of appetite gone
amok. Early showmen similarly advertise taboo gastronomic cravings. The
"good-tempered" Polish giant Charles Domery, for example, is reported
to eat raw flesh, four to five pounds of grass daily, and "in one year [to]
devour 174 cats (not their skins) dead or alive."[34] As a curiosity himself,
Gulliver likewise is exhibited as a spectacle of monstrous appetite for the
amusement of the curious Lilliputians. The connection between curiosity
and appetite is crystallized by the metaphor of consumption, whereby novelties are absorbed by the ever-hungry populace.

The curious appetite is primarily empirical. Empiricism was a rev-
olutionizing concept in the period covered by this book, as much for its
power to dress old ideas in fashionable garb as for its introduction of new
ones. Competing notions of curiosity sprang from the powerful, contemporary redefinition of reality brought about by John Locke's theories of
perceptual development in the *Essay Concerning Human Understanding*.
Written partly to confute the divisive religious enthusiasm of the English
Civil War, Locke's treatise rejected the concept of innate ideas and argued
that we learn everything we know only by sensual perception and rational
thought—since divine truth lies above (but not against) reason.[35] Informed
by this empirical philosophy and in the teeth of ancient warnings against
prying, the scientific method—investigation by disinterested observation,
analysis by trial and error, and the gradual separation of knowledge into
disciplines—was first institutionalized in 1660 with the foundation of the
Royal Society for the Improving of Natural Knowledge. At the same
time, the empirical method, however defined, was socially coded: there was
seeing and seeing—depending on where you stood. Seeing curious objects of intricate artistry or rarity was a privilege; stealing a sight at them
a crime.

This difference between honorable and criminal seeing partly reflected
traditional skepticism about the true status of the physical world. Medieval
and Renaissance natural philosophers feared that because they were untrained in philosophy, the uneducated might derive dangerous ideas from
the sight of certain things, particularly things pertaining to the guarded
areas of the occult, generation, and sexuality. Western philosophers had
long argued that seeing opens only superficial reality to the mind; it is a

Figure 4. "The capture and hanging of the 'Human Wolf.'" 1685. This very large etching
(13⅝ in. × 11⅜ in.) depicts in the background the vulpine human or humanoid
wolf killing children and animals near Onoltzbach and causing panic in the
countryside. The text explains that the monstrous wolf fell into a well while
chasing a rooster, whereupon the peasants stoned it, as shown. The central image
records the triumphant villagers punishing a creature—or a similar but human
one—by hanging it. The satirical ambiguity between man and wolf is apparent
in their physical interchangeability. Courtesy of the Art Collection, the Harry
Ransom Humanities Research Center, University of Texas at Austin

beginning, not the resolution of questions of cause and effect. Locke and Hume themselves articulated this principle by separating impressions or sensations from ideas, the aristocrats of perception. They proposed that sensations stimulate ideas, but these ideas are the transcendent solution to problematic experience. Yet, as both philosophers recognized, impressions, particularly visual ones, are forceful, whereas ideas are faint.[36] Paradoxically, under the sway of empirical science, seeing as a source of information was released from philosophical chains and did become an end in itself.

Visual delight—wonder at empirical beauty or skill—was thus an aspect of curiosity itself. This facet of curiosity as artistry flourished during the seventeenth century, particularly in the form of writing so artful that it paradoxically combined artistic representation and the symbolic representation of language. This was a novelty practiced especially on the Continent. Calligraphy that spiraled between words and figures, for example, or words in which each letter constituted a garland, cherub, or abstract pattern, used curious artfulness to make literary skill visual.[37] Micrographia was particularly popular, and it had an ancient origin: Pliny had discovered the *Iliad* written in such tiny letters that the entire epic poem fitted into a nutshell. Such artful renderings of writing blurred the margins between the pictorial and the symbolic: writing became simultaneously representational and nonrepresentational, like such sacred objects as the body of Christ or the monarch. In a parallel fashion, hieroglyphics, as both the icon and language of curiosity, symbolized the obscure and exotic Other, the remote regions of time and space. Similar forms of polygraphy, or ciphered writing, including shorthand, also had a dual function as decoration and meaning and were relatively inexpensive, unique, and easily learned.

The doubleness of cipher as both evident to the eye yet concealed from the mind reinforces its curious aspect: like microscopic or telescopic worlds, like sexuality, and like the occult, it is simultaneously seen and unseen.[38] These uses of language as decoration rather than signification enact the collector's economy, whereby the useful is rendered beautifully useless. Like items in collections, ciphered writings are secular relics of past meanings, lost time, irrecoverable importance, and thus play into the indictment of curiosity as luxurious excess.[39]

In several ways, this symbolic possession of experience through curiosity extends to time itself. Traditionally, virtuosi placed particularly high value on antiquities; coins and medals portraying rulers were especially popular as representations of past power. Charles I, a distinguished collector of art, exhibited his coins (unsuccessfully) to enforce his hereditary authority; and throughout the early modern period, the high price of the license needed to engrave images of royalty effectually limited their production—a practice that Princess Diana's estate currently seeks to revive. Since the Renaissance, many English elite had also collected autographs and holographs as relics of famous persons.[40] These precious objects, as Protestant equivalents of Catholic relics, reified the identities of the revered dead and gave timeless shape to past ideals. In the later eighteenth century, publishers exploited this custom by issuing "curious" biographies stuffed with decontextualized anecdotes of famous people. Such biographical curiosities preserve identity after death and out of time; they objectify the past into souvenirs of dead values.

Often, however, these values are not quite dead enough. Literary accounts abound of wonders, ghosts, and poltergeists who groan, knock, scratch, and boo interlopers out of the houses, or roles, that they once occupied. In the eighteenth century, such tales become published entertainment. As the famous stories of the Cock Lane Ghost and the Stokewell Wonder reach print, other tales of visits by the pious who had passed on, like Mrs. Veal, proliferate. These stories testify to the living about the reality of life after death. Despite religious promotions of these tales as proof of God's existence, in popular literature they often redress injustice by punishing interlopers. As manifestations of a rival spirituality, ghosts, like witches, push open the gates between life and death, and those that see them partake of their penetration of forbidden boundaries. These associations between the occult, the past, and curiosity infuse eighteenth-century literature, especially in the mode of the Gothic. Like those who collect relics, medals, signatures, and stories of the past, ghostly gazers possess the experience of the occult, the knowledge of life beyond death. Like virtuosi, they see beyond the visible. These curious creatures display the impious ambition to know their mortality.

Seeing rarities, occult or material, comes to represent the knowledge of the world, in the same way that Renaissance wonder cabinets displayed the universe; but in the age of exhibition seeing is not confined, as cabinets were, to the elite few. Symbolically, curiosities collected from overseas represent travel; seeing and possessing them demonstrates the knowledge of the world, particularly for those whose class and means prohibit them from travel itself. Collectors, like spectators or eyewitnesses, symbolically possess transcendent knowledge. The visual possession of curiosities either in cabinets at home or by seeing spectacles in the city endows the observer with the ownership of experience, and so with the experience of owner-ship.[41]

Although status-enhancing accumulation meant physical acquisition, it traditionally also extended to the mental possession of learning, and this forms one of the roots grounding spectatorship as an aspect of curious acquisition. From medieval times, monks and scholars were caretakers of past literature and practitioners of curious illustration. As literacy levels increased and cultural commodities burgeoned in the eighteenth century, the practice of prestigious accumulation by way of the mental acquisition of information extended to the middle classes. For these new bourgeois, publishers and promoters selected and packaged symbolic curiosities of language, literature, and biography into literary cabinets. Some people preferred to collect language themselves, like the author of the broadside "To the Curious," which lists 480 ways to spell the word scissors.[42] Most people, however, at least by the mid-eighteenth century, relied on the new, self-defined experts in culture: publishing critics like Oliver Goldsmith, Samuel Johnson, and Bonnell Thornton who presented themselves as literary connoisseurs. These professionals, in differentiating between valuable and worthless texts and topics for inquiry, defined the margin between the literary curiosity and high literature.

Early modern culture teases out the ambition in curious people and ridicules or reveres it as a rejection of social identity. Curious men—scientists, journalists, critics—are often depicted either as bourgeois, amateur collectors whose acquisitiveness is a feeble compensation for their sexual and social inadequacies, or as virile explorers boldly going where no man has gone before. Women, servants, laborers, and marginalized people like children and foreigners who collect, quest, or question usually appear as agents of pride, the central vice of mankind's fallen nature; their curiosity constitutes an attempt to poach the status of their social superiors. In satires that derive their idea of curiosity from biblical exhortations against the "lust of the eyes" and the "Athenian itch" to know more than God permits, curiosity is the mark of an upstart. Like Pandora, Oedipus, and Eve, these literary characters usurp God by seeking forbidden knowledge. People want to wonder, and it was feared this might make them want to wander. In contrast, works that use marginalized characters to celebrate curiosity are almost inevitably Romantic; these characters both suffer and expose social injustice. Curiosity sometimes runs against cultural conservatism, but the grounds for this opposition change in the nearly two hundred years that this book covers. Thus while the criticism of empiricism partly results from conservative resistance to ideals of self-advancement, literary treatments of inquiry do not fall neatly within political lines because different manifestations of curiosity evoke different kinds of objections. As I show, early modern literature uses tensions between several manifestations of curiosity to express cultural fears as new people and ideas gain social power.

Much of this tension was motivated by the collapse during the Civil War and Commonwealth (1640–1660) of the Renaissance ideal of learning as a blend of scientific and moral knowledge. In *The Advancement of Learning* (1603), Francis Bacon passionately contradicted the theological prohibition against curiosity as "the originall temptation and sinne" which "hath in it somewhat of the Serpent, and therefore where it entreth into a man, it makes him swel."[43] This work rebutted a panoply of traditional objections to learning: as fruitless busywork that fed anxiety, atheism, and disputation; as a presumptuous usurpation of God's province; as vanity and the misuse of time and talent. In their place, Bacon advocated a voracious learning that encompasses all areas of existence while honoring the supremacy of God. This learning keeps as its object the social utility of knowledge and blends contemplation and action to guarantee self-command, while providing the endless pleasure that the insatiable appetite of curiosity demands (43–44). Learning thus improved both morality and the human condition.

Despite the lucidity and appeal of Bacon's philosophy, however, all the arguments that he refuted reappear in the following two hundred years. Curiosity is blamed for the moral faults of sloth and pride, the intellectual flaws of over-subtlety and confusion, the religious sins of atheism and hubris, and the social errors of avarice, exploitation, and self-indulgence. Moreover, the political divisions and religious sectarianism of the Civil War produced a social fragmentation that encouraged the separation of classical humanism, still dominant in the universities, and scientific knowledge, the province of the Presbyterians and dissenters, even if these began to remix after the Restoration.[44] Severed into politicized factions, curiosity ceased to be an intellectual enterprise equally hospitable to natural, social, and artistic inquiries and became a charge leveled at those who tested the edges of their social sphere.

Whether interpreted as the masculine activities of collecting and of scientific experimentation, or as the feminine quality of impious peeping and unregulated spying, curiosity stirs up both cultural pride and resistance. Critics point to the waste of energy, imagination, learning, time, and money that could have been be spent on public good, complaining that instead these resources are frittered away on speculative concerns like lunar voyages or private collections, enterprises pleasing only to the practitioner. Similarly, curious people who ask impertinent questions, especially women and servants, abuse social decorum by winkling out private information for their own, prurient pleasure. This cultural hostility toward curiosity is directed at both the public activity of science and the internal quality of pride, even while elite discourse praises science as progress, identifies exploration and inquiry with divine reason, and argues that empirical investigation levels social inequalities and ensures the eventual triumph of a just society.

Within this pattern of opposing discourses, distinct historical attitudes appear that result from particular cultural events. For example, because it penetrated into origins, including the processes of generation, birth, and development, scientific inquiry in the late seventeenth century was viewed as a usurpation of the religious mystery of creation, and this objection gained force once the telescope and microscope seemed to set up a world visible only to the elite. In contrast, the mid-eighteenth-century frauds of Mary Toft, the Bottle Conjuror, Elizabeth Canning, and the Cock Lane Ghost staged the failure of medical and juridical expertise, opening a new legitimacy for alternate methodologies to explore the occult. And as collectors like Sir Hans Sloane popularized collecting, literature exploited the endorsement of what others deemed valueless—insects, dusty rocks, malformed people, secrets, and private histories. Even as the emphasis and shape of the attack on curiosity alters according to cultural circumstances, however, throughout the early modern period curiosity denotes the transgressive desire to improve one's place in the world.

Chronological classifications do not capture the fluidity of culture any more than labeling a row of rocks in a collection captures geographical history, but there are clusters of events and literary texts that express specific conceptions of curiosity at particular times. I have used these clusters to organize this book.

Chapter 1 shows that as curiosity emerged from wonder in the Restoration, literature depicted it as visionary ambition in the form of occult power, social authority, and hypocrisy. These manifestations of curiosity were embodied preeminently in the scientist, the archetype of the ambitious new thinker. Incarnate in the insect-scrutinizing virtuoso of the Royal Society, curiosity conveyed both political freedom and a deluded ambition to rival God by legitimizing scientists to see the secrets of generation and heaven itself. At the same time, however, wonder tales and texts by Christopher Marlowe, Thomas Shadwell, Lady Margaret Cavendish, and Aphra Behn represented inquiry as a paradox: an adamant belief only in empirical proof that yet spawned believers in the invisible. This chapter analyzes curiosity in Restoration literature as an ambitious attempt to re-create the world that spurs cultural regulation through satire.

My second chapter charts the construction of curiosity as modernity itself. It examines the ambivalent attitudes toward the curious man and the curious woman as both consumers and vessels of consumption. The first part shows that in the early eighteenth century curiosity was represented as taxonomic and sexual transgression, particularly in the "discovery" po-ems of the 1720s, prompted by the literature about Mary Toft, and in the poetry and drama of Jonathan Swift, Alexander Pope, and John Gay. These writings document that the new availability of finely wrought or rare ob-jects, whether consumed by purchase or observation, fed the indictment of curiosity as a sign of cultural presumption. The second part of the chapter analyzes spectatorship as curious consumption in the rhetoric and depic-tion of inquiry in newspaper advertisements, periodicals, and prose fictions by John Dunton, Daniel Defoe, Addison and Steele, and Jonathan Swift.

Although women appear as inquirers and curiosities throughout the period, a specific discourse also emerges that traces the reciprocal objecti-fication of curiosity and femininity. As chapter 3 argues, female curiosity designates a specifically sexual exploration that moves through the century from being a power of agency to a quality of character and that turns women from collectors to collectibles. Whereas early literature portrays female curiosity as the impertinent spying out of hidden secrets, by the mid-eighteenth century, changing social attitudes, discoveries in erotic classical art, and emerging printing conventions work to refigure curiosity as internal. Correlatively, whereas seventeenth-century curious women—witches, spies, and pandoras—threaten the status quo, eighteenth-century curious women are represented increasingly as aesthetic objects. By analyz-ing prose fictions by Aphra Behn, Delarivière Manley, and Eliza Haywood, as well as literary magazines and collections for and about women and am-biguous sexuality, this chapter shows that early modern literature shifts from portraying sexual inquiry as an impertinent disruption of the status quo to providing it as an opportunity for licensed transgression.

The mid-eighteenth century struggles with the institutionalization of the curious perspective. My fourth chapter explores the literary transfer-ence of curiosity to critical observers depicted as self-appointed connois-seurs. By analyzing public "wonders," newspaper commentary on curious exhibitions, literary "cabinets of curiosity," museum guidebooks, maga-zines, and novels by Horace Walpole, William Beckford, and Samuel Johnson, I explicate the way the contemporary anxiety to distinguish art from nature facilitates the professionalization of cultural inquiry at midcentury. The texts of such self-styled literary connoisseurs as Samuel Johnson and Bonnell Thornton prove that under the pressure of urban alienation the inquiring urge is refigured from material acquisition to connoisseurship of the curiosity cabinet of the world.

In the final chapter, I explore how at the end of the century curiosity was represented as a rebellious impulse that could endanger the state and the individual and that consequently required defusing through ridicule and reproof, spectacle and sententiousness. The spectacularization of inquiry appears in newspaper reports on conjuring, the birth of the circus, learned animal exhibitions, and hot air ballooning. At the same time, Romantic fictions by Ann Radcliffe, William Godwin, and Mary Shelley represent curious heroes and heroines ambiguously as violators of a corrupt status quo. This chapter argues that at the turn of the century, curiosity appears as a tyrannical desire to control others that creates monsters.

With its profusion of literary works and its tradition of free thought, England is a particularly rich area for research in curiosity and literature. In the Renaissance, England had the resources and cultural will in plenty to explore, acquire, and exploit; currently, critics are illuminating the way it manufactured means to possess colonial discoveries. But never was curiosity more openly debated than in England during the period beginning with the Restoration. Here it is that curiosity was reconceived as the very identity of mankind, the mark of our difference from both beasts and angels. This curious identity becomes the anxious subject of conflicting, emerging views of humanity, culture, and nature, and consequently of cultural examination through pictorial illustrations, live exhibitions, and writing. It is particularly the latter that occupies this study.

Early modern literature, no matter what its ostensible cultural rank, is always informed by competing cultural representations, and this is especially true in its exploration of the primarily visual issue of curiosity. Nonetheless, England historically has preferred written to emblematic popular texts, and the period I focus on here is the time when the increased literacy brought about by Puritan practice facilitated the shift from pictorial to written representations of wonders. Thus, this book examines textual representations in the widest sense, encompassing novels, poetry, satire, drama, journalism, trial transcripts, prints, and records and reports of experiments and experiences. Moreover, its central thesis seeks to embrace all these sorts of representation. This thesis is that early modern culture represents curiosity as cultural ambition, the desire to escape one's social role and to possess, control, or dominate culture, and that those who exhibit curiosity are depicted as upstarts who challenge the order of nature and society.

This study examines literary works as cultural documents. They are, nonetheless, cultural documents of a particular kind. Like the journalism and propaganda also examined here, literary works illuminate the historical issues and attitudes toward curiosity, but whereas most journalism is topical and ephemeral literature designed to spark contemporary responses, much of this now canonical literature was written with the additional aim of providing aesthetic pleasure for a sophisticated audience. Some of these texts are therefore cultural documents of a particularly rich, wrought, and thoughtful kind and merit a different kind of close analysis from documents written to be read quickly and without irony. Nonetheless, the primary role of literary works in this study is to clarify contemporary tensions around the impulse of asking and seeking.

In examining this range of documents, several issues of nomenclature and usage have arisen. My policy has been to correct compositor's spelling errors silently unless these contain significant *double entendres* or pertinently document the haste of the press. I have also used the anachronistic term "scientist" throughout the script. Although the social identity of the scientist did not exist before the nineteenth century, this identity begins to form through textual portraits just at this period from 1660 to 1820, fired into shape by 160 years of corrosive satire ignorant of the distinctions that became important later in history. I therefore use the term to underscore that the current, popular idea of the scientist springs from the rich tradition of representations of curiosity in the period before the systematization and professionalization of science in the nineteenth century.

Early modern literature depicts curiosity—the pursuit of information by empirical means—as cultural ambition that turns curious people into curiosities. In literary characters and discussions of curiosity in works from the seventeenth to the early nineteenth centuries, early modern writers contest the nature and value of inquiry. If, as Samuel Johnson remarked, curiosity "is one of the permanent and certain characteristics of a vigorous mind," it also killed the cat.[45] Flooded by new and newly curious men and women, early modern culture characterizes curiosity as cultural ambition: the longing to know more. And this characterization, as both praise and blame, remains with us today.

CHAPTER ONE

Regulating Curiosity

Curiosity at the start of the seventeenth century was considered an impulse that was thrillingly if threateningly out of control. Unlicensed, undirected, and spontaneous, it seemed to many writers and social thinkers to resemble the madness of the Furies or the hubris of Eve. They often portrayed curiosity as feminine because it was illegitimate, a force that operated outside the world of law and order. In 1611, Cesare Ripa encapsulated this idea in his image of *Curiosità* as a huge, wild-haired, winged woman, head hungrily alert, arms outflung as if to embrace the world (fig. 5). Declaring that "curiosity is the unbridled desire of those who seek to know more than they should," he depicts a "woman with a red and blue garment on which are spread many ears and frogs," the latter symbolizing human energy.[1] Ripa associates sharp sight and personal vigor with "Curiosity" by noting that "her head is sticking out, because the curious always stand thus . . . lively to know and to hear news from all sides." Curiosity's vestments colored for the body and sky imply that this desire to know is natural and boundless, both carnal and intellectual; the ears scattered on her dress "show that the curious [one] has only desire to hear and know things said by others." An outlaw impulse, curiosity feeds on gossip, absorbing the knowledge of others. It embodies the anticipatory fury of desire, and desire, by its very nature, remains unsatisfied and ambitious for something more.

During the Restoration and eighteenth century, voracious curiosity was increasingly seen as an ocular appetite. This reinterpretation of curiosity from an intellectual to a visual lust was stimulated by an explosively popular, new way to define and channel inquiry: empiricism. This philosophic method defined knowledge not as hearsay, information from received sources, or the statements of authorities, but as the outcome of sensual perception. Proponents of empiricism questioned the authority of all

Figure 5. Cesare Ripa, "*Curiosità.*" This image is one of a large series of figures embodying
vices, virtues, and passions in attitudes designed for quick apprehension by artists
and audiences. By permission of the British Library

received documents, even religious ones, and vaunted reason and especially observation over other human abilities. Empiricism itself extended
to all corners of English culture, transforming early modern natural science and flooding through literature via scientific texts and techniques.[2]
Prominent among these texts was Henry Oldenburg's polymorphous *Philosophical Transactions*, which disseminated the subjects and conclusions of
scientific experimentation to a general audience.[3] Similar enterprises that
adapted the method of scientific inquiry to people's daily religious, practi-

cal, social, and even sexual concerns followed, like John Dunton's *Athenian Mercury*. Publishers leapt to popularize the new method of solving problems. If Locke's entire *Essay Concerning Human Understanding* seemed too daunting or cumbersome, digesters were ready to render it readable.[4] In high and popular culture, empiricism was the promise of freedom, the bolster against tyranny, and the endorsement of individual ambition: anyone could master it, and it could master any problem.

Empiricism's very accessibility and democratic appeal intensified the threat of lawlessness that traditionally hovered around curiosity. Moreover, the circumstances surrounding the public establishment of scientific empiricism in the Royal Society strengthened the association of curiosity with subversiveness. Although recent work has shown that the New Scientific method of questioning characterized Jesuit as well as Puritan thought, nonetheless scientific empiricism arose during the Puritan Interregnum, and many key figures in the Royal Society were Puritans.[5] Moreover, the principles of the New Science were ideologically allied to Puritan values. Just as reformist thought rejected traditional biblical authorities and revered the individual interpretation of the Bible, so the New Science ignored Aristotelian logic and redefined the truth of natural philosophy as the result of experiment and demonstration. Like Puritan reformism, the radical philosophy of the New Science opposed state practice. Furthermore, both Puritanism and the New Science seemed hospitable to ambitious "new men" who sought social advancement on the basis of merit, not blood. Still more importantly, despite the political ambiguity of the method itself, the Royal Society remained triumphantly independent of the monarchy.[6]

While the institutionalization of curiosity coincided with the emergence of a new social order centered on Charles II that resurrected inheritance as a value, recent scholarship has shown that the fiercely contested lines between Puritan and Anglican, republican and Royalist, were actually rather blurred during the Restoration era.[7] Originally conceived in secret resistance to Aristotelian and theologically tinged science, the Royal Society advocated ideals that encouraged independence from official structures.[8] Despite its alliance with the king, the Royal Society was represented by its advocates as a free enterprise.

These circumstances made curiosity tremendously powerful and dangerous at the beginning of the modern period. Historically conceived as lawless and asocial, curiosity, newly legitimized as empiricism, swept to the center of culture just as England struggled to restore traditional order after the Interregnum. This popular curiosity invited readers to reexamine social "truths" and to consider themselves equal to those who determined them. During the Restoration, material, written, and social manifestations of curiosity challenged contemporary limitations of knowledge and definitions of evidence and value: what could or should make a secret, who could or should be curious (and about what), who was curious, and what curiosity allowed or entailed for the organization of moral and political power in society. Literary texts questioned the nature and significance of various kinds of seeing, of language, and of physical and metaphysical reality. Curiosity itself, rather than any invention, seemed the instrument for a progress that would launch unorthodox ideas and new people into power.

The power of this questioning to reform social reality prompted a simultaneous reaction: a thrust to discipline and regulate curiosity and thus turn it into a tool for elite use. Many cultural leaders, especially court-favored writers, represented empirical curiosity as a passion that fostered arrogance. They indicted the curious for inventing rival worlds that were simultaneously visible and invisible, detected only through the microscope, the telescope, or the ignorance and ambitions of the virtuosi.[9] To many writers, the empiricists' puritanical rejection of a classical education that would have taught them self-mistrust made them dupes of a range of kinds of trickery. To such critics, inquiring could be seen as a violation of nature, particularly as it was depicted in texts informed by the underground culture rooted in nonliterate forms of didactic art that stretched back to medieval times.[10] Many writers responded to this violation by devising ways to regulate curiosity through the demarcation of orthodox genres, topics, and approaches, and by invoking curiosity to satirize the illegitimately curious—the ambitious who violated public boundaries. In the process, these texts gave shape to the stereotype of the mad scientist that has flourished for three hundred years.[11]

THE DISCIPLINE OF FRAUD

The most urgent question confronting spectators and readers of curious explorations and experiments was whether to believe the writer. Travelers into new worlds had long earned suspicion, since homebound readers could not verify their tales, just as readers of esoteric experiments could not reproduce the laboratory's results. In the early modern period, however, writers of all sorts of texts, from advertisements to novels, deliberately invite the reader's skepticism as a way of verifying their own credibility. By framing their information in ways that flatter the reader's common sense and cunning, these writers suggest that readers' curiosity gives them the authority, irrespective of their own experience, to judge the author's credibility. Thus, both literary audiences and readers scanning advertising touts are represented as more curious—in both senses—than the authors they read: more careful, more inquisitive. They are investigators who both detect lies and exploit discoveries. Disciplined by the stylistics of invited doubt, rational readerly skepticism becomes the test of truth.

Geographical, if not literary, exploration traditionally brought fame to the bold who leapt over common boundaries. In the Renaissance, curiosity seemed to yoke individual and state ambitions. As investigation beyond the borders of England, nature, and the visible, curiosity could open terrae incognitae where the explorers became conquerors and their homelands sovereign. For the economic enterprises of a country looking beyond her borders for rich lands to plunder, the mobility of curiosity could prove highly useful—provided it could be controlled. Queen Elizabeth had channeled (or diverted) the ambitious energy of her male courtiers into overseas expeditions, depicting their piracy as patriotism and rewarding them with rank and land. Shaped into the exploration of the New World, curiosity itself could be applauded as heroism, just as wonder could be appropriated to authorize colonization.[12] Moreover, Elizabeth's favor gilded buccaneer barons like Jack Hawkins and Francis Drake with gentlemanliness. Similarly, both James I and Charles I sold the newfangled title of "baronet" to raise the rich into the gentry. Ostentatiously treated as favorite subjects, ambitious nobility were tamed and their mobility harnessed.[13] Licensed by mutual profit for the adventurer and the state, exploratory ambition could be reconciled with obedience to the rule of the monarch.

Travelers' testimony about unseen marvels, even shaped into patriotism, however, elicits curious doubt, the skeptical desire to usurp the writer's authority with individual reasoning. Curiosity thus denotes both the ambitious penetration of the unknown and the astute penetration of the untrue: curious writers challenge curious readers to define reality. Texts from the late Renaissance to the early Restoration represent this ambiguity as both enterprise and destruction, common sense and occult learning. These meanings combine to make documents of travel tests of readers' credulity.[14]

The anecdotal tome *The World of Wonders* (1607), for example, invites the reader to distinguish implausible from merely unperceived wonders. It defines the reader's method as curiosity: the cautious, self-protecting impulse to examine the improbable in the light of the known. This curiosity enables wise readers to detect and reject manipulation by such curiosity mongers as religious fanatics and spectacle salesmen who seek to profit from the public's appetite for surprise. At the same time, the reader's laudable curiosity binds him or her to the writer as a fellow explorer of the veiled worlds of the unexperienced, unseen, and undetected. The book achieves this feat of disciplining the reader's curiosity to serve the writer's end primarily by legitimizing Herodotus's travel myths as keys to expose hidden fraud and confute the rival occult of the Catholic Church. It defines wonders primarily as hidden, unorthodox, or illegal cultural and social practices—theft, gluttony, cruelty, sexual "perversion" from bestiality to lechery, murder, rhetorical manipulation, deception. Curiosity explodes this trickery by recognizing the pattern of self-interest beneath the wonder.

This practical instruction in the secret world of fraud identifies curiosity with the physical discovery of new lands. For example, *The World of Wonders* characteristically conjures the readers' powers of scrupulous inquiry to authorize the marvelous. Defending Herodotus's "fabulous" histories, the translator derides a pure empiricism that would deny the reality of unexperienced worlds by equating skepticism with atheism.[15] The author accuses the "mentall discourse" of distrusting the unseen of "tyrannizing" over historians by compelling them only to report what readers will believe from experience (6). Laudable curiosity in the reader thus avoids fussy dependence on the empirical. It welcomes the knowledge of that which the reader has not witnessed. At the same time, readers deploy their curiosity to avoid deception; they con human types to avoid being conned themselves. As John R. Clarke has explained, credulity and curiosity have an ancient kinship.[16] People who believe and people who inquire both have faith in an unseen world. Early modern texts use this paradox, whereby the curious are convinced only by what they see and yet devoted to what they have not seen, to structure the reader's curiosity. Instructed in the method of detecting a concealed reality, readers can apply the revelations of hidden fraud to their own social world. They discover a new land within the land they knew; other new lands become equally plausible. This technique redirects readerly curiosity from usurpation of to complicity with the writer.

Curious readers' thirst to believe in new, unseen worlds that they could master through secret knowledge challenged the authority of state institutions. In the post-Reformation world, curiosity stood in a tense relationship to religion, and it also threatened political authority and control—a threat that persisted into the Restoration, after England had witnessed violent changes in constituted state "authority." Thus, authors of travelogues and other curious texts were careful to inscribe limits on readers' curiosity in order to keep it orthodox and, correspondingly, to keep their texts in print. For example, even while relying on the reader's suspension of disbelief, the translator of *The World of Wonders* typically rejects credulity, scornfully differentiating his text from prognosticating almanacs and "any such rhapsodie of an undigested history" that might dangerously reread history (1). This rhetorical opposition persists throughout the early modern period and helps to make print the proof, the means, and the disciplining mechanism of curiosity.

Writers often elicited common sense to stage their credibility and arouse and channel the reader's curiosity. Henri Etienne, in his sixteenth-century preface "To the Reader," cites Thucydides' condemnation of the Greeks for "grounding their beliefe upon an uncertaine brute blazed abroad without taking further paines to search thereinto: which was the cause they so often entertained falsehood instead of the truth." Etienne condemns people's tendency to trust a speaker's authority, the inability "to discuss what they heare," and the blind belief in the opinions of received authorities (1). He suggests that open discussion and steady skepticism afford protection: publicly monitored inquiry becomes the means to avoid credulity. At the same time, however, it diverts curiosity into publicly acceptable topics and forms. While apparently applauding free inquiry, this radical rhetoric subjects investigation to public approval. Indeed, throughout early modern literature, habitual mistrust becomes a source of ridicule precisely because it rejects publicly accepted truth. Much literature thus depicts overscrupulous empiricists who either distrust their own eyes or scrabble at the obvious as examples of curiosity gone amok: people who doubt common sense itself.

To defuse this dangerous tendency to doubt the obvious and to discover concealed truths, writers also depict rational curiosity as the power to make the marvelous commonplace. Overused, however, this power can extinguish curiosity itself. *The World of Wonders* struggles to construct a definition of the curious that honors both the reader's reason and the observer's sense of the strange; the solution is to posit a universal, and thus comprehensible, humanity that nonetheless evolves according to circumstances. The author—scoffing at the proposition that "it is not probable, therefore it is false"—argues that difference proves the justice of curiosity. He explains, "If this were a good argument, nothing would seem either strange or wonderfull. For what do we use to wonder at, but that which falleth out against our expectation or opinion: that is, at that which we find to be true, and yet seemeth to be false, because it is not usuall, or above our reach, or against reason" (6). The author explains monsters as the power of the Omnipotent to create at will, yet his claim of historical evolution also accommodates changes brought by time (7). As proof, he relies on comparisons. By accusing them of a present-bound ignorance of the geographical and human scale of the ancient world, he condemns those who doubt that the Persian king's army drank rivers dry. He explains that the army was huge (and very thirsty) and the rivers small. His defense of Herodotus calls on the reader's knowledge of "the difference and dissimilitude which is to be seene betwixt us and our neare neighbors, as also the continuall strange alterations of customes and fashions in one & the same country" (9). Thus, curiosity indicates the reader's rationality as well as his credulity: it is the exercise of free reason.

This method of cultural comparison preserves the reader's understanding of humanity yet encourages the curious pursuit of difference. By viewing phenomena self-consciously—with an awareness of their own values—readers invent the curious: phenomena are defined as curious when they differ from the observer's norm. At the same time, travel writers knew that curiosity must remain within orthodox limits. They were aware that many thinkers deplored curiosity as irreligious. Montaigne, for example, finds curiosity part of man's "presumptuous" nature, even while it motivates understanding, because it refuses to recognize God's system.[17] In pointed contrast to such lawless wonder, he concludes after viewing a two-bodied "monstrous child" that hidden but divine logic explains all phenomena: "We call contrary to nature what happens contrary to custom; nothing is anything but according to nature, whatever it may be. Let this universal and natural reason drive out of us the error and astonishment that novelty brings us" (539). Properly disciplined, curiosity does not revel in the inconsistent but instead exposes the system beneath the aberration, familiarizes the rarity, and redefines as ignorance the curious relativism that admires difference. Montaigne dismisses curiosity as a presumptuous doubting of God's control. He sees it as a way of usurping God's system with a man-made system that reinterprets natural phenomena as "unnatural."

Montaigne's objection to curiosity as a kind of demystified wonder expresses the period's increasing anxiety about the power of curiosity to swallow up wonder itself and to promote a free thought that uses phenomena as material for a purely secular response and classification. In the English cultural imagination, the appetite of curiosity could easily extend from the physical to the social and intellectual. Restoration satirists thus depict the scientific insistence on finding a system to explain marvels as the self-aggrandizing desire to find the key to all mythologies. As England's cultural leaders recognized, desire that leaps one kind of boundary can surely leap another, just as the exploration of one kind of realm can induce exploration of others. This logic helped to characterize curiosity as treasonous usurpation. In popular culture this traditional indictment of presumptuous curiosity works to characterize impertinent people as "curious," and even as that most curious of creatures, the "monster."[18] These cultural monsters are represented, like Etienne's marvelous people, as adhering to customs or morals beyond the social norm; so offensive is their behavior that they are excluded not only from society but from humanity. Just as monstrous bodies combine two species in one, or swell or shrink beyond usual dimensions, people who desire or inquire beyond their place embody ontological uncertainty.[19] Their mobility across species or across social rank is seen as a transgressive sign of their ambition to transcend their place. By identifying ambitious people as monsters, early modern texts co-opt curiosity to support the status quo.

This connection between the appetite of curiosity, ontological transgression, and ambition appears in Renaissance texts as the original monstrous trait of ingratitude. As a violation of moralized, often naturalized, bonds of family, country, or religion, ingratitude symbolizes the rejection of human identity itself. Satan exemplifies this kind of violation of nature by betraying his father, God, and his own character when he rejects his angelic status, and King Lear excoriates his daughters and ministers for similar treachery with the phrase "Monster ingratitude!" (act 1, scene 5, line 40).[20] These texts reprove curiosity as antisocial ambition.

Early modern satirists, on the other hand, writing in an increasingly fluid social milieu, isolate hypocrisy as the preeminent human monstrosity.[21] Hypocrisy is ingratitude rendered political, ambitious, and invisible: it epitomizes mobility for personal gain. This is well shown in a political broadside entitled *A Character of a Turn-Coat: Or, The True Picture of an English Monster* (1707), adorned by an etching of the heads of a man and a woman who reverse roles when the sheet is turned upside down. As the writer explains, duplicity metamorphoses a man into a mirage, identity into illusion:

> For as the Times do change, they'll change their Face
> Forswear their Sex, their Age, their Name, and Race.
> As by these Pictures you may plainly see,
> He that was Man, a Woman seems to be,
> And she that did a Woman represent,
> By change into another Form is sent.[22]

Gender, age, nationality, even humanity itself are mutable in the turncoat. With no social location, hypocrites destabilize every conception of human identity; as living lies, they mimic the divine language of metaphor by showing the duplicity in surfaces. The curious art of this broadside by which the faces double for each other draws on the tradition of visual trickery. Indeed, doubleness is monstrosity itself insofar as the monster is both human and inhuman, divine and carnal, a clear sign of God's purpose and an unnatural phenomenon.[23] Such conceptions play on the tradition of exhibiting double-bodied "monsters" (fig. 6). These human curiosities corporealize ambition as physical excess: the usurpation of another body.

As curiosity incited to abhor monstrosity served to regulate political ambition, it also served to indict the impious. Religious exhortations condemn curiosity as the love of secular things. Notably, Christopher Marlowe's *Doctor Faustus* chronicles the quest for sensation, knowledge, beauty, and power that leads Faustus from the love of God to a love of man, and thus of himself. Marlowe identifies curiosity with presumption, as Faustus aims to be "on earth as Jove is in the sky, / Lord and commander of these elements!"[24] By seeking absolute power over "nature's treasure," Faustus mirrors Jove's passionate tyranny rather than God's divine understanding (1.1.72). As episodes throughout the plot show, this knowledge of nature is the knowledge of a human nature defined in opposition to the divine. Faustus's pursuit of natural knowledge indicates the rejection of spirituality that curious love entails.

Faustus also suffers from insatiability, the philosophical objection to curiosity. Haunted by boredom, addicted to visual delight, he devours wonder after wonder but is never replete. "O, how this sight doth delight my soul!" he exclaims upon quizzing the Seven Sins; later Mephistopheles shows him "what Rome contains for to delight thine eyes"; years he spends "with pleasure ta[king] the view / of rarest things and royal courts of kings" (2.2.178; 3.1.32; 4.1.1–2). Since the things of the flesh pass away, however, the curious can achieve no permanent contentment. Faustus is the image of a man consumed by consumption, starving from an overfed appetite. In search of the spiritual, he dabbles with spirits; in search of immortality, he achieves fame; but the essence of what he wants always escapes. The answer to this conundrum, argued contemporary philosophers, was not to locate reality in the physical world at all. Too late Faustus recognizes this: "what wonders I have done all Germany can witness, yea all the world, for which Faustus hath lost both Germany and the world, yea heaven itself" (5.2.47–51). Like Mephistopheles, Faustus exhibits the "aspiring pride and insolence" that wants all that God himself has. The final chorus warns the

Figure 6. "Nobilissimi Signiori." 1695. This good-sized (9¾ in. × 7 in.) representation, an advertisement for an exhibition at Venice, depicts a fashionably-dressed young man on stage exhibiting the head of a young woman growing from his stomach. Courtesy of the Art Collection, the Harry Ransom Humanities Research Center, University of Texas at Austin

audience "only to wonder at unlawful things" (5.3.4–8). *Doctor Faustus* advocates the humble admiration of "wondering" over a search for explanations that encroach on divine prerogative.

Through Faustus, Marlowe reiterates the medieval contention that curiosity constitutes a kind of intellectual parasite that wastes its host. Sebastian Brant explicates this idea in his account in *The Ship of Fools* "of the ouer great and chargeable curyosyte of men" (1509). Charting a direct connection between geographical and mental exploration, Brant links Alexander the Great's discontentment with the greed for immortality:

> As if all the erth were nat suffycyent
> For his small body by curyouse couetyse
> But at the last he must holde hym content
> With a small cheste, and graue nat of great pryce.
> Thus deth vs shewyth what thynge sholde vs suffyce
> And what is the ende of our curyosyte.[25]

In medieval and much Renaissance thought, curiosity exemplifies the irony of humanity's death-destined desire. Rather than leading to freedom, it entraps mankind. The agent made object, the curious body ends in the grave—itself the only fit subject for pious inquiry.

Despite these indictments, however, literary texts characteristically finesse both the religious prohibition against curiosity, and the punishment accorded to the curious hero-villains. Even while endorsing the church's critique, Marlowe expresses the popular recognition that curiosity can explode pretension. In a carnivalesque scene that reverses the power of the damned and the blessed, Faustus strikes the pope, beats the friars, and astonishes the religious throng with magical explosions.[26] By alluding to the wandering conjurer on whom Marlowe based the figure of Faustus, these feats allow the audience to triumph vicariously over the sanctimonious credulity of the church.[27] Cesare Ripa alludes to this context by exemplifying quick-eared curiosity through E. S. Bernardo's illustration of pride: "*if you see a monk walking with his head up and his ears up, you will know he is curious.*" Contemporary anticlericalism provided an added impetus to embrace a curiosity that was disapproved by religious authority.

Early modern England sought to regulate curiosity, taming it from political ambition and popular disorderliness into a careful skepticism that Lorraine Daston and Katharine Park associate with an elite work ethic.[28] While this effort largely failed, a great transformation in the cultural conception of curiosity did occur from the early seventeenth century to the

Figure 7. Thomas Jeffreys, "Curiosity." The costume has a rich, sensuous fabric; the upper garment is flesh-colored, trimmed with gold or silver lace, and the lower petticoat is white satin realistically emblazoned with calm, open eyes and perked ears. From *A Collection of the Dresses of Different Nations, Ancient and Modern*, vol. 4, no. 235: 37 (London: Thomas Jeffreys, 1772). By permission of the British Library

end of the eighteenth. Thomas Jeffreys' 1772 version of Ripa's image of "Curiosità," emblazoned on a masquerade dress, illustrates the change. As a means for masking identity to pursue pleasure, masquerade itself represents commercialized transgression.[29] Jeffreys replaces danger with decorous delight, tidying Curiosity's hands and hair and facing her to the reader, not enraged but smiling limpidly (fig. 7). Jeffreys' design accents sensual pleasure by replacing Ripa's frogs with ears and by elaborating the design of scattered eyes. Explaining that these "are emblems of [Curiosity's] eagerness to see and hear," Jeffreys employs a trompe l'oeil mirroring contemporary satire: the skin-colored torso of his figure resembles a face, with eyes placed over her nipples and a mouth between her legs.[30] This eager maid is a far cry from Ripa's flailing Fury. During the period from the

Renaissance to the late Enlightenment, curiosity is molded into a primarily visual, licentious indulgence, as well as into the emblem of legitimate consumption.[31]

This change is motored by the dissemination of empirical values through popular texts. Novel information, incalculably valuable, appeared in periodicals, newspapers, scientific treatises, and popular abridgments, but what defined information, news, "fact," or even "truth"—especially in contrast to a visual trick or intellectual confidence scheme—was still highly contested in all sorts of literature.[32] Unlike earlier travelogues, these texts address a medley of readers. Consequently, authors mingle various, sometimes contradictory, kinds of evidence in an attempt to establish their credibility by covering all the bases of belief. Nonetheless, they also incite doubt in order to get their readers to verify wonder.

Restoration writers saturate their texts with different kinds of evidence to placate the polymorphous curiosity of their readers. For example, the 1687 "Strange and Wonderfull News from Cornwall, being an Account of a Miraculous Accident that Lately happen'd neer the Town of *Bodmyn*, at a Place called *Park*" emphasizes its secular sources and scrupulous inquisition. It opens its account of a man who wakes from a deep sleep to find himself mysteriously transported from a seventeen-foot window to a field four miles away by asserting:

> The *Truth* of the Account here given of what lately occurr'd in
> *Cornwall*, is confirm'd by Letters from Gentlemen, of great Worth
> and Integrity, of the Neighbourhood where this Remarkable
> Accident happen'd . . . the strict Examinations and Enquiries that
> were made by the aforesaid Gentlemen, before they would write
> anything touching this matter, together with many other Passages
> that sufficiently demonstrate the *Reality of the Thing* [as does] the
> general Belief it hath obtain'd in the *West*.[33]

The specificity of the location, the testimony of local authorities, the methods of verification, and public acceptance authenticate the tale. Further passages point to historical parallels between this and other miracles in order to construct a pattern of probability. Such justification legitimizes inquiry into phenomena that violate nature.

Like travelogues, these wonder tales elicit skepticism to validate their marvels. *The* WONDER OF WONDERS, *or Strange* NEWS *From Newton in Yorkshire* (1675) vaunts its unlearned style as proof of unvarnished veracity.[34]

> We live in an age wherein so many Untruths are vended, not only
> Verbally, but likewise in Print, that when Truth it self comes on

the Stage, it shall hardly have Credence. The Reader is desired to excuse the roughness of the Stile, by reason the person that wrote the Letter, desired it might be done word for word according to his Coppy, he being an Eye-witness to part of this Subject and cautious to declare less or more than what really hapned.[35]

Artless writing, this author suggests, reproduces unmediated "Eye-witnessing." Moreover, details of identity, time, date, and source guarantee precision and verifiability. The story's truth is assured on several, competing bases: historical parallels, eyewitnessing by an accountable source with probity and proximity, "eminent" authority, sheer assertion, and a readerly sophistication that can tell a hawk from a heron, and a true from a tall tale.

This sophistication is conjured by a narrative strategy that becomes the staple of detective fiction: this strategy makes explanation the climax of the story. Even while the up-to-date evidence proclaims the subject fit for rational curiosity, it is instead depicted as a wonder until the final paragraph. Through a serving maid's testimony, the pamphlet recounts that Dame Wilford dreamed of a handsome gentleman, whereupon he appeared the following day amidst a shower of stones, and, despite her rejection, repeatedly pleaded with her in broken phrases, waiting all night in the courtyard. The following morning, the disturbed Goodman Wilford, her husband, confronted him to demand an explanation, only to discover that in the stranger's place stood a stone statue. His occult appearance in the Dame's dream, their cryptic exchange, the miracle of the stone shower, and the statue prove this a mythic marvel.

The conclusion of the narrative, however, changes from reportage to analysis. An apparently objective editor assumes the narrative and hints that human motives may explain the tale:

> The roads about *Newton* are crowded, people coming and going
> continually, day and night, to see this strange (but true) Prodegy,
> and return again with no less Admiration, *Goodman Wilford*
> remembring his wives dream, went to her and told her of it as she
> lay in her bed, but she (if not really) has framed her self speechless,
> and hath continued so ever since, where we will leave her and
> desire you to judge charitably of her untill we hear farther, which
> I am promised shall be if she makes any confession (7).

Inviting the reader to eschew "Wonder" or "Admiration" for more information, he insinuates that Dame Wilford's secrecy suggests something that may seem to the ignorant a wonder, but to the curious becomes a scandal.

The inexplicable becomes merely the unexplained, and the unexplained is easily explained by the curious: those who know what is "really" probable, who possess the knowledge of secret motivations, gossip, and hidden human nature. Once the tale becomes a human mystery, the miracle becomes a curiosity.

While travelogues and wonder tales called on common sense to regulate curiosity, scientific documents sought to define legitimate curiosity by forging a professional method. Popular literature, however, co-opted and collapsed the rhetoric of miracles, exploration, and meticulous experiment. As the dissemination of the *Philosophical Transactions* gave the reading public access to empirical science, newspapers were flooded with reports of marvelous medicines. Printing and popular medicine were so intimately connected, especially during plague times, that in the next century, Daniel Defoe used printed cures to represent superstition in the *Journal of the Plague Year* (1719). Advertisements underscored the rarity and exoticism of cures to authenticate them as new, while rehearsing a mishmash of evidence to massage the audience's curiosity. For example, "THE SOVEREIGN JULEP Which is universally esteemed in most Parts of *Europe*, as well as in other Parts of the World, as being first made and rightly prepar'd by that most eminent Physician *Shavilleir Borri*, lately deceas'd, and from whom a Noble Man in his Travels got the Receipt" presents the potion as a travel trophy.[36] Using the language of curiosity, such announcements depict remedies as works of both art and nature, proven by experiment but attained by exploration; moreover, details of provenance guarantee reliability. Readers are whipped up to believe wonders, but to believe them on the basis of physical evidence.

Many advertisements, quacks, and entrepreneurs brazenly fed off the prestige of the Royal Society, particularly its altruistic public physicking (*Medical Advertisements*, no. 226). Such offers as that of "D. Woodward, Professor of Physick and Astrology," to dispense advice and pills from ten in the morning until seven at night were legion (no. 162). Dozens of self-styled physicians were available, some of whom claimed the most respectable credentials:

> Dr Wells a Physician, a Graduate in one of our owen Universities, and a Member of the Colledge of Physicians in London, who has a Pill prepared . . . for the *running of the Reins*, which being neglected or unskilfully managed, occasions Ulcers in the *Mouth, Throat, Palatre, and Nose, Pains and Breakings out in many parts of the Body.* This Pill Cures the *runnings of the Reins* safely without leaving any

ill Dregs in the Body, and repairs all the parts and Senses when
they have formerly suffer'd Damage by *poisonous Medicines*. (no. 75)

This advertisement, unpleasantly like televised remedies, deploys medical
terminology for profit. Quacks leeched off Robert Boyle's identification of
medical experimentation with elite civic duty and portrayed medicine as
charity and themselves as selfless, and other entrepreneurial experts in
human problems followed. Their advertisements not only reinforced the
power of jargon to legitimize curiosity, but also validated inquiry into the
human body, especially when it went awry, as a topic for respectable inquiry by layman and expert alike.

Many topics that appeared in the *Philosophical Transactions*, especially
contentious ones, were recirculated in cheap cures, thus helping to demarcate legitimate subjects of curiosity. For example, "*The highly approved English Deaf curing Doctor*" who "has oftentimes cured those that have been
Deaf in half an hours time, and brought Coars out of their Ears some half
an Inch long, and some an inch long and upwards" vaulted off virtuosi's
explorations of deafness to perform an act that lies between curing and
conjuring, a conjunction that Eliza Haywood and Daniel Defoe revive in
their wonder narratives of the deaf-and-dumb Duncan Campbell (no.
169). Indeed, any invention that addressed the problems of nature or the
physical world was popular, like the announcement of a "Man preserv'd
from *Drowning* in any kind of Water, by a new, light, hollow Girdle, fill'd
with his Breath," which springs from the Royal Society's discussions of respiration and drowning (no. 172). Such mushrooming advertising, news
printing, and wonder-mongering, like satire, ate away at the distinctions
the virtuosi were forging between elite science and magical fraud by au-
thorizing elite topics of inquiry for curiosity and profit.

These topics were not confined, however, to scientific problems. They
traditionally also included objects of art, themselves reified investigations
into the human body, nature, or beauty. Curiosity in both journalism and
elite study often entailed the creation of objects—be they printed or
sculpted, mental or material—from subjects of inquiry. The power to authenticate such objects rested with the connoisseur or the creator, and virtuosi were eager to assume these roles. Leisured gentlemen like the socially
ambitious Samuel Pepys and the inquisitive John Aubrey, inheriting from
the Renaissance an ideal of voracious inquiry that implied cultural power,
epitomized the fashionable curiosity of the virtuoso as both investigator
and collector. They adapted the new reverence for minute observation and
empirical thoroughness to a pursuit of learning that yet avoided profes-

sionalism.[37] Significantly, both wrote diaries that focus on human curiosities and that contain both autobiographical and biographical remarks. After scattered memories of Venetia Stanley's charms, including descriptions of her face and portraits of her, Aubrey records:

> About 1676 or 5, as I was walking through Newgate Street, I saw Dame Venetia's bust standing at a stall at the Golden Cross, a brazier's shop. I perfectly remembered it, but the fire had got off the gilding: but taking notice of it to one that was with me, I could never see it afterwards exposed to the street. They melted it down. How these curiosities would be quite forgotten, did not such idle fellows as I am put them down![38]

In an ironic parallel to the stone intruder in *The* WONDER OF WONDERS, Aubrey's "curiosity" memorializes the past, memory, history, and narrative. For him, the object frozen in time makes the lost concrete and concretizes the loss: object and meaning inspire one another, like the relics of saints. Since, however, he records information that only he remembers, his personal curiosity creates curiosity in and curiosities of other people. From "idle" leisure, Aubrey manufactures value—but only for the elite, like his companion, since the merchants melt the denuded statue to get their kind of value from it. Aubrey claims the gentlemanly prerogative to make the commonplace a subject of inquiry by his act of choosing to value it; as both he and Pepys make clear, they form the center spring of the curious value.[39] This power to objectify life, both one's own and others, to turn process into product, marks curiosity as a capitalistic enterprise that occupies an ambiguously symbolic sphere. Aubrey's curiosity makes the lives he discusses "goods" for examination. Like royalty or divinity, he has the power to make meaning.

Aubrey and Pepys were two of the first writers to participate in the early modern process of turning social relations into written cabinets of curiosity, but they were following a practice already firmly established in the world of fairs and shows. There, human oddities or "freaks"—limbless artists, giants and dwarves, those with strange appetites or features—already had their curiosity value enhanced by the biographical flourishes provided by their own publicity or by their touts and managers.[40] In print, however, people claiming irregular bodies relied on biography for their claims to marvelous status. "The *Wonder of Wonders*: or the Dumb MAID of WAPPING Restor'd to her Speech again," for example, consists of the "Impartial Relation" of Sarah Bowers's recovery from seven years of speechlessness. While the testimony of "Ministers" and the ultimate call to repentance legitimize both the wonder and the pleasure of reading it, the tale derives its interest from the paradox of imaginatively hearing "the Girls own Words."[41] Similarly, the enormously popular account of "*The ENGLISH HERMITE, or Wonder of this AGE.* Being a relation of the life of ROGER CRAB" makes secular life a mystery parallel to that of religious martyrs.[42] These biographical wonders enact through the reader's complicity the thrill of comparison in which observers confirm their normality by contrasting themselves with human marvels. Like Aubrey and Pepys, readers become the center while the curiosities form the margin. This taxonomic act defines curiosity as power. At the same time, it reinscribes conformity to "normal" limits as the condition for this power.

Curious texts and displays thus both enhance and shape the reader's power, status, and social value. By watching or reading them, audiences enter the rarefied world of the curiosity-maker: their own interest confers value on the curiosities they witness, as these curiosities, once witnessed, reciprocally raise their status. Roger Crab's strange appetites—his refusal "to eate any sort of Flesh, Fish, or living Creature, or to drinke any Wine, Ale, or Beere," and his "constant food [of] Roots and Herbs"—for example, define him as a curiosity for moral consumption. By reading about Crab, readers experience humility, but they also reassert their difference from excessive piety. The act of defamiliarization whereby others become curious buttresses the observer's normality. Thus, showmen and curious texts sell what Aubrey and Pepys record: the experiential frisson of comparing one's own to others' existence. In a period when identities were shifting according to new social bonds and ideologies, the desire for such comparisons burgeoned, and so did the texts providing them. Biography intensified curiosity by depicting the relationship of the observer to the observed, the maker of curiosity to the thing or person made curious. This power also lay in texts like witch trials and wonder narratives, where reading of testimony, empirical phenomena, and experiments reenacted observation and alerted skepticism. Print defamiliarized life into art for the curious reader and regulated curiosity as the means for cultural superiority.[43]

The endorsement of the observer's authority by means of printed curiosity was both maintained and monitored by the proponents of the New Science. Most notably, Thomas Sprat's *The History of the Royal-Society of London, For the Improving of Natural Knowledge* (1667), like Dunton's *Athenian Mercury* and John Tradescant the Younger's *Catalogue*, regulated inquiry by explaining its rules to the public, albeit for political not commercial ends. Despite its mixed reception, the concept of publishing a genealogy that would explain the virtues of curiosity so appealed to Charles Gildon that he did the same thing for Dunton's Athenian Society. His *History of the Athenian Society* (1691), like Sprat's *History of the Royal Society*, was propaganda for both an ideology and a publication.[44] Whereas Dunton and Gildon sought to profit from curiosity, however, Sprat claimed that true curiosity was disinterested. He asserted that the dominance of gentleman in the Society was designed to prevent the "*two corruptions* of Learning": the instant and premature application of discoveries to profit-making enterprises, and the ossification of some men into "*Masters*" and others into "*Scholars*; some imposing, & all other submitting; and not as equal observers without dependence."[45] Because of the contemporary panoply of profiteering ventures, this claim spawned a host of slurs on virtuosi as hypocrites.

Recent critics have attacked the claim of scientific disinterestedness; Sprat's contemporaries, however, never accepted it. Despite Charles II's unprecedented distance from the Royal Society, traditionally he still represented the source of social preferment and prestige.[46] In the wake of Hobbes's cynical definition of human nature as selfish, moreover, many satirists bluntly discredited the idealistic notion that anyone would labor without self-interest; instead they interpreted the virtuosi's disinterested posture as repression or perversion of the most fundamental animal impulse of all: sex. Hobbes himself regarded curiosity as distracting and delusive, if also the motivating force behind the establishment of the institutions of society.[47] Satirists used their own claim of disinterestedness to discredit the virtuosi on the basis of Platonism: if the first duty of the cultured citizen is to know himself—"The proper study of Mankind is Man," as Pope put it—then the virtuosi failed from the start. Unable to identify their own physical impulses, how could they possibly be trusted to explain the physical world? This criticism persisted for three centuries.

Sprat's declaration of the ideals of the Royal Society sets the stage for subsequent satire of science as fraud. *The History of the Royal Society* represents inquiry regulated by the Society as the means for rational, social unity.[48] Sprat defines science as both monarchical conquest and political liberty, "An *Enterprize* equal to the most renoun'd Actions of the best *Princes*. For, to increase the Powers of all mankind, and to free them from the Bondage of Errors, is the greater Glory than to enlarge *Empire*, or to put Chains on the necks of Conquer'd *Nations*"(dedication). Not only does he promise Charles that "Your *Majesty* will certainly obtain *Immortal Fame*, for having establish'd a perpetual Succession of *Inventors*," but he traces "Civility and Learning" to the Society itself. Since science calms the spirit, the virtuoso occupies a world quite separate from the political one, contemplating "*Nature* alone," detached "from past, or present misfortunes" or from "*Men*, and *humane affairs*" (56).

To the traditional objection that the contemplative life breeds envy and fantasy, Sprat, like Bacon, replies that the flaw lies in individual excess, not in the practice; indeed, he claims that the pursuit of science liberates men from repressive society. This defense avoids the fundamental contention that activity itself shapes the man, that indeed the human identity is social, and that such solitary studying breeds ambition—a contention that traditional humanists used to indict virtuosi for pride.[49]

As Stephen Shapin and Simon Schaffer have argued persuasively, members of the Royal Society co-opted the posture of the aristocracy particularly by claiming disinterestedness.[50] Thus, self-interested scientists were derogated as bad scientists. For example, in refuting William Holder's "Cavils" about the education of a deaf and dumb pupil, John Wallis typically accused Holder not only of a bad memory, but of interested motives: guilt, fear, and desire for profit.[51] To avoid polluting experiment with self-interest, scientific societies proposed rules of argument forbidding speculative or religious discussion and specifying "modesty."[52] This insistence on disinterestedness fed the satirical indictment of virtuosi as both rebelliously antisocial and as decadent students of things of no use.

The social composition of the prominent Royal Society deepened the identification of science with fraudulent ambition. Sprat figured empirical investigation as a public contract like serving the country in foreign wars: men "will not be able, handsomely to draw back, and to forsake such honourable Intentions" (3). Most members were indeed well born or connected, yet they had no political role. Sprat assured the public, "But, though the *Society* entertains many men of *particular Professions*, yet the farr greater Number are *Gentlemen*, free, and unconfin'd" (67). Such freedom echoed the licentiousness of curiosity itself. Moreover, members of the society sought "Universal Importance," rather than political or social advancement per se, an amorphous fame outside the king's power to give. And the founders had established their rebellious tradition by forming their society in opposition to prevailing theory and in a secret fashion, while the Society itself touted its sovereign independence from the monarchy. Filled with the desire "of breathing a freer air, without being engag'd in the passions and madness" of the Commonwealth, they wanted a "*free way* of reasoning" (53). The Society's very independence prompted attacks on the virtuoso for arrogance and a mad ambition to be a king himself.

Furthermore, virtuosi seemed to contemporaries to pander to charlatans. In his autobiography, Boyle defended commerce with those of lower rank: "titular greatness is ever an impediment to the knowledge of many retired truths, that cannot be attained without familiarity with meaner persons."[53] Like Aubrey, he described himself as solitary and studious, inclined to socialize with workmen rather than wits. This model of sociability violated traditional, courtly principles of political relationships. The Royal Society, particularly through Boyle, extended a public profile, even a social legitimacy, to members of social classes conventionally deemed beneath a gentleman's friendship. These people included professional doctors, chemists, foreign inventors, and artisans, who, if they did not receive membership, often at least received money from instrument-besotted virtuosi.[54] Boyle wrote an entire treatise, "Of the Usefulness of Mechanical Disciplines to Natural Philosophy. Shewing, That the power of Man may be much promoted by the Naturalist's skill in MECHANICS," essentially advocating philosophical status for laboring craftsmen (*Works* 3:162–66). In another pamphlet, he declared that learned men should learn from "illiterate mechanicks" because they produce works of art that illuminate principles of nature.[55] This transgression of social rank and bold redefinition of art hints at rebellion and private ambition. Consequently, it appears in satire as credulity: the virtuoso's inability to detect fraud or to distinguish culture and nature. Ultimately, this transgression turns the curious man into an object of curious, or artful, exploitation by cunning men, conjurers, hypocrites, and masqueraders.

Shadwell's *Virtuoso* (1676) definitively dramatizes the humanistic objection to science as fraud. It attacks the virtuoso not for "Natural imperfections," but for a self-construction that breeds bad manners, misuses social resources, including the virtuoso's own wit, and attempts to transgress boundaries of art and nature.[56] The virtuoso's false self-image erupts as a tempting credulity that fertilizes fraud in others. Here, Shadwell borrows from literary tradition. From Ben Jonson's satire *The Alchemist* (1610), popular during the first twenty years of the Restoration, he derives the device of the cunning man who preys on learned fools, a scenario that would be freshly sharpened by the spectacle of the rich members of the Royal Society.[57] Like a picaro, this figure punishes vice by conning victims with mystified science. Indeed, Jonson's address to the reader begins by warning against a duplicity that gluts on the victim's self-deception: "If thee beest more, thou art an Understander, and then I trust thee. If thou art one that tak'st up, and but a Pretender, beware at what hands thou receiv'st thy commoditie; for thou wert never more fair in the way to be cosned then in this Age."[58]

In Jonson's play, an astrologer and an alchemist dupe characters seeking

illegitimately to advance themselves through magic. Promising the philosopher's stone that turns all metals to gold and other charms to guarantee
success in trade, gambling, and marriage, they exploit their victims' ambition. These fools want more than the world offers, so they prefer to believe
in a false, magic world. A traditional symbol of scientific fraudulence, alchemy embodies the desire to forge value from nothing by transforming
material. *The World of Wonders* similarly exposes merchants, physicians,
apothecaries, clothiers, and usurers as robbers "who cloke their thefts under cover of traffick or trade" (114). Such significance was easily trans-
ferred to the new practitioners of substance transformation, the virtuosi
who located new worlds in a moldy cheese and many of whom, like Elias
Ashmole, did believe in alchemy and astrology despite contemporary contempt for them as false science.[59]

In updating Jonson's play, as Claude Lloyd and others have shown,
Shadwell closely parodies the specific activities of the Royal Society, often
with detailed allusions to the *Philosophical Transactions*.[60] He mocks Boyle's
experiments with the air pump, blood transfusions, respiration, and motion, as well as discussions about luminescence, the possibility of human
flight, and the discoveries of the telescope and microscope. Tied to his
ridicule of such intellectual abuse is the moral charge that science undermines traditional values. In *The Virtuoso*, Shadwell dramatizes this point by
contrasting classical humanism and social sophistication, represented by
the sparks Bruce and Longvil, with the search for novelty, embodied in
the virtuoso, Sir Nicholas Gimcrack. Like the two modish rakes, a host of
charlatans, scholars, and virtuosi desire the favor of the wealthy but deluded Sir Nicholas. The opposition between classical humanism and novelty dramatizes the opposition of two kinds of identity and authority. Shadwell portrays the virtuoso as an example of a man who sinks himself
beneath his social inferiors because of a misguided belief in the authority
and prestige of the new enterprise of experimentalism. When Sir Nicholas,
prone on a table and under the tutelage of an attendant, tries to learn to
swim by imitating the spasms of a frog—the ancient symbol of energetic
curiosity—he fails to recognize his absurdity because he relies on the
praise of the scholar he has hired. Just as he will never test the success of
his "theoretical" method of swimming in the dangerously real medium of
water, so he will never hear people's real opinions of him.[61] In trusting the
bought flattery of mobile "experts," he abandons his own authority and
accords dangerous power to an amorphous group resented from both
above and below: the protoprofessional classes.[62]

Shadwell articulates contemporary unease about the unprecedented influence of these tutors, instrument-makers, and scholars by underscoring Sir Nicholas's spendthrift habits. Clarinda, one of Gimcrack's nieces, reveals that he has spent a staggering £2,000 "in Microscopes" (act 1, p. 12). Snarle, his uncle, reveals that Sir Nicholas has bought wondrously hairy eggs for ten shillings each, only to discover that the hairs were inserted by a fine needle (act 1, p. 34). His search for one kind of curiosity has promoted the production of another, but he prefers monstrous nature to fine artistry. His credulity makes him a mark for confidence tricksters: he boasts of his collection of "*Microscopes, Telescopes, Thermometers, Barometers, Pneumatick Engines, Stentrophonical Tubes,* and the like" (act 2, p. 36). At what some feared was a great social and financial cost, the new mongers of wonder tools seemed to be pandering to the asocial appetites of curious men. The virtuoso's ambition and credulity prompts the ambitious fraud of others.

Shadwell indicts the virtuoso's philosophy as useless. He immediately opposes it to classical values by opening the play with Bruce, one of the play's two truewits, dressed in a "Gown" and reading a text emblematic for its traditional wisdom, Lucretius's *De Rerum Natura* (On the nature of things). Bruce praises both the classical scientist for fidelity to nature, and the reconciliation of "Poetry and Good Sense," in contrast to the "natural philosophy" of scientists (act 1, p. 1). Shadwell's argument is that Sir Nicholas's philosophy breeds superstition rather than self-knowledge and that it transfers responsibility to physical nature away from moral nature. In the central scene featuring the frog, the truewits Bruce and Longvil and Sir Nicholas openly articulate the opposition between humanistic and scientific philosophy. "I seldom bring anything to use," Sir Nicholas, the student of speculative not practical knowledge, asserts grandly, "'tis not my way. Knowledge is my ultimate end" (act 2, p. 30). Bruce responds with the ironic citation of a classical dictum: "You have reason, Sir; Knowledge is like Virtue, its own reward" (act 2, p. 30). Sir Formal chimes in: "To study for use is base and mercenary, below the serene and quiet temper of a sedate Philosopher" (act 2, p. 30). Ignorant of their flattery, Sir Nicholas concludes, "You have hit it right, Sir; I never studi'd anything for use but Physick, which I administer to poor people" (act 2, p. 30). His natural philosophy thus keeps him vulnerable, credulous, and useless to society.

The differentiation of kinds of philosophy determines identity. Rather than seeking moral distinctions, Sir Nicholas differentiates between classes of life. In earnestly imitating a frog, "the most curious of all amphibious animals," he betrays an amphibian ambition to transgress his humanity; his study of the lower orders of nature in place of man makes him less than a man himself (act 2, p. 28). Such a rejection of identity resembles rebellion, hypocrisy, ingratitude. In contrast, Longvil and, especially, Bruce adopt a philosophical resignation that marks them as true gentlemen, as both their language and their behavior demonstrate. Whereas the followers of the New Science engage in experiments in a fashion perilously similar to manual labor—indeed, Sprat suggests that children learn by applying their eyes and hands, and he explicitly advocates "a *Mechanical Education*" over a "*Methodological* one" (329)—truly philosophic gentlemen lounge about in dressing gowns planning *affaires*. As Bruce beseeches Longvil, they need time to think deeply about eternal truths (act 1, p. 2). While Shadwell satirizes contemporary fashion through these beaux, he also echoes a distinction with class overtones between classical and scientific values.

Shadwell also satirizes the contemporary exploitation of science as popular medicine. Like Sir Hans Sloane, Sir Nicholas physics the poor for no fee, but Shadwell, echoing contemporary skepticism about scientific disinterest, pinpoints a concealed self-interest in his benevolence. Shadwell uses Sir Nicholas's experiments to symbolize the virtuoso's dereliction of social responsibility by showing the social consequences of his new role. Gimcrack's experiments resemble Dr. Moreau's violations of species on Huxley's island. Parodying Boyle's experiments in transfusing the blood of animals, Sir Nicholas dabbles in species transformation: as Bruce ironically explains, "excellent Experiments may be made in changing one Creature into the nature of another" (act 2, p. 34). According to Snarle, Sir Nicholas has killed four of five people by transfusions from other animals, although Sir Nicholas claims these patients were already doomed from internal complaints, including "cacochymious." "Pish!" snorts Snarle, "I do not know what you mean by your damn'd cacochymious canting; but they dy'd in sadness" (act 2, p. 34). But Sir Nicholas is deaf to Snarle's demand for humane care: he cares only for the physical. His language marks him as a specialist who attends to one part of the body and ignores the rest.

Indeed, Sir Nicholas's self-appointed expertise virtually ordains him: scientific replaces spiritual attention as the virtuoso turned doctor mutates professions to become a kind of priest. In a hilarious example, one grateful patient calls himself "the meanest" of Sir Nicholas's "Flock"; his religious jargon is comically literalized when we learn that he has been saved by an infusion of sheep's blood. Transformed, if not spiritually at least physically into one of Sir Nicholas's stock, he now sends Sir Nicholas his own wool. Indeed, as Swift suggested fifty years later when in *A Modest Proposal* (1729) he recommended that landowners make gloves from Irish baby skins, such procedures can bring profit: Sir Nicholas plans to make "all my Cloathes" from this wool (act 2, p. 34). His exploitation of his dependents extends to their very skins. The poor are depicted as hapless victims of this aristocratic misuse of traditional power. The virtuoso, in turn, exemplifies the abuses of the nouveau riche, men given social power without the conventional training in social responsibility.

Sir Nicholas's experiments evoke a European folk tradition of monstrosity in which the physical represents the moral. Since the ancient period, moralists had interpreted deformities in the body as portents from heaven that warned of human vice and that were historically authenticated by Herodotus's stories and the Bible. *The World of Wonders* identifies bestiality, a confusion of human and animal parallel to Sir Nicholas's transfusions, as the "sin against nature," according to common usage.[63] In the early modern period, this discourse, wavering between metaphorical and empirical meanings, questions ontology itself. What is a human? Broadsides available throughout the later seventeenth century frequently employ the trope of species fluidity for satirical purposes. In Shadwell's play, the scientist aids regression when he inverts the chain of being. As Sir Nicholas here meddles with natural categories, so other kinds of demonic dabblers like Dr. Frankenstein attempt to violate God's order by impertinent experiments. Their activity parodies divine creation and marks Satanic ambition. In showing that, by valuing monstrosity, scientists applaud ontological transgression, Shadwell links science and monstrosity as violations of humanity. He thus identifies the scientist with a physical aberration that fatally attempts to improve on nature.

Sir Nicholas exemplifies the early modern charge against curious men: their pursuit of monstrosities and curiosities has made them monsters or curiosities themselves (fig. 8). Through Sir Nicholas, Shadwell expresses the contemporary fear that society applauded freakishness. The way to combat such distortion was by co-opting the stance of spectating scientist for oneself. Longvil does just this when he identifies Sir Formal with a tout, and Sir Nicholas with a public curiosity: "I would rather be the Trumpeter to a Monster, and call in the Rabble to see a Calf with Six legs, than shew such a Blockhead [as Sir Formal does Sir Nicholas]" (act 1, p. 10). When he sees Sir Nicholas swimming on the table, Bruce remarks wonderingly, "He is the most curious Coxcomb breathing" (act 2, p. 27). Longvil calls him "the rarest Fop that ever was heard of" (act 2, p. 27). Sir Formal himself underscores the social ambiguity of curiosity. When he commends Sir Nicholas as "the finest speculative Gentleman in the whole World, and in his Cogitations the most severe Animal alive," he interlards categories

FELLOWS OF THE ZOOLOGICAL SOCIETY

Figure 8. George Cruikshank, "Fellows of the Zoological Society." (Colored etching, n.d.)
This print depicts scientists transformed into the creatures they study. Courtesy
of the Art Collection, the Harry Ransom Humanities Research Center,
University of Texas at Austin

to define the virtuoso in terms of an oxymoron (act 1, p. 9). While Sir
Nicholas is a "Gentleman" who "speculates," he also becomes only a theoretical or speculative gentleman: a man of dubious or unrealized status. By
hinting that curious self-indulgence undermines class, this joke underscores the social cost of virtuosoship. Moreover, Sir Nicholas jeopardizes
not only his class affiliation, but his species membership: he becomes an
"Animal" instead of a human, a monster instead of a gentleman.

The satirical transformation of virtuosi into curious items within their
own curiosity cabinets co-opts their very power of collecting. Such satires
allow audiences to turn inquiring subjects into objects. Thus satires discipline curiosity, turning it into the popular condemnation of elite fraud.
This fraud is located in the virtuosi's habit of inventing value. By idiosyn-
cratically valuing objects like rocks or people like artisans, virtuosi undermine the fixed values of society. Historically, this confusion of means and
ends appears in the regard for instruments like microscopes, compasses,
and clocks as themselves curious items.[64] In contrast, satires suggest that

the pursuit of things interferes with the pursuit of knowledge: items obscure the scientific purpose of collecting; objects defeat the object. They thus grant the audience's free-floating, savvy curiosity power to condemn the specialist's acquisitive curiosity as fraud.

CURIOSITY AS SECOND SIGHT

As Restoration satires show, science can be read as fraud in many ways. One of the most resonant in early modern English culture was the derogation of curious vision as a version of the oldest con game of all: second sight. This trope neatly mocks a rich cluster of scientific traits. It explodes the virtuosi's claim to disinterestedness and identifies them as witches, cunning men, and scam artists, dressed in empirical—or in the emperor's— new clothes. Alternatively, sometimes even simultaneously, this trope attacks the virtuosi for credulity, naive idealism, and a superstitious belief in obvious impossibilities. By describing the fabulous lands and creatures revealed by this suspect vision, the trope exposes the ambition of the virtuosi for new worlds to conquer. Finally, it contrasts instrument-aided vision with the traditional form of second sight: the holy perception of the moral visionary, the poet or priest blessed with an understanding close to God's. Unlike traditional second sight, however, this new kind of fine sight could be shared by the common person if she had access to the tools to achieve it. Such sight could enable the sensibly curious, the rationally empirical, to see behind deception.

The indictment of scientific empiricism as second sight reflects the cultural anxiety to regulate curiosity for social use. As either a noble pursuit or as entertainment, the curiosity represented in English early modern culture threatened to disrupt social order. It seemed to preoccupy potential leaders with experiments, co-opt intellectual and social activities—especially classical learning and charity—encourage masquerade and vice, and blur taxonomic and social distinctions. To those excluded from the elite world, it appeared to promulgate an exclusive sociability and perspective that entailed seeing reality in ways that were unverifiable by common sight or common sense, by means only of specialized information or elite instruments like the microscope and the telescope. Moreover, curious men seemed to express their discoveries in an exclusive jargon. To many people, scientists seemed to be brushing aside the traditional values of society.

This anxiety centered on language. By embracing literal language as the means to avoid disputation, Sprat and others seemed to some to marginalize the moral language of poetry. Although several virtuosi themselves wrote in verse, they seemed to conservatives merely to be extending their usurpation of culture into traditional forms. To defend or make their own cultural place, university-trained poets thus sought to deploy curiosity for their own art, just as medical practitioners, journalists, and practitioners of a host of other skills were doing. Revising religious arguments against curiosity and enlisting popular mistrust of the New Science, these poets attacked as naive the conviction that language can represent truth as clearly as the eyes can see reality.[65] Instead, they advocated the artistry of poetry. By lampooning virtuosi for destructive self-indulgence, they defended the traditional view that poetry speaks to the people and nourishes social and sexual relations. By linking blurred sight and crippled expression, they indicted virtuosi for preferring strangulated jargon and mediated vision to piety, society, and common sense.

The trope of blinded sight pervades English culture. Blurred vision or seeing something that is not there marks the saint, the fool, and the visionary. The association of curiosity and the occult partly derives from the medieval tradition of science that mingled magic—the supernatural—with natural philosophy, conjoining astrology and medicine. This conjunction draws particular animus after the Civil War when Puritan fanaticism was depicted as rarefied wonder-mongering. Despite the public definition of curiosity as the pursuit of truth by empirical means, its other meaning as the pursuit of the unseen persists. The cultural logic behind this apparent contradiction lies in the early connections between the two ideas. Both curiosity and the occult are seen as offering false versions of the world that rely on what is conceived of as unreliable evidence: the evidence of the eyes. But, as traditional culture repeatedly proves, nothing is so easily hoodwinked as the eyes. Nonetheless, curious people believe themselves rather than conventional wisdom: curious and credulous characters are twinned in culture as examples of self-absorption.[66] Moreover, curiosity seeks concealed knowledge, and so attempts to find a new world. The occult offers such a world, full of mysteries above nature. The curious become susceptible to superstition.

The connection between the occult and the curious is etymological as well as cultural. Rooted in the Latin word for concealment and related to "occlude," "occult" signifies things hidden, obscured from sight, or secret and pertains to aspects of nature only science or alchemy can reveal.[67] A word with much currency during the early Restoration, it connotes a belief in the imperceptible and therefore in the preternatural, supernatural, or unnatural. Thus, cultural doubts about the reliability of empirical perception find expression in literary treatment of the supernatural, from lunar satire to Gothic romance. These explorations of the occult also inform genre since they address the function of metaphor itself. Is seeing literal or imaginative, a function of the body or of the mind, faith, and spirit? Can sight create value from nothing, or change the very nature of material? Both popular and learned texts fret at the border of the empirical and the occult in order to define curiosity for their own ideological ends.

Early modern witches and the reports of their detection and punishment notably pit curiosity against wonder. Throughout modern culture, they (along with tales of ghosts and poltergeists) provide the opportunity to stage the battle between common perception and unseen power. At the turn of the century, the conflict between the belief in witchcraft and the new empirical philosophy appears in trial narratives. The notorious case of Richard Hathaway demonstrates that secret observation and careful inquiry could reveal common deceptions behind strange possessions, as in the case of the Cock Lane Ghost. In 1701, young Hathaway charged Sarah Morduck with bewitching him so that he succumbed to various diseases, lost the use of his senses, starved, and vomited nails and pins. A suspicious doctor exposed him, but the public remained unconvinced. Hathaway, his master Mr. Welling, and others hounded Morduck from her home, forced her to move to London, and, accompanied by a rabble of observers and soldiers, rioted in front of her house there, making such a commotion that her case was brought to court. Instead of punishing the rioters, the Aldermen of London searched her for secret signs or teats, permitted her to be scratched by Hathaway to confirm her witchcraft, and then committed her for a witch, refusing £500 bail.

But others doubted Hathaway. After Morduck's indictment, suspicious officials immured him in the house of a Mr. Kensey, where they quickly discovered that he had taken sustenance when the urine he had hidden in a box lid began to drip onto the bedclothes.[68] By directing a supposedly sympathetic chambermaid to trick him into eating while "several Persons of Reputation" watched "through a Hole fit for the Purpose," they exposed him. Unaware of the trick, when examined by these reputable doctors, "*he made signs, that he had fasted twelve Weeks, and clung up his Belly as a proof of his Emptiness, according to his common Practice, though he had in their sight just before eaten a plentiful Meal.*" In addition, a skeptical observer discovered his method and his motive. The prosecutor reports, "He practiced his Trick of Vomiting Pins several times, but pretending to [do]it once before one who did not take every thing upon Trust, but was curious enough to observe Nicely, and search him; *after some resistance, several Rows of Pins were found in his Pocket."* His doom was sealed when the investigator discovered that "upon his first pretending to vomit Pins . . . he had prepared *a Narrative of his own being Bewitched,* and *he himself carried it to a Printer"* (3).

At Hathaway's trial, the judge demanded that the public "consider with yourselves whether you have any evidence" of devilry sufficient

> to enable a man to fast beyond the usual time that Nature will
> allow [since witches] cannot invert the order of Nature: And if the
> thing is impossible, and he endeavour all this while to make the
> world believe he has fasted so long a time, it is most evident he is
> a Cheat. (3)

The public account of Hathaway's imposture dramatized that observation and shrewd curiosity could expose not only witchcraft, but all kinds of deception, just as *The World of Wonders* had argued. Public trials of fraud could use rational curiosity to explode the false occult.

However, other trial narratives that, in contrast, verified the occult also used circumstantial details. Only two years after Hathaway's trial, Sarah Griffiths was committed to Bridewell as a witch. Living in a garret, she inflicted distempers on her neighbor's children, causing them to vomit pins, contort their bodies, and see "strange Apparitions of Cats, which of a sudden would vanish away."[69] Although she "was a long time suspected for a bad woman . . . nothing could be prov'd against her, that the Law might take hold of her," until one day a "jolly" apprentice selling her soap joked that his uneven scale was bewitched. Falling into a fury, Griffiths ran from the shop threatening revenge, and that night the shop goods tumbled from the shelves and the apprentice fell ill. A few days later, after he had recovered, he saw her, seized her, and threw her in the river to see whether she would swim as a witch would, or drown as would an innocent woman, "but like a Bladder, when forc'd under Water pops up again, so this Witch was no sooner in but Swam like a Corke," pulled herself upon the shore, and hit the jolly apprentice in the arm where her handprint remained in black until, shortly afterwards, he died. His master, Mr. John, brought her before the justice, who "had evidence" of the apprentice's vomiting nails and gangrenous arm, and so condemned her.

These trials show that like many members of the Royal Society, the public believed in invisible power at the same time that they accepted empirical rules of evidence. Produced as material for the reading public, witchcraft texts reveal that although the fundamental question of the existence of witchcraft remained moot, juries believed that they could examine physical evidence with clear minds, and readers were sure that they could similarly balance belief and skepticism. Juries' evidence often constituted not only diseased victims, but empirical phenomena: objects moving without agents, unaccountable sounds, smells, and sights, and proof of the unnatural appetites associated with evil curiosity. These texts thus demonstrate the persistence of belief and interest in unseen worlds that project curious power: the power to sweep through ontological boundaries and overturn categories. Significantly, witches' victims frequently vomit indigestible objects, demonstrating witches' power both to compel people to perform against their natures, and to transform material from one category to another—from metal to food. As examples of a double nature like the hypocrite and the monster, witches challenge the dominance of the public definition of nature. Similarly, their printed stories, hearkening to a world of alternative values and powers, become curious tales that prove the invisible.[70]

In the late seventeenth and early eighteenth centuries, witches embody the fraying margin between public and private belief. Despite increasing skepticism about their existence, including Sprat's vigorous disproof of them, some virtuosi believed in witches precisely because their unseen power could manifest itself and so be proven empirically.[71] Encouraged by Boyle and Henry More, Joseph Glanvill authenticated witches when he recorded his expedition to a haunted house to verify tales of strange signs and ghostly voices and then published an account in *A Philosophical Endeavour towards the Defence of the being of Witches and Apparitions* (1666), expanded two years later into *A Blow at Modern Sadducism in some Philosophical Considerations about Witchcraft*. Glanvill relies on reason and his own scientific objectivity to validate his empirical experience. As a cleric, Glanvill had a further reason for believing in witches. Like many Puritans, Methodists, and religious enthusiasts, including John Wesley, he interpreted apparitions as tangible proof of God's existence. Belief in the occult thus blended with adherence to traditional piety. The posthumous edition of his work, *Saducismus Triumphatus* (1681), extends Glanvill's defense of the existence of the supernatural by identifying skepticism with atheism in a host of recent works.

Even in the following century, witches fascinated pious thinkers and writers. Joseph Addison and Samuel Johnson, for example, only awaited proof of their existence.[72] Narratives of the occult thus allowed readers and writers both to ally themselves with experimental and empirical philosophy, and to maintain a public belief in the divine, whatever their innermost doubts about witchcraft.[73] Moreover, the widely published debates of the

Royal Society about witches' existence legitimized a printed tradition of ambiguous accounts of the supernatural that tell of witchcraft yet hint at fraud. Because they visually demonstrate invisible power, witches constitute a phenomenon that borders both empiricism and faith, curiosity and wonder.

Tales of witchcraft allowed writers to exploit religious superstition either to defeat or to buttress empiricism. Catholicism, however, offered a polemical topic to test curiosity against "curiousness." For late seventeenth-century Englishmen, alienated from the Continent by the Reformation and the Civil War, Catholics embodied credulity and superstition. Not only could the religion be seen as relying on curious rituals and antirational mysteries like the transubstantiation of the flesh during Mass, but the obedience to priests and the preservation of a Latin service full of rituals seemed to mystify not only religion but also the body, the natural world, and language. In "Notes Conferr'd: Or, A Dialogue betwixt The Groaning Board and a Jesuite: Demonstrating the Ambiguous Humour of the one, and Curiosity of the other" (1682), a broadside published during the Exclusion crisis in the 1680s, a Jesuit interrogates a table for news of dead friends: he believes that the board holds oracular truths veiled by "Ambiguous Words."[74] Although he attempts concealment, his curiosity exposes him as a Jesuit—a credulous believer in an unseen world. The unknown, unseen world of the occult that yet yields itself to the curious eye was represented as a Catholic world.

Marvelous narratives of witches and wonders generally employ simple, denotative language to veil metaphorical interpretation and claim empirical accuracy, but some authors attempted the contrary: to use the poetic idiom to make the empirical marvelous. None did so more passionately than "Mad Madge," Margaret Cavendish, the Duchess of Newcastle, in her book of scientific verse, *Poems and Fancies* (1653). This volume is a bold attempt to invent an empirical mythology, a poetic language to describe and explain the natural world in literal, scientific terms.[75] Her fifth dedication, to "the Reader," defends her enterprise for its thrifty and decorous use of language and opposes Puritan simplicity and connoisseurship: "It [this Worke] is not *Excellent*, nor *Rare*, but *plaine*; yet it is *harmlesse, modest*, and *honest*."[76] At the same time, she argues that "if you *judge*, and *understand* not, you may take / For *Non-sense* that which *learning Sense* will make." She tiptoes between rejecting elite philosophy, the province of men and scholars, and embracing curiosity as the rightful province of the general public. Similarly, she dutifully rationalizes her focus on the natural world by explaining, "For *God*, and his *Heavenly Mansions*, are to be *admired, wondred*, and *astonished* at, and not *disputed* on." By her elaborate prefaces and modest posture, she attempts to evade philosophical quarrels, but her attempt drew a great deal of criticism, albeit muted out of respect for her high status or out of fear of her stately spouse.[77]

Not only did Cavendish encroach on the preserve of men by dabbling in scientific affairs and contriving the publication of her own verse, but her curiosity revealed her ambition. She herself teasingly acknowledges this when she puns that her fear grows bulky, fed on her tiny poetic *"Atomes,"* yet "if I am condemn'd, I shall be *Annihilated* to nothing; but my *Ambition* is such, as I would either be a *World,* or nothing" (fourth dedication). Using the images of her own verse, she articulates one of the central charges against philosophers, later used by John Wilmot, Earl of Rochester, and against the curious: that they invent, even become, their own worlds, setting up a universe to rival that of God for their own aggrandizement.[78]

Cavendish identifies the hidden world of science with the religious world of unseen faith. The curious endeavor not only penetrates the origins of human and animal life and the nature of the universe, but it identifies the inner space of the mind with the supernatural. Imagination and religion coalesce. In another poem, *"Of many* Worlds *in this* World," Cavendish compares the infinite interior open to science with a *"Nest* of *Boxes"* decreasing in size:

> Although they are not subject to our *Sense,*
> A *World* may be no bigger than *two*-pence.
> *Nature* is curious, and such *worke* may make,
> That our dull *Sense* can never finde, but scape.
> For *Creatures,* small as *Atomes,* may be there,
> If every *Atome* a *Creatures Figure* beare.
> If foure *Atomes* a *World* can made, then see
> What severall *Worlds* might in an *Eare-ring* bee.
> For *Millions* of these *Atomes* maybee in
> The *Head* of one *small,* little, *single Pin.*
> And if thus *Small,* then *Ladies* well may weare,
> A *World* of *Worlds,* as *Pendents* in each *Eare.*

Cavendish's curiosity plunders science for poetic license and female power. More ambitious even than telescopic adventurers, it leaves no space, however trivial or private, unexplored. In *The Rape of the Lock* sixty years later, Alexander Pope derides a feminine inquisitiveness reduced to a fetishizing acquisitiveness, but Cavendish seamlessly matches inquiry and commodity, investigation and possession, empiricism and mystic imagination. Cavendish's numberless worlds express a desire for unlimited power—and her adaptation of the scientific mode demonstrates that it allowed even women to dream of conquest.

Cavendish defines curiosity as an intellectual drive with a physical form. Glossing Bacon's concept of the mind as God's storehouse, she imagines it as a cabinet of fashionable curiosities. One "Fancy" identifies "The *five Senses*" as "*Natures Boxes, Cabinets*," unlocked by nature's keys, but "The Braine" is "her chiefe *Cabinet*" (126):

> In *Natures Cabinet*, the *Braine*, you'll find
> Many a fine *Knack*, which doth delight the *Mind*.
> Severall *colour'd Ribbons* of *Fancies* new,
> To tye in *Hats*, or *Haire* of *Lovers* true.
> *Masques* of *Imaginations* onely shew
> The *Eyes* of *Knowledge*, t'other part none know.
> *Fans* of *Opinion*, which wave the *Wind*,
> According as the *Heat* is in the *Mind*.
> *Gloves* of *Remembrance*, which draw off, and on . . .
> *Black Patches* of *Ignorance*, to stick on
> The *Face of Fooles:* this *Cabinet* is shewn. (126)

This mental curiosity cabinet holds works of social art—love, opinion, memory—that are simultaneously nature's knickknacks. Here, Cavendish dissolves the distinction between the physical and the intellectual underlying much contemporary argument. Moreover, this logic allows any observer to be a collector of intellectual rarities, qualifying her as a connoisseur. Although this concept surfaces more strongly in the middle of the eighteenth century, even in the Restoration, the potential for empiricism to unravel formal social categories by enfranchising everyone with eyes was perceived as a threat.

Whereas *Poems and Fancies* idealizes the investigation of nature as a form of devotion at once physical and intellectual, religious and rational, Restoration satirists identify it with a devotion to the unseen that is far from sane. Samuel Butler's *The Elephant in the Moon* (c. 1676) and Aphra Behn's play *The Emperor of the Moon* (1687) exemplify the reaction against the Royal Society. Informed by the contemporary genre of utopian voyages, they mold the anthropological idealism of such lunar explorations as Francis Godwin's *The Man in the Moone: or, Discourse of Voyage Thither by Domingo Gonsals The Speedy Messenger* (1638) into scientific satire. In Behn's play, for example, Harlequin, dressed as ambassador to the moon, astonishes the idealistic doctor by describing the lunar world as equally corrupt as ours, full of hard-drinking women and mercenary and faithless men (3.2.235). Whereas early seventeenth-century fantastic voyages both disseminate scientific information and fantasize about the possibilities for human perfection, these Restoration works use realms newly discovered by science as arenas to expose human folly, exemplified by scientific credulity.[79] Behn and Butler, moreover, express a new antagonism between poetry and science as alternate modes of moral apprehension informing social behavior. These texts question the reliability of sight and the status of the unseen.

Behn contrasts the different ways of seeing: idealism, love, empirical curiosity, and exploration. Her farce *The Emperor of the Moon* blends the multiple contemporary meanings of curiosity in the figure of Doctor Baliardo, the peeping scientist who believes in an ideal, lunar world. Baliardo satirizes the virtuosi of the Royal Society. We first meet him, "*all manner of Mathematical Instruments, hanging at his Girdle*," as he is mounting his telescope to peer at the Emperor of the Moon in his private closet.[80] When Baliardo's servant, Scaramouch, reproaches him for indecency, he admits, "it were flat Treason if it shou'd be known, but thus unseen, and as wise Politicians shou'd, I take survey of all: This is the States-man's peeping-hole, through which he Steals the secrets of Kings, and seems to wink at distance" (1.2.7). Notably, the political words "States" and "Steals" receive capitals here, but in the eighteenth-century version, "Peeping" and "Secrets" are both capitalized instead—printing changes that reflect each period's special sensitivity.[81] This alteration reveals how, historically, the secrets of the closet differ. Whereas the Restoration audience sheltered statesmanship from peepers, early eighteenth-century readers shielded sex; the first era sexualizes politics while the latter politicizes sexuality.

In both cases, however, visual or empirical pretension facilitates social ambition. If early eighteenth-century writers conceived of upstarts as gender-crossers, particularly public women, Restoration upstarts were political-crossers, scientists who ignored traditional court manners, hierarchies, and kinds of truth. Both inquiring types become curious by their impertinent disregard for conventional boundaries. In this play, Behn emphasizes the transgression of scientific peeping by her figurative representation of the distinction between the ambitious Baliardo and the (literally) outlandish role he desires. His telescope enacts the upstart's desire to penetrate the state, particularly through its body, the body of the king. Moreover, the distance the doctor "winks at" is more than physical; it is the distance between divine royalty and common mortality, between ruler and subject. By foolishly trusting his eyes, he blinds himself to symbolic truth.

Dr. Baliardo, furthermore, remains ignorant even of his own ambition. His daughter Elaria blames his belief in a lunar civilization on his reading *Lucian's Dialogue to the Lofty Traveller* and other fanciful adventures describing voyages to the moon, which he takes literally. Behn here touches on a powerful theme that flourished throughout the early modern period: conservative distrust of Romantic fiction for confusing readers and stimulating impossible or inappropriate desires and self-images. In the Restoration, this fiction includes travelogues, scientific utopian visions, and fabulous histories; in the late eighteenth century, it concerns sexual love and Gothic adventure. Both kinds of romance prompt the reader to credit the unusual, unseen, or ideal, and thus both subtly criticize social reality and flatter readers as superior to it.

Aphra Behn punishes Baliardo for this vanity and idealism by a device. Baliardo's daughter and her friends prepare a farce called *The World in the Moon* to cure the credulous doctor of his delusion. Like Shadwell's impractical Sir Nicholas Gimcrack, who prefers insects to humans, Baliardo believes that "man was not made for Woman" and enthusiastically welcomes a lunar philosophy that circumnavigates procreation. Whereas Gimcrack falls to amphibious depths by promoting himself to studying more than man, Baliardo, in conceiving of a humanity born, like Christ, without sex, credits salamanders and fairies with conferring life and immortality (1.2.9). His scientific curiosity dovetails with folk superstition. This foolish credulity results from more, however, than a naive trust in the eyes or in what those eyes have read in fiction. It also reflects an inflated sense of his own importance.

Although Baliardo's vanity lies concealed more deeply than Gimcrack's, it still prompts him to accept readily the fantasy that he has been chosen above all men to become the father-in-law of the lunar emperor, for like the members of the Royal Society, he considers himself "devout and pure of Spirit; free from Sin" (1.2.9). When the sparkish Don Charmante, masquerading as an ambassador from the moon, explains that the qualifications for admission to the Society of divine *Caballa* are "an absolute absence from carnal thought" and adherence to secrecy, Baliardo eagerly accepts the challenge (1.2.10)—moments later hoping for a "Hero" as a "Grandson" (1.2.11). Indeed, in the panting Baliardo, "Refining his Thoughts" in order to clear his eyes properly and peer secretly at the emperor through the rigged telescope, Behn incarnates her central criticisms of Restoration scientists for vanity, naive empiricism, prurient curiosity veiled as disinterest, self-ignorance and idealism (1.2.11). Through this image, Behn mocks the Royal Society's solemn assertions of disinterested perception.

Behn interweaves skepticism about the power of sight with disbelief in the objective scientific personality. As Restoration theater repeatedly dramatizes, looking and liking are intricately, often causally, associated, and never more so than in questions of love. Lust itself arises from visual stimulation. Educated by romances and scientific treatises, Baliardo understands nothing of this moral truth. Thus, he believes Don Charmante's assurance that he will see divine nymphs if he is free from sin. Peering hopefully through the telescope, he is deceived by a quickly inserted picture of a sprawling lady, lit from behind. Convinced of his own purity, he rhapsodizes at her beauty and is reproved for "peeping" at the nymph when she is reposing (1.2.10). Here, Behn throws sight itself into doubt: the doctor cannot be sure whether he is seeing something close or far away, whether he is seeing something ideal, real, or rigged, or whether he is seeing beauty, art, or sex. His ignorance of what he is seeing stems from his ignorance of his own human nature: like Sir Nicholas Gimcrack, he does not study man, and, denying his own desires, he denies his humanity.

Equating illicit looking with the virtuosi's endeavor, Behn suggests that telescopes make virtuosi see something invisible, particularly by annihilating distance. In her farce, when the doctor peeps again at the supposed emperor in a "private" "Love-fit," brooding on his passion for a mortal woman, his peeping serves to demonstrate the ease with which scientific objectivity becomes prying. As well as a prurient joke, these episodes express contemporary questions about artificial visual aids; more generally, they call into doubt the morality of assisting fallen human nature to achieve its desires. Behn dramatizes the Hobbesian refutation of the possibility of disinterest by revealing that the doctor hopes for the nymph's (platonic) love in order to be immortalized with his niece and daughter. He cannot accept the common, if metaphorical, method of immortality through procreation but wishes for absolute immortality by becoming divine.

Behn shows that trust in seeing conjoins the scientist and the lover, the traditional archetype of self-delusion, blinded by the blind Cupid. To reinforce the indictment of curiosity as lust, in the same scene, set in a garden, Behn depicts Bellemante writing of "a great Curiosity" (capitalized in the eighteenth-century edition) or love-longing of a shepherd for a maid (scene 2, act 2, p. 207). His kind of curiosity parallels the Doctor's, but he knows he is seeking pleasure, whereas the Doctor believes he is seeking truth. Moreover, Behn devoted her two subplots to the sexual machinations of servants. When the jealous Don Cinthio finds his rival hiding with his mistress from the Doctor in the closet, Scaramouch placates him by calling his discovery self-deception and blaming it on the eyes: "*Deceptio visus*, Sir; the Error of the Eyes" (scene 2, act 2, p. 240). By using the Latin phrase, Scaramouch underscores the paradoxical flaw in both science and love: misplaced trust in one's eyes, and equally misplaced mistrust in them. Scaramouch's folk wisdom coincides with the wisdom of traditional learned culture to reproach the credulous scientists who trust themselves too much. With its reliance on the duplicitous senses and its proud ignorance of culture and tradition, science is depicted as yet another means for human self-deception.

With similar allusions to specific scientists like Kepler, John Wilkins, and Sir Kenelme Digby, Samuel Butler's earlier mock epic, *The Elephant in the Moon*, burlesques the telescopic pretensions of the Royal Society.[82] Originally written in octosyllabic form, Butler revised the poem into heroic couplets, and it was published immediately. While this revision may have been intended to ironize contemporary poets like Dryden and Davenant, it was not an uncommon practice for poets to dignify their verse by rewriting it in the longer meter, and Butler may also have aimed to make the poem more satirically suitable to the pretensions of the Society. Certainly the form works with the language to mock the ambitions of the virtuosi. It portrays a deluded scientist, possibly Sir Paul Neal, who, clapping "to th'optick glass his judging Eye" (1.32) to survey the moon, mistakes proximate flies and a mouse for lunar armies and an elephant. The credulity of scientists who believe in their own fictions, the profitable symbiosis of their association with one another, and their hidden avarice all emerge in the symbolic shape of deluded vision.

In this satire, Butler identifies the distortions of sight offered by scientific instruments with the grandiose social claims and speculative tales of the virtuosi. After explaining the "glorious ... Design" (1.16) of the "Learn'd *Society*" (1.1) to survey the lunar landscape for purposes of imperialistic cultivation equivalent to those employed in Ireland, the narrator describes the instrument of observation as if it were a noble weapon of combat:

> And now the lofty Tube, the Scale
> With which they Heav'n itself assail,
> Was mounted full against the *Moon;*

And all stood ready to fall on,
Impatient who should have the Honour
To plant an Ensign first upon her. (1.21–26)

These modern warriors exercise their heroism by mere observation and ambitious dreaming, rather than by physical contest. Indeed, they imagine epic battles on the moon, but they remain in the safe realm of intellection. By the mock heroic mode, Butler implies a contrast between traditional standards of physical valor and social duty and the Royal Society's vicarious bellicosity, self-interested values, and febrile activities. He ironically identifies the chief *"Virtuoso"* as a type of Nestor, revered for his "deep Belief" (1.27) as "the most profound, and wise / To solve Impossibilities" (1.29–30). In the blink of an eye, the eye peering through the telescope, this virtuoso chief has conceived an entire lunar society whose elite dwell in dark, civilized cellars protected from the sun and their enemies, the ground-inhabiting "rude Peasants," whom they are perpetually battling (1.51). Another passage ridicules a "great Philosopher" for defending the perceptions of the blind over those of normal men (1.60). Butler targets a rarefied kind of vision that excludes common "sense," and that, manipulated by ambition, endows virtuosi with disproportionate influence in both the scientific and literary worlds.

Indeed, in this lampoon, scientific empiricism grows into more than a false religion. As philosopher after philosopher elaborates on the customs and history of the lunar inhabitants, the society constructs a false reality verified by the consensus of each member, as, "Proud of his Int'rest in the Glory / Of so miraculous a Story," he contributes his own lie to the construct in order to increase his own glory (1.165–66). Butler is very clear on the self-justificatory imperative of the Royal Society, as well as on its colonization of literary as well as cultural values. One virtuoso,

who for his Excellence
In height'ning Words and shad'wing Sense,
And magnifying all he writ
With curious microscopick Wit,
Was magnify'd himself no less
In home and foreign Colleges, (1.169–72)

represents the spread of the contagion of the Royal Society's boasting into literary culture. This philosopher argues that the discovery of lunar civilization compensates for "all our unsuccessful Pains, / And lost Expence of

Time and Brains" (1.176–77). As the virtuosi are plotting their fame, however, their footboys peer in the telescope and discover the elephant to be a mouse. Butler's satire attacks the self-generating authority and self-referential standards of truth-testing of the exclusive Royal Society.[83] Common perception outstrips learned peering.

In his *Characters*, Butler distills his doubts about the social consequences of scientific curiosity. He identifies a "Virtuoso" by his "Humour," an "Inclination" that, ignorant of true "Art," leads him to treat all men as if they were as engaged in his "Arts and Sciences" as himself.[84] The virtuoso's megalomania makes him socially incompetent. Moreover, ignorant of himself, expending great labors on fruitless activity, and "dazzled" by display, he loves "Rarities" and "strange natural Histories," which he deliberately tempts himself to believe, "forgetting that Belief upon Belief is false Heraldry" (122–23). According to Butler, virtuosi construct entire systems of untruth, rival worlds that resemble "Romances," but deny their fictional status. This misguided belief partly results from the virtuosi's ambition. As Butler explains, these pedants are preoccupied with "Wit and Knowledge," determined to impress others; the result is a form of learning that values appearances above truths and that, couching itself in indecipherable language, prefers to mystify rather than communicate. Moreover, Butler's "Virtuoso" desires applause above all, regardless of who applauds. He thus disregards the intellectual and moral distinctions drawn up by public opinion. Using art, language, and knowledge for his own glory, he is the incarnation of the social vice of pretension (122–23).

This Virtuoso resembles "The Curious Man" or collector, the very emblem of false valuation. This character defines value as personal possession. Like the Virtuoso, he "Values things not by their Use or Worth, but Scarcity" with the intention only of winning applause "because the Rarities are his own" (104–5). Butler condemns curiosity as hoarding: it is a misuse of wealth, but more importantly it is a device whereby the individual collector raises his own worth at the expense of social values. Like the Virtuoso, the Curious Man believes he sees more than others: "That which other Men neglect he believes they oversee, and stores up Trifles as rare Discoveries." In his confidence in his private system of valuation, the Curious Man treads on the edge of a faith in the unseen: "He admires subtleties above all Things, because the more subtle they are, the nearer they are to nothing; and values no art but that which is spun so thin, that it is of no Use at all" (105). As an example of this precious uselessness, Butler offers the copy of Homer's *Iliad* that Pliny discovered written in a nutshell, a classic and classical example of micrographia that reflects on the current passion for microscopic natural investigation. This character's predilection for useless art, for invisible wonders, demonstrates an antisocial valuation that makes him socially valueless himself: "His perpetual Dotage upon Curiosities at length renders him one of them" (105). For Butler, curiosity, like scientific investigation, manufactures an occult world in the face of the public world that all uninitiated men value.

These satires seized on what appeared to be a contradiction in the empirical method. The contemporary "dispute over the reliability of the eye, and of witnessing, as the basis for generating and warranting knowledge" spilled into distrust of elite curiosity.[85] Even while plain seeing was defined, in opposition to rarefied metaphysics, as the scientific test of empiricism, scientists apparently required the aid of expensive instruments. *Philosophical Transactions* bristled with debates, resembling advertisements, concerning the merits of different telescopes and microscopes.[86] Some issues printed arguments by instrument-makers fresh from Europe and eager to prove the superiority of their products. In the index to the issues from 1665 and 1666, the listing of "Artificial Instruments" occupies twenty-two lines, more space than almost any other single entry.[87] Reports devoted to such wonders as "An *Optical* Contrivance for strange visions, or Apparitions" opened the possibilities of scientific fraud, credulity, and impiety.[88] Many entries specify the uses of "Glasses" by Campani, Helvetius, Huygens, and others, while subsequent indexes include reviews of books advocating certain optical devices as well as directions for using them and the results of experiments conducted with them.[89] Scientific exclusivity provided commercial opportunities. Moreover, virtuosi encouraged exhibitions. In 1673, John Evelyn had recorded, "I went to see Paradise, a room in Hatton Garden, furnished with the representations of all sorts of Animals, handsomely painted on boards or cloth, and so cut out and made to stand, move, fly, crawl, roare, and make their several cries. The man who shewed, made us laugh heartily at his formal poetrie."[90] The scientific appetite for the new and spectacular linked high and low curiosity.

Whether vision is belief or proof crystallized several sensitive points for advocates of and against empirical curiosity. Before Butler and Behn's satires, many virtuosi had argued in favor of instrument-aided sight. In his chapter on "The Credit of *Optick-Glasses* vindicated against a *Disputing Man, who is afraid to believe his Eyes against Aristotle*," Joseph Glanvill finessed the distinction between unaided and instrument-aided sight. With the common sense of a plain folk tale, he mockingly refutes complaints by a clergyman *"that our Glasses were all deceitful and fallacious"*:

[This] Answer minds me of the *good Woman*, who when her
Husband urged in an Occasion of difference, [*I saw it, and shall I
not believe my own Eyes?*] Replied briskly, *Will you believe your own
Eyes, before your own dear wife*: And it seems *this Gentleman* thinks it
unreasonable we should *Believe ours*, before his *own dear Aristotle.*[91]

By identifying adherents of Aristotelian speculative reasoning with unreasonable old women, Glanvill claimed masculine independence for empiricists, as Thomas Sprat and Robert Boyle had done.[92] He defended perception first by arguing that microscopes and telescopes alter only the
proportions of objects, not their appearance, and then by questioning the
reliability of anyone's eyes: "we all have the like reasons to *distrust our Eyes*"
(*Plus Ultra*, 66). Sensitive to contemporary skepticism, Glanvill attempted
to normalize scientific vision.

   This defense of science as the logical way to understand man also ran
against the popular ridicule of virtuosi for vaunting brain over brawn.
Whereas traditionally the aristocratic class supplied military or diplomatic
support, the Royal Society offered theoretical gains in understanding, remote promises of the conquest of nature, and, most practically, eventual
improvements in industry and trade. This separation of mental from physical capacities echoed Puritan theology, in which the superiority of the soul
over the body had led to extreme physical discipline and extremely complicated metaphysics.[93] Particularly absurd to satirists like Butler and Rochester seemed the contradictory claim of scientists or devotees of reason that
they could understand the physical world although their own physical natures remained repressed or ignored.

   No one better represented this apparent fallacy than Robert Hooke.[94]
Hooke came literally to embody what satirists saw as the flaws of science.
Central to the Royal Society for thirty years, he acted as Curator of the
Repository in 1676 and of Experiments; since he was regarded as a me-
chanic who acted as caretaker of the products of experimental philosophers, his centrality seemed to epitomize scientists' febrility.[95] Pope, Gay,
and Arbuthnot gave his role to a malevolent dwarf in *The Memoirs of Martinus Scriblerus* (1741).[96] Hooke's physical disabilities seemed to parody his
intellectual pretensions. Author of the widely popular *Micrographia*, setting
out the discoveries of microscopic investigation, he could see in front of
him only by peering through thick spectacles, and he walked with a stoop;
his prominence in the internecine world of the virtuosi to some seemed to
show his snobbism.[97] Hooke's dedication, physical disabilities, and ascetic
habits provided images for several of the objections to science: its exclusiv-

ity, its Puritanical antagonism to pleasure, its perverse interest in the body purely as a machine, its self-absorption and shortsightedness, its hypocrisy of disinterestedness, and its narrow or esoteric focus on issues apparently far from the concerns of the common citizen.[98] Through satire of such virtuosi, Restoration culture indicted science for an ambitious attempt to reconceive, even remake, humanity and reality itself.

ﻝ

Curiosity found a new credibility and a new popularity in the Restoration, but at the same time it earned its indelible mark as a sign of cultural desire. Because of the peculiar combination of independence and social influence that characterized the Royal Society, scientists early on became colored with the charge of ambition: like impious seekers, they wanted to usurp traditional power. At the same time, since the Society lacked the formal regulation of Continental academies, its members could be seen as embodying the uncontrolled formlessness of curiosity itself. Mysteries and unseen worlds became legitimate topics of inquiry as new instruments and discoveries opened new ways of seeing the world. In the face of this riot of questioning, early modern literary culture struggled to mold curiosity into forms that would preserve public values. The Royal Society and provincial scientific organizations avowed an ethic of scientific disinterest that defined curiosity as public service. Accounts of travels and experiments employed a rhetoric that defended inquiry as public good. Such techniques, however, also fed the tradition indicting curiosity as illegitimate and selfish, and writers exploited this contradiction by mounting their own definitions of laudable curiosity. Witch and wonder narratives tiptoeing between piety and skepticism incited readers to hone their curiosity into a tool that could differentiate devotion from deception, and truth from fraud, while touts and quacks advertised their goods by enlisting scientific terms. Satirists reveled in the medley of voices claiming truth. By identifying the New Science with old frauds, they sought to return curiosity to common sense.

The competing world of popular marvels and contemporary skepticism undermined the New Science's moral authority and made its claims of intellectual liberation seem a new form of profiteering. The *Philosophical Transactions*, like Sprat's *History*, was an advertisement for this science and its practitioners, in competition with other kinds of print and ostentatiously independent of the Royal Society. Its promotional language, recommendation of new instruments, emphases on wonder, visual delight, and personal authentication by purchase or attendance all made scientific papers resemble popular marvelous exhibitions. The idiom it employed in descriptions, book reviews, and reports resembled the touts in newspapers. Indeed, as the printed vehicle of the latest information, the *Transactions* was a kind of newspaper itself. The prolific Glanvill credited the moderns' superiority to "*Printing*, the *Compass*, and the *Royal Society*" and named the improvement of "INTERCOURSE and COMMUNICATIONS" as the second method to advance knowledge, following only scientific investigation itself.[99] Dunton and other publishers seized on this idea to make print the vehicle of liberty and truth.

Moreover, the *Transactions* promoted the printed transmission of new experiments and results. Like novels, it sold printed novelty constructed by close observation of common life.[100] Blurring selling and explaining, the *Philosophical Transactions* cornered the marvels market, and like broadsides and woodcuts it included illustrations. Some of these, like depictions of two-headed human "monsters," even commanded a price in the market on their own. Mirroring the written representations of curiosity, these illustrations portrayed the marvelous as the normal expanded or extended to the abnormal.[101] Devices to advertise shops and pubs through the lust of the eyes connected empiricism with purchase and spectatorial pleasure. One display of a model of Amsterdam that took twelve years and "a vast Sum of Money" to complete offers an eagle's-eye view of civilization, an empowering diminution and fetishization of the culture, especially the rural world.[102] These shows and publications elided distinctions between entertainment, commercialism, and science in language, printing venue, and purpose. In confutation of satire, they vaunted scientific second sight as entertainment, profit, and wisdom.

This literary culture stitched together competing traditions of curiosity to make it the vehicle of advertisement, wonder, and self-promotion. Whether advanced by mystics or virtuosi, claims of special sight and the discovery of new worlds allowed writers to update traditional wonder into a new commercial prompt: curiosity. For Behn, Butler, and Shadwell, the New Science reenacts the impious inquiry that Marlowe indicts, but their ambitious scientists do not lose their souls in their lawless quest because they have already lost their minds. However, they do lose their identities by compromising their status and dignity in the pursuit of the wrong kind of knowledge. These portraits of the scientist identify their key flaws as mistaking esoteric or simplistic information for wisdom, reversing or denying social values, and making the material immaterial and vice versa. These are the very qualities of Butler's Curious Man:

> That which other Men neglect, he believes they oversee, and
> stores up Trifles as rare Discoveries, at least of his own Wit and
> Sagacity. He admires subtleties above all Things, because the more
> subtle they are, the nearer they are to nothing; and values no Art
> but that which is spun so thin, that it is of no Use at all.[103]

Such pig-headed refusal to value the things society values makes the virtuoso arrogant, as well as credulous. Galvanized by the social threats represented by the Royal Society, these satirists revive a religious discourse that characterizes curiosity as Luciferian arrogance, but they charge it with a secular desire: the ambition to change nature, including one's own.

Curiosity openly denoted ambition in the Restoration: ambition for new truths engineered by new methods and wielded by new men. In its capacity to create value through creating, collecting, and revering rarities, curiosity, like advertising, entailed a power unallied to traditional institutional structures. Writers attempted to control this power by defining what and how to analyze, and by regulating sight itself. Satirical literature indicts curious men for distorting public values, for naiveté, corruption, and arrogance, and for mistaking the real for the ideal, the seen for the unseen. Advertisements, wonder literature, witch narratives, and poetry exploit curiosity by manufacturing value from print. Like related documents that trumpet the colonial enterprise, these genres mingle traditional and new principles of authority and evidence to tout curiosity as power to penetrate and master the unknown. Curiosity becomes the method by which readers can detect fraud and enact piety; it even links the two as complementary sides of man's divine nature, reason. These kinds of writing aim to regulate curiosity and make it a commodity: they attempt to turn the amorphous hunger to know and to be more into a product for perpetual resale, and to channel the ambitions of the curious into the desires of the consumer.

CHAPTER TWO

Consuming Curiosity

At the beginning of the eighteenth century, curiosity defined fashion. New exhibits were the emblem of London's increasing power and wealth, and observing them demonstrated the power and wealth of the new class of consumers: the urban sophisticates, themselves the very archetypes of cultural ambition. Curiosity thus defined the fashionable personality itself. This new man looked beyond himself, out toward fresh horizons, conquering, collecting, and classifying phenomena from a range of new social, physical, and geographical worlds, all replete with objects for analysis and control. Language, ideas, even morality itself were reified by print into items for manipulation.

This fashionable curiosity, however, whether manifest in objects, print, or people, still challenged traditional social values, and writers allying themselves to such values sprang to turn curiosity against itself. The explorer Robinson Crusoe is re-represented as the fool Lemuel Gulliver. Such satirists as Swift and Pope represent the curious man as a collector, a spectator, an anatomist of the social world whose scientific skill destroys what it would explain and whose appetite devours what it seeks. A victim of his own inquiry, this new man empties himself into the vast maw of inquiry and vanishes. Frequently, satirists depict the curious man's obverse as the curious woman who is subject to rather than the mistress of curiosity: she becomes a collectible, a spectacle, a composite of artificial limbs.

Whether praised or damned, the curious personality is characterized by a drive for knowledge that entails scientific objectification, Scriblerian complexity, cataloguing, the "discovery" of new truths, impious peeping, the collection and witnessing of objects and subjects that destabilize art and nature, and an investigation beyond temporal and material borders that is either heroic or deluded. Early eighteenth-century literature both embodies and thematizes these quests as a contest between novelty and tradition, between the power to forge curiosity and the weakness of becoming one. Contemporary writers, struggling for the cultural authority to claim the curious perspective, vaunt their own curiosity to turn opponents and their literature into monstrosities while they claim curious value for their own art. Poetry is touted as "curious" in its intricate artistry; prose is curious in its dedication to explaining mysteries.[1] Conservative rhetoric represents curious objects and human curiosities as proof of modern devolution, but the curious personality also appears as the triumph of modernity itself. The "curious maid" emblematizes self-distortion; the curious man symbolizes self-realization. This literature contends that curiosity, by its voracious consumption of information and novelties, makes the inquirer a consumer, a commodity, a master, or a monster.

The charge of monstrosity implies the embodiment of a desire so impertinent that it transgresses humanity. This monstrosity appears in exhibitions of people, animals, art, and machines that confuse art and nature. Contemporary naturalists, writers, and audiences were mesmerized by phenomena that seemed to chronicle the occult, and both monster-merchants and writers capitalized on this fascination by contrasting physical abnormality and cultural mastery.[2] To many writers, hybrids, giants, and dwarfs provided metaphors for the commodification of identity wrought by modern consumption, the excessive desire for experience or acquisitions. Like ontological "monsters" whose bodies violate human limits, yet whose verbal skills prove their humanity, both acquisitive consumers and exploitative writing that oversteps formal categories challenged distinctions between art and nature.[3]

Not only monstrous people but also curious exhibitions could be seen as symbolizing monstrous consumption by interfusing art and nature. As life seems art in monsters, art comes to life in moving exhibits. Many displays enact modern progress. Miniature mechanical marvels—Wistanley's water theater, peep shows of optical illusions, miniature cities replicated from wood or plaster—mold curiosity into the display of power.[4] These shows, however, simultaneously enact the proximity of false and true, art and nature, humanity and inhumanity, proving the difference unnervingly undetectable. The "Moving Skeleton," for example, brings death to life. A life-sized skeleton that emerges from a curiosity cabinet, something between a grave and a *wunderkabinet*, it raises an hourglass in one hand and a dart in the other, gestures menacingly at spectators, then groans thrice, lights a pipe, and blows out a candle. This "*wonderful Piece of* ART . . . *To be seen without Loss of Time*" combines the mechanical and the occult.[5] A memento mori in its own cabinet that offers a peek at the forbidden, this mordant exhibition celebrates humanity's power over nature—art—in the form of nature's power over humanity—death. Such exhibits negotiate the public appetite for novelties and the conventional attack on frivolous consumption.

The ambiguous status of curious exhibitions as fusions of art and life that encourage consumption and feed the popular appetite for entertainment echoes conventional attacks on curiosity as limitless and ambitious. Religious discussions figure curiosity as the desire to burst through proper limits, often pleading for intellectual restraint with the text Dr. Johnson quotes from Ecclesiasticus: "Be not curious in unnecessary matters: for more things are showed unto thee than men understand" (3:23). In 1629, the cleric Thomas Adams identifies curiosity as "Disease 17," an intellectual promiscuity that spins out endless questions and mixes "the skimme" of the brain with "the broth."[6] Adams censures curiosity as an extravagance that wastes time and labor and deranges social space, a charge reiterated throughout the eighteenth century. In his *Essay against Unnecessary Curiosity in Matters of Religion*, William Newton defines curiosity as "irregular and inordinate" desire with "no measure nor no end."[7] Also commonly cited was Acts 17:21: "For all the Athenians and Strangers that were there spent their Time in Nothing else, but either to tell or to hear some new Thing," which Dunton triumphantly cites as praise in *The Athenian Mercury*. These discussions condemn curiosity for elevating individual pleasure above communal good, and they deride fashion for replacing production with entertainment.

Using these arguments and pointing to burgeoning fairs, museums, and exhibitions, cultural conservatives claimed that the commodification of the body as a curiosity showed modern corruption: a love for the distorted and ugly instead of the symmetrical and divine. In fact, the long tradition of court dwarfs, hunger artists, "discovered" human hybrids with elephantine throats, hedgehog skins, fish scales, or cat's tails, and other physically unusual performers show that the body had been displayed for money for well over two hundred years. Rather, the sudden urgency of resistance to these displays reveals other cultural changes. Partly, the diffusion of genteel culture blurred the stratification between popular and high entertainments so that newly sentimental values clashed with older traditions of ontological display.[8] Also, the use of leisure began to mark social status, so that the consumption of entertainment assumed a class stamp.[9] Discoveries of new species and lands intensified the public interest in and the availability of rarities, pulling spectatorship into the center of culture. In the early eighteenth century, the domestic implications of this exhibition of the body came home.[10]

The notorious case of Mary Toft underscores the reciprocity of curious object and curious subject as signs of ambition. As Dennis Todd shows, her case publicized the fundamental uncertainty about the nature of identity.[11] Mary Toft was reported to have given birth to seventeen and a half rabbits and various parts of cats after being imaginatively moved by seeing these creatures. Her account brought doctors flooding to her bedside, at first believers but later skeptics. Questions arose about the story's truth or even possibility, the witness's reliability, Toft's motives, and her doctors' authority. As the story emerged under the rigorous examination of the king's physician, it became clear that some of the doctors had conspired for fame and reward. The exposure of scientific credulity and graft revived both the tradition of indicting doctors for ignorance, pretension, and fraud, and the debate over the nature of mankind and the ways to understand it. The "DISCOVERIES" around Mary Toft concerned generation: the secrets of birth itself, which made women curious in one sense, and men in another (fig. 9). To empiricists, the story proved that science could conquer fraud if exercised by reputable men. To satirists, it showed that the more impious the search, the more credulous the seeker. These conclusions reflected the contemporary concern about the people who made new "DISCOVERIES": collectors, critics, scientists, and peepers. All seemed new men pushing impertinently against the status quo.

MONSTROUS MODERNITY AND CURIOUS ART

While mocking science, much eighteenth-century poetry adopts its characteristics, particularly cataloguing, objectification, repetition, and collecting. Even as these procedures spur moral criticism, they contribute to the construction of a professional, authorial identity. This identity is also informed by changes in the book trade, as verse in print becomes both unique and a replicable commodity. As items of high culture, books, especially early poetry, are a subject of *virtu*, and thus poets themselves become art incarnate, a commodification of identity that touched Alexander Pope closely.[12] Pope represents himself as a moral virtuoso whose collection of his own identity in print makes him simultaneously the object and subject of his own virtuosoship. In contrast, he characterizes the "modern" identity of others as "curious": a jumble of acquisitive and exhibitionistic appetites that turn the curious subject into a curious object. This modern man

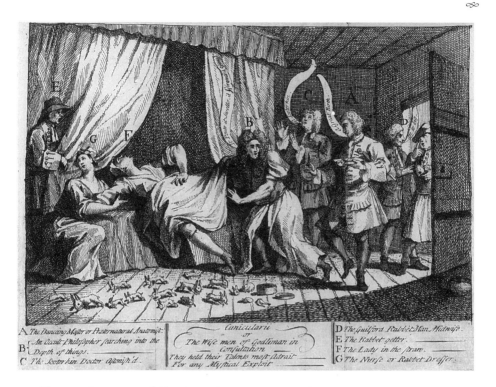

Figure 9. Frontispiece of *The Wonder of Wonders* (1776), a collection of the documents
written by Mary Toft and her physicians. This engraved illustration of Toft being
investigated by doctors shows "An Occult Philosopher searching into the Depth
of things." By permission of the British Library

resembles William King's Virtuoso: "a Man [of] no real Parts [who] is Master of only Scraps pick'd up from one and from another, or Collected out
of this Book or that."[13] The figure of the virtuoso is himself a collection of
others' stale ideas. For Pope and other writers, the collector of curiosities
and novelties embodies the fragmentation of ideals of order, beauty, and
character.

Pope's symbol of the virtuoso as a promulgator of false values centers
on his usurpation of cultural values. This was a common criticism. One
anonymous satire, comparing collectors to cardsharps, scolds "Chief" virtuosi for encouraging "Fools" to spend their "Fortunes upon *dry'd Butterflies, speckled Adders*," or "like trifling Curiosities" in order to profiteer from
them by supplying insignificant insects at immense prices.[14] These unscru-

pulous "Men of *Wit*" are collectors who collect fools, indeed, create them by mesmeric mental control: "These wily Wretches, the leading *Virtuoso's* of the Age, by unheard of kinds of Strategems, have made a tyrannical Usurpation, and arrogated to themselves, with *lawless Power*, a sovereign Dominion over the Minds of the Ignorant; and now they have got to Lord it at large over the Sense of the weaker and wealthier Part of Mankind" (47). As well as usurping the role of cultural leaders, these virtuosi, according to this Rambler, promulgate the waste of wealth by the same means as other cunning men: "The Art is an upstart kind of Deceit that succeeded *Alchymy*, when the Jest of that was grown stale, and would take no longer" (47). Like alchemists who swear they can turn stones into gold, credit merchants, bubble brokers, and virtuosi, by turning toads into rare and precious jewels, spin value from air and pretend that it materializes in objects. "This *Itch* of curious Folly" usurps value (47).

In *The Rape of the Lock*, Pope articulates this resistance to the contemporary commodification of value by giving a mocking attention to the seductive surfaces of a world of things. This critique of false values centers on Belinda's beautiful body, prepared with "*Combs, Bodkins, Leads, Pomatums*" that blur the line between life and art.[15] Belinda's beauty relies on commodities that make her identity a display of consumption. She is not alone: "(*Sir Plume*, of *Amber Snuff-box* justly vain, / And the nice Conduct of a *clouded Cane*)" is defined by his fashionable accouterments, one of which is an action—conduct of the cane—entirely dependent on the object (4.123–24). Pope retains this text exactly from the two-canto 1712 edition. Moreover, Pope tucks Sir Plume into parentheses, cabining him in syntax. Human parts can be similarly objectified. Belinda's virginity is not merely represented as the lock; the lock becomes the public manifestation of that virginity, as, circled by diamonds in a ring on the Baron's "Rapacious Hand," it is "Expos'd thro' *Crystal* to the gazing Eyes" (4.116, 114).[16] In this image, Belinda is confined within a travestied wedding band, an object of precious consumption. Ironically, the more that she makes herself a beautiful thing, the more she invites the rape that apparently destroys that beauty. When the Baron refuses the lock, he vows, "That while my Nostrils draw the vital Air, / This Hand, which won it, shall for ever wear" (4.137–38). Pope represents body bits—the nostrils, the hand—as operating independently of the man. This conception of the body dissipates human integrity.

Pope reinforces the equation of the body with objects through a carefully descriptive style that epitomizes curious art. His catalogue of cosmetics on Belinda's dressing table places "Unnumber'd Treasures" in a "mystic

Order" resembling that of a virtuoso's collection (1.122, 129). Just as virtuosi admire themselves in the mirror of their collections, Belinda surrounds herself with objects acquired "with curious Toil" to exhibit her body (1. 132). Like objects in a curiosity cabinet, their meaning derives from their function of aggrandizing the collector:

> This Casket *India's* glowing Gems unlocks,
> And all *Arabia* breaths [*sic*] from yonder Box.
> The Tortoise here and Elephant unite,
> Transform'd to *Combs*, the speckled and the white.
> Here Files of Pins extend their shining Rows,
> Puffs, Powders, Patches, Bibles, Billet-doux. (1. 133–38)

Within these caskets lie trophies from overseas, some, like Arabia's "breaths," puffs of scented wind, as insubstantial as the contents of parodied curiosity cabinets. In this collection, exotic species "unite" to become monstrous offspring, "combs," while replicated specimens lie classified in "Rows." Belinda's female curiosity cabinet exemplifies the collection of material relics in a world mesmerized by ownership. Whereas virtuosi's collections testify in absentia to ownership of land, expanding identity to vast territories, her armory frays her ownership of her own body.

In a commodity-mad economy of value, things stand for values and stand in for them: the material replaces the moral. Indeed, so fluid is the exchange between subject and object that, as bodies become objects, even physicality dissolves into idea.[17] Pope emphasizes this point in the Cave of Spleen, where moods and traits such as ill-nature and affectation are embodied:

> Unnumber'd Throngs on ev'ry side are seen
> Of Bodies chang'd to various Forms by *Spleen*.
> Here living *Teapots* stand, one Arm held out,
> One bent; the Handle this, and that the Spout:
> A Pipkin there like *Homer's Tripod* walks;
> Here sighs a Jar, and there Goose-pye talks;
> Men prove with Child, as pow'rful Fancy works,
> And Maids turn'd Bottles, call aloud for Corks. (4. 47–54)

This passage shows the fluid exchange between the literal and the metaphorical in contemporary literature. It both literalizes the belief in the power of the imagination to transform the body, and portrays the fluid exchange between identity and commodity.

This exchange relies on the objectifying and disaffected perspective that marks the scientist and the satirist, both of whom make men monsters. Pope shows that by transformative imagination, the observer turns subjects into objects, people into goose pies, fellows into curiosities. Indeed, the Cave of Spleen represents a cabinet of curiosities—here it is not only the objects that possess spleen, but the collector who has transformed them through his own spleen. As Ernest B. Gilman has shown, this shift in viewpoint has a correlation in art, where curious paintings distort familiar images to decenter meaning: "The curious perspective undermines the viewer's authority by dislocating him from a 'centric' point and obliging him to see the work of art from multiple 'perspectives' before he grasps it fully."[18] Similarly, observers, particularly of human curiosities abroad and at home, seem to eighteenth-century satirists to lose their moral footing. At the same time, the fantasy of an identity that embraces multiple perspectives proves enticing for many writers, including Pope. This epistemological uncertainty, exploited in the Cave of Spleen, resembles Gulliver's vacillation between familiarizing the peculiar and defamiliarizing the banal. Seen simultaneously from within and without, these human curiosities are both objects and subjects of curiosity.

In the revised version of 1714, Pope presents his poem itself as a curious object. He complicates his representation of materiality with the "machinery" of the sylphs. Like other scientific "laws" of nature, sylphs's presence or power can be deduced only from their occult effects on human beings, but their efforts to save Belinda merely produce physical phenomena ignored by blind humans: "A thousand Wings, by turns, blow back the Hair, / And thrice they twitch'd the Diamond in her Ear," but the sylphs fail before Belinda's preoccupation with carnal—or at least human—desires (3.136–38). Like women such as Mary Toft who conceive monsters by witnessing, imagining, or dreaming of them, Belinda's own hidden desires, "th'Ideas rising in her Mind," transform physical laws (3.142). Sylphs simultaneously inhabit a symbolic and a material world. As invisible agents playing on the margin between cause and effect, the real and the fantastic, these semiphysical sprites intensify the text's baroque existential titillation.

Published as a single work embellished with a sophisticated subtitle— "an Heroi-Comical Poem"—the 1714 edition includes six illustrations by the popular French artist Louis Du Guernier. This unusual feature represents the poem as both a mental game for readers and an art object.[19] Almost all the illustrations center on scenes with a curious feature. Two are erotic: one shows Belinda waking to her dog's "Tongue" and Ariel's whispers, with a cosmetic table bearing a mirror that would reflect her exposed breast in the foreground; another portrays a fainting Belinda, supported on either side, as the Baron bears the lock aloft. This interpolated scene indicates that these illustrations offered entertainment in their own right and were not merely visual cribs to the verse.

Other plates possess other curious features. In the second plate, Belinda floats down the Thames in a boat distorted like the Ship of Fools to evoke the curious perspective, while sprites spiral out of the clouds above, evoking the visual play of micrographia. In the plate depicting the Cave of Spleen, small monsters crawl before tiny bottles and teapots with the heads of people protruding from their necks; in the foreground, a small pie casket holds a recumbent figure (fig. 10). These objects elide commodity and identity and present monstrosity as the hidden desire of the female body.

The frontispiece, as Robert Halsband explains, most brazenly combines various curious themes and icons. It is "synoptic," a visual puzzle whose "mixture of symbols and allusions piques the reader's curiosity."[20] Images allude to the most heavily catalogic scenes in the poem: the card game, Belinda's dressing table, and the Cave of Spleen. Indeed, the card game and the dressing table often appear in collections of poetic "beauties," anthologies that reprint excerpted literary passages suitable for memorization and recital. In addition, the frontispiece depicts items from the text associated with curiosity: a putto in high heels and a satyr wearing a mask, both indices of monstrosity, transgression, and the concealed erotic, as well as an open casket and small bottles, the items of a collector. *The Rape of the Lock* becomes simultaneously an analysis of art and an art object, a dissertation on curiosity and a curiosity itself.

The matrix of kinds of curiousness in Pope's *Rape of the Lock* prompts later treatments that reveal its status as a text brimming with subversive or hidden implications. In 1717, Giles Jacob produced *The Rape of the Smock*, a pun-pocked attack on Pope that yet documents the erotic value accorded possessions in the poem.[21] It connects stylistic "curiousness" with illicit watching. In this poem, like the discovery poems, the naked Caelia "sitting to pull off her Shoe, / Exposes all her under Parts to view" to the peeping Philemon (lines 79–80). This prurient association between peeping and penetration, keyholes and female exposure, reappears in later poems and novels, like *Tristram Shandy*, but in *The Rape of the Smock* its purpose is to undermine Pope's pretensions to high art. The first edition of Jacob's poem is even embellished with a frontispiece depicting the rival beaus dueling over the smock while Caelia rages in her dressing room. Later in the century, however, William Hogarth, Henry Fuseli, Thomas Stothard, and

i.ud. Du Guernier inv.   C. Du Bose sculp.

Figure 10. Du Guernier, "The Cave of Spleen." From Alexander Pope's *The Rape of the Lock* (1714). Courtesy of the Clark Library, University of California at Los Angeles

their imitators consistently work the twin aspects of Pope's poem as a concealed erotic allegory and—particularly as the Romantic period approaches—as occult fantasy or dream vision.[22] By exploiting the duality of curiosity as elaborate visual artifice and hidden significance, these illustrators preserve the status of Pope's text as a work of curious art.

Contemporary distrust of oxymoronic "new truths" embraced cultural as well as physical "discoveries." The relations between the cultural and the physical remained ambiguous. This ambiguity forms the subject of a cluster of "discovery" poems of the 1720s: pornographic satires that use the empirical method and the sexual theme to point out that new methods reveal old truths. As Felicity Nussbaum has argued, dressing room poems sabotage women's claim to importance and thus function to curb their assertion of cultural power.[23] Discovery verses reflect a similar hostility to women's new prominence as consumers of pleasure, particularly unregulated visual pleasure. Moreover, these poems figure women's pleasure as a usurpation linked to moderns' claims of cultural authority. They show that apparently startling revelations merely reenact Eve's discovery and repeat the fall into carnality, making curiosity the power to turn body into object. In addition, discovery poems contrast the language of naive "discovery" with a devious language of double meanings signaled by the subtitle "A Tale," so that their artful method as well as their subject makes them curious. Observation, scrutiny, peeping, and watching exhibit an ambition analogous to scientific exploration—the penetration of the human body. The human body becomes a consumable curiosity. By locating the site of false discovery in female genitalia, these poems allude to the fraudulent wonder of Mary Toft and reassert the conservative credo that there is nothing new under the sun and that empiricists are merely peepers.

The forerunner of these satires was *The Curious Maid* (1720), a poem that spawned many imitations.[24] Like *The Rape of the Lock* and *Three Hours After Marriage, The Curious Maid* popularized "curiosity" as a sexual innuendo.[25] It uses the erotic trope of the self-scrutinizing woman to condemn as masturbation the hunger to see mystery. Through the concept of curiosity, this trope condemns women's ambition in seeing themselves for themselves. In the jargon of touts, it opens by ironically distinguishing appearance from truth, the empirical lure from the moral content:

> Beauty's a gaudy Sign, no more,
> To tempt the Gazer to the Door;
> Within the Entertainment lies,
> Far off remov'd from vulgar Eyes.[26]

The poem mockingly identifies the human body as a "Sign," a commercial advertisement that "tempts" the curious "Gazer" to sin. This sin-sign-sight resembles the banners hung outside public houses to lure customers in to drink, but the customers of beauty seek gratification of a different appetite, a rarer sight than the one "vulgar" "Eyes" perceive.

The poem concentrates its attack not on the public consumer of beauty but on Chloe, the commodified beauty herself. Dozing in bed, Chloe contemplates herself through the refracted lust of her "Conquests" (line 8). She is created victor by a social creed that idolizes sexual pleasure, but like Psyche, Chloe is not content merely to receive love. Desiring knowledge of what makes her the thing of "Beauty," she struggles, as "perplex'd" as a "*Chymist*," to see her genitals, attempting to understand a moral impulse by physical examination (30–31). When she manages to peer into herself, "the curious Maid" discovers a fundamental cultural truth, "*Hell's Portal*," the seat of birth and death, the horror of human flesh (46, 47, 50). Her discovery shows the monstrous disproportion between the physical cause and the social consequence of human desire: "And is this all, is this (She cry'd) / Man's great Desire, and Woman's Pride" (51–52). Revolted, she banishes the sight to darkness: "Like other *Myst'ries*, Men adore, / Be hid, to be rever'd the more!" (61–62). While reproving the penetration of "mysteries," the poem degrades female power and targets the scientific enterprise to understand human nature both by means of the physical and as physical itself.

The argument that the mysteries of life—love, God, sexuality—escape objectification is a traditional one, but the contemporary fascination with empirical pleasure gave it a new application. A poem of the same period entitled "On Caelia's saying she had no SECRET" uses a similar conceit—the scientific objectification of sexuality in women's bodies. When "Damon" hears Caelia assert that she has no "*Secret*," he declares he must die or "something more Discover." While his "discovery" is Eve's discovery—sexual difference—the language again enlists the rhetoric of the new experiments in physical nature:

> The Chymist searches in the Fire,
> And tries and tortures with his Art,
> Thro' Nature's Mazes he'll enquire,
> Her wond'rous *Secret* to impart.
>
> Bright *Caelia*'s Charms I'll ransack so,
> I'll pierce her to the Heart,

Even when her self she does not know,
And Penetrate *each Part.*[27]

Whereas the author of this poem suggests that male curiosity can penetrate secret nature, the effect is deliberately iconoclastic. Secrecy becomes material rather than moral, but the act of penetration in both cases smacks of violation. Here, the violation is licensed as a form of revenge against Caelia's impertinence. A related poem, *The Contest*, depicts vying "Lasses" surveying each other's "Gift" or pubic hair with "curious set Eye."[28] Their competitiveness makes their careful scrutiny a transgressive kind of curiosity that again licenses the masturbatory peeper/reader to enjoy watching them. In his different but related treatment, the author of *The Curious Maid* suggests that the real mysteries of human existence can be approached only through religion and culture, not by the crude empiricism of the prying eye.

The ambiguity of visual curiosity as a sexual appetite is crudely underscored in *The Peeper: being a Sequel To the Curious Maid.*[29] The existence of this dreadful work testifies to the notoriety of the original poem—the lines, "And is this all? No, Curious Maid, / It is but Half (the *Peeper* said)," appear twice in the poem—and to the contentious interest that the issue of looking aroused (lines 1–2, 24–25). This poem gives voice to the hidden observer, a peeping (tom) cat, who points out that beauty lies in the seer's eye and that Chloe thus needs another pair of eyes, those of a lover, to complete the sexual mystery. The poem's lurid imagery of "Ruddy Pear" and "mossy Brow," the double entendre of "puss," the conceit of the cat wandering beneath ladies' skirts, and the reification of Chloe's sexual organ itself as the puss that, well plied with male "milk" or sperm, becomes lovable, link illicit curiosity, sight, and sexuality to warn women that their peeping makes them objects of others' violation.

Another of these poems compares scientific and sexual quests by reference to the well-publicized competition to determine longitude, which was still unresolved. *The Longitude Found out: A Tale* interprets the scientific quest as the search for sexual fulfillment. The poem recounts how the frustrated Sylvius "Brood[s]" on "vast Designs" and privately "measure[s] out the *Longitude*."[30] The poem equates scientific ambition with masturbation. Rather than patriotism and lust for honor, it is plain lust that drives Sylvius toward the "Secret" and "welcom Wonder" (42–43). In recording "how when all his Projects fail'd / The weak *pretended Stoic* rail'd," the poem shows that Sylvius's mental "Project" is a feeble diversion of his physical impulses (51–52). When Sylvius finally embraces a nymph, however, he indeed discovers "*new Longitudes*" (34). These occur in the human body rather than in the external world that natural philosophers explore. The poem thus mocks scientific ambition as the misdirection of physical impulses.[31]

The satiric transformation of curiosity into a search for pleasure veiled from the searcher resurrects the familiar charge against curious men that they destroy their own delight by impious probing. In the early eighteenth century, this charge was used to target a naive faith in reality as an empirical phenomenon and a corresponding idealization of things, embodied in the antiquarian analysis of artifacts as vessels of human history. Jonathan Swift explores this confusion over the moral and ontological status of the ideal. Whereas earlier discovery poems focus on the illegitimate quest, Swift anatomizes not only ambitious peeping but also the curious urge to make values from, or into, things. Swift's three discovery poems attack the cultural commodification of female beauty and its correlative propagation of prurient curiosity.[32]

"The Lady's Dressing-Room" (1730) examines the relationship of the body and social identity by the technique of cataloguing. After Caelia has dressed, Strephon, the type of a curious youth, "Stole in, and took a strict Survey" of her discarded clothes.[33] The poet's ensuing "*Inventory*" burlesques Belinda's dressing-table collection in *The Rape of the Lock* by heaping filthy objects upon each other in abrupt, octosyllabic couplets (line 10). Beginning with "a dirty Smock," (11) possibly an allusion to Giles Jacob's parody of Pope's *Rape of the Lock*, the poem specifies Caelia's cosmetics, several of which are also items on Belinda's dressing table: "various Combs" (20), "A Paste of Composition rare, / Sweat, Dandriff [*sic*], Powder, Lead and Hair" (23–24). Whereas Belinda culls her combs and perfumes "with curious Toil" from the profits of world trade, Caelia's cosmetics are homegrown, distilled from her own pet: she has "Night-Gloves made of *Tripsy's* Hide" (29). Rather than silver vases, Caelia owns "Gally-pots and Vials"; in place of "Puff, Powders, Patches," and the rest, she possesses "Pomatums, Paints, and Slops" (33, 35). Rather than standing as a beautiful if hollow museum in its own right, Caelia's collection resembles a dusty heap of refuse, gathered and deployed to enhance the possessor. The poem catalogues not the objects Caelia uses as much as the remains of Caelia clinging to them: her "Snuff and Snot," "the Moisture of her Toes" (50, 52). The scrapings and leavings of Caelia's body constitute a collection themselves. Her "Chest," which reveals Caelia's excrement instead of the gems Belinda hoards, is contrived to seem "A Cabinet to vulgar Eyes" (70, 78). It symbolizes Caelia's body, a cabinet of natural curiosities hypocritically decorated. Caelia becomes a composite of objectified elements.

In all discovery poems, the revelation concerns not only the object disclosed, the female body, but also the prying investigator.[34] Whereas the natural philosophers envisioned themselves as disinterested observers, Swift and many early eighteenth-century poets depicted seeing as something that engages both seer and sight in a moral relationship, a concept sentimentalists would later endorse. Swift stresses, "No Object *Strephon's* Eye escapes," but Strephon perceives his own physical nature differently from Caelia's (47). When he peers into the magnifying mirror, it shows him "the Visage of a Gyant" (62). By his impious peeping, Strephon, like a virtuoso, magnifies his identity into monstrosity. Moreover, he makes Caelia a monster too. When Strephon opens Caelia's "*Pandora's* Box," he remains unwilling to dirty his hands by scrabbling for hope (83). Instead, he implores, "O! may she better learn to keep / Those *Secrets of the hoary Deep!*" (95–98) Despite his curiosity, the "peeping" Strephon, like the curious Chloe, prefers mystery, and when "finishing his grand Survey, / The Swain disgusted slunk away," he is doomed always afterwards to see women as stinking carcasses (115–16).

This empirical tyranny fractures the surface to make monsters. Although "to him that looks behind the Scene, *Statira's* but some pocky Quean," the alternative is to admire the artful surface contrived with curious toil (131–32). Instead of "impiously" blaspheming Caelia, he should "bless his ravish'd Eyes to see / Such Order from Confusion sprung'" (135, 140). Sight "ravish'd" by beauty worships the careful art that makes meaning from the chaotic catalogue of body parts or vicarious desires. Swift suggests that unregulated empiricism can prove destructive, particularly because the idealistic empiricist knows his own nature so little that he rejects what he discovers. Art, in contrast, makes integrity: Caelia's body, and by extension the human body, becomes in two senses a work of curious art, whittled and wiped of its sheddings and oozings into a thing of beauty.[35] Similarly, in Swift's "A beautiful young Nymph going to Bed," the sight of Corinna undressing does not arouse the lust of the peeper; rather, it reveals the ambiguity between thing and flesh, object and subject. In the evening, the nymph divests herself of artificial hair, a "Chrystal Eye," eyebrows, teeth, breasts, and so on.[36] After a night tormented by nightmares of imprisonment and pursuit, she wakes to discover her artificial body ruined, and she must invent herself anew—"recollect the scatter'd Parts" and begin "gath'ring up her self again" (lines 68, 70). Like her body, her selfhood consists of parts skillfully conjoined.

The fragmentation of identity reflects the anatomizing, empirical perspective. "Strephon and Chloe" and "Cassinus and Peter. A Tragical Elegy" (1731) both excoriate the peeper for the empirical flaws of credulity and lack of faith. In the first poem, Swift ridicules the curious urge to destroy by examination, depicting Strephon's plunge from romance to revulsion when he witnesses the "wond'rous Maid" urinating (line 29). Swift catalogues women's charms—"Hair," "Mein," "Shape," "Face," "Arm-pits," "Toes"—to parody an objectification of the body both scientistic and paradoxically idealistic (6, 7, 22, 23). "Cassinus and Peter" narrates the tale of how the lovestruck "College *Soph*" Cassinus peeps into Caelia's chamber and discovers her physical nature (1). The contrast between his tragic denunciation of Caelia for betraying him because she "shits" and his mirroring but unrecognized physical excretions as he leans over his "Jordan" (chamber pot) either to "spew or spit in" reveal the hypocrisy of the observer who disconnects himself from what he sees (lines 118, 21–22). Cassinus remains blind to his own similarity to Caelia at her most degraded. Although these poems take romantic love rather than scientific quests as their example of idealism, they both center on the hazards that confront peepers who confuse empirical with moral discovery. Like other discovery poems, they identify the curious gaze and the scientific quest with masturbation.

The satiric equation of modernity, sexual diversion, science, and monstrosity peaks in the Scriblerian farce, *Three Hours After Marriage* (1717). Here, the antimodernist Scriblerians depict curiosity as the symptom of a culture that is confusing self-improvement with consumption. Written at the height of the battle of the books, the play, by tying science to sexual inadequacy, stages the contemporary charge that curiosity is perverted power.[37] Many of the play's devices are borrowed: Samuel Butler's motif of the scientists jostling each other to peer through a telescope, unable to tell north from south while villains escape under their noses; the episode of the solipsistic virtuoso performing medical quackery on hapless patients; Aphra Behn's scene of the duped doctor discoursing on nature with a masquerading mocker; and the visit to the virtuoso's museum of grotesqueries that stir the audience to marvel at the bizarre and exotic, a theme later travestied in Colman's *Blue-beard*.[38]

This libertine drama resurrects the Restoration equation of power and sexuality in order to disempower the moderns. It depicts Dr. John Woodward, the archetypal modernist virtuoso, as the deluded and impotent Fossile.[39] At the time the play was staged, Woodward himself, backed by his academic friends, was engaged in defending the empirical methodology of the New Science.[40] Renowned as an encyclopedic collector who organized his massive collection of some 9,400 fossils by fiendishly complex classifications, he advocated the diluvial origins of geological processes.[41] Modeling their play on Shadwell's *Virtuoso*, the Scriblerians gave a topical shape to scientific discourse as the emblem of modernity. Science appears as the refuge of the pretentious bourgeois, whose experiments in generation and archaeology ineffectually compensate for his failure in the bedroom. This play adumbrates the growing rift between humanistic and scientific curiosity: between the exploration of man's social and physical nature.

The duping of Dr. Fossile indicts scientific inquiry. A physician and natural philosopher, the fifty-year-old virtuoso marries Mrs. Townley, a bigamist and flirt. Repeatedly, he is persuaded out of believing the evidence he finds of her true character, the "circulation" of her "Snuff-Box."[42] Like Aphra Behn's Dr. Baliardo, his "Credulity is the Cause" and also the "Cure of his Jealousy" (act 1, p. 14). As a scientist, he questions the world about him, but always the wrong parts of it, in the wrong way. When, disguised humiliatingly as a footman, he discovers a stash of letters to his wife from various people begging for love or money, he muses:

> Why is Nature so dark in our greatest Concerns? Why are there
> no external Symptoms of Defloration, nor any Pathognomick of
> the Loss of Virginity but a big Belly? Why, has not Lewdness its
> Tokens like the Plague? Why must a man know Rain by the aking
> of his Corns, and have no prognostick of what is of infinitely
> greater moment, cuckoldome? Why is the Enquiry allowed only
> to *Jews*, and deny'd to *Christians*? (Act 2, p. 31)

These questions, heaped on each other like inquiries in the *Philosophical Transactions*, underscore the difference between materialistic and moral interpretations of reality. By depending like the Jews (or Othello) on physical evidence, Fossile invests the empirical enterprise with the hopeless task of gauging morality by external proofs. His conviction that physical evidence could or should expose true nature in fact emphasizes that successful interpretation rests on the moral knowledge of human behavior and desire, a knowledge attainable only by self-scrutiny.

Fossile, however, remains blind to his own weaknesses. Despite witnessing the perfidy of his bride as fops vie to seduce her, he is easily convinced to distrust his own experience by a false letter. "How true is that saying of the Philosopher!" he rhapsodizes with unconscious irony, "*We only know, that we know nothing*" (act 2, p. 35). Gay, Pope, and Arbuthnot symbolize Fossile's naiveté through his "curious" attitude of collecting and objectification. In attempting to understand human nature through the examination of fossils, chemicals, and relics, the debris of man's merely material shell, Fossile remains blind to man's active nature: sexuality. Moreover, he cannot differentiate natural from artificial, or cultural, objects. When he is trying to woo his bride to bed, he calls her "thou best of my Curiosities" (act 1, p. 2). This endearment reveals the central flaw that contemporaries saw in science as a method for defining mankind. By identifying Mrs. Townley as a collectible, Fossile discloses his egocentric possessiveness and his isolation from the world of public meanings and values. She, however, is not the relic in the room; he is. Rather than adding her to his collection, Fossile must learn that she has collected him. Indeed, he himself notes, "Should this Fellow get to my Bride before I have Bedded her, in a Collection of Cuckholds, what a Rarity should I make!" (act 1, p. 11). Mrs. Townley has indeed made her own cuckold collection, including a foreign rarity—her husband from the Indies. The collecting attitude that reduces humanity to objects reverses nature and risks making consumption, rather than production, culture's central activity.

The point appears most compellingly when Mrs. Townley, reluctantly entering Fossile's museum, discovers Plotwell stuffed in an Egyptian mummy and Underplot rolled into a preserved alligator. Once the property only of princes but now a popular rarity throughout the eighteenth century, when travel to Egypt remained hazardous, the mummy represented both mankind's past and his future: it was the body after death, expired yet preserved—a theme that reappears in the literature of curiosity throughout the early modern period. Traditionally, crocodiles and alligators represented God's wonders.[43] At the same time, both mummy and reptile violated eighteenth-century concepts of nature, beauty, and use. As the poet Imlac remarks in Samuel Johnson's *Rasselas*, the pyramids seemed a monument to mankind's vanity, his emptiness and hopes, and the mummies they contain similarly seemed to represent the overweening ambition—familiar to the virtuoso—to defeat death. Further, the very popularity of Egyptian rarities had long encouraged forgeries.[44] Egyptiana epitomized deceptive appearance, the promise of rarity but the reality of fraud. Fossile's possessions literally "embody" his deception.

By confusing living subjects and collected objects, Fossile dramatizes what the authors saw as the moral danger of collecting. The confusion of natural and cultural objects was commonplace in contemporary museums and curiosity cabinets. Both kinds of object merited the same analytic scrutiny; to Scriblerians, both showed the collector's redefinition of value.[45] The equality of the two classes of objects seemed to equate trivial and significant discoveries, challenging or even leveling traditional hierarchies of value and use. The visiting virtuoso, Dr. Nautilus, demonstrates this disjunction when he recommends that women cultivate their minds by decorating their closets "with preserv'd Butterflies, and beautiful Shells, instead of *China* Jars, and absurd *Indian* Pictures" (act 3, p. 61).[46] Nautilus believes knowledge comes from studying nature rather than admiring art.

The symbol of the rakes in the rarities implies that within the collection lurks the libertine who exploits others' bodies for private gain. It is the emblem of the new, curious man's usurpation of culture. By juxtaposing Fossile and the fops, the Scriblerians link illegitimate sexuality and collecting, both forms of self-pleasure that colonize others' possessions.[47] To the Scriblerians, the grandiose self-mirroring within collecting epitomizes the modernists' substitution of private for public values.[48] Fossile declares that the "*Musaeum* of the Curious is a lasting Monument," but it reverses the hierarchy both of the living and the dead, and of the noble and the bourgeois, for Fossile adds, "I think it no Degradation to a dead Person of Quality, to bear the Rank of an Anatomy in the Learned World" (act 3, p. 62). Such curious virtuosi as Fossile and his niece represent the new spread of the previously elite privilege of acquisition and material accumulation to the middle classes, as well as the spread of what the Scriblerians saw as the resulting reversal of values.

The retort of satirists alienated by this objectification of humanity is to make the upstart objectifiers themselves objects: to make curious men and women curiosities. The satirists depict the commodification or objectification even of beauty as something that makes social ambition dangerously possible by severing signs of value from the people who should embody value itself. In the *Moral Epistles*, Pope differentiates the love of beauty from the love of curiosity or the ugly. The four poems treat several of the topics historically identified with the errors of curiosity: monstrosity, the distortion of identity through acquisition, and the misuse of wealth. In the *Epistle to Bathurst*, "Of the Use of Riches," Pope blames "Paper-credit" for concealing the transactions that really move society and depicts such credit as a kind of supernatural sprite, the Ariel of gold.[49] His attack focuses on hypocrisy, the trait that designates a divided identity, represented by the vicious Chartres and by the cheating "Director" of the South-Sea Company (117). In the same vein, he indicts the "Glorious Ambition" of those who seek to possess or rule the nation by means of money (125). As his illustration of people maddened by their ruling passion shows, the true danger of wealth lies in its ability to indulge monstrous appetite or ambition. Pope advocates the sensible use of riches "with the Art /

T'enjoy them, and the Virtue to impart, / Not meanly, nor ambitiously persu'd" (213–15). This philosophy endorses artful consumption over a frenzied acquisition designed to enhance the acquirer.

Pope excoriates accumulation most fully in the *Epistle to Burlington*, also called *Of False Taste*. A bold assertion of Pope's ambitious status as an aristocrat of taste, this poem attacks greed and display through the bourgeois sophisticate who attempts to imitate "men of taste" by filling his house with fine objects. The poem opens by equating the "strange" Miser with the "strange" Prodigal.[50] The key repetition of "strange" signals the contradictory pretension of the fashionable collector who both spends and hoards. This type manifests two of the traditional flaws of the curious man: he commandeers fine goods for private gain, removing them from the public sphere, and he accumulates without discrimination, unable to differentiate the beautiful from the popular. The result of the collector's physical zeugma is, as in other cases of monstrosity, loss of identity. The collector sinks to a mediator of others' desires:

> Not for himself he sees, or hears, or eats;
> Artists must chuse his Pictures, Music, Meats:
> He buys for *Topham* Drawings and Designs,
> For *Fountain* Statues, and for *Curio* Coins,
> Rare Monkish Manuscripts for *Hearne* alone,
> And Books for *Mead*, and Rarities for *Sloan*. (Lines 5–10)

By cataloguing the objects of others' desires in repeated noun phrases—"for *Topham*," "for *Fountain*," "for *Curio*," "And Books for *Mead*," "And Rarities for *Sloan*"—Pope mimics the meaningless compulsion of collecting, in which the activity of acquiring things substitutes for the purpose of them.[51] In his revision, he intensified the clutter of nouns denoting objects, replacing the reference to Curio with "For Pembroke Statues, dirty Gods, and Coins," and the reference to "Rarities" with "Butterflies."[52]

The repetition of "Rare . . . Rarities," however, in the original edition significantly underscores rarity as a material value of its own, an innuendo reinforced by the type "Curio." While Curios embody the evils of wasted energy and indiscriminate desire, such collectors as the man of false taste present a deeper threat. They ape the aristocracy—both the traditional aristocracy whose inherited estates contain wonders acquired by generations, and the new (self-declared) aristocracy of taste that values selection over collection, to which Pope belonged. Instead, these greedy collectors cherish objects over ideas: "In Books, not Authors, curious is my Lord"

(118). Similarly, Timon's grandiose "Villa" wastes wealth, becoming a monstrosity that instead of making the owner grander contextualizes him, too, as a monster surrounded by "huge Heaps of Littleness around!" (92–93). By violating proportion—a point Pope reinforces with the ironic capitalizations of "Heap" and "Littleness"—Timon, as the epitome of the bourgeois collector overwhelmed by his collection, abandons his own nature to become an "Insect" (92).

Pope's solution to the quandary of how to avoid vulgar accumulation and also avoid being "collected" by others is to become a collector himself—an advocate of natural curiosity, the skillful creation of "pleasing Intricacies"—who catalogues not physical species but rather social types in his poetic cabinet (line 99). Scientific observation simultaneously attracts and alerts Pope. Even while he adopts it, he distrusts its seductive claim of objective authority. In the *Epistle to Cobham* (1733), a treatise on classifying humanity, he cautions, "To Observations which ourselves we make, / We grow more partial for th'Observer's sake" (11), conceding the "Diff'rence . . . between / The Optics seeing" and "the Objects seen" (23–24).[53] Nonetheless, he favors scientific precision: "Shall only Man be taken in the gross? / Grant but as many sorts of Mind, as Moss" (17–18). And his own footnote points out, "There are above 300 Sorts of Moss observed by Naturalists" (4).[54]

Further on, Pope cautions that man's reasons for behavior vanish in the moment of perception: "Like following Life thro' Creatures you dissect, / You lose it, in the Moment you detect" (39–40). He also warns against trusting the "retrospective Eye" that "from th'apparent *what* conclude[s] the *why*" (51–52). Yet his project to dissect and categorize the types of men and his cautious skepticism concerning his instruments of empirical observation echo contemporary science. Moreover, he identifies a grand principle equivalent to gravity to explain man's contradictions: that the most proximate "Image" or passion serves as a cause (45). Pope simultaneously gathers scientific authority for his own project and transcends it.

The alternative to fragmented identity, monstrous ambition, and meaningless acquisition is self-possession. Pope idealizes the woman who remains "Mistress of yourself."[55] His own close negotiations with Lintot enabled him to design his own miscellanies: to accumulate himself in a collection. But his most baroque collection must be his final work, *The Dunciad*. This catalogue of monstrosity was published anonymously with an elaborate preface that underscores its hidden meanings. By adjuring the reader not to puzzle "if he cannot decypher" the semi-veiled references, the poem depicts a decaying civilization crowded with abortions, excrement-strewn villains, and demons.[56] Through this printed cabinet, with its bal-looning roster of names and encroaching torrent of footnotes, Pope parod-ies the Renaissance practice of collecting the universe in cabinets, but in place of representative items from the natural world, Pope, like his scien-tific contemporaries, finds a limitless supply of subtypes and unique spec-imens.

Poets of the early eighteenth century depict modernity as a monstrous dereliction of human identity; nonetheless, they co-opt the power that col-lecting entails. While Pope specifies the false collector as a medley of oth-ers' desires, Swift locates the fracturing of the self in the body. The stylistic device of cataloguing underscores the meaningless fragmentation of iden-tity in the collector of art and in the beautiful body. Both poets anatomize their moral complaint—lack of integrity—by showing the despised other as a composite of objectified elements.

THE CURIOUS EYE

While Scriblerians were speaking as the voice of integrity pulling together a collectible world, prose was rapidly becoming synonymous with novelty, and a rival interpretation of the curious personality was emerging.[57] Dur-ing the early century, prose works, often composed quickly in response to the day's events, sometimes by men with little formal training, are defined as commodities to stir readers' curiosity, whether through novelistic ac-counts of individual experience or information supplied by journalists. These journalists portray themselves as passionate for knowledge, yet dis-interested. By asserting an ideal of unedited inquiry, they also create audi-ences in their own image: readers flattered into defining themselves by their thirst for encyclopedic knowledge. Fertilized by the periodicals and pamphlets popularizing all kinds of previously esoteric topics, a new kind of fashionable personality begins to develop: the self-defined curious man avid for recent information. Information becomes the most prized com-modity; correspondingly, the capacity to ask penetrating questions be-comes the cultural stamp of the rising man. Nourished by print entrepre-neurs, curiosity, rather than denoting forbidden desires, begins to mark those whose intellectual ambitions objectify the world and lift them above the mob.

Nonetheless, there remain questions that elite men—or nice girls—do not ask. The explosion in the means and areas of inquiry prompted the kinds of concern with which people today face information on the Internet. Several central questions arose, many familiar, some new. Are all topics fair for inquiry, or for inquiry by all people? If there are limits, what and why are they, and how could they be enforced? And what are the means for inquiry? Does empiricism provide answers for every kind of question, or are there different ways of inquiring, suited to different topics? And how can one tell whether a question is genuine or an answer true? Such doubts color the literature of the period. Writers who favor traditional, humanistic approaches excoriate inquiry into the unseen—sexuality, monstrosity, religion, the occult—as illegitimate, confused, and self-aggrandizing; others, hotly enthusiastic about progress, hold out for a method by which inquiry could be perfected past danger into a universal tool. Many writers tiptoe between these poles, but all identify cultural excellence with their own kinds of literary inquiry. While some writers reveal the unseen or explain the unknown, others mystify areas of conventional inquiry to stimulate sales; some, like Defoe, do both. In this period, literary excellence itself becomes defined as the skillful and decorous manipulation of curiosity and information: fine artists elicit, mold, and direct the reader's questions to fit the answers they possess.

Central to this elevation of curiosity as the essence of fashionable modernity are periodical publications. These battle to define the means, ends, and words of curiosity. As formal embodiments of novelty, new serial publications sold questions, answers, and commentary prompted by the most recent events, and fresh from the press. Using the formula Dunton established in the 1690s, several periodicals invite readers to submit questions or quips in order to establish a dialogue with the contemporary audience. While other literary endeavors like miscellanies also exploited novelty by inviting readers to contribute to the enterprise, periodicals permitted replies and publicized witty exchanges. Curiosity, whether manifested as questioning the world around one, as informing oneself about the latest discoveries, commodities, and debates, or as inventing artful literary items for publication, became the mode for manifesting identity in the public arena.[58]

These early periodicals mimic the scientific project of disinterested description and observation, but their quasi-scientific analyses address the social world. They reorient curiosity away from nature to social affairs. Almost all title themselves after the paramount organ of curious perception, the eye. One of the earliest, Ned Ward's *London Spy* (1698–1700), imitates *The Turkish Spy*, a late seventeenth-century work that described the familiar world from the perspective of a foreigner.[59] The image of "spy" signals unbiased inquiry into the affairs of the capital by means of unperceived perception, pure empiricism. Ward's spy, tiring of fruitless "enquiry" in old books, succumbs to "an itching inclination . . . to visit London."[60] He witnesses London's curiosities with a fresh eye as he is conducted around the sights by his sophisticated friend, a sometime surgeon without a fixed occupation who diagnoses both physical and moral diseases. By the structure of these two personae, Ward defines curious observation as both watching and analyzing. The "spy" of the title is simultaneously a naive empiricist and a trained analyst. While readers vicariously enjoy both the freedom of unrestrained curiosity, and the superiority of understanding the subtext, they also use the periodical as a key to understanding life. Curiosity becomes more than an idle pleasure in spectacle; it becomes the mode of urban survival.[61]

Whether Spy, Spectator, or Tatler, the periodical persona is a social scientist who catalogues the species of human beings. *The London Spy* originates the method of these personae. The spy's device for revealing fraud is categorization by type: an astrologer, a moralist, a captain, an Irishman, a gossip, and others. These types serve as classifications of modern "characters," people whose moral natures are defined by their occupations. The urban spy can identify the species and diagnose the disease of numerous social types at a glance. For example, the distracted posture of "a vertuso" turns him into a monster, peered at by the ignorant. Further anecdotes reveal that he has lost a fortune trying to manufacture a crackbrained potion and that he eats only at noon because his appetite accords to the sun. As his mesmerized gaze at the flickering candle exemplifies, so alienated is this virtuoso from the social and sensual world that he has transformed his own body into an instrument. The later description of a self-absorbed "peripatetic," or wandering philosopher, at Gresham College reiterates the satire against virtuosi for ignoring their social presentation (chap. 3, p. 45). Like other urban riffraff, these characters have lost their humanity through obsession; their occupations have made them monsters.

The spy differentiates legitimate and illegitimate curiosity. Particularly by indicting the virtuoso, but also in other sketches, he contrasts the inefficient, self-injuring experimentation of the professional inquirer with his own self-protective curiosity. Whereas the virtuoso has "faith" in fantastical means to raise himself above others, the careful adventurer distrusts the quick-rich schemes of sharpers and quacks, which are actually based on robbery. Virtuosi, hints Ward's guide, fritter away their resources on useless "projects" intended to project themselves ahead of others. He emphasizes the point by describing the curiosity cabinet of this "wonderful antiquary . . . that out-does Gresham College" (chap. 1, p. 11). Along with

Epicurus's humming-bird-claw toothpick, Diogenes' lantern, Heraclitus's frozen tears, and an Ark nail, the virtuoso "pretends" to have a piece of silver from Judas's thirty: "A mighty collection of these sort of trinkets he tells the world he's master of, and some give credit to his ridiculous romances" (chap. 1, p. 11). These material manifestations of the virtuoso's "pretension," these items incarnating his delusions, win him "credit," a commodity valuable only for ensnaring the credulous.

Although curiosity eviscerates the virtuoso, the lust for curiosities infects all of society, forcing those who yearn for advancement to sell themselves as fashionable curiosities. The trick to avoid becoming a curiosity, for Ward, is to choose the right topics of inquiry. These topics lie in the social reality that surrounds the inquirer. In the contest between social and scientific analysis, the virtuoso loses; he shrinks to a specimen, identified, collected, and analyzed in the spy's cabinet of London curiosities.

The attack on people who sell entertainment, themselves, or themselves as entertainment is a form of social criticism.[62] Ward's cabinet includes a wealth of other spectacles that exhibit freakish identities, notably tumblers, dancers, touts, drolls, and waxworks at Bartholomew Fair. Many are women described as impinging on the limits of their species. One tightrope walker "waddled along the rope like a goose" (chap. 10, p. 182). Another sword dancer has skin that, but for lacing, "would have hung down in folds like the hide of a rhinoceros" (chap. 11, p. 196). Several of both sexes so lack artistry that, in disgust, the spy declares:

> I thought it an abuse to human shape for anything that bore the
> proportions of either sex to behave themselves so ostentatiously
> foolish, so odiously impudent, so intolerably dull and void of all
> humor, order, or design. There would [be] no more diversion
> in the accidental gestures of one ape than in all the studied
> performances of the whole company of pretending vagabonds.
> (Chap. 11, p. 197)

This self-distortion violates "proportionality" and makes monsters both of those who participate in it and of those who admire them. The women's self-sale echoes that of other female actors who use their bodies to entertain the mob: prostitutes, another subject of the urban spectatorship that Ward attacks.[63] These women embody the reciprocal waste of humanity as consumers and consumed. Like Restoration virtuosi, women in particular challenged social roles and occupations—and even, albeit differently, categories of human identity—early in the seventeenth century.[64] In contrast, *The London Spy* attempts to dissever spying (the curious perspective) from self-display (the curious personality) in order to shore up curiosity for the new consumers: those who watch or read, rather than those who do.

However, since watching engages the spectator in a dynamic with the spectacle, this distinction remained contested. The two-week August festival of Bartholomew Fair epitomized this problem. As the lure of London, it offered things to see that included those who came to see. It had long drawn criticism for making people, whether performers or perceivers, into playthings. In *Bartholomew Fair*, Ben Jonson uses the fair to dramatize the human adoration of spectacle and object, as people stand "scandaliz'd at toyes, / As Babies, Hobby-horses, Puppet-playes."[65] Such festive sights test various kinds of vision—even, given the criminal parasites, peripheral vision. In William King's *A Journey to London, In the Year 1698*, the French persona outlines the relationship between buying and theft:

> I was at *Bartholomew Fair. It consists of most Toyshops, also Fiancé and Pictures, Ribbon-shops, no Books; Many Shops of Confectioners,* where any Woman *may commodiously be treated: Knavery is here in perfection, dextrous Cut-Purses and Pick-Pockets . . .* I met a man that would have took off my Hat, but I secur'd it, and was going to draw my Sword, Crying out, *Begar! Damn'd Rogue! Morblew,* &c. when on a sudden I had a hundred People about me, Crying here Monsieur, see the *Tall Dutch Woman;* see the *Tyger,* says another; see the *Horse and no Horse,* whose Tayl stands where his Head should do; see the *German Artist,* Monsieur: see the *Siege of Namur,* Monsieur: So that *betwixt Rudeness and Civility, I was forc'd to get into a* Fiacre, *and with* an air of Hast, and a full Trot *got home to my Lodgings.*[66]

The shops, showmen, beasts, monsters, tricks, and thieves profit from the visitor's seeing. They also make those who come to gawk subjects of theft, both within and outside the booths. As a symbol, Bartholomew Fair suggests that through the manipulation of desire and illusion, anything can be made into a commodity—even those who come only to look—as long as there is a buyer.[67]

With its profusion of goods and unrestrained class mixing, Bartholomew Fair was a stage for the struggle between people's appetite for novelty, visual delights, and commodities, and the state's attempts to supervise consumption.[68] Its power to promulgate drunkenness, robbery, rebellious behavior, and all kinds of profligacy had become so strong that in the first decade of the century, puritanical Londoners and members of the Societies for the Reformation of Manners agitated to limit it from the two weeks to which it had recently been expanded to three days. *Reasons . . . for the Punc-*

tual Limiting of Bartholomew Fair (1708/11) defines the fair as the "contrary" of the "good *Order* and good *Manners*" that constitute rational and religious happiness.[69] Much of this vaunted order may refer to these merchants' own steady sale of goods, which was clearly compromised by competition from the fair. Still, the primary reasons they provide concern the dangers of the fair's encouragement of "Extravagance," leading to "Disorder" and "Ruine" from the unchecked, "exorbitant *Lusts* and *Passions* of Men"—all exemplified by the exhibition of an erotic book (4, 10).

To these merchants and others, the fair's excess, the mark of monstrosity, open sexuality, and profligacy denote rebellion. Indeed, the writers of *Reasons* contend that the performers form a *"Political Body"* rivaling the government in order to regulate their own methods of robbery (5). Other witnesses reinforce this charge. The rambling narrator of the poem *Bartholomew Fair* (1717) records the mob's organized anti-authority in rescuing a pretty prostitute from a police constable trying to haul her to Bridewell.[70] Citing such offenses against authority, the London protesters against the fair argue that its purpose no longer concerns "fair" trade: "Every Body knows it to be a meer *Carnival*, a Season of the utmost *Disorder* and *Debauchery* by reason of the *Booths* for Drinking, Musick, Dancing, Stage-Plays, Drolls, Lotteries, Gaming, Raffling, and what not" (11).[71] To them, the fair is the symbol of unrestrained curiosity: consumption.

The answer of those who oppose the fair is institutionalization. In order to control and reform criminals and to ensure the legitimate government's authority, the protesters propose "the Multiplication of *Workhouses*, with a due Inspection and Government," a solution that resembles the inspection and closure of infected houses in Defoe's *Journal of the Plague Year* (1722). The urgency of the task derives from the conviction that the fair instigates an attitude dangerously close to "*Rebellion*" against God (7). Significantly, the opponents of the fair unearth as the basis of their legal argument a charter from Charles I licensing the fair for only three days, a precedent that hints at the civil disorder that may result from unmonitored assembly. The order of 1708 indeed recommended the three-day limitation in order to reduce "Tumults and Disorders" (8, 24). Moreover, the entire collection of arguments, including the order itself, was reprinted three years later, testifying to the continued vitality of objections to the fair. The anxiety surrounding the fair recorded by these documents manifests the pervasive cultural identification of curiosity and consumption with rebellion.

The intersection of the meanings of curiosity as opulent commodity and free inquiry infuses periodicals—texts that encapsulate both qualities.

Periodicals play a key part in regulating the way in which questions are asked and the forms curiosity can take in the public arena. While queries about matters pertaining to mathematics, natural science, and spiritual or religious doctrine already possessed a format established by schools, the pulpit, and the Royal Society, questions pertaining to cultural, sexual, or traditionally forbidden matters needed to find a public language.[72] The periodicals provided one. In order to legitimize a curiosity focused on social affairs, authors struggled to design a mode of inquiry that avoided both the traditional indictment of gossip, and the new resistance to thoughtless consumption and objectification. Their solution for circumnavigating cultural hostility was the technique Dunton initiated of projecting the responsibility for curiosity away from writer onto the audience, while also advertising the social advantages of current knowledge.

The British Apollo; or, Curious Amusements for the INGENIOUS. To which are Added the most Material Occurrences Foreign and Domestick (1708–1711) was important in defining inquiry as a fashionable attitude. Its first subtitle conjoins curiosity and amusement as equivalent activities for the "ingenious," those who have intellectual ambition; the second subtitle advertises the project's empirical focus with the pun on "material," conceived to mean not only significant, but also "consisting of matter; corporeal, not spiritual."[73] Rather than citing an author, its attribution claims that it is "Perform'd by a Society of GENTLEMEN," casting the enterprise as an elite, cooperative act.[74] By such a pronouncement, the authors project an audience who wish to be identified as opulent enough to need diversion. Likewise, the persona of King's *Journey to London* claims "Curiosity" as his motive, and King, too, assumed that there were enough similarly idle people to ensure him an audience (1). In both cases, such an audience appeared. *The British Apollo* was—unusually for a periodical—sold by subscription, and it enforced its paradoxically public conjuration of a coterie of readers by including relatively elaborate information on how to submit inquiries.[75] Several changes in format and price were justified as benefits for subscribers. One such change involved the inclusion of concert tickets, which prompted an outraged response because of the class mixing and cultural ambition it encouraged. The paper was thus structured as an exchange of information simultaneously public and elite. This exchange threatened contemporary distinctions of class, knowledge, and social contact.

This simultaneously elite and public function also colors the periodical's mode of legitimizing what was previously considered illegitimate inquiry. The authors of *The British Apollo* stress that in contrast to other periodical authors, they occupy the gentle ranks of society. They note that "this

Design was incourag'd by several Persons of Quality and others of the Brightest Parts, before it was Publish'd, and a great many have Subscribed since the first paper."[76] Readers are invited to participate in the enterprise by questioning, so that their curiosity inducts them into the gentlemen's "Society"—a formula imitated by the popular *Gentleman's Magazine* later in the century. Defining the journal as an activity of fact-finding and novelty-collecting, *The British Apollo* subsumes all kinds of announcements and performances as "curious amusements for the ingenious," including extempore poetry; political news; advertisements and solicitations for new books; rentals; and lost, stolen, or escaped people, animals, and things. Thus, science, new devices, literature, art, music, and possessions become equivalent kinds of knowledge. Answers prompted more questions; print fed the appetite for print; and the *Apollo* happily offered a regulatory mode—vetting by gentlemen—to channel this profusion.

This riot of querying did not entirely lack a structure. The tripartite division of topics into religion, science, and other matters, although not announced in *The British Apollo*, follows the practice of *The Athenian Mercury* (1691–1697). This segregation of topics inscribes a hierarchy of questions. Ostensibly, scriptural questions are of primary importance, but in practice *The British Apollo* sometimes begins with popular questions that inform readers about "curious" social practices. In number 6 (27 February to 3 March 1708), for example, a question concerning gaming odds precedes one about religion. New questions are preeminent. Readers, at least initially, are directed by references to find the replies to repeated queries in back issues or in other papers; they are told to look, for example, in the *Athenian Oracle*, no. 4 (20–25 February 1708). Moreover, despite the increasing lack of space, many replies take the form of entire paragraphs that usually set out authoritative references or evidence and argue the solution from that proposition. This formula evens out knowledge to a way of reasoning from available information and thus tends to counter the emphasis on technical specialization present in the *Philosophical Transactions*. *The British Apollo* treats almost all questions, irrespective of their topic, as equally important.

Whereas Dunton and his fellow Oracles weeded out insincere inquiries, the writers of *The British Apollo* welcome all comers by shifting their tone to meet their topic. Some queries the Apollo answers in short shrift. These exceptions show how the Apollo distinguishes between legitimate inquiry and illegitimate curiosity. For example, the question *"Who was Job's Father?"* elicits only "He that begot him" (no. 15, 31 March to 3 April 1708). Again, *"Is it true that a Fool may ask more Questions than a Wise man can answer?"* earns "You had best ask a dozen or two as fast as you can, and find out the Matter of Fact by your own Experience" (no. 15). Modeled on exchanges published in courtesy and jest books, these readers' riddling queries are designed to play on curiosity as intricacy; the Apollo's "reply" is designed to turn curiosity against the querists and make them foolish themselves. At the same time, the Apollo offers another, social kind of "answer" to such questions. By witty riposte, he not only engages the querist in a social exchange, but inscribes the limits of scientific authority.

By far the most common topic to win this kind of riposte is the one that the Apollo thinks defies logic: love. For example, the question *"Tell me most Learned and Polite Assembly, what is the killing and fatal Cause, that persevering Love, and tenderest Demonstrations only excite to more Indifference the Charming Conqueror?"* elicits "O Charming Fair! The fatal filling Cause of your Misfortune, is that your Choice has fall'n too much below your Merit; Your Conqueror wou'd else in floods of rapid Joy sail swiftly to your Call" (no. 9, 10–12 March 1708). The abandonment of logical argument for poetic metaphor signals that romance cannot be tackled with the tools of rational inquiry. Instead, the verses sprinkled throughout the periodical complement such inquiries by voicing romance in its own language, the language of poetry, while crude inquiries on bodily functions adopt the formula of satiric verse. As was common, questions in doggerel receive rhyming replies. This stylistic flexibility provides a mode for topics that cannot be asked about in empirical prose, and it identifies novelties of form with new information. Such mutual joviality gilded inquiry with politeness. The Apollo's tonal modulation shows that much of the real knowledge and entertainment provided by this journal lies in manner, not matter. Verbal art will show off the speaker's ingenuity, rather than only his knowledge. Moreover, readers ought to recognize wit themselves. When one earnest correspondent asks whether Isaac Bickerstaff's prophecies, spun by Swift, *"were writ in jest or earnest?"* Apollo replies testily:

> In jest Man! fie, fie! In earnest, you may lay you Life on't, Esq.;
> *Bickerstaff*'s a downright Conjuror; the Dumb man's [Campbell]
> a Fool to him. He's as great a Conjuror as Dr. *Faustus*, or the
> *Brazenhead* of *Friar Bacon*, and if you are one of those Unhappy Souls
> his Prophecies threaten Death to, e'en set your House in order,
> take leave of your Friends, and die without grumbling. (No. 15)

The ingenious reader should differentiate fraud from both science and wit.

Although the Apollo establishes a stylized language to answer illegitimate curiosity—prurient or artful questions—one category of questions is not answered so kindly. Women who inquire into matters of love in a way that the Apollo interprets as hunting for compliments receive mockingly gallant responses that trivialize the inquiry. The Apollo prefaces his replies to such questions with elaborate and usually offensive courtesy. Olivia's request, "*I desire you will tell us how we may distinguish between a real Passion and a feign'd one*," elicits, "*Madam*, the Society will with all Chearfulness attempt your Satisfaction, if you have the Courage to stand the shock of it; for it is with all the regret imaginable when we advised a Lady to part with any thing so dear to her as Vanity and Affectation" (no. 6, 27 February to 3 March 1708). When another querier demands, "*How many things are required in a Woman to be perfectly Beautiful, or whether can [sic] a Woman be said to be perfectly so?*," the Apollo answers reprovingly, "Now, Madam if you think *Apollo* a Beau or a Courtier, and Expect to be sent to your Looking-glass for an Answer, we shou'd be sorry to stand in the place of the poor Chamber maid who must bear the shock of your disappointment" (no. 5, 25–27 February 1708). Throughout the periodical, women's requests—or requests made under the guise of women—are used as opportunities to excoriate women's ambitions to turn inquiry on themselves—their desire for self-exposure, sexual knowledge, and sexual power. As an increasingly influential audience, women threatened to monopolize curiosity.[77]

Periodicals continually redraw the boundaries of legitimate inquiry. Defoe's *Review* (1704–1713), primarily a political journal, supplemented its news with a feature like Dunton's Secret Oracle, a section titled "*Mercure Scandale*: or, Advice from the Scandalous Club." This club, supposedly held in session in Bartholomew Fair, is created as a disinterested moral court, "to censure the Actions of Men, not of Parties . . . not . . . to expose Persons but Things."[78] One issue reports that the *Review*'s publishers were summoned to the club to justify printing a physician's advertisement "for the Cure of a Scandalous Distemper."[79] Thus, the dissemination in periodicals of open commentary on social and sexual matters flourished.[80]

Because it discussed loose morals, if only to condemn them, Defoe's "*Weekly History of* Nonsense, Impertinence, Vice *and* Debauchery" gained a profitable reputation as licentious, but Sir Richard Steele transformed gossip into a legitimate source of public information when it was structured in the form of social criticism. *The Tatler* (1709–1711), as Steele asserts in his first number, takes its name as an "Honor" for the "Fair Sex," defined by their desire to hear secret tales about town matters.[81] Reversing the practice of *The Athenian Mercury*, which made all topics matters for serious answers, this title profits from *The British Apollo*'s appeal to class and equates all kinds of inquiry as "idle talk." Curiosity becomes the privilege of the leisured. Steele copies the *Athenian Oracle*'s division of knowledge by promising something in every issue for women and by systematizing knowledge into categories, each issuing from a different coffeehouse: "*Gallantry, Pleasure* and *Entertainment*," "*Poetry*," "*Learning*," "*Foreign* and *Domestick News*," and his thoughts on "any other Subject" (16). These coffeehouse categories multiply and classify the topics for fashionable consumption, simultaneously defining readers by their curiosity and equating political "news," literature, and social criticism. Furthermore, all become topics for "tattling," unregulated talk.[82] Steele thus acts himself as the conduit and mediator of curiosity.[83]

Addison and Steele's hugely successful periodical, *The Spectator*, epitomizes the device of funneling wide-ranging curiosity through a single sensibility. Each issue examines a scene of life in a single essay, written from a single point of view.[84] The Spectator's accountability is guaranteed by his unaffiliated status. A member of the gentry, not bound to any occupation, single, and apolitical, he appears to incarnate free empiricism. Nonetheless, as skeptical readers know, all observations are colored by the eye that sees them, and therefore the reader's own "curiosity" about the source of all reports shows wisdom. By revealing the genealogy, affiliations, and idiosyncrasies of the central intelligence channeling curiosity into information, Steele makes the curious eye accountable. In contrast to this accountable observation, Mr. Spectator inveighs against gossip and spying. While reluctantly granting spies a political necessity, he cautions rulers that "a Man who is capable of so infamous a Calling as that of a Spy, is not very much to be relied upon. He can have no great Ties of Honour, or Checks of Conscience, to restrain him."[85] Mr. Spectator's real target, however, is not political but social spying. Spies are a manifestation of unregulated curiosity, since they have no fellows to verify their information, no context in which to place and therefore understand it. In contrast to spies and "Vulgar Souls," "great and heroic Minds . . . are altogether free from that Impertinent Curiosity of Enquiring" about rumors (44). In this formulation, the social curiosity that anxiously defends its own status through either prying or spying is déclassé because it violates the distinctions between public and private spheres of informational exchange.

Mr. Spectator embodies laudable curiosity: the detection of the divine. He praises the "Discovery of [the] secret and amazing Steps of Providence" as a pious "Entertainment" suited to creatures in whom "Curiosity is one of the strongest and most lasting Appetites" (vol. 2, p. 420: no. 237, Saturday, 1 December 1711, Addison). Like a scientist, Mr. Spectator analyzes nature, but his purpose is the worship of God and social reform: albeit similar to the "insatiable desire" of inquisitiveness that lacks "any Use in the World," his own "Curiosity" is a mental storehouse of items "which cannot but entertain when they are produced in Conversation" (388). In contrast to this analytic hero stands the "inquisitive" man, a "Creature" who, despite having learned much, "cannot trust to the Range of his own Fancy to entertain himself upon that Foundation, but goes on still to new Enquiries" (vol. 2, p. 368: no. 228, Wednesday, 21 November 1711). His "Vacancy" of imagination makes the Inquirer a parody of the Spectator, collecting information for no purpose (388). Mr. Spectator scoffs, "The Inquisitive are the Funnels of Conversation; they do not take in any thing for their own Use, but merely to pass it to another: They are the Channels through which all the Good and Evil that is spoken in Town are conveyed" (387). As dealers in secondhand information, inquisitive men spread malice, invent secrets, breed divisiveness by turning public facts into private gossip; they colonize information and reverse the public categories of meaning and insignificance. Parodies—or rivals—of the moral mediator of information, they embody unregulated curiosity.

Periodicals defined the consumption of information as a means for social mobility, and they made the fashionable identity of the curious consumer widely available, encouraging an intermixing of different kinds of inquiry and information that many Restoration scientists had resisted. Questions or answers that carried class or gender stamps, especially concerning the occult and sexuality, leapt between texts that had recently been segregated loosely into 'popular' and learned or technical categories. This cultural fascination with the empirical description of the unseen helps the narrative of wonder infuse the new form of the novel.[86] Early eighteenth-century prose fictions, like periodicals, jumble together a medley of aspects of curiosity: the quest into the unknown, the revelation of hidden parts of contemporary society, empirical detail.[87] Although the unseen that these record tends to be the psychological, sexual, historical, or exotic, contemporary writers recognize the kinship of these areas to the supernatural; Jonathan Swift and Daniel Defoe, in particular, treat the overlap between the supernatural and other areas of the unseen. Swift distrusts the moderns' claim to use language with transparent honesty, just as he distrusts the worship of novelties and wonders associated with "progress."[88] Defoe exploits both the moderns' use of language and the worship of wonders by fictionalizing numerous facets of curiosity: exploration and conquest, commodification and advertisement, the penetration of forbidden secrets, the occult, ideologically untethered speculation on inexplicable phenomena, and the protection against fraud.

Conflicting attitudes toward curiosity structure Defoe's *Journal of the Plague Year*.[89] The book portrays the popular appetite for sensational information in the process of being bifurcated through middle-class practice into useful empiricism, on the one hand, and self-indulgent peeping, on the other. Defoe's *Journal* disciplines inquiry, honing investigation into public service.[90] While the saddler, H. F., displays dangerous curiosity in his role as spectator and protagonist-victim, he exercises rational empiricism and authority as a licensed "examiner" of suspected houses. H. F. exemplifies this authoritative role by marshaling data, debating evidence, conceding the dubious nature of his sources, and comparing different stories; he models Locke's negative ideal of inquiry: "not entertaining any proposition with greater assurance than the proofs it is built upon will warrant."[91] The role of examiner, which demands close contact with the infected, however, conflicts with the saddler's private interests, not only of self-preservation but also of independent judgment. H. F. admits that he loses his "courage" for the task of inspector and retreats to watching "spectacles representing themselves in my view out of my own window" (189–90).[92] This retreat symbolizes his withdrawal from the aggressive personality of curiosity to that of spectator, full of wonder, and so of fear.

This perverse, spectatorial curiosity induces H. F. to hazard his life to witness more than he needs to see: death. He confesses that "curiosity led me to observe things more than usually, and . . . where I had not business" (38). Notable among these things is the pit of the dead, the very symbol of hell: "A terrible pit it was, and I could not resist my curiosity to go and see it" (77). Rather than a spiritual journey to the underworld, however, this visit shows an enlightened recognition of the physical nature of evil. As a vessel of the human sin of pride—inquiring into the forbidden and eating from the tree of knowledge—the saddler returns to the forbidden sight/site:

> My curiosity led or rather drove me to go and see this pit again . . .
> and I was not content to see it in the day-time . . . for all the
> bodies that were thrown in were immediately covered with earth
> . . . but I resolved to go in the night and see some of them thrown
> in. (79)

The sexton urges the saddler against his visit, since "I had no apparent call to it but my own curiosity," but the gawking saddler cannot resist. As both spectator and examiner, H. F. records statistics yet ruminates on signs.[93] He represents the conflict between two methods and modes of inquiry.[94] Whereas one reproduces the evidence of "strict examination," the approved method of enlightened science, the other represents the traditional method of untrained appetite (27). As an examiner, the saddler adopts the first method; but as a spectator, he also adopts the second: he is both regulative and curious.[95]

The conflict between regulated inquiry and undisciplined curiosity is exemplified by Defoe's treatment of superstition. Superstition, including astrology, dream visions, and the belief in miracles and predictions, models false interpretation by means of false empiricism: it breeds wonder, not curiosity. When the saddler "joined with [the people] to satisfy my curiosity" in attempting to see an angel in the sky, he exhibits the appetite for wonder—the pious need for redemption—but in rejecting the vision he demonstrates the triumph of regulated empiricism (43). As a propagandist himself, Defoe works the connection between superstition and people's naive faith in false language. He disciplines the language of advertising or publicity throughout the novel with H. F.'s skeptical stance: as John Bender explains, Defoe's text orders disorganized perception as the state orders society. He accomplishes this partly by exposing the superstitious uses of language: the pyramid of "ABRACADABRA," thought equivalent to an amulet; advertisements bearing "Capital Letters" promising free cures; "flourishes" and touts (50–56).[96] By setting advertisements off from his own text as evidence of the plague's disruption to be evaluated objectively, Defoe bids readers to deconstruct the language of publicity. This hieroglyphic use of language is exemplified by the words cut on a gate by the friend of a victim, whose disorder Defoe represents in print:

> O mIsErY!
> We BoTH ShaLL DyE.
> WoE, WoE. (165)

The jumble of capital and small letters represents the writer's confusion but also resembles the inversions of hierarchy characteristic of duplicitous advertisement.[97] To combat these lies and frauds, suggests Defoe, readers should trust only what they see—or the word of God imprinted in the only reliable mystical text, the Bible. Readers' own curiosity becomes a means of empowering them against deception.

The debate over curious language reaches a peak (or nadir) in Swift's *The Wonderful Wonder of Wonders; Being an Accurate Description of the Birth, Education, Manner of Living, Religion, Politicks, Learning, &c. Of mine A — se* (1721), published the year before Defoe's *Journal*. In this mock biography, Swift alludes to the narrative of Mary Toft, but its central point reaches farther than topical criticism.[98] By degrading "wonder" to designate not the unrepresentable divine but the unmentionable behind, Swift links Scriblerian obfuscation, political paranoia, and popular credulity. The entire tale of the tail works the disparity between sign and signified to indict the exploitative methods of popular curiosity: astrology, science, monstrous exhibition. Reading for curious meanings becomes peeping. The pun-riddled preface announces that since "Curiosity, inquisitive of *Secrets*, may, possibly not enter into the *Bottom* and *Depth* of the Subject," the author will remove the "Veil" to improve the reader's "*Insight*."[99] Mocking credulous readers and fraudulent writers, Swift defends this curious artistry by claiming the ancient authority of "Emblem and Riddle" (vi–vii). Swift's Scriblerian reply to his own text, *The Blunderful Blunder of Blunders, &c.*, mocks the assumption of this authority by scientists:

> 'Tis true indeed, that in the early Ages of Learning, *Scholars*
> through an affected Vanity of appearing Wiser than the rest
> of Mankind, disguised their Knowledge under the Cover of
> *Hieroglyphicks*, but as *Philosophy* acquired more Heat and Luster,
> these Clouds began to vanish, and the Rays of *Truth* more
> universally diffused themselves to all such as was earnest to
> search and pry into the *Secrets of Nature*."[100]

This curious speaker illustrates the correspondence between mystifying language and gullibility by recounting a popular deception that also functions as allegory:

> A certain cunning Fellow who had been reduced to his last Shifts,
> and knowing the World to be very fond of *Wonders*, gave out that
> he had found a terrible Monster in a Wood, which he took Care
> to chain up in a dark Corner of his Room; People flocked in
> abundance, and the Man made a very great Advantage of his Show;
> for he managed it so dexterously, by the dreadful Accounts which
> he gave of its Fierceness, that no Body durst approach near enough
> to see what it was, till one Day, a Pot Valiant Fellow, who knew
> how to value his Six Pence, rushes upon the Monster, swore he
> would see what he was to have for his Money, and in short, drags
> out a *Dog in a Doublet*. (7)

Although impertinent peeking can expose fraudulent mystification, ironically it merely cures the disease it promotes. Curiosity fosters curiosities.

As these works deconstructing superstition show, while elite disbelief rose, texts chronicling the underside of empirical curiosity, the occult, continued to flourish. These texts record the transgression of the borders of life and death, selling themselves as tests of readers' faith. The account, putatively by Defoe, of the visitation of Mrs. Veal to her friend Mrs. Bargrave epitomizes this application of empirical verification to the unempirical. Opening the tale by asseverating that "this relation is Matter of Fact, and attended with such Circumstances as may induce any Reasonable Man to believe it," the editor testifies to the authority of his source and the credentials of the reporter—a "discerning" witness need not "be put upon by any Fallacy."[101] The opening sentence defends the tale as a precious item of knowledge: "This thing is so rare in all its Circumstances, and on so good Authority, that my Reading and Conversation has not given me any thing like it; it is fit to gratifie the most Ingenious and Serious Enquirer" (1).[102] Such careful verification simultaneously placates the skeptical reader and guarantees the value of the work.

During the decade of the 1720s and into the early 1730s, a series of six accounts of mystical fortune-telling appeared, centering on the deaf and dumb Duncan Campbell who could prognosticate people's fortunes merely by setting eyes on them and who recorded his visions in writing. These chronicles enlist the language of empiricism; all justify themselves on the grounds of public "Curiosity"; all persistently note the objective confirmations of each extraordinary act of divination, usually through the disinterested narrator; all invoke wonder repeatedly to emphasize the lack of any rational explanation for the phenomena. In his collection of biblical and modern ghost stories, *The Secrets of the Invisible World Disclos'd* (1727), Defoe promises to bridge the two "Extreams" of obstinate disbelief in demonstrations and superstitious terror by "setting things in a true light, between Imagination and solid Foundation."[103] His efforts to define "this undetermin'd thing" entail examples of "real Apparitions" and frauds imposed on the credulous (preface).[104] Throughout the collection, references to the "Eye" abound: it is the organ of discovery, but what it discovers is invisible to sight. Similarly, his accounts of Campbell, like Eliza Haywood's *Spy upon the Conjuror*, recount the seer's magical feats: Campbell sets eyes on a newcomer and instantly reveals by silent looks that he knows of his or her secret fate. For example, in another of Haywood's narratives, *The Dumb Projector* (1725), when an old gentleman approaches Campbell, "the Sight of him had more Effect on Mr. *Campbell's* Resolution, than all the Persuasions [that] had been made use of—He cast his Eye full upon him, and seem'd struck with Wonder and Amazement."[105] These books make vision the avenue to the unseeable.

Apparitions and second sight are attempts to penetrate the borders of morality that make the subject—mankind—the object of inquiry. Traditionally, for example, second sight can foresee only two events reliably, according to Duncan Campbell: death and marriage, the supposed precondition for offspring.[106] Historically, apparitions have been taken as evidence of the immortality of the soul.[107] Both aspects of the occult thus partake of the contested curious desire for immortality. Indeed, Campbell identifies second sight as the "Power of discerning incorporeal Beings" who inform him of secrets out of time (*Secret Memoirs*, 63). This "Power" allows him to participate in an alternative reality, but unlike a witch, a devil, or a God, he cannot influence these apparitions himself. It is for this reason that Campbell proved so fascinating to eighteenth-century audiences and customers. He represents a disinterested, benevolent investigator into the unseen, a scientist of the spirit world.

By guaranteeing the persistence of the self beyond mortality, beyond birth and death, beyond both the physical and the temporal world, these occult phenomena provide empirical evidence of the unempirical nature of the self. They de-materialize identity itself, even while such identity appears a physical or psychical phenomenon that can be observed. In the body of Campbell, empirical investigation transcends time, overleaps physicality, and certifies the existence of subjectivity outside the body itself. This curiosity liberates identity from time and space: albeit bound in simple ways by providence, the self is free.

The radical potential of inquiry to make the subject immaterial shapes many of the fictions of identity that litter the period, especially Defoe's fictional biographies. The enormously successful *Robinson Crusoe* (1719) exemplifies the contemporary appetite for a curious hero whose identity is released from social bonds. Even while he receives severe punishment for his curiosity, Crusoe embodies the constant quest of the free intellect.[108] As H. F. initially embodies the unregulated appetite to probe the forbidden, to transgress into the realms of death, so Robinson incarnates a wanderlust; as H. F. himself becomes an agent for ordering curiosity through examination, so Robinson forges from his willfulness a constructive curiosity that masters the physical world. Robinson's head is always filled "with rambling Thoughts," thoughts of rambling that themselves are disorganized (2). Survival gives them shape. His imprisonment on the island not only compels him to stop wandering physically, but induces him to wonder psychologically, to use his inquiring urge to analyze and thus to take control of his own destiny.[109] When a lightning storm strikes the island, "a Thought . . . darted into my Mind, as swift as the Lightning it self," the realization that "at one Blast all my Powder might be destroy'd" (70). As a result of this "Impression" of the fragility of his "pow[d]er," Robinson provides for future contingencies; notably, he "discover[s]" wild goats, the species which becomes the basis of his farm (71). When his curiosity turns to his fate, he satisfies it with an empirical survey of his past, buttressed by religion (108–9). His capacity to analyze and control the world around him—characterized by his appetite for information and desire to survive—becomes his identity.

At the same time, Robinson Crusoe incarnates the cultural ideal of transcendent curiosity. Even more than Defoe's other explorers, he escapes time and space; even more than other conquerors, he emblematizes cultural ambition. Discontented with his social place, disobedient to his father, thirsting for new experience, he rejects society to invent a new culture in which he stands as priest, lawyer, merchant, and ruler. While he accumulates possessions, Crusoe is never possessed by them: he conquers new lands—from his island to the rich coasts of the New World—colonizes natives like Friday, and accumulates a wealth that yet never entails responsibility. By portraying a hero who is essentially free of memory and grief, Defoe undermines the importance of society's institutions. Indeed, by triumphantly ignoring history to offer readers, through their identification with Robinson, the fantasy of constructing culture, he represents ambition and curiosity as the means for power. The voracious desire for novelty and sensation that such satirists as Swift read as vacancy, Defoe interprets as the limitless spring of an energy that kicks away the past and propels the curious seeker hungrily into new experience.

Defoe expresses this thrilling resilience and movement through a narrative that eludes temporal distinctions. Critics have long complained about the instability of Defoe's form, pointing out that the narrators' moral retrospection clashes with their enthusiastic account of immediate experience. Defoe's form, however, does not betray clumsiness; rather, it carries vital cultural significance. By evading remorse, Defoe makes experience always immediate and narrative always novel. As in *Moll Flanders*—the female version of the fantasy of adventure, exploration, and conquest—Defoe's narrative style in *Robinson Crusoe* elides past and future tenses: Crusoe's journalistic method renders every day as present experience. Moreover, the novel itself lacks formal distinctions like chapters that demarcate experience as units for contemplation. Instead, the narrative tumbles through events chronicled mainly in the order of their occurrence, each equally important precisely because it happened. *Robinson Crusoe*, indeed, initiated the novel as a genre that made presentness the essence of narrative. It fostered repeated sequels and inspired ever-incomplete novels, from *Clarissa* to *Tristram Shandy*, that made memory itself a present sensation. In characterization, genre, and style, *Robinson Crusoe* epitomizes the eighteenth-century idealization of modern curiosity.

Both this idealization of curiosity and the success of the book irritated many competing writers. The cycle whereby curious publishers create curious consumers who promote more publishers proved profitable to writers from Defoe to Pope, but it also epitomized for many the decadence of a civilization that feeds off its own products. Critics charged that by eating up printed novelties, eighteenth-century audiences were becoming inquiry addicts. Answers merely prompted more questions; when practical inquiries ran dry, impractical, ludicrous, or even insincere inquiries sprang to replace them. To conservative writers, notably Swift, contemporary readers seemed to feed off information without putting it to social use. Questions about the snow, or the genus of moss, or the cause of earthquakes seemed not to speed any practical solutions for the victims of avalanches, disease, or disaster. Rather, such information seemed merely to drop into the bottomless yaw of the reader and vanish.

Indeed, by raising curiosity, as the defining mark of mankind's divinity, to an ideological pinnacle, philosophers like Locke, promoters like Dunton, and authors like Defoe define readers by an absence: the absence of knowledge. Such a definition plays into traditional attacks on curiosity as limitless desire. Swift exploits the credulity that such desire encourages in his Bickerstaff predictions, imitation almanacs that spoof both predatory con men and superstitious readers. To satirists with traditionalist leanings, these news-hungry readers, consumed with an insatiable intellectual appetite, seem ultimately to be seeking their own identity: the understanding of themselves as physical creatures in a world theoretically legible to the eye. However, by defining themselves by curiosity, an intellectual desire always chasing its retreating fulfillment, they annihilate any concrete self. The self becomes a vacuum whose sucking implosiveness is intensified by the novelties poured into it. These readers' consumption of curiosity becomes all-consuming—in the end, in fact, consuming them.

This cultural charge that curiosity consumes the consumer shapes the period's most thorough anatomy of curiosity: *Gulliver's Travels* (1726). This work brims with satiric targets that embody curiosity: the violation of boundaries for the purpose of self-advancement.[110] Through Swift's satire, these curiosities mirror the grotesque curiosity of the reader who, quite literally, buys them. The book portrays humans who, like teratological monsters shrunk or swollen to disproportionate size, reveal humanity's hidden vices and warn of culture's impending collapse. The malicious and minute Lilliputians incarnate political corruption as they bicker to conquer Blefescu and leap over each other. The Brobdingnagians have grown gigantic by devouring spectacle; they exhibit mankind's ambition in full. In Laputa, scientists and scholars, deformed by self-absorption, reverse production and consumption through such experiments as extracting sunlight from cucumbers. They seek to rule nature itself. Both Glubbdubdrib, the land of ghosts, and Luggnagg, the land of the immortal Struldbrugs, dramatize the reader's quest to confute death itself. In Part 4, Swift depicts man's utopian ambition as the loss of his very nature. Gulliver so strongly identifies with another species, Houyhnhnms, that he becomes a monstrous hybrid himself—and so does the reader who identifies with him. *Gulliver's Travels* is a catalogue of curious subjects that satirically exploits the reader's own cultural ambition through curious spectacle.

Through his metaphorical form and rhetoric, Swift condemns both the commercialization of wonder through print, and the gullible reader who buys it. As a whole, the book, with its clichéd title and meretricious preface, mimics the exploitation of readers by travel writers and profiteering publishers. The preface consists of a letter from the ostensible publisher, Richard Sympson, "to the Reader." The letter, with its passing reference to a personal relationship between Sympson and Gulliver, alludes to the contemporary publisher Lawton Gilliver, and so underscores the self-interest of the book trade. Skeptical readers will notice the connection, as they should recognize the deception in such books as *Robinson Crusoe*. For Swift, as for Pope, these voyages usurp sophisticated art and kidnap audiences. *Gulliver's Travels* mimics Defoe's limpid and lying empiricism through the consistent application of curious art that implies a concealed meaning. Swift thus ridicules the naiveté that accepts the visible as truth. In the publisher's prefatory letter, Swift parodies the self-promoting bombast accompanying wonderful biographies:

> The Style is very plain and simple; and the only Fault I find is,
> that the Author, of the Manner of Travellers, is a little too
> Circumstantial. There is an Air of Truth apparent throughout
> the Whole; and indeed, the Author was so distinguished for his
> Veracity, that it became a sort of Proverb among his neighbours
> at *Redriff*, when any one affirm'd a Thing, to say, it was as true as if
> Mr. *Gulliver* had spoke it.[111]

Not only does this disingenuous passage indict Defoe's novels as simplistically written, dully detailed, and improbable, but it also lambastes readers who swallow such fictions as fact.[112]

However, the reader's understanding of language as metaphor makes

Gulliver the victim of his own empirical prose. Empiricism, here as in Swift's poems, remains a central theme. The book mocks travel in foreign lands as a curiosity in motion that deludes the traveler and the reader; just as such texts whip audiences to consume lies as curiosities, so authors, including experimental scientists, delude themselves. Gulliver embodies the self-importance, pretension, and ignorance of Whiggish explorers. Too bashful to wear the spectacles he needs to see properly, he remains correspondingly unreliable as an observer. His pedantic style and obstinately superficial perspective present one side of delusive empiricism; scientific sight provides the other. Swift represents the delusions of telescopic and microscopic vision in the Lilliputian and Brobdingnagian parts, where the human body becomes a subject of intense scrutiny. Pleasingly reduced and seen from afar, the body in Lilliput stimulates wonder as minute seamstresses weave invisible threads into fabric; magnified in Brobdingnag, the body prompts revulsion as it displays gigantic tumors, pimples, and spots, all meticulously recorded by the physician Gulliver.

Part 3 parodies other forms of scientized sight. Here, Swift, by depicting the most learned Projectors as those who substitute "*Things*"—repeatedly capitalized and italicized—for words, literalizes the charge that modern men materialize value. When Gulliver notes that the Projectors can thus construct conversation from the material about them, Swift mocks Defoe's practice and ideology of opportunistically presenting only the present itself. Another experiment enables ignorant readers to write on an encyclopedic range of topics cheaply and quickly by having them analyze fragmented sentences that result from the chance conjunctions of words stretched in folios on a frame that is shaken periodically and violently by attentive students. The new collections of words produce new texts. Such satire collapses collecting into writing, makes writing itself collecting, and indicts the entire modern culture of print as meaningless acquisition. These and Swift's many other hilarious examples not only thematize the abuses of empiricism, but also gleefully demonstrate that readers find more meanings in words than are dreamed of in scientific philosophy.

Swift's scientific satire resurrects several of the vital themes of *Three Hours After Marriage*. Like the Scriblerian authors, Swift intended parody, specifically of Defoe and of travelogues vaunting the odd over the true, but more generally of the moderns' credulity, pedantry, and unacknowledged appetite for notoriety and power. In this mock travelogue, Swift brings to life the myth of the antediluvian giant, documented by his gigantic appetite. Rather than providing teeth from the giant, like Fossile and other early collectors, Swift shows Gulliver as a Brobdingnagian hogging Lilli-

putian food by the barrelful. He does more than discourse on the morality
of Egyptian mummies and pyramids, like both John Gay through Fossile
and Samuel Johnson through Imlac in *Rasselas;* Swift puts Gulliver himself
in the land of the dead to hear the questions of rank debated. Particularly
in the Voyage to Laputa, Swift satirizes the rise of science in both new and
old terms. The sexual inadequacy of the Projectors, whose wives escape to
the land below for satisfaction, reworks a familiar motif in the history of
curiosity. Swift's invention of Flappers to awaken the abstract philosophers
to social reality reveals the new intensity that this period gave to the traditional complaint that scientists remove themselves from the daily grind. In
Swift's vision, this abstraction does not prove the philosophers impartiality
and reliability but rather their incompetence and solipsism—points reinforced by Gulliver's own dubious posture of academic disinterest in describing foreign lands and cultures.[113]

The Projectors and Gulliver's empirical method of classifying experience plays with the familiarizing and defamiliarizing maneuvers of science.
On one hand, phenomena are deliberately described in details that make
them new to the observer, and therefore available for logical, nonpreju-
diced analysis; on the other hand, Swift's pervasive satire reminds readers
of the metaphorical meanings underlying all observed phenomena. The
Lilliputians' leaping and creeping for office provides one of the best examples. Another is Gulliver's precise description of a Brobdingnagian's gigantic breast, provided in lieu of a comparison "so as to give the curious
Reader an Idea of its Bulk, Shape and Colour."[114] The Lilliputians' technical description of the contents of Gulliver's pockets especially ridicules the
language of spying, be this prurient, political, or scientific:

> a Globe, half Silver, and half of some transparent Metal: For on
> the transparent side we saw certain strange Figures circularly
> drawn, and thought we could touch them, till we found our
> Fingers stopped by that lucid Substance. He put this Engine to
> our Ears, which made an incessant Noise like that of a Water-Mill.
> And we conjecture it is either some unknown Animal, or the God
> that he worships: But we are more inclined to the latter Opinion,
> because he assured us, (if we understood him right, for he
> expressed himself very imperfectly) that he seldom did any thing
> without consulting it. He called it his Oracle, and said it pointed
> out the Time for every Action of his Life. (Pt. 1, p. 53)

The interfusion of the literal and the metaphorical by both the meticulous
Lilliputians and the inarticulate Gulliver proves that the two languages de-

pend on one another. No pure language exists since no phenomena exist outside a social context. Moreover, the Lilliputians' narrative positions all phenomena around themselves like the narratives of Royal Society experimenters.[115] The entire book works on the same principle.[116]

Nonetheless, Defoe's *Robinson Crusoe* represents the most important target for Swift, and not merely for its form. While burlesquing the appetite for and exploitation of curiosity in Defoe's stories, *Gulliver's Travels* focuses on the heterodox fluidity of Robinson Crusoe's character. Crusoe's very emptiness—his identity as the curious urge, his function of heroizing irresponsible inquiry—makes him a repellent curiosity for Swift. By incarnating him as Gulliver, Swift excoriates misdirected curiosity. His laborious opening—"My Father had a small Estate in *Nottinghamshire*; I was the Third of Five Sons. He sent me to *Emmanuel-College*"—reproduces the curious style of meaningless specificity (pt. 1, p. 39). As a printed lie, a distortion of language and values, the character of the analytic, investigative traveler is, for Swift, monstrous; moreover, this monstrosity derives partly from the audience's prurient appetite for the distorted, ugly, and untrue.

Throughout the book, the public's curiosity not only for printed voyages but for curious sights receives satiric treatment. Gulliver's retreat from "the Concourse of curious People" who visit him indicts both people's undisciplined appetite for wonder, and Gulliver's self-creation as a monster, for his own curiosity has made him into one.[117] This dynamic is progressively worked out in the book. Both in Lilliput and Brobdingnag, Gulliver is literally monstrous. As Aline Mackenzie Taylor notes, he is exhibited as a monster in Brobdingnag precisely the way peculiarly formed people were displayed in contemporary England, and his identity as a monster is proved by the physical evidence of his tiny, mouse-skin breeches.[118] Once again, curiosity proves a mirror in which consumer and commodity, in eternal reflection, perpetually become each other.

Gulliver not only becomes a monster of corrupted humanity, however; he also loses every form of identity, even his species identification. With a virtuoso display of the ways in which Gulliver's physical being can be made a spectacle, Swift plunders the early modern tradition of the wonders and exhibitions of the body. Despite his asserted indignation at being "exposed for Money as a publick Spectacle to the meanest of the People" and exhibited "to the Wonder and Satisfaction of all People," he seems proud of his monstrous status as he struts and bows as a performer on stage (pt. 2, p. 102). Yet this public curiosity almost consumes him: "The more my Master got by me, the more unsatiable he grew. I had quite lost my Stomach, and was almost reduced to a Skeleton" (pt. 2, p. 106). Without a social context, he loses his class identity, becoming a noble "*Nardac*" and would-be colonial breeder in Lilliput, a "Slave" to be bred himself in Brobdingnag, and something between a servant, a pet, and a pest in Houyhnhnmland (pt. 1, p. 106; pt. 2, p. 138). When, after his rough treatment and in an unconscious parody of courtesy, Gulliver kisses the hand of his Brobdingnagian tormentor, his master induces his son, as a reciprocal sign of friendship, to "stroak" him like an animal (pt. 2, p. 97). His flourishes and gestures make him both a showman and a show in the tradition of Bartholomew Fair.[119]

Gulliver's monstrosity is a manifestation of his cultural ambition: he is curiosity personified. As he aims to rise in each society he joins, he apes its cultural values and in the process parodies them: urinating in the Lilliputian palace, offering the Brobdingnagian king deadly gunpowder, projecting in Laputa, whinnying in Houyhnhnmland. He is proud of his *Nardac* status in Lilliput, and he boasts of his physical displays on the table in Brobdingnag. Unencumbered by the past, like Crusoe, he mirrors his present context, yet his identity ripples on the margins of whatever culture he inhabits. For Swift, such mutability exemplifies the monster. Gulliver's concluding praise of the rationality of the Houyhnhnms who expelled him and his arrogant raving against people with "any Tincture of this absurd Vice" of pride show that he has no stable context in which to define himself (pt. 4, p. 266).

In foreign lands, Gulliver even loses his ontological identity. In Brobdingnag, the king believes him to be a clockwork toy "contrived by some ingenious Artist"; a monkey embraces him; the farmer examines him as "a small dangerous Animal" like "a *Weasel*"; the farmer's wife screams at him as "a Toad or a Spider"; the farmer's son views him as a sparrow, rabbit, young kitten, or puppy; and the natural philosophers conclude that he is a "*Lusus Naturae*" beyond nature (pt. 2, p. 107–8, 95, 97, 108). In Houyhnhnmland, he is embraced by a Yahoo while he attempts to become horsified. By dramatizing Gulliver's instability of identity through physical shifts in perspective, *Gulliver's Travels* argues that unrestrained, other-seeking curiosity—the appetite that Steele excoriated in the Inquirer—empties the self. Gulliver's efforts ironically exclude him from the society he would join. A giant in Lilliput, a dwarf in Brobdingnag, a rube in Laputa, a Yahoo in Houyhnhnmland, a horse in England, throughout, he is the spectator and the spectacle, the exhibitor and the exhibit.

Robinson Crusoe and *Gulliver's Travels* dramatize the contemporary opposition between curiosity as an ambition that is heroic and curiosity as an ambition that is monstrous. By a narrative focused entirely on the present,

Defoe represents experience itself as novelty. While Crusoe embodies the modern heroic quest to control the world through analysis, his tale of the independent construction of civilization thematizes curiosity as the ambition to remake culture; and Defoe's present-propelled narrative genre and style formalizes the ideology valuing the new. Like readers of detective stories, Defoe's audience participates in making a world by anticipating and solving each of Crusoe's difficulties. In *Gulliver's Travels*, Swift ironically imitates this device. He details degrading incidents such as Gulliver's urination and defecation to satirize the reader's curiosity as prurient; he invites readers to identify with a monstrous hero; his narrative insistently, doggedly repeats the term "curious" so that is becomes the degraded litany of modernity. Whereas Crusoe forges value from his new world, not merely finding but making both food and wealth, Gulliver serves to parody the conjuration of value from the valueless. Afloat on a boat of Yahoo skin, he symbolizes the cannibalistic perversion of a curiosity that supports itself by self-consumption. As a comprehensive indictment of curiosity, *Gulliver's Travels* depicts culture itself as the deluded pursuit of novelty. Most powerfully, the two books narrate the very definition of curiosity itself. They definitively demonstrate that curiosity is cultural ambition, manifested by ontological transgression—transcendence or monstrosity—and registered by empiricism.

In the first decades of the eighteenth century, writers saw empiricism as the method of modernity, but its power to capture and collect the world as a jumble of material items seemed to threaten humanistic values. The scientific urge to dissect and classify the physical universe marks a new subjectivity: a selfhood projected outward, explaining phenomena beyond the inquiring self, not reflective except insofar as the self can be objectified as an item for analysis. The self thus expands to occupy the world, and to obsess narrative: it consumes novelty, information, experience, and, to many, seems consumed itself and thus transformed into something dehumanized. Defoe's heroes as well as the satirized collectors in contemporary poetry exemplify this idealized identity. These characters shrug off traditional contexts and envelop new ones with a limitless flexibility that defines them only by movement, either through the world or in response to the fashion of the day. This movement enacts their survival, a survival that, although physical, depends on the mental appetite to explore, to exploit, to know, to conquer: it is survival by curiosity.

Even while this curiosity seems to allow an infinite choice of mutable identities, it paradoxically seems to objectify identity itself by making the sign of investigation the accumulation of *things*. Modern language, touted by self-promoting novels, erodes boundaries between advertisements and information, wresting authority from social consensus and resting it in the assertion of the writer alone. Questioning simultaneously shapes and explodes the subjectivity of authors and readers. While the appetite for information proves the entrée to modernity, it also reflects the subject's internal vacancy: the hollow within that needs furnishing with the things, ideas, and topics of contemporary society. Even as they prize linguistic skill, writers condemn the objectification of value, the materialization of morality, and the rendering of ideas into printed products that is ironically exemplified by curious art, and that turns the writer into a commodity. This paradox whereby art becomes product and inquiry becomes identity commodifies curiosity itself. Curiosity fragments identity even as it defines the modern human.

CHAPTER THREE

From the Curious to the Curio

Impertinent curiosity, particularly sexual snooping, is an impulse traditionally attributed to women. From Pandora's peeking and Eve's eating
to Alice's anxiety in Wonderland, female curiosity in religion, myth, popular culture, and high literature has meant a perverse desire to spy things
out, particularly to know what makes men, men. In the eighteenth century,
however, female curiosity attracts a passionate new derogation. It is represented as the co-opting of knowledge: the seamy obverse of elite inquiry.
Whereas the public if unstable institutions of journalism and the Royal
Society could be seen monitoring male inquiry, female curiosity, precisely
because women were traditionally excluded from public life, seemed to riot
behind the scene.

For many people, such enterprises as Dunton's *Athenian Spy* merely
verified a feminine tradition of subversive inquiry: untutored, irrational,
irreverent, beyond regulation.[1] Hester Piozzi in *British Synonymy* (1794)
differentiates between men "ADDICTED TO ENQUIRY" and "the people we
call INQUISITIVE, and in the language of low female GOSSIPERS"; thus she
characterizes base curiosity as female attention to minute inquiries about
other people.[2] As women began to encroach on the masculine arenas of
politics, literature, and consumption, eighteenth-century culture represented as female curiosity the whole host of traditional disparagements
of curiosity that scientific, institutionalized inquiry had attempted to
dispel. Female curiosity was idle, ignorant, prurient, useless or even socially destructive; it sneered at the higher claims scientists made; indeed,
eighteenth-century culture feminized objections to scientific reasoning.
Curiosity without method and without justification became female. Most
of all, female curiosity epitomized illegitimate cultural ambition.

In a replay of the Restoration satirists' revenge, eighteenth-century
culture attempts to control this subversive tradition by transforming

women from inquirers into objects of inquiry—a process that culminates in the Victorian ideal of the living doll. Eighteenth-century literature represents women as possessing a hidden "Secret" that turns them into objects of a curious search; the virtuoso's imperialistic curiosity co-opts the curious female to make the questioner the question.[3] In this capacity to become objects, women exemplify the definitive trait of curiosity: the ability to shift beings, to violate ontological categories.

The literature from the Restoration to the Regency wrestles with the relationship between these two representations of women: as priers and as precious objects. Much of this literature configures women as rebels whose inquisitiveness and bodies enable them—literally and figuratively—to receive a carnal knowledge that defies social and religious rules and invites men to transgression. This transgression involves secular devotion, a love of the sensual or material epitomized by collecting—even collecting women themselves. Correlatively, the double role of women as inquirers and collectibles links them to virtuosi, satirically figured as monsters from their own cabinets. Women writers exploit this double role. While as women they participate in the underground culture of illegitimate questioning, as writers they belong to the regulatory institution of journalism; they form the subjects of their own inquiry.[4] Thus, writing about and by women in this period vacillates between external and internal description, as the female subject wavers between object and agent.

Gender borders many of the central issues surrounding curiosity. It frets at the margins between man and non-man, between private and public interest, between physical and social humanity. During the early modern period, gender draws heightened scrutiny because it constitutes a central battlefield of cultural power. As they came to incarnate cultural ambition, women were increasingly represented as curiosities. Such female curiosities as Mary Toft, Elizabeth Canning, the Cock Lane Ghost and her medium, Jane Wenham and other female witches and managers of the occult, including Eliza Haywood's Spy, and a miscellany of performers with odd bodies test current definitions and limits of proper inquiry. Their very bodies become the sites of transgressive desire: the desire to transcend their proper place (fig. 11).

While men also act as tricksters and exhibitions, women attract particular attention in this period as they begin to penetrate and thus challenge the male arenas of empiricism. Many depictions of curiosity thus attack sexuality as the emblem of monstrous cultural corruption, notably by portrayals of the women of Bartholomew Fair, prostitutes, transsexuals, and the violent Monster of 1790. The hostile equation of aggressive and re-

Figure 11. Kilian Wolffg, "Magdalena Rudolfs Thuinbuj of Stockholm." 1651. (Engraving, 11 1/8 in. × 6 1/8 in.) This poster displays the armless woman's pedal dexterity in twenty-one vignettes depicting tasks ranging from card playing and hair combing to the caretaking of her baby. Her domestic labor appears as a marvelous exhibition that proves the female will to be monstrously powerful over the body. Courtesy of the Art Collection, Harry Ransom Humanities Research Center, University of Texas at Austin

ceptive curiosity peaks in the late-century caricature of curious females questing for sex in a society thinned of men by the Napoleonic wars. This caricature is epitomized by Thomas Rowlandson's "The Advertisement for a Wife," depicting Doctor Syntax overwhelmed by underdressed beauties in pursuit.[5] Such depictions identify the female body as the agent of cultural usurpation.

As the bourgeois ideal of the self as owner or connoisseur develops, a host of immaterial aspects of culture become commodified through print.[6] Women's inquiry, with its frisson of violation and sexuality, takes the form of subversive publications, collections of scandal tales, and secret histories blending stories of the political cabinet and private "closet." Not only do these print vehicles sell unlicensed inquiry, however, but they make the subject of that inquiry itself an object of inquiry. The sensibility and particularly the corporeality of the penetratingly inquisitive female itself becomes a site of transgressive exploration.

In exploiting female curiosity as empiricism's underside, much eighteenth-century literature employs traditional and conservative tropes. Pandoran plots that oppose prying to love, mock the supremacy of sight, and associate curiosity with a decadent sexuality that devastates women reinforce the conventional moral opposition between feminine fulfillment and curiosity. Many texts, however, use female curiosity to question, undermine, or ridicule the newly dominant masculine modes of scientific empiricism. These texts often use the structure of gossip. Like other forms of curiosity—witchcraft, science, the occult, monstrosity, pornography—gossip inquires into forbidden territories beyond nature, religion, life, and sexual boundaries. Culturally figured as feminine in its social and sexual orientation, gossip escapes regulation, eludes established structures, and gratifies private agendas that, once published, enter the public sphere. As Patricia Meyer Spacks has shown, gossip shares other curious traits: it legitimizes idleness, spices up voyeurism, and threatens usurpation of others' lives.[7] Most significantly, it motivates a genre for women's inquiry in which women serve as both subjects and narrators. As women moved into public culture as writers, actresses, and consumers, the narrative form of printed gossip became a central means for the expression of a subversive curiosity that vaunted the cultural power of women.[8]

THE INQUIRY OF EVE

Even as eighteenth-century literature refigures women's curiosity, it reworks traditional literary forms that warn of the dangers of prying women.

Pandora—who, like Eve, the Christian mother of evils, looks on the forbidden and brings grief and corruption into the world—infuses eighteenth-century texts, sometimes as the harbinger of monstrosity. In *Callipaedia*, Samuel Cobb blames her prying for the benighting of Reason and the distortion of true form.[9] Other texts deploy the myth of Psyche, whose prying ruins love, and occasionally of Lot's wife, whose backward glance at Sodom symbolizes disobedience.[10] Of course, not all sly priers are female, but scenes in paintings, gossip, and literature in which women become willing sights for Peeping Toms attribute agency to the women rather than the men.[11] This marginally licit voyeurism reenacts the curiosity that marks the prying woman: an officious interest in sex that spurs men's reciprocal interest and that translates into a general prying into others' "affairs."

The opposition between curiosity and love symbolized by Psyche reappears in an ancient fable freshly popular in Restoration literature.[12] The story runs that a lover, usually male, cannot accept the fidelity of his beloved and insists on testing it by persuading a friend to try to seduce her. Repeated attempts fail, until finally, either to punish her lover or because his jealousy has alienated her, the beloved succumbs and the jealous lover has the ironic satisfaction of having his worst fears realized. Aphra Behn summarizes the theme as "too much curiosity lost paradise."[13] It may also be the source of the mot "curiosity killed the cat," a revision of the Renaissance maxim "care killed the cat." The myth dramatizes not only the hazardous folly of trying to prove what must be taken on faith, but the evils of personal manipulation. Curiosity indicates over-anxiety as much as too much inquisitiveness.

In *The Amorous Prince, or The Curious Husband* (1671), Aphra Behn uses this plot to mock social and gendered attitudes of possessiveness.[14] In one of the play's two main stories, Clarinda's jealous husband, Antonio, has beseeched his friend Alberto to try to seduce his wife and thus prove her faithless. Alberto pretends to agree but in fact refuses to flatter or bribe Clarinda as the perverse Antonio demands. Meanwhile the two sisters, Clarinda and Isabella, discovering that Alberto actually desires Isabella (whom he believes to be Clarinda), have dressed identically without informing Alberto of Isabella's existence or allowing Antonio to see their identical costumes. Their purpose is to stimulate Alberto to love through jealousy and to punish Antonio by contriving love scenes between the blameless Isabella and Alberto, as the concealed Antonio watches in agony. Alberto, however, is reluctant to try to cuckold his friend, although he begins to fall in love with Isabella (whom he thinks is Clarinda) in earnest.

Repeatedly, Antonio urges Alberto to greater efforts; and repeatedly Alberto's failure leads Antonio to weep, embrace his friend, and bless his fortune in possessing so fine a friend and so true a wife. Nonetheless, he begins (with justice) to doubt his friend's sincerity in attempting to seduce his wife: is he *really* trying? Or—worse still—*is* he really trying? His self-induced comic dilemma is neatly encapsulated thus: "this uncertainty disturbs me more, / Than if I knew *Clarinda* were a—Whore."[15] Antonio embodies the dilemma of curiosity, sharpened in the first flush of empiricism, which would rather destroy love, faith, and trust than live in a world where such things remain beyond proof.[16]

As Behn's tale shows, the conventional link between jealousy and curiosity strengthened during the Restoration. Both are seen as passions that reject reason and insist on an unreal world. Moreover, both jealousy and curiosity also involve possessiveness: amassing novelties or colonizing others. Prince Frederick, the titular "Amorous Prince," collects women: his decadent desire to see Laura, whom he believes to be a new beauty, is described as "curiosity," and one scene portrays his examination of a bevy of beautiful women, disguised as courtesans, as an exercise of connoisseurship. Nonetheless, the traditional association of curiosity and possessiveness loses much of its moral animus in Restoration court literature—a loss doubtless aided by the scientific collector Charles II's enthusiastic womanizing. In many Restoration dramas, the objectification of women as sexual collectibles exhibits the pursuit of novelty that marks modernity.[17] Indeed, women on the stage—themselves a novelty—did perform as collectibles, exhibiting themselves to aristocrats questing for a new mistress. In response to this libertine portrayal of curiosity as possessiveness during the Restoration, religious objections to curiosity as the worship of materiality and of sex resurface with the aim of condemning the many texts that portray novelty as a new sanction for treating people as objects.

At the end of the seventeenth century, popular versions of the fable about the jealous lover abound, but their emphases fall on different aspects of the weakness of jealous curiosity. John Crowne's *The Married Beau; or the Curious Impertinent* (1694) traces Mr. Lovely's trial of his wife to a vanity that demands, "My Eyes shall wander o're her Face to spy / If, when I kiss her, she's entranced with joy."[18] The prose version of Behn's play, entitled *The Curious Impertinent*, equates domestic curiosity with scientific irreligion in opposition to faith. Here, as usual, the amorous Anselmo's curiosity to test his lover's fidelity destroys love itself.[19] Despite his friend Lothario's advice to "consider how vain and impertinent a Curiosity it is to stir the Humours that now lye settled in your Wife's Breast," Anselmo, in his passion, demands "proof" of his wife's affection: empirical evidence of the empirically unverifiable—the heart. Lothario explains the grounds of hostility to curiosity:

> Methinks, *Anselmo*, you are at this time just like the *Moors*, who are not to be convinc'd of the Error of their sect by . . . any thing grounded on Matters of Faith; but they must have Instances brought them that are palpable, easy, intelligible, undoubted, and like the Mathematical Demonstrations not to be deny'd. . . . It must be shewn them by Operation, and lay'd before their Eyes, and yet no Man can convince them of the Truth of our holy Religion. The same form and method will be proper for me to use with you; for your present Curiosity is so wild and remote from anything reasonable that it will be but a loss of Time to shew you the Extravagancy of it. (146–47)

Lothario equates Anselmo's domestic jealousy with an enveloping attitude of resistance to authority—specifically with the distrust of religious and social authorities, notably the arguments of speculative or metaphysical thinkers, the Scriptures, the word of man. The text here suggests that curious men, like heretics or heathens, demand a private showing of eternal truths. Their intellectual passion is at once arrogant and irrational.[20]

Women's curiosity—the curious attribute of females—can redeem male curious prying, whether through love or through lust. Reinforcing their conservative resistance to curiosity, texts that condemn male sexual accumulation represent women's sexual curiousness as divine mystery, the just corrective of male vice. Since women introduced pain and evil into the world, they also served as the occasion for Christ's redemption. In Sir William Killigrew's comedy *Pandora*, Pandora's action redeems carnal curiosity from monstrosity and transforms it into the blessing of love, as the eponymous princess reforms the rake Clearcus. The more licentious dramas of the Restoration that revel in the motif of sexual collecting show female appetite as the cause of male behavior. Many of these dramas celebrate sexual exploitation as cultural mastery, whether exercised by men or women. Famously, William Wycherley's satire *The Country Wife* (1675) portrays the seduction of the newly married country naïf, Margery Pinchwife, as proof of women's irrepressible and natural sexual curiosity, but the main pull of the play lies in Horner, the cynical libertine who puts horns on others. A collector of sexual experience and self-declared impotent, Horner, the masquerader or hypocrite, embodies decadent desire. Employed in pleasuring women to the point of exhaustion, he acts as a facilitator of female inquiry, a version of Rochester's town tool, Signior Dildo, whose dedication to women's pleasure entails becoming a kind of curio. Horner's service to women makes him a servant and a collectible: in the act of possessing them, he is possessed by ambitious women. This satire shows female curiosity as the agent for lawless duplicity and as the ironic justification for licentiousness.

The representation of female curiosity as the destruction of social institutions also nourishes the tradition that monsterizes women, incarnating their curious appetite as curious object. The medieval belief that women's distorted imaginations or desires have the power to produce—or reproduce—cultural horrors in the form of monstrous children lingered throughout the eighteenth century. Albeit often questioned, even ridiculed, this belief in imaginative imprinting drew strength from teratology and emerging empirical science. In popular literature, just as moralized monstrosity differentiates Protestants, Catholics, and others, so it can be used to differentiate the sexes. Indeed, monstrosity often collapses culture and gender because the female, by definition, violates masculine proportionality: she is the ridicule of the revered, the alternate form of the human whose disproportionality impinges on the mock heroic.[21] As one satire explains:

> If man the greatest Brute on Earth was made,
> And Woman with that monst'rous Clay allay'd;
> How vile a thing must such a Creature be,
> The hated Cause of Man's lost Liberty?
> . . . Shew me a Woman, I'll a Monster find.[22]

Susan Gubar has argued that for Augustan writers, women emblematized the duplicity of a fair façade disguising death: they are the cursed part of human nature, the flesh.[23] However, in the eighteenth century, their threat lay equally, if not more urgently, in their power to co-opt culture. Especially through their role as mothers, women were depicted as morally monstrous or as bearers of monsters, responsible for the degeneration of the culture—or embodying it in their derogation of maternal duty.[24] Moreover, eighteenth-century theory held that female imagination and suppressed desires could be made flesh in the child.[25] Women's most compelling desires, suggest these satires, were for commodities.

As usurpers of the male province of consumption, women stimulated satirists to deploy both religious and quasi-scientific discourse to combat the threats presented by other cultures and exemplified by the ambitious woman. For example, in *"Pride's Fall; or, A Warning to all English Women,* by the Example of a Strange Monster born by a Merchants proud Wife at *Vienna* in *Germany*," a 1710 broadside, a vain *"Dutchland* Frow" conceives a "strange Monster" with two faces, one hand shaped like a mirror, and breasts, neck, and body all formed as if decked in fine clothes.[26] This off-spring makes fashion flesh, publicly revealing the mother's interiority. Thus, it divulges not only the concealed "truth" of female vanity, but the cultural danger of foreign opulence. Indeed, female otherness and national otherness coalesce: the body of the self-loving mother whose vices deform her products warns the falling English of the danger of consuming and thus producing a false kind of nature, a duplicitous nature—fashion. Simi-lar arguments against fashion, appearing in protests against dress, perfume, linguistic affectations, and consumer items throughout the century, often blame foreign countries for turning English women into monsters and pol-luting native culture.[27] The Dutch beauty in the satire warns the English against propagating their own pride and making monsters from children, or children from monsters.

The preeminent new product for female consumption was literature, especially prose fiction. Since early modern scientific institutions excluded women, print became the only public venue for women's questions: even the Duchess of Newcastle communicated her theories about scientific matters through poetry, not through fellowship in the Royal Society.[28] Whereas poetry often rehearsed traditional indictments against women's questions, new print forms provided a structure for writers to explore sex-ual issues traditionally of particular interest to women yet conventionally suppressed. The genres of popular inquiry—novels, newspapers, and peri-odicals—appealed directly to female audiences, as well as to men.[29] To some people, indeed, the promulgation of print seemed itself a monstrous feminization of culture.[30] In *The Courtesan* (1765), Edward Thompson identifies literary composition with prostitution, dubbing the "Pen" a "cu-rious maid" and "wonder of the town."[31] This satire equates the appetite for composition, consumption, and female curiosity as examples of devious art leading to debauchery, the devouring of wonder, and decay: all are whoredom.

This theme inspires a central novelistic plot derived from Cervantes' *Don Quixote*, feminized in Charlotte Lennox's *The Female Quixote*, and cul-minating in Jane Austen's *Northanger Abbey*. The plot blames women's cor-rupt curiosity on an inadequate education that prompts a licentious long-ing for sensation that can be satisfied either by reading or romance. Indeed, reading and sexual experience form such a tightly interwoven definition of female curiosity throughout the eighteenth century that they become a satiric cliché in Richard Brinsley Sheridan's *The Rivals* (1775).[32]

The ambition to uncover truth and rule men that female curiosity implied, however, also provided journalists and women writers with rich opportunities. John Dunton masterfully exploited them with his *Athenian Spy*, a periodical that legitimized public inquiries into sexuality.[33] As the title indicates, the primary sense with which to apprehend reality was the eye, and the lust of the eyes became the primary sensual pleasure thematized by novels, particularly women's amatory novels. These novels problematize the relationship of the seen to the unseen.[34] Correlative satire genders rebellious empiricism as female and rebellious females as curious. Such satire depicts women in masculine roles engaging in a mirroring rebellion that verges on monstrosity as they approach ontological, as well as social, transgression.[35] While exploratory penetration of the natural world for man's uses becomes increasingly associated with male inquiry, the revelatory curiosity that peeps behind the green curtain to see what is manipulating the Great Oz becomes female. Women's curiosity in the seventeenth and early eighteenth centuries designates the desire to unsettle the status quo.

Dunton's *Athenian Mercury* provided a forum "to satisfy all *ingenious and curious Enquirers* in to Speculations, Divine Moral and Natural, Etc. and to remove those Difficulties and Dissatisfactions, that shame or fear of appearing ridiculous by asking Questions may cause."[36] By answering private inquiries in public and by preserving the anonymity of both the inquirer and the respondent, Dunton applied the empirical method to the most common areas of life.[37] In the revived *Mercury*, called *Atheniae Rediviae* (1704), Dunton classified knowledge into divisions that seemed to gender phenomena: "The Divine Oracle," resolving questions of conscience; "The Philosophick and Miscellaneous Oracle," tackling all empirical matters; and "The Secret (or Ladies) Oracle, Giving a Modest Satisfaction to the Nicer Questions, relating to the *Arcana Naturae*, and such *Love Secrets* as are privately sent to the *Athenian Society*." While assuring readers that he had "refin'd [the Ladies' Oracle] from every Indecency . . . Obscenity and Smut," in practice Dunton exposed a censored area of social interaction to general inspection.[38]

Equally alarming, the questions he received unraveled conventional boundaries. One question asked whether a woman might abort her child if its father reneged on marriage, a remarkably honest expression of a peculiarly female dilemma (*Atheniae Rediviae*, no. 3, p. 108). Other questions slipped between material and social factuality. In one *Mercury*, for example, a correspondent inquired whether love was a chemical or spiritual condition (*Atheniae Rediviae*, no. 6, p. 224). Another correspondent—in asking whether "the first Motions of Love are in our Power, and afford the Mind Time to deliberate?"—questions the relationship between will and sexuality, implicitly invalidating romantic rhetoric. Dunton replies by excoriating the poetic ideal of "blind Love" and claiming that there is always a cause for falling in love, if we search deeply enough (ibid., p. 223). Empiricism was so central to his method that he denied the possibility of blind people falling in love. Although Dunton's Athenians, like their imitators, reassert public sexual standards vilifying abortion and urging the regulation of sexual (especially female) imagination and desire, their printed and serious discussions of "private" matters propelled female issues into the public arena.[39]

Dunton's Athenian ventures and the periodicals that imitated them opened a public venue for the airing of challenges to traditional sexual hierarchies and relationships. One querier wondered whether "one Sex [is] less needful for Procreation than the other?" and Dunton's reply, if sycophantic, equalized the sexes:

> As Nature hath appointed Generation for continuing the Species,
> so it hath appointed Distinction of Sexes, aiming as well at the
> Female, as the Male, and not at the Male Alone, as some think,
> who would make the Female an imperfect thing, and an Aberration
> of Nature: For the one Sex is no less needful for Procreation than
> the other. (*Atheniae Rediviae*, no. 4, p. 154)

Not only did Dunton's Private Oracle—later extended into *The Ladies Mercury*—place female curiosity on a cultural par with male curiosity (or almost), but it filled a social function. Women writers applauded it as the only public space to air private, particularly female, concerns.

In its analytic empiricism, skepticism about distinctions between social and physical phenomena, female advocacy, and sexual themes, the printed literature of periodicals powerfully resembles another venue of female inquiry: the novel. It also resembles pornography. Indeed, in his attempt to put female curiosity on a par with the male sort, Dunton faced moral censorship. While he believed he was differentiating "genuine" curiosity from the prurient kind, the boundaries between pornography and inquiry were not at all clear.[40] Simply reading about sexual matters seemed equivalent to stimulating sexual response. Furthermore, periodicals, pornography, and the novel were all results of the explosion of print culture, which opened up new audiences with new expectations.

The genre of female curiosity also borrowed techniques from the printed vessels of male curiosity: travelogues and catalogues of curious items. Many women writers adopt these techniques while they address the topics of female inquiry. In their amatory fiction, Behn, Delariviére Manley, and Haywood enumerate the physical signs of arousal in the style of a catalogue, and like travelogues, they chronicle sensual phenomena in the course of recounting an adventure through experiences, albeit their arena is domestic and bodily.[41] The thrust of their fiction, however, ridicules scientific objectivity and returns curiosity to the sphere of prurient subversion.

In her opus, Aphra Behn represents curiosity in several modes.[42] *Oroonoko: or, the Royal Slave* (1688) melds travelogue, the genre of men's exploration, and romance, the genre of women's, through a narrative voice that often mimics scientific disinterestedness. In its dedicatory epistle, Behn, "beseech[es]" Lord Maitland to absolve her from seeming "Romantick" by considering "the unconceivable Wonders" of far countries.[43] To verify her scientific accuracy in describing Oroonoko's sentimental passion, she lists the "Rarities" of Surinam, describing birds, beasts, and people in anatomical detail, comparing Surinamese marvels to those in "His Majesty's *Antiquaries*," and portraying herself as a collector by recounting that her gift of a feathered dress from the country to the king's theater was "infinitely admir'd by Persons of Quality" (3–7).[44] In the Athenian style, she confutes the apparent opposition of empiricism and romance by denying that nakedness promotes lewdness and arguing instead that in naked bodies there is "nothing to heighten Curiosity" because "all you can see, you see at once, and every Moment see; and where there is no Novelty, there can be no Curiosity" (7–8).

Behn centers curiosity in the paradoxical figure of Oroonoko himself: the ruler made rebel, the natural hero cultured into a criminal, the enslaved prince who symbolizes the reversal of nature and culture. Indeed, throughout the following century, captured kings were displayed to the public as curiosities. "The tall Black, called the Indian-King," for example, demonstrated the wonder of royalty reduced to service, and again "The Painted Prince," a tattooed African king, exhibited the paradox on his body itself: his very skin, originally decorated to signal his status as royal and precious, became an exhibit for pay in a public cabinet of curiosities.[45] Behn's narrative perspective reveals the contradictions between cultural assumptions and the facts proved by experience.[46] She uses the methods of scientific curiosity to revitalize ideal love.

Similarly, eighteenth-century amatory novels attempt to use empirical means to scrutinize romance. Delariviére Manley pushes Behn's ambiguity into satire by portraying the conventional reproof of women's curiosity as hypocrisy. Parodying Bacon's *New Atlantis*, the idealistic site of male inquiry, her New Atalantis characterizes empiricism through the narratives of a figure called Intelligence and of an old woman narrator, the very archetype of a gossip. The term "intelligence," as social jargon for rumor glossed with the claim of verification through observation, itself parodies empirical presumption. This amatory fiction exploits curiosity in several ways. Not only does Manley allude to court scandals and, by publishing thinly veiled fictional accounts, make secret sexual affairs public in print, but her stories openly endow the mythic figure of gossip with moral and empirical authority.[47] In *Secret Memoirs and Manners Of several Persons of Quality of Both Sexes from the New Atalantis*, Astrea, the goddess of Justice who seeks knowledge to educate her ward, stands in for the reader—particularly the female reader who supposedly shares Astrea's naive morality. Both Astrea and this reader listen to the tales of sexual corruption explicated by the mythic figure of Intelligence, the "Groom" of Fame.[48] For Manley, this figure, later replaced by the traditional gossip, an old woman, embodies the social impulse: prurient inquiry into private affairs simultaneously sexual and political.

Moreover, the opportunity to print these scandals celebrates the new value of empirical discovery, openness. Manley employs print and stylistic techniques designed to stimulate the reader's appetite for novelty, fashion, and sensual experience—all aspects of the "lust of the eyes" denigrated by religious opponents of empiricism. As Dunton remarks in 1701, writers need to provide material to "gratifie the curious Palate of the Nicer-Reader, who is for New-Lives, (as well as for *new Expresses, new Fashions, and new Projects*)."[49] Like many early eighteenth-century writers, Manley and Dunton lavish their prose with italics as visual markers of variety, emphasis, and concealed meaning, contrived to incite readerly excitement. By detailing the sensual luxuries available, if only in fantasy, to the consumers of her novels, Manley advertises high fashion:

> The Dutchess softly enter'd that *little Chamber* of *Repose*, the
> Weather violently hot the *Umbrelloes* were let down from behind
> the windows, the Sashes open, and the Jessimine that cover'd 'em
> blew in with a gentle Fragrancy; *Tuberoses* set in pretty Gilt and
> China Posts, were placed advantageously upon stands, the Curtains
> of the Bed drawn back to the *Canopy*, made of yellow Velvet
> embroider'd with white *Bugles*, the Panels of the Chamber

> Looking-Glass, upon the Bed were strow'd with a lavish
> Profuseness, plenty of *Orange* and *Lemon Flowers*, and to compleat
> the Scene, the young *Germanicus* in a dress and posture not very
> decent to describe; it was he that was newly risen from the *Bath*,
> and in a lose Gown of *Carnation Taffety*, stain'd with *Indian Figures*,
> his beautiful long, flowing Hair, for then 'twas the Custom to wear
> their own tied back with a Ribbon of the same Colour, he had
> thrown himself upon the Bed . . . (33)

Like modern sex-and-shopping paperbacks, this novel directs readers in up-to-the-minute elite entertainment. Manley's emphasis on the interrelationship of objects, bodies, and experiences, however, triumphantly contradicts metaphysical conceptions of love. She explains this point in the voice of the cynical count who stage-manages Germanicus's encounter with the Duchess: "tho' we surely know we shall be sated, we can't help desiring to eat, 'tis the Law of Nature, the pursuit is pleasing, and a man owes himself the Satisfaction of gratifying those Desires that are importunate, and important to him" (32–33).

Manley also alludes to print as the vehicle of sexual knowledge.[50] When, for example, she recounts the story of a lascivious Duke's seduction of his ward, Charlot, she documents this corruption through the changes in Charlot's reading. When the Duke desires Charlot to remain innocent, "he banish'd far from her Conversation whatever would not edify, Airy *Romances, Plays*, dangerous *Novels, loose* and *insinuating Poetry*, artificial Introductions of *Love*, well-painted Landskips of that dangerous Pyson" (53). By these significant italics, Manley humorously compares the reading she provides her own reader with what the Duke supplies Charlot, thus advertising her own novel as a vehicle of female information. She deepens the joke, indeed, by details that adumbrate the hypocrisy of this conventional prohibition. In his program to eradicate all hope, fear, self-love, vanity, and coquetry from Charlot, the Duke "sometimes permitted her those [pleasures] of *Poetry*, not loose Descriptions, lascivious Joys or wanton heightnings of the passions; they sung and acted the History of the *Gods*, the Rape of *Proserpine*, the descent of *Cores*, the Chastity of *Diana*, and such pieces that tended to the instruction of the Mind" (56–57). The difference between these permitted tales of jealousy, incest, rape, and seduction and the forbidden reading, Manley implies, is in the eye of the beholder. In fact, it is when Charlot is performing the role of Diana that the Duke becomes overwhelmed by lust for her. Furthermore, once he decides to seduce her, after reading a maxim from Machiavelli's *The Prince*, the Duke

gives her access to "the gay part of reading" in all languages in his library
(62). Manley suggests that the real knowledge that literature provides is
the knowledge of sexual relations, and this knowledge should be available
equally to both sexes.[51] In Manley's stories, both reading and sex offer
knowledge of the other—of the world and of male nature.[52]

Despite her comic endorsement of sexual exploration, however, Manley also reflects the conventional reproof of asking to know forbidden
things. In her collection of stories entitled *Court Intrigues In a Collection of
Original Letters, from the* ISLAND *of New Atalantis*, published in 1711 to capitalize on the success of her earlier novel, the first story openly reverses
gender roles by casting a man as Psyche. Advertised on the flyleaf as the
most "Curious and Entertaining" tale of the collection, the story, narrated
by an embittered woman servant, records the affair between a noblewoman
and a soldier. Seeing and desiring him, she arranges for him to come to
her between midnight and two in the morning for sexual encounters, during which he never sees her face; in return, she supplies him with a lavish
allowance. Her stipulation is adamant: he must *"Ask no Questions"* nor ever
seek to identify her, or he will pay with his life. Eventually, however, he
chafes at the restriction and pesters her to reveal herself. His importunity
disgusts her: she admits she might have revealed herself "whilst my Passion
had yet the gloss of Novelty; but I see him now with the Eyes of Custom"
(17). He has already, however, discovered her identity, and in admitting as
much to her, he seals his doom. He is killed in a mysterious fashion. Again,
cultural power is manifest in the ability to indulge novelty and curiosity
while retaining secrets, albeit here the woman rather than the soldier
possesses the power. Significantly, this soldier—Mr. Wilson—had been
cashiered for cowardice abroad: inhabiting the symbolic space of a woman,
he is the victim of curiosity both internal and external.

In reworking the mythic materials of the Ovidian story of Psyche, this
tale anticipates one of the most striking modern myths of curiosity: the
French story of Bluebeard. By opposing masculine acquisition with feminine disobedience, this story dramatizes the cultural struggle over the
definition and status of curiosity. Bluebeard himself encapsulates the abuse
of power and the arrogant desire for eternal life at the expense of ordinary
reproduction.[53] Bluebeard collects wives—or their bodies, at any rate. An
early modern fairy tale by Charles Perrault, translated into English by
Robert Samber in 1729, and introduced into high literary culture by
George Colman the Younger at the end of the century, this story embodies
the contradictory attitudes toward inquiry as a political and cultural phe-

nomenon. Briefly, the tale recounts the marriage of a mysteriously power-ful and wealthy, blue-bearded landowner to a local woman who, hearing disturbing rumors, disobeys her husband by entering a forbidden chamber while he is away. There, she finds the corpses of his numerous previous wives, beheaded for their curiosity, and learns of her husband's dealings with the supernatural. Bluebeard returns and, discovering her perfidy through his magic and her changed manner, is just raising his ax to behead her when she is saved by her brother (later refigured as her lover, a role that was freshly endorsed as a bond that permits social opportunity), who storms the castle, kills Bluebeard, and inherits the estate. Thus, the story traditionally connects women's curiosity with the overthrow of a tyranny at once domestic, political, and economic.[54]

Late eighteenth-century English versions of the tale, however, relocate the political tyranny in the orient and tend to dissever its collapse from the female impulse to inquire. Much of this orientalism derives from the contemporary popularity of *The Arabian Nights*, which itself contains a version of the Bluebeard tale of illicit curiosity in the story of "the wonder-ful one," Agib, whose curiosity costs him an eye.[55] Set in Turkey, Colman's "Dramatick Romance" *Blue-Beard; or, Female Curiosity!* (1798) satirizes women's culture in broad.[56] Repeated jokes play on the idea that beheading cannot cure gossip: when Fatima, the curious heroine's sister, reports that "'tis whispered that he beheaded the poor souls one after another:—for, in spite of his power there's no preventing talking," her socially ambitious father Ibrahim replies, "That's true indeed;—and, if cutting off women's heads won't prevent talking, I know of no method likely to prosper!"[57] Nor can threats change women's nature: "That Curiosity should cost so much!" laments Bluebeard's confidante, the effeminate musician Shacabac, "If all women were to forfeit their heads for being inquisitive, what a number of sweet, pretty, female faces we should lose in the world!" (act 1, scene 3, p. 16). Such humor attempts to defuse the unnerving parallel between the power of women's unregulated culture, manifest in gossip and curiosity, and the male power of political regulation. Indeed, woman's innate prying is portrayed as man's burden: Bluebeard's destiny is to have his life "endan-gered by the Curiosity of the woman" whom he marries (1.3.16). To avert this danger, his ghastly chamber of horrors bears the superscription "THE PUNISHMENT OF CURIOSITY," which is death (1.3.17). Ironically, however, this prophesy fells Bluebeard himself: when the devilish dagger slays him, the "Tyrant" is punished for his ambitious curiosity in dabbling in the black arts. Popular versions of Colman's drama, even while adhering to the plot, emphasize the risks of curiosity rather than its rewards.[58] As women increasingly penetrate culture, their inquiry increasingly represents a threat.

In eighteenth-century literature, women's curiosity becomes both an aspect of and an invitation to illicit inquiry and collection.[59] As an impulse, it presents a rival empiricism that challenges institutionalized curiosity. Once objectified, however, it is transformed into material for subjugation by male curiosity. For example, in the 1682 edition of *Admirable* CURIOSI-TIES, Nathaniel Crouch tells the traditional tale of Lady Godiva, whose long golden hair hid her "so that no part thereof was uncivil to be seen" (208). However, by the cheaply produced 1710 edition, a woodcut has appeared illustrating Lady Godiva, enveloped in hair, riding in front of a row of houses, all with empty windows except one, in which an eager face appears staring out. Crouch has added to the text, "I here [*sic*] it a Tradition that this Lady commanded all the People to keep their Houses that day, and not to look out of the Windows, which one presuming to do was hanged or struck blind, and his Effigies in a peeping Posture to be seen in a Belcony near the Cross to this day."[60] The bookseller John Newbery, according to Austin Dobson, jotted a note on this tale in his travelogue, along with a "curious and very useful machine" for "ducking scolds."[61]

As these material manifestations of peeping both commemorate curiosity and act as curiosities, so literature that portrays women's "Secret" serves to sell and enact transgression. This secrecy is commodified as a form of cultural capital, and women, transformed from iconoclasts into icons, are fetishized into secrets themselves.[62] These uses of femaleness as forms of curiosity parallel other reifications of inquiry. At the same time, they trace a powerful tradition of female objectification, possession, and punishment. Women embody and enact ontological transgression, the very power of curiosity itself, and that ability manifests the fundamental impulse of the curious: cultural ambition.

WOMEN AS CLOSETED CURIOSITIES

Just as curiosity in general slides between functioning as a quality of people and of things, literary curiosity is always both a subject and an object. Literary curiosities include works of literature that possess curious features, as well as literary works that discuss curious subjects. Significantly, almost all such works are, in fact, various kinds of literary collections. The genre or subgenre of the literary "cabinet"—a compilation of separate items linked by topic, tone, or use—burgeoned during the late seventeenth century, but it was Haywood who first exploited it as a vehicle to sell sexual collection. As literary containers like the elite curiosity cabinet, these books were accumulations of all sorts of linguistic and literary odds and ends, compiled usually by their publishers—printers or booksellers—and variously addressed to segments of a very wide audience. Some of these compilations were directed particularly to women, as containers of household hints or "secrets" concerning cooking, housekeeping, husbands, cosmetics, and cures. Others were courtesy primers for would-be courtiers, filled with compliments and formulae for spontaneous witticisms. Many such collections, for children or adults, featured jests, linguistic puzzles, and poems for amusement and education. Conveniently for publishers, the contents of these books could be expanded, condensed, rearranged, and reclassified to make them serve different functions and draw new audiences. Like their material counterparts, these collections of literary objects, designed for both use and admiration, demonstrated the intellectual ambition of their readers.

Such cabinets, however, could also accommodate subversive curiosity: collections of forbidden inquiries into sensitive material. Moreover, they allude to another context: the political or physical "cabinet" or closet of secret consultation used by monarchs and potentates. As a secret space in which relationships were negotiated (or categorized), the closet metaphorically twins the cabinet. Both indicate a privileged area in which relationships escape conventional classifications and humans think, speak, and act in unregulated, even unlicensed, ways. Although the metaphors of closet and cabinet center on social rather than ontological connections, they share with the curiosity cabinet the release of phenomena from established hierarchies and the corresponding transgression or "queerness" this release implies. As explorations of new relationships, early novels or tales often use these metaphors to authenticate their spicy mix of scandal and sex. The preface of *The Cabinet Open'd, or the Secret History of the AMOURS of Madam de Maintenon, with the French King* (1690), for example, differentiates the book from other "Romances" because "the better part of the Memoires, from whence this little History is drawn, came out of the Cabinet of Madam *de Maintenon,* and were partly written with her own hand."[63] The secret source verifies the value of the content. Both Delariviére Manley and Eliza Haywood also use the metaphors of "cabinet" and "closet" to guarantee their amorous fiction—not its veracity, but its titillation. Secrecy, like curiosity, eludes the regulative and supervisory structures of society and thus offers readers something rare, authentic, exotic.

The long, disjointed titles of these books also characterize their method. Literary cabinets or closets contain multiple items, only loosely associated. Even adventures like those of Robinson Crusoe are touted in the plural to stress their more-for-the-money value. The title of *Moll Flanders* not only promises her "Fortunes and Misfortunes," but itemizes the numerous events to come: "Who was Born in Newgate . . . was Twelve Year a *Whore*, five times a *Wife* (whereof once to her own Brother) Twelve Year a *Thief*, Eight Year a Transported *Felon* . . ." (title page). Similarly, Roxana's biography contains not merely "A History of the Life," but her "Vast Variety of Fortunes."[64]

Such plurality also suggests the way curious books were represented as reading experiences. Even these continuous narratives contain episodic events, incidents that begin and end with little causal effect on the rest of the tale. By their titles, these books advertise variety and portability— incidents, scenes, or characters that stand separate in the mind and can be collected and arranged by the reader. Like the items in a physical cabinet, literary cabinets sever causal connections between items. And the two types of cabinet often combine. For example, like Haywood's fiction, the biography of Madame de Maintenon includes separable items: poems, songs, prayers, letters, lists of resolutions. All of these items are collected and printed in one volume, which is itself then part of another collection, number eleven of a series of adventurous, political, and amorous tales called "Modern Novels" by R. Bentley (1692). These collections of novels use the method of the curiosity cabinet to incite readers to a particular kind of pleasure, strongly identified with sexual pleasure: the pleasure of the frisson of elusive difference, of the close comparison of similar items. Haywood's novels appear in reprinted, multivolume collections where addicted readers may linger over minor differences in the arrangement of their repetitive format of awakened desire, frustration, betrayal, and regret. This kind of pleasure in contrast, difference, and the violation of symmetry or order links sexuality, curiosity, and the spectatorship of monstrosity as manifestations of unregulated desire. These cabinets and collections solicit and tout an unregulated, individualistic method of reading associated with the intellectual restlessness of curiosity.

The rejuvenation of female curiosity as a derogated quality rather than an action dates from the eighteenth century. As sentimentalism began to reinvent women as innocent, they became victims or icons of the evil of the world, instead of perpetrators of it. Pandora's dangerousness contrasts with the praise of women as emblems of a modernizing economy. As Ronald Paulson has shown, the aesthetic category of the novel—curious and surprising—gathered advocates and vehicles in the eighteenth century as tastes moved away from the pallid symmetry of the neoclassical to a heterodoxy associated, among other things, with the female shape and taste.[65] Moreover, the aesthetic connection between curiosity and art has another, specifically female application rooted in the primary meaning of the word "curiosity" itself: skillfulness. The prototype of the virtuously curious woman is Penelope, who fended off greedy suitors by nightly unweaving her tapestry, a care parodied and reviled in the archetypal witch who uses pins to elicit or prick out evil. Using this image, neoclassical writers reconstruct the curious maid as an emblem of virtuous femininity, the woman engaged in domestic art rather than in occult, uxorious, or luxurious arts. Jabez Hughes identifies women's care with the creation of a universe in his translation of Claudian's *The Rape of Proserpine*: "Neat in th'embroidered Ground, the curious maid / Her native Heav'n and th' Elements display'd" (lines 355–56).[66] Even as late as *Sense and Sensibility* (1811), Jane Austen credits the sensible Elinor Dashwood with the skills of weaving social as well as fire screens.[67] This notion of female care as domestic application idealizes female inquiry as legitimate labor, the parallel of the scientist's controlled experimentation.

These attempts to feminize curiosity as obedience, however, clash with the cultural power that women exercised in the new world of novelty, consumption, and freshly mutable social roles. Literature depicts this conflict between the newly fetishized female and rebelliously demanding women in a burst of new kinds of texts of sexual and cultural exploration: travelogues, pornography, literary cabinets of curiosity, and, of course, novels. These texts increasingly embrace the cultural hostility to women's power by exhibiting female sexuality as a licentious opportunity for vicarious pleasure by the reader. Indeed, these narratives border textual pimping. In eighteenth-century England, prostitution is identified with female curiosity because of its association with a panoply of contexts of curiosity.[68] Both prostitution and female curiosity entail sexual investigation, artifice, and collection, a manifestation of impulses to explore, elaborate, and acquire in the sexual realm—although in historical fact most of this exploration was male. As Tassie Gwillam explains, in early modern culture, women were represented through metaphors of duplicity—as agents of a concealed desire and as emblems of the difference between the beautiful surface and the disease-prone depth of the body—and these metaphors colored their representation in a host of texts, notably Samuel Richardson's *Pamela* (1740).[69]

Even while these prose forms share themes with dramatic or poetic treatments of female curiosity, they clearly differ from traditional genres.

As scholars have long recognized, the forms of prose fiction that developed in the eighteenth century are deeply indebted to empiricism, yet novels do not use the same idiom as scientific treatises. Rather, like poetry and drama, they elicit metaphorical meanings. This mixed mode facilitates their double representation of women as subjects and objects of curiosity. Much early eighteenth-century fiction represents women's impulse to find out as the desire to find out about others, especially about others' sexual histories: Eve's inquiry is fictionalized as gossip or scandal narrative that plays on the margins of political and sexual revelation. Novels by Behn, Manley, Haywood, and Defoe, notably *Roxana, or the Fortunate Mistress* (1724), variously treat the dangers of letting women learn and of admitting them into the male informational space, be this the secret life of politics, the court, or the public man.[70] By the last third of the century, women's prying becomes almost entirely commodified. Women are portrayed as desiring not histories but things; indeed, histories, be they biographies or gossip, become things themselves, packaged into novels. Despite these historical shifts, eighteenth-century prose fictions persistently play with the interaction between the channeling of desire, especially the desire to know, into curiosities and the correlative power of curiosities themselves to incite desire.

Critics for three hundred years have commented on the connections between females and fiction. Although they were read and written by men, eighteenth-century novels were regarded as a peculiarly woman's genre. The reasons for this association are multiple, but central among them is the association of print with a new audience ripe for novelty, consumption, and informal knowledge. Eighteenth-century cultural commentators gendered the genre by blaming it for women's unlicensed desires. For example, in Richard Brinsley Sheridan's play *The Rivals* (1775), the heroine, Lydia Languish, imitates the romantic rebellion that she has encountered in circulating library fiction by planning to elope with a penniless soldier.[71] In novels themselves, even by women, as Jane Austen famously remarks, heroines denigrate novels as intellectually and morally misleading.[72] Most notable, perhaps, is Charlotte Lennox's *The Female Quixote* (1752), in which the heroine, Arabella, risks her fortune, chastity, sanity, and life because she is immersed in the fantasies of seventeenth-century romances.

Especially at the end of the eighteenth century, in reaction to the French Revolution, English writers represented women's reading pleasure as a threat to conventional social relations, and women were urged to return to the texts that, at least in social myth, they had read traditionally— religious doctrine, household hints, and, more recently, conduct literature.

Whereas twentieth-century critics have emphasized the ideological endorsements of empiricism and individualism in the novel, contemporaries
pointed to its depictions of love, courtship, and sex, matters in which gender was definitive.[73] These two approaches, however, make related points.
What unnerved critics about the novel was its valorization of ambition,
specifically social or—for women—female curiosity.

It is, indeed, not until the eighteenth century that women writers find
a cultural space for this female ambition, with its gendered social spying
and its discourse of gossip: the novel.[74] Novels link the desire to find something out, curiosity, with the desire to be aroused, and they plant both
firmly in the social sphere. Indeed, the two impulses mirror one another as
explorations of the unknown for personal gratification.[75] Exploiting the
seepage from mental to physical arousal, early novelists co-opt the objective authority of inquiry to the end of fictional pleasure.[76] Haywood, in
particular, negotiates the two poles of curiosity to endorse inquiry while
condemning credulity, and to exploit the delight of sexual exploration
while intoning its costs. "Curiosity is the most prevailing passion of the
human mind," remarks Haywood's Magical Adept, echoing Samuel Johnson; and many of Haywood's works openly praise novels as social handbooks for women.[77] In the mirroring subplot of *Love in Excess*, Haywood
portrays the exemplary Melliora reading Fontenelle's philosophy for "Improvement" but Ovid's *Epistles* when lounging in enticing dishabilleé.[78]
Both kinds of reading exhibit her admirable thirst for knowledge. Indeed,
the noble Frankville falls in love with her in a library (41–42). In addition,
Haywood connects the reader's impulse to find out what happens with the
sexual impulse of the characters: the curiosity of the reader—spectator,
narrator, or audience—reflects that of the protagonists, and vice versa. In
this process, Haywood represents women simultaneously as readers and as
subjects, inquiring minds and yearning bodies, agents and objects of curiosity. Novels, in turn, offer both information and illicit pleasure.[79]

This curiosity spans both reading and amatory adventure. The popular
Love in Excess; or the Fatal Enquiry defines inquiry strictly as the quest for
sexual knowledge. *The Fatal Enquiry*, *The Masqueraders*, and most other
texts use the term "enquiry" to mean sexual desire, usually of women. This
reduction of "enquiry" to conventional sexual appetite reflects the cultural
pressure to confine women's cultural power itself. Indeed, in *Love in Excess*,
as in many of Haywood's novels, questioning or questing entails danger,
exploration, and a damning self-discovery that usually results in destruction. *The Fruitless Enquiry* varies the theme by linking female inquiry with
the impious desire for a better world than God has granted.[80] One story

within this text, moreover, graphically represents the consequences of illicit knowledge: the ostensibly happy Anziana, confessing that she betrayed her lover, shows Miramillia into a secret cabinet containing the skeleton of a man "with arms extended wide, as if in act to seize the adventurous gazer," with a label on his breast warning Anziana of her coming fate (8). This Christ-like memento mori indicts curiosity by revealing that all inquiries eventually lead to betrayal and death.[81]

Even while she rehearses the cultural resistance to restless women, Haywood plays on the subversive pleasure that female curiosity promises. Her use of the term "enquiry" mocks the distinction between scientific and prurient interest and plays on the double role readers inhabit. In *Fantomina; or, Love in a Maze*, the narrative revels in the eponymous heroine's "Frolick" to satisfy her "Curiosity" for Beauplaisir, leaving moral reproach to a paragraph banishing the heroine to a convent at the end.[82] This novel makes clear a dynamic that is pervasive in Haywood's other work. The pleasure that her texts offer readers results from the transgressive invitation both to enjoy the sexual arousal and to enjoy punishing the heroine. The title of *Love in Excess* works this ambiguity by punning on the meanings of "excess"—as a moral designation or as a publishing promise. In *The Secret History of the Present Intrigues of the Court of Caramania*, the narrator coyly introduces the hero's hidden lust with reference to the reader's narrative desire: "But not to detain on the rack the Curiosity of my Reader, who by what I have said cannot but imagine there was some other and more powerful motive for this Prince's Behaviour, than . . . was publickly known."[83] While acknowledging the "realistic" rejection of spiritual romance implicit in amatory fiction, John J. Richetti interprets Haywood's work as the facilitation of erotic pleasure through the myth of persecuted female innocence and aristocratic male villainy, but this analysis overlooks the tonal ambiguity in her works.[84] Like Defoe, Haywood slips between moral positions. She renders female curiosity simultaneously as a sign of blameable cultural ambition in her women characters and as a route to transgressive pleasure in her readers.[85]

Thus, for Haywood curiosity leads to a knowledge of sexual nature both informative and dangerous. In the plot of both *The Masqueraders* and *Fatal Enquiry*, empirical inquiry remains an inevitable part of social initiation for women, even as it turns them from agents to subjects. Both stories open with a woman stirred to "Curiosity" by the sight of an attractive man, a reversal of conventional gender roles imitative of Manley. This sight stimulates their physical and emotional responses, characterized as the exploratory impulse to find out about the new thing. Although *Love in Excess* shows the vulnerability opened by female curiosity, it also attacks the ways in which women become subject to this appetite.[86] As Ros Ballaster has pointed out, political and sexual meanings interfuse each other in amatory fiction, and Haywood often characterizes sexual vulnerability by allusion to Puritan ideals and romantic conceptions.[87] *Love in Excess* dooms Alovisa for concealing her identity in order to preserve pride. Throughout, she repeats Eve's error: "finding the Door lock'd, her Curiosity made her look thro' the Keyhole."[88] Her death dramatizes the dangers of curiosity for women in both social and symbolic terms. So desperate is she to learn her rival's name that she pretends to consent to an affair with Baron Espernay if he will find it out for her: "What will some Women venture to satisfy a jealous Curiosity?" (93–94) Although she desires only D'Elmont, "her ill Genius, or that Devil Curiosity, which too much haunts the Minds of Women" drives her into consenting to adultery (104). In a confusing scuffle, she dies on the Baron's sword, symbolizing the sexual hazards of an undisciplined curiosity.

By becoming subject to sexual desire, women become commodities in print. Alovisa in *The Fatal Enquiry* dresses her face as she does her body: "her Eyes, the gay, the languishing, the sedate, the commanding, the be-seeching Air were put on" (5). Borrowed from Congreve, this catalogue of female attitudes mechanizes the body in a comic explosion of Petrarchian conceits. As Lynn Hunt has noted, such techniques link pornography and the novel as satirical exposures of social pretense.[89] They also provide publishing opportunities. Women are associated with commodities, especially printed ones, in many eighteenth-century contexts.[90] The shift from women as consumers of novelties to curiosities for consumption themselves is not an absolute one, nor is it confined to a single historical era. But the flow between the consumption of and consumption by curiosity does have a specifically gendered application. As cultural conservatives generally identified curiosity with idleness and luxury, so they saw women's appetite for novelties as a demonstration of the corruption of their traditional roles.[91] Such corruption carried a specific sexual meaning. The desire for novelty or experience entailed the desire for sexual encounters.

Manley documents the ambiguous relationship between women as curious and as curiosities. This dual role is founded on the functions of women as consumers and consumables and, notably, on their role as writers.[92] In her autobiographical *Adventures of Rivella; or, the History of the Author of Atalantis*, Manley depicts the inquisitive conversation of a young Chevalier with Sir Charles Lovemore as centering on her own sexual adventures. As he explains, the "Curiosity" of D'Aumont "puts me upon enquiring after the ingenious Women" of England, and this kind of inquiry, or sexual tourism, is depicted as beyond condemnation.[93] It leads D'Aumont to explore "amongst other Curiosities, a Lady who made her self admired by all the World," Madam Dacier (2–3). His impulse to "admire" human wonders induces a minute physical description of Rivella—feature by feature, including her growing bulk—and a narrative of her life. In this humorous introduction, Manley depicts men gossiping about women, more admiringly, perhaps, but in the same manner as women gossip about themselves. Sexual, social, and narrative curiosity are shown not only to feed off curiosities, but to create them. It is, furthermore, specifically as the writer of sexual stories, particularly the Germanicus scene, that Rivella becomes curious; and her curiosity includes sexual attractiveness, since Chevalier D'Aumont cannot but believe that her descriptions come from her own experience (4). He asks, "Do Her Eyes love as well as Her Pen?" (8). By tracing women's commodification to their role in the luxury market of fiction, Manley reiterates the cultural charge that women's penetration of the public sphere makes them curiosities.

As curiosities, women follow the same rules that govern other rarities. They are collectible, removed from public use, and examples of labor as display, not profit. Representations of women have long been collected, from classical statues of Venus and images of the Virgin Mary to secular portraits of nudes.[94] For centuries women's bodies were depicted as objects of aesthetic admiration, collected in art galleries and even, in the case of some monarchs like Charles II, in person as well as in pictures. In public fairs and circuses, too, women contributed an extra frisson to monstrosity. From the Renaissance to the Regency, not only bearded ladies and similar ontological oddities, but also women who manipulated their bodies in artful ways, like hunger artists who lived on the scent of flowers, became public curiosities. In the eighteenth century, however, prose fiction, inspired by the contemporary fad of empiricism, also opened as an exhibition space for spectacular femininity: women who transgress.

Both sexual and scientific inquiry explored physical nature for personal gratification by means of a kind of seeing that afforded peculiar kinds of pleasure. This overlap between kinds and causes of exploration tainted the new science by impugning the motives of the men engaged in it. Popular culture frequently ridiculed virtuosi for looking at art or nature and seeing (or not seeing) sex. To peep or "keek"—meaning to glance illicitly or to look furtively—became a popular term in the eighteenth century. Like "curious," it slides between objective and subjective applications. Johnson's *Dictionary* initially defines "peep" as "first appearance," the sudden presentation of a new sight, like a bird, to the observer's eye, but subsequently explains it as "curious looking." Finding no etymology for it, Johnson derives it from either the Dutch "to lift up" or the Latin for "spy." Eighteenth-century meanings of the word burgeon to designate a looking-glass, an eye, and a one-eyed person; "Peeping Tom" acquired its meaning as "an inquisitive person" at midcentury.[95] As a term for unauthorized empiricism, this "peeping" in literature often signifies social information presented without a moral organization, snapshots of other lives or social circles. "Peeps" or texts that squint at a scene, so to speak, become a minor subgenre in themselves.[96] Like early modern women's amatory and occult fiction, they shake the status quo by means of secret spying. The rebelliousness of curiosity is correlated with the lust of the eyes.

The contemporary valorization of inquiry, however, did open new ways of thinking about peeping and could be deployed to sanction sexual curiosity. It provided a public ideology for the traditional topic of female interest in the novels of Aphra Behn, Delariviére Manley, Elizabeth Haywood, and Ann Radcliffe, whose heroines act as active probers and priers. These heroines are Pandoras whose curiosity into social, sexual, and religious matters is, albeit ambiguously, legitimized in the fictional sphere. At the same time, this contemporary endorsement of curiosity provides a marketing strategy for this kind of fiction: the cabinet or collection. These literary cabinets imitate the private collections of the virtuosi, be they natural philosophers or connoisseurs of art, by supplying a complete or at least representative collection of private materials. As Walter Kendrick points out, pornography or forbidden, erotic material is associated with elite collecting from the early modern days of archaeology, when scientists accumulated the idols of the cult of Priapus and other rare and erotic artifacts from archaeological explorations and permitted gentlemen alone access to them.[97] In addition, the cultural association of female genitalia with secret cabinets enforced the association of pornography and collecting.[98]

If Haywood's female curiosity designates unfulfilled sexual appetite, this appetite often takes the form of gossip morally shaped into fiction. Gossip functions in a way parallel to collecting: it removes people or items of information from their public sphere and refigures them to form private or alternative meanings. Gossip represents women and men as agents and objects, not of public duty, but of private desires, particularly of sexual desire. It thus makes people objects to be rearranged in a cabinet of private, often prurient, meanings, just as collections of rare or erotic objects were recombined in the private cabinets of virtuosi. Periodicals from *The Spectator* to *The Lounger* exploit print's power to make gossip public discourse;

similarly, Eliza Haywood uses gossip in prose fictions of various kinds. Borrowing Manley's devices of topical allusion, she portrays a world dedicated to female sexuality, more particularly to its destruction, through the cultural commodification of women's sex, which becomes the object of collection, the curiosity itself. In *The Tea-Table: or, A Conversation between some Polite Persons of both Sexes, at a* LADY'S VISITING DAY, Haywood ironically equates novels and tea parties as sources of information about men's machinations; both inform women about men, but both stimulate sexual desire rather than caution. Gossipers accumulate stories about others' mistakes just as readers do, and to Haywood neither form of curiosity brings improvement.

Haywood further exploits the slippage between gossip and reading by her device of the "spy": an unobserved observer who, like Addison and Steele's Spectator, reports on the moral and social doings of society. Haywood's spy, however, not only reports others' hypocrisy, but also exposes the contradictions between many layers of society's systems of evaluation. In *The Invisible Spy*, the narrator, "Explorabilis," is veiled by an invisibility that allows investigation of the social world. Quickly, Explorabilis discovers that a model couple's exemplary public behavior conceals their private discord. This revelation at the same time questions deeper moral schemata. The narrator reports that Marcella sensibly advises her cuckolded husband, Celadon, to treat her with courtesy and affection in public for both their sakes. This advice juxtaposes opposed social values: for sexual freedom and for social decorum, for practical rationality and for sentimental honor, for experience and for love. Haywood's spy is more than the naive satirist of *Candide* or *Gulliver's Travels*, however. Ambiguous and undefined in every way, even in gender, s/he embodies the moral ambiguity of invisible spying.[99] Such spying, which allows the observer to watch without being held to account, complicates the quest for knowledge itself. This device sets into conflict two ideals about the value of learning: as moral instruction and as amoral—even immoral—delight. Such a conflict between the *utile* and the *dulce* of Horace's maxim infects the narrative method of reportage itself.[100] Objective or disinterested reporting is tainted with self-interested self-pleasuring, just as the elite practice of collecting specimens becomes colored with prurient self-scrutiny, because social information acquired in an antisocial spirit hints of rebellion.

Indeed, Haywood herself associates narrative spying with curious collecting.[101] Explorabilis attains his/her invisibility by magic. S/he informs the reader that s/he was the friend of a descendant of "the ancient Magi of the Chaldeans . . . well versed in all the mystic secrets of their art," who "found something in my humour and manner of behaviour that extremely pleased him."[102] This "something" constitutes a blend of moralism, prurience, and social alienation, together identified as curiosity and shared by the philosophical magician and the exploring narrator. When the old man nears death, he promises Explorabilis a gift from his private curiosity cabinet, built like a turret at the top of the stairs and furnished with antiquarian and magic items, including globes, writing paper, hieroglyphic manuscript books, telescopes, horoscopes, talismans, and spells. Several of the rarities function as political and cultural satires. Among them is a crystal ball filled with "The Illusive Powder" that "raises splendid visions in the people's eyes" if scattered when the moon is in Aries but that "spreads universal terror and dismay" when the moon is in Cancer (*The Invisible Spy*, vol. 1, p. 3). Another is "The Sympathetic Bell" whose tinkle sets all the bells in the country ringing to the owner's chosen tune (1:3–4). Explorabilis wishes to give the "Salts of Meditation, Which . . . corrects all vague and wandering thoughts, fixes the mind, and enables it to ponder justly on any subject that requires deliberation," to "divines, lawyers, politicians, or physicians" (1:5). These curious items promise power over human nature, both social and physical. They link the narrator's exploration into occult remedies for moral failings with the ambitious and satirical desire to control and reform humanity.

For Haywood, narrative licenses the free exercise of curiosity. As the embodiment of the fantasy of pure recording, Explorabilis attains two rarities. "The Belt of Invisibility," a gathering of free atoms, transcends materiality, promising a vision beyond sight that induces Explorabilis's "covetous emotions. . . . I could not persuade myself it was a real substance, till I took it down, and then found it so light, that if I shut my eyes I knew not that I had any thing in my hand" (1:5). The belt represents pure sight that vanishes when the eyes are closed. The second rarity, a tablet capable of shrinking or expanding to "imperial" size, "receives the impression of every word that is spoken, in as distinct manner as if engraved, and can no way be expunged, but by the breath of a virgin, of so pure an innocence as not to have even thought on the difference of sexes . . . exceed[ing] twelve years of Age" (1:6). The tablet offers transparent transcription; it records knowledge, and specifically sexual knowledge of the "difference of the sexes." Such information can be erased or lost only by those who have never found it, mythical virgins who live in Edenic ignorance of their own sexual nature. Like the belt that vanishes when the beholder refuses to see, this "pocket-book" grows blank when touched by the breath of those who know no sex. Both devices give knowledge only to those who desire it. Just as curiosity is the inscription of the difference between self and other, writing is the sign of this difference itself. The Spy is given both.

This spectatorial power to control curiosity characterizes Haywood's narrating spy in *A Spy Upon the Conjurer,* "Lady Justicia," who defines her very identity by her overarching curiosity. This identity, however, does not guarantee her authority. As the reporter to an anonymous "Lord" on Duncan Campbell's feats of second sight, Lady Justicia makes him the object of her scrutiny. She claims "*Curiosity,* which in my greener years I had as large a Share of as most of my Sex," makes her penetrate sexual secrets, which are his topic.[103] Repeatedly, she excuses her actions by this motive: it is her "natural Propensity" (80), one of her "resistless Passions" (81). Since her "old inextinguishable Curiosity" will "suffer me to stick at nothing," it propels the narrative as well as the narrator (133–34, 168).[104]

Her curiosity translated into print gradually comes to control her. She both demonstrates and boasts of a satirical humor that mocks the misfortunes of others (67, 103). At one point, she confesses that, "my Curiosity getting the better of my good Manners," she interrupted a private conference (70); at another point, she spends four hours piecing together the torn fragments of a confidential note she pilfered (59); further on, she eavesdrops, spies, and breaks into locked boxes of Campbell's correspondence and copies the letters she finds there (65–66, 123, 125). Explorabilis similarly becomes the "Invisible Thief" of a correspondence discussing love (*The Invisible Spy,* 1:220). Indeed, Justicia's curiosity seems to grow more and more ruthless and uncontrollable, like the corruption of Defoe's Roxana. A servant girl loses her place "only for assisting me in the Gratification of my foolish Humour of Curiosity"; nonetheless, Justicia persists in prying, questioning, writing (78). Increasingly, her curiosity also seems to entail her complicity in Campbell's prognostications, to the degree that his clients, the reader, "my Lord," and even Haywood's audience grow suspicious of her role in promoting the deaf and dumb oracle. One lady grows convinced that Justicia has betrayed her and ignores her socially forever afterwards (47). In another case, the devotion and support of a client with a fatal secret to hide resembles the pattern of blackmail (59). Justicia's increasing credulity parallels that of skeptical visitors who come to mock and stay to marvel. She becomes enmeshed in the curious narrative.

Central to the book is the question of Campbell's method, and this is closely linked to the limits of the novelistic genre itself. Early in the narrative, Justicia debates how and how much Campbell knows (44–45). Astrology, witchcraft, second sight, and divine inspiration are all considered. Although the nobleman to whom she purportedly writes does not, Justicia believes in witchcraft, and many serious female and some joking male clients refer to Campbell's *"Familiar,"* or satanic agent, as she does herself (64). Witchcraft works as a contagious instance of unverifiable empirical wonder that problematizes the credibility of the narrative and the narrator by signaling her gendered credulity. Justicia slides from investigator to advocate. In one instance, sympathizing with "my Lord," who apparently suffers for love, the narrator equates women's cruelly infatuating "Charms" with "Spells," thus linking curiosity to witchcraft in the traditional context of psychological evildoing (33). She reports that Campbell himself called her "a greater Witch than the Conjuror himself" for knowing a secret (173). When her correspondent forbids her to talk of witchcraft, Justicia tries the alternative explanation of divine intervention through angel-aided guardians, which had been parodied by Pope in *The Rape of the Lock.* Adopting the discriminatory language of reason, she admits that some dreams are prompted by "our Desires of the Day," and that the superstitious trust all dreams when only some hold meaning (27). Her defense of the intervention of the divine into daily life introduces traditional beliefs in the occult into empirical narrative.

Campbell's only evident source of information is vision. Haywood, however, constructs a slippery definition of this vision—"the Wonders of his Discernment"—as simultaneously natural and supernatural, empirical and occult (163). In debating his use of fortune books, accounts of people's futures that resemble astrological charts, Justicia differentiates Campbell's method from pure astrology on the basis of empiricism: "'Tis certain that when he first looks on People, he conceives a Knowledge of what Accidents will happen to 'em," she explains, and only afterwards tries to map this knowledge by using astrological "Science" (101). Moreover, the narrator quickly denies that *"Second Sight," "Natural Magick,"* or *"Diabolical* Means" can explain his talent, preferring to attribute it to divine favor (17). Some instances suggest that Campbell guesses the people's preoccupations by their appearance or conversation. In one case, he writes, "I see a natural Propensity in this young Woman to ruin herself" (137). As in the "science" of physiognomy, decreasingly popular until the end of the eighteenth century but still employed, faces tell fortunes. Other instances suggest that sympathetic listening informs Campbell of ladies' desires.

Just as Campbell's talents differ from the deceptive trickery of fortune-tellers, so he pointedly employs plain language, eschewing the enigmatic riddling of most fortune-tellers (89). At the same time, Justicia defines the marvels as social revelations aided indirectly by God. Campbell's curiousness makes him a sight/site for pious wonder, not a specimen for dissection. Indeed, the narrator derides the cruel tricks of some doctors and skeptical inquirers who torture him to make him speak, and she satirically compares the visit of a "great Man" to Campbell with the inquiries of "Virtuoso's" into insects (144, 145, 171). In contrast, she presents Campbell as someone who supplies useful social information, especially for women. Moreover, believers must similarly mediate credulity and incredulity: she avers that her narrative proves "that there is a Knowledge in that man, infinitely superior to what is generally believed, or indeed more than can be *imagined* by any one, who has not suffered himself to be convinced by an undeniable Demonstration" and who is free from prejudice (35). By rejecting categorical supernatural or preternatural explanations, Haywood sanctifies the marvelous and blends wonder and empiricism.

The vehicle to exploit this conjunction of wonder, especially regarding forbidden topics, and empiricism is print. Campbell communicates by writing, and Haywood's narrator uses the same means, as does Haywood herself. The inquiries and methods of Campbell's visitors thus correlate with those of Haywood's readers; and Haywood makes amorous anecdote represented in prose the genre of curiosity. One anecdote even asks whether a dumb man is able to feel love, echoing Dunton's discussion of whether blind people can fall in love (154). Coyly, Justicia dissolves the conventional distinction between male and female inquiry by writing to "my Lord": "I know now, in spite of the Contempt your Sex pretends to have of Curiosity, you will be plaguing me to Death the next time I see you, to tell you the Name of this lady" (48). Haywood thus redefines her own audience for scandal as both male and female. Several times, Justicia recommends *The Life of Mr. Campbell*, thus encompassing biography with amatory, epistolary fiction as genres of wonderful adventure (61, 111). Italicized typescript reproduces the epistolary effect, reinscribing intimacy (124). The second and third parts of the novel—entitled "All Discover'd"—are constituted by letters from clients to Campbell that reproduce Athenian inquiries. In particular, one exchange unsettles the definition of rape (184–87); another questions whether a child can be born after only six months (187). Whereas the Athenian society attempted to weed out such evidently prurient or satirical inquiries by a rigorously scientific tone, Haywood provides a printed space for them as examples of the conflict of credulity and curiosity in the sphere of sexuality.

Spinning off the associations between curiosity, idleness, disobedience, and the social malfeasance of witchcraft, amorous fiction often links curiosity with scandal. Scandal, libel, or "Tittle tattle" harms others by the occult means of gossip, eavesdropping, and baleful spying, a form of the evil eye exercised by members of the social circle with nothing else to do.[105] If Haywood's narrative persona identifies curiosity specifically with sexual desire, her characterized speakers usually use the term to connote a frivolous or malicious desire for novelty and sensation—especially the sensation of witnessing or hearing about others' sexual pain. This fusion of occult and empirical curiosity reinscribes gendered differences between agency and subjectivity. Justicia confesses:

> I believe if Mr. *Campbell* had known the Pains I took to find out
> the Affairs of those who came to consult him, he would have
> forbid me his House: But his Art of Divination did not stoop so
> low as to give him any Idea of the little foolish Curiosity I was
> then possess'd with. Not but he gave me Hints sometimes that I
> was of an inquisitive Nature; and when I have shew'd myself more
> forward than indeed became a Woman who pretended to good
> Breeding, in pressing into the Company of People who seem'd not
> desirous of being seen by a Stranger, he would often smile and
> write to me, *O Woman! Woman! Woman! The Sin of Eve taints thy
> whole Sex.* (73)

Justicia's curiosity searches for the illegitimate and partakes of the social meddling of gossip, whereas Campbell's second sight partakes of the divine. It is her curiosity, nonetheless, that drives the mode of fiction.

In the next sixty years, curiosity as a printed commodity implies self-exposure or other kinds of sexuality deemed irregular because they are self-pleasing rather than reproductive. In *A Curious Collection of Novels* — eight sexual stories—"The Grand *French* Marqui: or, a Dinner for a Dog" tells the tale of an emigrant who tries to lure a dog by "pulling out what Nature should not be Exposed to publick View"; the story links French "frugality" or miserliness with self-pleasuring.[106] Curious sexuality, culturally located in the secrecy of Priapic cults and in the monstrous collections of private cabinets, in literature spills over to a range of unorthodox sexual proclivities that either fail to reproduce or produce social aberrations. Often, this secret sexuality was associated with social resistance, either to conventional or religious rules of behavior, or to state policies.[107]

Especially, but by no means exclusively, during the later eighteenth century, when social regulations were tightening in response to rebellion abroad and free thinking at home, the printed exhibition of sexually transgressive people as embodied curiosity burgeoned.[108] A "living curiosity" from the final quarter of the century exemplifies the permeability of the margins of the term: Mademoiselle LeFort, the Strong (fig. 12). This

MADEMOISELLE LEFORT.
Exhibited in Spring Gardens, 1818.
Published for R.S.Kirby, 10, Warwick Lane, Oct.1,1819.

Figure 12. "Mademoiselle LeFort, Exhibited in Spring Gardens, 1818." This Regency woman bridges soldierly masculinity and feminine beauty; although she exhibited herself for a circus, this text analyzes her appearance in a tone of scientific disinterest. From *Kirby's Wonderful and Eccentric Museum*, vol. 3 (1 October 1819), frontispiece. Courtesy of the Harry Ransom Humanities Research Center Library, University of Texas at Austin

woman violates not only gender boundaries, but boundaries between enlightened and popular inquiry; she is a monster shown at a fair, a case of ontological fluidity whose meticulously reproduced image evokes scientific illustration; she is also an omen who parodies effeminate soldiers and aggressive women, thus exhibiting transgressive sexuality as cultural decay.[109] Her curious feature, the beard, confuses natural and cultural sexual distinctions, making sexuality itself a question determinable only by unlicensed peeping.

Cross-dressers represented in print similarly collapse satire and a teratologically infused inquiry, freeing spectators to indulge a variety of unsocial responses.[110] As Jessica Munns points out, clothing, now a matter of widespread interest as market improvements and shop displays stimulated consumption, involves a performance and transformation of identity that shakes social and gendered taxonomies.[111] *The New, Original and Complete* WONDERFUL MUSEUM *and Magazine Extraordinary*, which bristles with wonders, devotes a high proportion of its stories and illustrations to surprising sexualities signaled by violations of the dress code. The issue for 1803 presents "An Eccentric Character.—The Walking Bookseller and Teacher of Languages," illustrated by an engraving of a stooping gentleman carrying a folded parasol and books under his arm. As the text beneath and other stories testify, this character is "John Theodora De Verdion," a German woman who dresses as a man in London, teaching and selling books. Another engraving bids us:

> Stop gentle Reader, and Behold
> A Beau in Boots who loves his Gold
> A Walking bookseller, an Epicure,
> A Teacher, Doctor, and a Connoisseur.
>   *Alias*
> Doctor V—in his Wrigling attitude, hawking old Books as Moses
>   does old Cloaths.[112]

Several tales relate the drinking and gormandizing of "Dr. V"; indeed, in these accounts her taste for learning merely demonstrates her uncontrolled appetites. As a foreigner, a collector, a miser, a "connoisseur," and a cross-dresser, the "Chevalier Verdion" combines many of the traditional meanings of curiosity. She recycles value like antiquarians and usurers; she deceives sight and violates categories; and she inquires into areas of male curiosity. Even while the text denounces her, it permits readers to indulge in the carnivalesque pleasure of vicarious masquerade. Like the example of Mademoiselle LeFort, here the body becomes an area for the display of culture in contest with nature.[113]

In looking, peering, asking, and collecting beyond the sphere of fashion legitimized in the late century, women as sexualized or unconformable bodies, feminized men, and humans who infract categorical boundaries are portrayed as usurping cultural privilege and defining the limits of respectable inquiry. In place of sanctioned consumption, they display prohibited exploitation.[114] Readers, however, are invited to act as voyeurs who surmount, yet also experience, these violations by possessing them in printed form. These printed depictions of transgressive bodies and themes transform inquiry into the double act of owning and hiding secret knowledge. The "Curious Maid" who explores her own genitals exemplifies the transformation of curiosity into the hidden object. In these satires, the maid's quest for self-knowledge thus leads to knowledge of her shameful sexual nature. On the other hand, the quest also leads to the self-discovery of a secret identity hidden from public view. The instrument of self-exposure, furthermore, is a mirror, the symbol of vanity.[115] Secret histories, published curiosity museums, and erotic texts similarly function to elicit the reader's secret self, manifested by the enjoyment of unlicensed or uncanny identities, transgressions, sensations.[116] Even as such texts liberate this impulse, however, they reassert the owner's control over that self through the fact of his or her possession of the text. This possession proves the reader's self-possession and the confinement of curiosity itself.

The cultural tension between legitimate and illegitimate curiosity flourishes in late-century literature that frequently associates dilettantism, sexual curiosity, scandal, print, and travel in order to spoof high culture. "*A Court Lady's Curiosity*; or, the VIRGIN *Undress'd. Curiously surveying herself in her Glass, with one Leg upon her Toilet . . .*" figures women's "curious attitude" as straddling a mirror, but it recounts the adventures of a Casanova.[117] Set in the early Restoration and highly imitative of Haywood, the novel chronicles the exploits of the captivating Gentleman Davila, who seeks amorous experience under the guise of a Christian companion of the Jesuit Fathers out to convert the Chinese. By acting decorously until his reputation for virtue is strong enough to protect him, he serves to mock the ideal of religious purity and to expose the universality of sexual curiosity. Early in the book, he asks, "What has the largest Share / I'th Composition of the Fair"? And he discovers " 'Tis that Propensity to pry / In each forbidden Mystery," the same impulse as "the Reader feels": "CURIOSITY" (p. 4, lines 1–2, 11–12, 18, 22). This "Passion" (20) marks all women, "in every Age, in every Clime" (24). As the appetite to "taste the Tree" that defines womankind, curiosity transcends difference. The "curious Itch" is both an itch in a curious place and an itch to explore: thus, female curiosity becomes sexual or masturbatory exploration.[118] This exploration extends to the "Reader": reading transgressive tales is parallel to sex, since it promotes desire and discontent with boundaries. Female curiosity denotes the usurpation of public value for private use: the pleasure of their own bodies. This text ridicules emerging sentimentalism by finding sexual appetite the universal language.

This "CHINESE Novel" resembles a literary collection of sexual adventures that parodies high art. In the adventure illustrated in the frontispiece, the cavalier hides all night in a Chinese jar with the help of the maid or confidante and then surprises the woman as she is dressing. Other tales metaphorically interchange sexual action and aesthetic object in similar ways. In listing the "curious" antiquities he sees, the bard identifies the woman with the elaborate art of the Chinese palace, "the Tyle-resplendent Wing! / That holds the vain, the wanton Thing" (lines 73–74). Other artworks underscore the identity of aesthetic and sexual accumulation. Along with lewd portraits from the classics, the Bible, and contemporary society, references to Ovid, Rochester, and treatises on raising the dead, and two Aristotles, the narrator describes material collectibles:

> One has a Curtain drawn before it;
> The Belles are ready to adore it!
> A * *Priapus* — And next to that,
> Another, cover'd with a Hat.
> *Diana* bathing; and a *Helen*,
> Whom *Paris* is all over smelling. (Lines 87–92)

The footnote underscores the association between virtuosoship, cultural exploration, and prurience by explaining that the narrator has adapted the original "*Chinese*" allusions describing his "Cabinet of Curiosities" to "*European* Literature, as being more familiar." Like Hildebrand Jacob's "Curious Maid," the protagonist strips herself to find "the mighty Cause" of love, politics, history, and battles in her genitalia, but she is stirred to this inquiry by her love of high culture:

> The Books—the Paintings—all conspire
> T'excite this new—this odd Desire.
> In fine, her Fancy prompts to see
> The World's great *Primum Mobile*;
> That Master-piece! That Source of Passion!
> That Thing! That's never out of Fashion.
> (P. 25, lines 241–46)

By contrasting fashionable art with the timeless female "Thing," this author objectifies female sexuality as a collectible and ridicules the hypocrisy of high art that merely diverts sexuality. Women's subversive sexuality, their capacity for ontological fluidity, and their social prominence coalesce in this popular image of female inquiry.

Impertinent sexual curiosity feminizes the curious man or dilettante in eighteenth-century satire: the man with threatening cultural ambition.[119] Late eighteenth-century caricaturists portray the curious attitude in men and women as a sexual peeping that links them with other curious people—

collectors, connoisseurs, virtuosi—who pretend to look at naked figures to
see only art, not sex. Caricatures of connoisseurs ignorant of their own
motives, in which they are portrayed as examining fractured relics or un-
clothed women, both ridicule collectors and condemn the prominence of
women as objects of cultural scrutiny. James Gillray's 1778 portrait of "female curiosity" shows a woman staring at her buttocks, which are adorned
with a stylish wig perched on her hips, by looking over her shoulder at a
mirror her kneeling servant holds. The portrait indicts women's self-
exploration as decadent fashion.[120] Gillray designates female sexuality as
peeking, yet his print identifies the spectator's gaze with the woman's. In
peeking at sex or sneering as connoisseurs who look at women as art, the
spectator himself exercises transgressive curiosity. The spectator can see
what women and feminized men cannot, their true faces or feelings. The
association of women's curiosity and cultural ambition was seen as endan-
gering traditional sexual relations, and one solution was the excoriation of
sexual spectatorship as inversion.[121]

ﬁ.

Female curiosity indicated both women's investigation and the investigation of women, and in the eighteenth century both sprang into urgent visi-
bility through novels, satires, periodicals, and broadsides. The prominence
of feminized inquiry reflects the new prominence of women and their
threat to established social conventions and hierarchies. Indeed, as the new
social force, women epitomized cultural ambition at midcentury. In response, many writers and cultural critics, including women themselves, revived biblical indictments against curiosity as impertinent. This charge
allowed them to condemn women's power as a perversion of nature that
made women monstrous. Particularly, it sexualized the tendency to pry
into matters outside the public and masculine realm: the cultural charge
implied that women who ask are asking for it. In the competitive dynamic
of inquiry, curious women or sexually curious people were thus commodified by curious spectators into consumers, "queers," collectibles.

Literature capitalizes on this cultural transformation of inquiring
women into topics and readers of printed investigation. Revising the tone
of the "The Curious Maid," Samuel Richardson in *Pamela* (1740) lauded
women's self-scrutiny in print. By examining herself morally, not physically, Pamela purifies her own nature. Richardson's *Clarissa* (1747) more
openly opposes the heroine's epistolary self-evaluation to the sexual impulses of her nature, as her letters become proofs of her sexual and spiritual

virtue. Even as such novels celebrate a female curiosity that counters the innuendos of the "curious attitude," they still edit the rebellious potential of women's power by portraying puritanical heroines whose inquiry concerns self-improvement not social reform. While self-knowledge remains respectable, investigation of other affairs remains forbidden: William Kenrick's premier warning in *The Whole Duty of Woman* (1753) is to "avoid . . . the bewitching claims of curiosity" and "thirst not after prohibited knowledge" (5). The commodification of women as topics for print leaves a complex heritage for women writers.

Early modern cultural critics depict female inquiry, whether enacted by women or men, not as an act of impiety or insanity shaped by a corrupt culture in way the male quest could be, but rather as an act of transgression that endangers society or the individual. As beings closer to the occult than men, women in literature signal the subversively spiritual—increasingly repressed in enlightened England. At the same time, in the early novel, women's inquiry takes the form of penetration into illegitimate areas.[122] Female curiosity was culturally conceived of as a phenomenon closer to superstition and antirational wonder than to the scientific enterprise; indeed, one critic has suggested that the Gothic genre is the result of a contemporary historical alienation from empiricism and a revival of an older, anti-empirical discourse.[123] Early prose fictions that capitalize on curiosity exploit this permeable boundary between superstition and empiricism. As a new audience fostering new prose forms and social issues, and as the ancient embodiment of disobedience, women were figured as disrupting, at least potentially, formal and social conventions. The fictional representation of women's participation in an unlicensed world of sexual, hidden, or occult investigation contributed to the objectification in literature of female experience as a rarity and of women as curious objects—corporeal displays of secret sexuality.

The morally ambiguous appetite to uncover secrets structures the empirical impulse in other genres that portray and feed women's desire to know: early narratives, travelogues, and literary cabinets. Haywood exploits this connection between writing and sexual inquiry as forms of collected experience. Many of her spy novels are composed of anecdotal or episodic narratives in which incidents are accumulated for thematic, not plot-connected, purposes. Publishers, in a related fashion, collect stories with similar themes into cabinets of literary curiosity. Indeed, the term "cabinet of curiosities" became as powerfully associated with literary collections as with material ones, even designating in the Victorian period reprinted studies of sexual peculiarity.[124] Increasingly, curiosity bifurcates into applauded categories of investigation of nature, the display of male control, and derogated categories of sexual or impertinent inquiry, the exhibition of feminine weakness. Thus, later eighteenth-century culture revives the biblical notion that female curiosity symbolizes the moral hazards of inquiry. Beginning as a strictly sexual category, one that overleaps conventional behavioral restrictions of modesty, piety, marital contracts, and so on, inquiry transmutes into a representation of dissatisfaction with society—either for its limitations or for its abuses. This searching, associated with novelty, frivolity, and the attraction to the unproved and new over the traditional, threatens the hierarchy, status quo, and institutions of society. These new values imply the rejection of classical values—the past, history and, therefore, obedience, duty, social class and role; they suggest a love for the novel and the secret.

Early fictions by Manley and Haywood portray carnal curiosity, the defeat of spiritual for social exploration. Their narratives are structured on the unlicensed desire to fulfill the self by knowing the physical truth about other people, and they violate emerging ideals of teleological and causal narrative by their repetitive patterns and rejection of closure.[125] This fiction exploits transgressive appetite by depicting and inciting physical and asocial desire, the same device used in "curious" collections of monstrosities, erotica, and scandal. Female amatory fiction alludes pointedly to contemporary social scandals, for it is the vehicle both of female curiosity—sexual exploration in print—and female discourse, gossip. While fiction throughout the century reinterprets the epic plot of the revelation of the hero's identity, worked out at length in such novels as *Tom Jones, Humphry Clinker,* and *Camilla,* detective fiction originating in the Gothic deploys curiosity to reveal hidden corruption. However, these early fictions also depict, even symbolically incite, this corruption by portraying and compelling readerly pleasure in violation.[126] The pornographic elements in Haywood's fiction license readers to revel in sexual exploitation, intensified by the overt moralizing of the heroines as they fall. These generic traits mark readers of curious histories as rebels against social conventions.

At the same time, elite curiosity became a means of controlling illicit desire. Cabinets of collected rarities, whether literary or physical, acquired the frisson of forbidden eroticism safely cabined away from public use. Sanctioned by the discovery of erotic artifacts, collectors represented the conquering scope of Don Juan through materiality. Sexuality, the defining trait of women, became a central ingredient in the collector's arsenal. These connections between investigation, possession, and sexuality worked to make women's curiosity into curiosity about women: the habit of collecting sex. Women were transformed from the curious to the curios; sexual collections turned the inquiring female into the acquired one. Whereas early virtuosi were condemned for sexual sublimation, later collectors and virtuosi were represented as *raffiné* fetishists. By the end of the eighteenth century, female curiosity, especially as it was manifest through literary consumption, represented a hazard to social convention. It pushed sexuality before spirituality and identified the flesh beneath the fine.

Connoisseurship in the Mental Cabinet

By the mid-eighteenth century, the consumption of curiosity through experiences and objects denoted connoisseurship. As more and more people "improved" themselves by witnessing and collecting curiosities—examples of categorical transgression in life, art, and nature—curiosity itself acquired a new social power. Rather than betraying the curious watcher's monstrosity, an involuntary slide between species, the observation of transgressions implied the observer's superiority: the deliberate power to transgress limiting social categories. Seeing curiously thus denoted cultural superiority, and not solely in scientists, but also in cultivated social observers. Although satirists continued to lampoon virtuosi for self-absorption, credulity, and decadence, forty years of consumer products had changed the discourse on the material aspects of curiosity. Vitalized by the Grand Tour—a journey (as long as three years) through Italy, France, and other European countries that young gentlemen took to complete their education—and protocolonial enterprises abroad, the enterprise of collecting exotica began to signal power and learning instead of monstrous perversion: laudable rather than impertinent ambition.[1] This change was motored by the increasing prestige of collection as artistry, exemplified in the new British Museum, and by the rise of a new class of professional cultural monitors. Pressured by consumerism, commercialism, and skepticism, curiosity receded from designating a quality of the external and became a quality of the observer. This is the period that marks a fresh shift in the weighting of the meaning of curiosity from objects to subjects.

Authorized by scientific precedent and popularity, the manner of informed, refined inquiry into contemporary as well as historical matters legitimized the subjective quality of curiosity as social ambition—at least for some. Matching the benevolent connoisseurship of physical wonders epitomized by Sir Hans Sloane, midcentury authors, journalists, and critics—notably, Oliver Goldsmith, Samuel Johnson, Bonnell Thornton, and George Colman—manufactured legitimizing underpinnings for a new kind of connoisseur: disinterested monitor of the social arts. In their responses to the contemporary ambivalence toward aristocratic ideals, they redefined the "connoisseur" as a fashionable expert in classics and British literature.[2] If Sloane had the Royal Society, these writers had various clubs for literary experts who set themselves up to classify the beautiful and the true by blending empirical investigation with learning in both traditional and new literary forms. Whereas conventional virtuosi evaluated material culture, these new experts inquired into language, cultural history, contemporary manners, and literature.

Once more, however, not all who inquired into contemporary affairs were praised for their curiosity, for such inquiry endangered conventional hierarchies. As in the Restoration, cultural critics scorned this fresh legitimation of curiosity as sanctioning credulity, so that although faith in the unseen could signify humility and humanism, it could also denote discontent, impiety, or superstition. Thus, curiosity garnered a new class signature even while the classes practicing it changed. Occult investigation, admiration of the strange, and literary experimentation indicated enlightenment only when practiced by the enlightened individual; when the "public" flocked to admire or rose to question, curiosity indicated rebellion or usurpation: an uninformed rejection of enlightened explanations, a threatening co-opting of public space, discourse, and value through the domination of the press or the courts. Curiosity in private was very different from the curiosity of the crowd.

These tensions are played out in the struggle during the midcentury to define a method of legitimate inquiry that would prevent the indiscriminate spread of the power of social advancement through information to anyone, or any group, who asked questions. This struggle shapes contemporary public culture and literary form. As the rooted English habit of discussing everything in print pulled a wide audience into fashionable controversies, events, reports, and literary genres that induced or attacked public duplicity spiraled. The confusion between inquiry and naiveté was deepened by the emerging ethos of sentimentalism. Endorsed by literary connoisseurs, this ambiguous literary style, with its valorization of heroes of febrile feeling, blurs the lines between benevolence and impertinence, stupidity and faith. Moreover, its genres include popular forms: wonder tales, parodic fiction, and literary collections designed to encourage individual interpretation. To many people, these forms seemed to flout the moral uses of literature, just as superstitious stories seemed to promote impiety; yet fashionable proponents like Goldsmith wrote and defended sentimental literature for its social value. The question of how much curiosity, how much violation of social and literary norms, was safe for the public galvanized contemporary culture.

Significantly, proponents of sentimentalism often acted as key figures in the mediation of public curiosities of the period. Three such curiosities were particularly notorious from 1749 to 1760: the case of Elizabeth Canning, the incident of the Bottle Conjuror, and the appearance of the Cock Lane Ghost. Like Mary Toft's mystery twenty years earlier, these highly publicized incidents, by testing mankind's physical and moral limitations, pitted public beliefs against those of professional arbiters. Literary critics sprang to fill the gap in cultural leadership by asserting a rival professionalism to that of legal, scientific, journalistic, and medical practitioners: the detection of social truths. They forged a new method of investigative sophistication and redefined rarities as experiential possessions—souvenirs in the mind, objects rendered valuable by the memories clinging to them, recollections, memories of the self.[3] Co-opting the disinterestedness of the scientist, literary critics spread an ideal of encyclopedic knowledge as privileged, rarefied, and authoritative judgment that humanized scientific curiosity.[4] By channeling transgressive fantasy into literature, these writers and interpreters became mediators of the occult and connoisseurs of human practice.

The three cases of Canning, the Conjuror, and the Ghost spectacularly staged the failure of enlightened methods for determining human veracity. In so doing, they revealed the need for a systematic method of inquiry: a taxonomy of questioning that would make curiosity scientific. Since the Restoration, audiences had doubted scientists' ability to read human motives. When William King's spokesman asks Sloane, "you have a peculiar faculty of believing almost any thing: But pray what Reasons can be given to justifie the sincerity of your Correspondents?" the natural scientist has no answer—nor did the participants in the cases of the Conjuror, Canning, or the Ghost, or at least none that held.[5] This failure to find a reliable logic of human motive prompted writers to retool empiricism to suit their subject, the subject that escapes direct observation: humanity. Melding the new method to old beliefs, some journalists touted a legalistic procedure of checks and questions to verify the gifts of seers and the reliability of spirit tales. Elite sentimental writers instead internalized both empiricism and second sight. Their new systematic scheme for enlightenment was the acquisition of moral expertise through the individual collection of experience: a curious quest that openly scoffed at established truths. These ostensibly divergent quests of questioning and watching both molded empiricism to endorse instinctive impression. Both high and popular curiosity thus resisted public systems of order.

This public validation of an essentially impertinent curiosity in mid-century England depends vitally on print. Innovations in writing and publishing make possible the paradox of a culture that endorses transgression, that lauds a social ambition that it fundamentally forbids. The primary mode for this paradox is sentimental literature. This literature applauds rebellious inquiry yet does so with the sad conviction of its impotence to change the world. Instead, the curious heroes expire. Like curiosity, sentimentalism trumpets the private as the source of value. Its stylistic signature is a fragmented impressionism evocative of cataloguing that reflects the protagonist's chaotic reception of meaningless, modern life and simultaneously empowers the reader to assemble his or her own meanings.[6] In Henry Mackenzie's *Man of Feeling* (1771), for example, disconnected episodes, some unfinished, formally reproduce the inconclusive experiences both of the hero Harley, and of the shadowy narrator, the Ghost. This Ghost, spokesman from a past world of lost values who appears in a churchyard, narrates the tale as a heroic fable, now forgotten. Both the Ghost's morality and Harley's sensitivity—so acute that he feels literally like others—make them curiosities in sophisticated London. Mackenzie implies that only idiosyncratic readers of life or art can find its context.

Similarly, poetry from Blair's *The Grave* to Johnson's *Vanity of Human Wishes* urges readers to find their happiness in the immaterial.[7] Several fictions, notably Sterne's *Travels through France and Italy* (1768), portray inquisitiveness into others' situations and histories as a sympathetic identification that impinges on the hero's identity. These fictions suggest that the desire to know about forbidden matters, if exercised by well-intentioned men, demonstrates distrust of corrupt social institutions and an admirable, if naive, determination to engage in social intercourse on a level beyond class. The protagonists of these stories are collectors of rare impressions, yet at the same time they are themselves curiosities because of their emotional rarity. Like virtuosi, they turn nature into art by the power of mental collection or recollection.[8] Like virtuosi also, however, they are fools. Their desire to overleap the bounds of time, class, or physicality is sanctioned, but only as hopeless idealism, confined to thought, impossible to act on: safe.

Other literary innovations similarly express the paradoxical fascination with curiosity as deception, transgression, and ambition. Gothic fictions deliberately inhabit an ambiguous literary status by blatantly violating contemporary literary values in order to alert and challenge the reader's faculties of aesthetic judgment. As curiosities themselves, they position readers as connoisseurs—but also as fools for buying blatant deceptions. In particular, Horace Walpole's *Castle of Otranto* (1765) and William Beckford's *Vathek: An Arabian Tale* (1786) exploit curiosity in form and theme by satirizing wonder and violating realism. Just as the passion for Egyptiana and other collectibles had long lined the pockets of counterfeiters, so this literary taste for the rare prompted some authors to manufacture fakes, notably James Macpherson's *Fingal, an Ancient Epic Poem,* purportedly by the bard Ossian (1762), and Thomas Chatterton's poems, ostensibly by the fifteenth-century Bristol poet Thomas Rowley (1768). Gothic fictions and frauds share three curious traits: close attention to details or skillfulness; a self-conscious "rarity" achieved by defamiliarizing techniques; and the solicitation of the reader to entertain unfamiliar standards.

Literary "Cabinets of Curiosity" employ the same device. Their catalogued contents deliberately vitiate narrative logic: one item follows the other in no rational order in order to reproduce the aesthetics of dislocation, irrationality, impressionism. As entries are severed from public meaning and free for use as private pleasure, the reader may recombine them in his or her own mental cabinet. Some novels employ this technique. In both *Joseph Andrews* (1742) and *The Vicar of Wakefield* (1764), Fielding and Goldsmith insert independent narratives whose moral application the reader alone determines. Nonetheless, novels formally present causality, a moral sequentiality that rewards virtue and punishes vice. In contrast, literary curiosity cabinets ignore causal connections by randomly juxtaposing items addressing different themes and by linking them under the antimoral rubric of pleasure. Often, these literary "rarities" compile secret phenomena pertaining to the natural and human world.[9] Popular cabinets, like Thomas Hill's *Natural and Artificial Conclusions* (1649, 1670), for example, contain domestic spells and show readers, among other skills, how to walk on water.[10] In both high and popular culture, such cabinets offer readers a transgressive power over the public world.

Written cabinets of curiosity facilitate intellectualized consumption. As literary analogues to the museums and repositories all over England, these cabinets celebrate the elite ownership of nature and culture enacted through observation: the extension of material possession to symbolic possession by means of the eyes. Such cabinets reproduce for readers the experience of museuming, the patriotic admiration of acquisition. This purpose organizes John Tradescant's *Catalogue* describing his father's garden of botanical wonders, collected for Charles I and representative of the English monarch's power over land.[11] Just as visitors toured the museum to witness tangible evidence of exploration and conquest, so readers perused the *Catalogue*. Moreover, such museuming touches visitors or readers with the virtuoso's dream of immortality. Tradescant's epigraph asserts, "The body may, and must: ARTES CANNOT DIE."[12] As Tradescant's *Catalogue* exemplifies, the enterprise of compiling a catalogue parallels that of collecting, and both are reproduced in the mind of the visitor or the reader by experience. A prefatory poem warns Tradescant to remain modest like his father, and he himself describes his principles of augmentation and order as intended to "preserve . . . together" the collection. Thus, Tradescant's cabinet becomes a memorial to his father's rarity and uniqueness, unalterable by time. Such English versions of the European display of power in the noble curiosity cabinet spur the association of curiosity with sublime transcendence. The collection dramatizes the collector's sensibility, reverentially reified, with an order based on historical chance, not classification or logic. It makes the collector himself the curiosity, but it also creates a collector within the reader.

The greatest curiosity is thus the curiosity of the collector. All items are conquered by the collector's most powerful use of curiosity: collection. Indeed, curiosity makes the curious themselves explorers, conquerors, scientists, and phenomena in their own collections, their own ultimate example of fine art. In section 7 of Tradescant's *Catalogue* on "Mechanick artificiall Works in Carvings, Turnings, Sewings and Paintings," precious items such as embossed agate and "several curious paintings in little forms, very antient," are represented as empirical phenomena whose value, albeit high in the world of commercial exchange, is boldly redefined by the collector's eye (37). This ontological magic, this spectatorial philosopher's stone by which observation makes value and turn dross to gold, lifts the collector himself over social boundaries. Still, drenched in midcentury nostalgia, the collector's revision of the world remains private—unless he has the social power to convince others to see or to question as he does: the power that leads to revolution in the next decades. In the museums, cultural exhibitions, journalism, sentimental fictions, and literary cabinets of the midcentury, writers and cultural leaders vie to exercise this power. They promise that by employing their methods of curious inquiry, by rejecting public values for theirs, by reading, witnessing, and acquiring, and by refining impressions into a classification of humanity, the curious reader may advance—at least in his or her own mind.

CURIOSITIES OF ARTFUL NATURE

Popular curiosities promise witnesses the experience of transgression. These curiosities include both people and objects that, by moving between spheres of value or reality, challenge observers to differentiate simple nature from devious art, artifice, or artfulness. Promoters use human monsters to thrill spectators by hinting at a forbidden alliance between the human and the excessive, or by reasserting the spectators' normality by staging the abnormal. Human curiosities also test observers' powers of classifying normality, nature, and art, and of detecting the artifice in human nature. Curious or skeptical observers thus define curiosities, examples of nature turned into art. The episode of the Bottle Conjuror, in particular, documents the way curiosity becomes a quality simultaneously rarefying an object or event and its observer.

In January 1749, an advertisement appeared in the newspaper for a magical performer who would—among other tricks, such as raising the dead in seances—appear on stage with a bottle of ordinary size, disappear into it, and pass the vessel containing him around the audience (fig. 13). Londoners, including the Duke of Cumberland, flocked to the theater. After they had checked their canes and cloaks and paid their entrance fees, they sat patiently for over an hour staring at the empty stage bearing an empty bottle on an empty table. Meanwhile, however, their fees, hats, cloaks, and sticks had vanished with the Bottle Conjuror, the latter perhaps indeed into a bottle somewhere else in London.[13] When they finally saw that they had been taken in, the enraged mob destroyed the theater.

This fraud, indebted to the 1714 illustrations of *Rape of the Lock* portraying maids turned into bottles, drew instant publicity because it illustrated the unchecked spread of scientific credulity to all social ranks—and the dangerous results. Uncertain about the physical status and limits of humanity, audiences tutored by eighty years of *Philosophical Transactions* and lifetimes of superstitions were prepared to believe in outlandish physicality, convinced by the publicity and the attendance of gentry like the Duke that they were witnessing a rare event. Moreover, the trick invoked socially reproved desire in the name of curiosity. Playing on the tale of the genie in the bottle from *The Arabian Nights*, the Conjuror's trick enticed audiences with the fantasy of immense power as they manipulated a man shrunk to Lilliputian size. This fantasy enacted a prohibited form of sexuality.[14] The public handling of a masculinity that could swell or shrink at will dramatized the masturbatory license of curiosity, yet the literalistic advertisement and the inclusive rubric of entertainment stifled criticism.

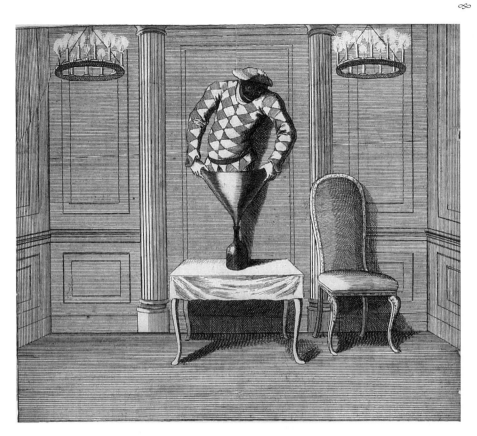

Figure 13. "The Bottle Conjuror," 1749. This newspaper illustration purports to be "an exact Representation of Harlequin's Escape into the Bottle; introduc'd in the Pantomine Entertainment of 'Apollo and Daphne,' or the *Burgo master Trick'd*, acted at the Theatre Royal in Covent-Garden, to crouded and polite audiences." By Permission of the British Library

The Bottle Conjuror also offered the disenfranchised classes the chance to co-opt elite curiosity and literally play with another man's body.[15] The Conjuror promised to bring literature to life; to reverse power relations; to incarnate onanism; to make monstrosity—the transgression of physical boundaries—humorous. Instead, he made the audience fools of their own desire. When balked, furthermore, this unleashed desire turned violent. The explosive result revealed the danger of unmonitored curiosity.

The Conjuror represented himself as a hybrid between nature and culture, a creature who could transcend physical limits. He resembled a scientific curiosity, particularly in a period when artisans were fashioning mechanical dolls that performed cultural tasks like piano playing and sewing, and thus usurped the roles of humans.[16] He also resembled a sometime dwarf, another legendary creature who exemplified the mutability of the margin of the natural and the cultural marvel. In *The Memoirs of Martinus Scriblerus*, Pope, Gay, and Arbuthnot make the keeper of "the gates of the Show-room" in which human and animal curiosities are exhibited a "perfidious" dwarf.[17] While dwarves' primary fascination was their "unnatural" size, advertisements stressed their marvelous imitation of life—their skills of dancing, acrobatics, singing, conversation. In popular culture, they represented the paradoxical disparity between external and internal power. One dwarf—who derived his name from *baiocco*, the smallest Roman denomination of coin—modeled for eminent artists.[18] As something between the genuine coin and a counterfeit, he, like the Conjuror, embodied the ambiguous permeability of body and symbol, nature and art.

This ontological ambiguity, this interfusion of life and art, characterizes the public curiosities of the midcentury and stimulates widespread skepticism about elite expertise. Four years after the Conjuror disappeared, the case of Elizabeth Canning further vitiated the public trust of social leaders and approved methods of evidence. The story is still famous.[19] The eighteen-year-old servant disappeared on 1 January 1753, for a month, reappearing thin and bedraggled. When neighbors demanded her story, she claimed she had been robbed, beaten, seized with a fit, and marched to the bawdy house of Susannah (Mother) Wells, where she was solicited, mocked by two prostitutes, and imprisoned without food by a knife-wielding gypsy whom she identified as Mary Squires. Had it not been for the penny mince pie in her pocket, she would have had to survive the entire month on a single loaf and a pitcher of water. All London debated her digestive and deceptive abilities. On the plea of friends, Henry Fielding entered the case, elicited corroborating testimony from the witness, Virtue Hall, and condemned Wells and Squires to Newgate. Despite the original charge for only theft and disorder, after the public furor, the judge sentenced Wells to imprisonment and branding, and Squires to be hanged. But contradictory evidence surfaced. Witnesses located Squires a hundred miles away at the time of the crime, and Sir Crisp Gascoyne, the Lord Mayor, elicited a different story when he reexamined Virtue Hall in private. Although Fielding in turn reexamined Canning and reiterated her innocence, she was arrested. The following week, Fielding published *A Clear State of the Case of Elizabeth Canning*. It was so popular a second edition appeared two days later.

What fascinated Londoners so much about the Canning case? The opposing versions of Canning's conduct and the contradictory evidence tested both competing definitions of human nature—physical, moral, sexual, and social—and competing applications of logic. Adherents of both sides enlisted "Reason" to prove their arguments. *The Unfortunate Maid* supplies a five-page catechism showing readers how to resolve dubious cases by detecting "Prejudice, Partiality and Ignorance," while Dr. Daniel Cox describes the perfect "middle character . . . form'd for reasoning, judgment, and determination."[20] Two years before he wrote his *Enquiry into the Causes of the late Increase in Robbers*, Fielding declared that he would rather believe in "one great Monster of Iniquity . . . than . . . a Gang of Wretches" eluding justice (61–62). Sentimentalists saw art turned to life in the Richardsonian tale of a poor young woman, who, despite harassment by gypsy bawds, preserves probability of character and prefers starvation to sexual defilement.[21] One letter in *The Genuine and Impartial Memoirs of Elizabeth Canning* terms her "my Heroine . . . a realized *Pamela*" (4–5). Believers in Canning chivalrously defended her in the press. Speaking of the rescue the "poor Girl" from powerful enemies, including Gascoyne and Hill, a "Gentleman, well known to the learned World," *The Unfortunate Maid* inveighs against the "repeated Injuries" that brand her "a Woman . . . capable of all the Vices, that can make a Man sink below the Degree of an Animal" (10, 4). Female nature was at stake.

Canning's narrative thus brought to life a fantasy opposing divine virtue and bestial evil, in which people acted with a dramatic irrationality and sexual violence that strained enlightened ideas of the logic of human behavior. Fielding describes it as "a very extraordinary Narrative . . . consisting in many strange Particulars, resembling rather a wild Dream than a real Fact," a passage repeated in *The Unfortunate Maid*, and Hill sneers that it is, "a Piece of contradictory Incidents, and most improbable Events; a waking Dream; the Reveries of an Idiot."[22] The author of *Genuine and Impartial Memoirs of Elizabeth Canning* records that some considered it the latest example of public deception: "You ask, Whether it is not a Tale invented on Purpose to try how much farther *British* Credulity may be imposed on? Now, tho' the Bottle-Conjuror was far from engaging my Curiosity . . . yet give me leave, without being superlatively credulous, to suspend my Judgment concerning this young Woman."[23] *A Refutation of Sir Crisp Gascoyne's Address to the Liverymen of London* ironically denies that Canning's friends have sufficient "CREDULITY" to believe that she starved and stripped herself.[24] The case staged the drama of the judiciary's attempt to defend the public against either fraud or force—a drama based on whether the young woman had told the truth.

Like the Bottle Conjuror's trick, the tale also dramatized contemporary class tensions. It revived fears about violent and lawless usurpation of property, sharpened the previous year by an upsurge of murderous smuggling often condoned by the working classes.[25] The story featured an organized yet lawless "gang" given not to theft alone, but to compelling women to its will. The presence of gypsies, outlaws with a popular history as "barbarous," intensified the battle between the prejudices of traditional and enlightened culture (*Maid*, 23). Gypsies symbolized both exotic and hazardous curiosity. Known as members of a diasporic culture that openly rejected English law, they represented the preference for private over public values—a clear threat to legal professionals and to a public fearing disorder. During the period when England was forging a national identity, this threat seemed to deepen: broadsides and publications depict Squires as a witch, wearing a peaked hat and escaping from justice on a broomstick.

Fielding himself identifies gypsies with criminals in his pamphlet on contemporary robbery.[26] Throughout the narratives supporting Canning, Squires is called merely "the Gipsy." *A Refutation of Sir Crisp Gascoyne's Address*, which prints key points in small capitals (one of the authors was the printer), stresses the appearance of "a TALL SWARTHY OLD WOMAN" who swears "d - - n you, you b - - h" and slaps Canning (4). This publication articulates the public fear of gypsy usurpation of the wider culture by denouncing the associates of "vagabond gipsies, wretches who subsisted only by breaking the laws, and who at Enfield were the inmates of a bawd, the companions of thieves and prostitutes" (12). The authors condemn one pro-Wells witness in balladic language as someone "who became a vagabond with the Gypseys for love of Lucy" (16). Cox opens and closes his argument by attacking the king's pardon of "this criminal," although he stresses "*that it is by the Testimony of evidence alone that the truth of any fact can be absolutely determined*" (6, 9).

With its traditional features of a gypsy mother, imprisoned maid, sudden escape, and magically sustaining meal, the Canning case exploited popular myths, absorbed by learned and unlearned alike, of changelings switched by gypsies—a theme Fielding uses in *Joseph Andrews* (1742)— maids locked in towers, compelled conversions, witches, and fairy feasts.[27] On the other hand, tales of lying servants—impostors like Richard Hathaway, to whom *The Unfortunate Maid* refers (21–22)—and plump eighteen-year-old women who disappear for a month were equally familiar both to readers of *Moll Flanders*, and to those who could not read; but these tales offered nothing uncanny, no strange correspondence between dream and life, past and present.

The public curiosity that the case licensed worried many, since this curiosity scrutinized authority. Those who entered the press on the question had their own motives examined. All claimed disinterest, assumed the role of public defender, and attempted to control turbulent speculation by their authority. As a "writer," Dr. Daniel Cox, reproaching readers and "the bulk of the species" for lacking the "quite impartial mind" needed to see Canning's innocence, assumes fitness for the task (*An Appeal*, 2–3). In contrast to those who supposedly attacked her, Fielding explains his own "Motive" for entering the case as "Curiosity" leavened by "compassion" (*A Clear State*, 286). Hill blames such "compassion" for gullibility, but for Fielding it bleaches curiosity into disinterested love of justice (Hill, *Story*, 17). This "Curiosity" resembles Christian chivalry, "something within myself which rouses me to the Protection of injured Innocence, and which prompts me with the Hopes of an Applause much more valuable than that of the whole World" (*A Clear State*, 286). Fielding's declaration became common cant: *Memoirs* explains the interest of Canning's nosy neighbors as "Compassion and Curiosity" (7). Dr. Hill opens his refutation of Canning's story by asseverating the "Honesty of my Intention," and that, being "disinterested," he has "acted . . . only on the Principle of real Honesty and public Utility" (*Story*, 4–5). On the other hand, the author of *The Unfortunate Maid* attacks the prosecutors for "Bribery and Corruption" (3).

Once Canning's case hit the press, as in like cases of witchcraft or lawless desire, the processes of careful, judicial fact-gathering clashed with the public's desire to scapegoat those who transgressed the borders of the public and private by abusing women's bodies. Fielding participated in this demonization. Distrusting both superstition and abrupt shifts in character, he explained the ontological anomalies by expanding the definition of humanity to include metaphorical monsters: "doth not History as well as our own Experience afford us too great Reason to suspect, that there is in some Minds a Sensation directly opposite to that of Benevolence, and which delights and feeds itself with Acts of Cruelty and Inhumanity?" (14).[28] Since such people are "very little removed, either in their Sensations or Understandings, from wild Beasts," their motive must be to increase their breed (14). As the details of the case and the disputes between experts emerged, they suggested a different narrative from Canning's, one in which duplicity and obfuscation triumphed over elite expertise. Virtue Hall's testimony was proved the result of Fielding's bullying; witnesses located Mother Wells a hundred miles from the scene at the time of the abduction; skepticism about the power of a single mince pie to fend off starvation rippled through the city (Hill, *Story*, 19, 39). While what Canning actually did or where she went remained a mystery, professionals, contesting who could deliver the "Public" from "a most horrible Imposture," savaged each other's authority (7). The press became the venue for competing explanations of the inexplicable in which the revelation of truth seemed to lie in the occult issue of motive.

The publicity of the case also alarmed Fielding because it allowed power to seep from the courts to the printed page, from private to public means of persuasion. Although "the Wit of Man could invent no stronger Bulwark against all Injustice, and false Accusation, than this Institution," he exclaims in his pamphlet defending Elizabeth Canning, nonetheless should a false accusation come about, "a proper and decent Application, either to the Judge . . . or to the privy Council . . . will be sure of obtaining a Pardon" (3–4). Instead, however, of such "proper and decent Manner, by a private Application to those with whom the Law hath loaded a Power of correcting its Errors," Hill has resorted

> immediately to the Public by inflammatory Libels against the
> Justice of the Nation, to establish a kind of a Court of Appeal from
> this Justice in the Bookseller's Shop, to re-examine in News Papers
> and Pamphlets the Merits of Causes which, after a fair and legal
> Tryal, have already received the solemn Determination of a Court
> of Judicature, to arraign the Conduct of Magistrates, of Juries, and
> even of Judges, and this even with the most profligate Indecency,
> are the Effects of Licentiousness to which no Government, jealous
> of its own Honour, or indeed provident of its own Safety, will ever
> indulge or submit to. (4–5)

In contrast to Fielding's stress on legal proceedings and judicial institutions, Hill considers published "Notices" primary evidence (13). If ontological transgressions—fiction into fact, the body defeating its own nature—supplied one example of curiosity, the subsequent spectacle of a power struggle between experts, bruited in the popular press, provided a second.

Eventually, Sir Crisp Gascoyne released Wells and Squires and instead arrested Canning for perjury. While the original charge remained popular, the new charge had the virtue of transferring the public threat from Squires to Canning, and so containing it. The indictment accuses Canning of "being moved and seduced by the instigation of the devil, and having no regard for the laws and statues of this realm, nor fearing the punishments therein contained, and unlawfully, wickedly, maliciously, and deliberately, advising and contriving, and intending to pervert the true course of law and justice" by accusing Mary Squires.[29] Here Canning rather than Squires appears the rebel, indifferent to the law and insensible to fear. Repeatedly, her acts are attributed to "her own most wicked and corrupt mind" (3). Both motive and means remained mysterious, but by portraying Canning as evil, the trial publicized a kind of supernatural motive that banished any private, natural one from public discourse. This demonization made the story an example of the private abuse of the public trust, and thus refigured public curiosity as the appetite, not for fantasy, but for justice.

At the trial's conclusion, Canning was convicted of perjury as "a crime attended with the most fatal and dangerous consequences to the community" (200). Attempting to dispel the shadows of the occult, the judge suggested motives, from Canning's desire for compassion and profit to her friends' encouragement (200–201). Attributing the initial credulity of the public to "resentment" whipped up by "surprize" at "this almost miraculous tale," he praises the public service of the magistrates involved and derives a lesson from the case: "as evil actions have sometimes been productive of unforeseen, nay, even good effects; so, this iniquity of yours will, I hope, instruct mankind not to suffer their credulity to get the better of their reason" (201).

This reason, honed by the elite, becomes the device to control curiosity, the ambition of the masses to define human nature themselves. While Fielding relies on physicians' expertise to adjudicate the physical possibility of her experiences, he positions himself as the authority to pronounce on the moral possibility of her treatment (17–18). His logic interweaves public information and his own humanistic beliefs. Declaring that the explanation deduced from her absence and emaciation constitutes "Evidence" that compels belief from "every Man, who hath Capacity enough to draw a Conclusion from the most self-evident Premises," he imposes enlightenment ideals of logic on seemingly inexplicable "facts" (20). At the end, if he has been imposed on by Canning, he can find his only flaw "an Error in Sagacity" (57). Fearing the violence prompted only a few years earlier by smugglers' riots and the Bottle Conjuror's fraud, Fielding seeks to return the genie to the bottle by redefining credulity as spiritual superiority.

Five years after the Canning case, another mystery of ontological transgression tested competing methods of determining truth. Again, a prominent member of society took up the cause, but now he evoked the authority of common sense, rather than that of scientific or legal expertise. The occasion was the celebrated case of the Cock Lane Ghost, who appeared after a mysterious death. After his wife died in childbirth, Mr. Kent, a sometime usurer, and therefore not popular, sought to marry his sister-in-law, Fanny, but a legal prohibition compelled the couple to rent rooms in London from a compliant landlord, Mr. Parsons. There, they wrote reciprocal wills in each other's favor, shortly after which Fanny died. Instantly rumors began.

It was learned that although Parsons had heard knocking earlier, which even then he had strongly suspected to be Kent's first wife returning from the dead, Fanny's death led him to pursue the matter, assisted by a Methodist preacher, John Moore, and Fanny's family, balked of an inheritance. In the winter of 1759–1760, Parsons held public seances, attended by the most fashionable gentry, and fully believed by at least one prominent noble, William Legge, Earl of Dartmouth. These seances featured Parsons's young adolescent daughter, Elizabeth, who, put to bed in her own room, answered by mysterious knocks questions about Fanny's death posed by the people who nightly bought tickets to see her. Accused as a murderer, Kent was finally arrested. The Cock Lane Ghost won instant notoriety. Two newspapers, *the Public Ledger* and the *St. James's Chronicle*, embraced the cause of the Ghost, while the *London Chronicle* remained skeptical. Each of the three published long, detailed accounts of the phenomenon, while the hapless Kent was under public suspicion as a murderer and was hounded from his house.

Because of the shame brought by the Elizabeth Canning affair, the magistrate of the Cock Lane Ghost case, Sir Samuel Fludyer, remained reluctant to intervene. In February, however, an apothecary, a new physician, a justice of the peace, clergy and reputable people attended a test at Mr. Stephen Aldrich's house, away from Elizabeth's familiar bed, and discovered that here no knocking occurred. Careful eavesdropping exposed her tearfully confessing her fears about disappointing her father—and sealed his fate. At the public trial, after the Lord Mansfield's hour-and-a-half harangue, the Ghost conspirators were condemned in fifteen minutes: Parsons got two years in prison and three times at pillory, his wife a year in prison, and the others, with those who had stirred up public sentiment in the papers, were fined £50 each. Nonetheless, at the pillory the glib Parsons so convinced the public of the reality of the Ghost that they tended him kindly and even took up a collection for him.

The Cock Lane Ghost scared up again a host of concerns about who should or could command enough public respect to sway opinion on occult matters. Like the Bottle Conjuror and the Canning case, the Ghost, albeit adjudicated publicly, escaped neat closure. It continued to haunt public memory as an ambiguous example of the profitability simultaneously of exploiting curiosity and of duping experts. Much contemporary literature sought to control the damage by ridiculing public credulity. As Douglas Grant notes, the Ghost appears in many contexts: in play revivals, caricatures, novels, and poetry. In March of that year, the *London Chronicle* published a verse mocking the vulnerability of the educated for faith in "a something, a nothing, yet mark'd with a name," which even scoffers credit "in private."[30] The following year (March 1761), Charles Churchill, adapting spiritual to political fraud, published *The Ghost*, a satire on the progress of superstition. These texts identify common sense with educated skepticism. Nonetheless, the popular longing for mystery that the three cases reveal inspires contemporary popular and high literature, from wonder narratives of rural marvels to Walpole's *The Castle of Otranto* (1764). Belief in the occult showed aesthetic or spiritual sensitivity.

As another example of the dangerous power of unmonitored curiosity, the Ghost invited cultural leaders to mediate between high and public culture and to inscribe the limits of legitimate inquiry. Stepping in like Fielding, with a similar purpose of rescuing an innocent victim from public abuse, Oliver Goldsmith published an elaborate argument blasting the Ghost and clearing Kent's reputation. This document exemplifies the critic's new role as connoisseur of public culture. As a sentimentalist convinced of individuals' fundamental decency, irrespective of class, and as a proponent of the antirational aesthetic set out in Edmund Burke's *Philosophical Enquiry into the Origin of Our Ideas of the Sublime and Beautiful* (1757), Goldsmith wrote proto-Romantic literature and edited literary collections that crossed class boundaries. His novel *The Vicar of Wakefield* (1766), the Persian letters of *The Citizen of the World* (1762), and the nostalgic *The Deserted Village* (1770) all articulate the themes of social discontent and spiritual yearning that appear in contemporary wonder narratives and Gothic fictions. When in 1762 Goldsmith entered the debate about the Ghost in the voice of common sense, he intended to defend Kent rather than to prosecute Parsons, for, like Fielding, as a novelist whose forte was the scrutiny of individual motives, he trusted the individual over the mob, assuming that many had lied rather than one. This conviction that ignorant or evil groups persecute defenseless individuals thus not only animates sentimental literature, but also supports the author's public role as detective and defender of the innocent.

Like the participants in the Canning case, Goldsmith stresses his disinterestedness, and he relies on witnesses he believes and on the established institutions of society to confute the alternative reality offered by the occult. Throughout, he appeals to people's common sense and senses—hearing, sight—to explode the fraud. Repeatedly, he indicts others' "idle" or malicious "curiosity" as the cause of the silent Kent's miserable plight, especially in contrast to his own motive of "public duty," recording that "thousands, who believed nothing of the matter came, in order, if possible, to detect its falsehood, or satisfy curiosity."[31] By linking the furor against Kent to the fanatical attacks on magicians and witches, and by defending Kent as a Christ-like sufferer, Goldsmith opposes ghost mongering to the enlightened sentimental defense of the underdog. Once more, an elite, disciplined, and responsible questioning is evoked to curtail the danger of the mob's undisciplined curiosity.

In defending the British system of justice, Goldsmith also defends a related set of institutions and practices: medical expertise, the verification of witnesses' credibility, the learned dismissal of the supernatural, and, not least, the authority of those in charge of interpretation. He sneers that the "interpretation" of the young girl's knocks are spiritual readings of the unrecorded that parody Catholic interpretations of God and therefore insolently assert a truth invisible to others. While he stresses the couple's fondness for each other, the triviality of the legal bar to their marriage, the doctors' testimonials of natural death, and witnesses' accounts of Fanny's deathbed gift of her inheritance to Kent, his most vehement passages attack what he sees as the true cause of the Ghost: gossip. Evading legal restriction, this gossip is vicious, unaccountable, and unregulated: "[Kent] was attacked from a quarter, that no person in his sense could in the least have imagined, in a manner, that but to mention, would have excited the laughter of thousands. . . . Who is his accuser? Why, a ghost! The reader laughs; yet, ridiculous as the witness is, groundless as the accusation, it has served to make one man compleately unhappy" (17). Claiming he knows he is preaching to the converted, he demands:

> The question in this case, therefore, is not, whether the ghost
> be true or false, but who are the contrivers, or what can be the
> motives for this vile deception? To attempt to assign the motives
> of any action, is not so easy a task as many imagine. A thousand
> events have risen from caprice, pride, or mere idleness, which
> an undiscerning spectator might have attributed to reason,
> resentment, and close laid design. (25–26)

As a discerning analyst of human nature, however, Goldsmith points out that the attackers initiated the story of the ghost at the same time as the chancery suit against Kent began. His pamphlet articulates the attempt of the new amateur professionals to establish themselves as elite judges of the real.

Correlative to this power to judge the real is the power to channel fantasy.[32] Through the sanctioned space of literature, literary connoisseurs purvey the unreal: they convert superstition to fiction, and they legitimize transgressive pleasure in an area outside the social sphere. Horace Walpole's *The Castle of Otranto* proclaims its ambiguous status with a subtitle stressing its supposed antiquity and rarity: "*A Story Translated by William Marshall, Gent.* From the Original Italian of Onuphrio Muralto, Canon of the Church of the St. Nicolas at Otranto." Presenting the story as a curiosity—a historical art work, full of occult marvels—the preface explains that it no longer has any public meaning or use. Since "miracles, visions, necromancy, dreams, and other preternatural events, are exploded now even from romances," it "can only be laid before the public at present as a matter of entertainment."[33] The "miraculous" is defined as the remnant of superstition converted in the age of reason into pleasure: it is a curiosity because its original "use" to evoke terror and reprove sin is now converted to idle entertainment. Thus, most of the preface analyzes the literary aspects of the story—its characters, diction, and moral tendency—and reduces its themes to aesthetic events.

As in *Gulliver's Travels*, *The Castle of Otranto* literalizes metaphor. The clearest example occurs when a gigantic helmet, parodying Manfred's swollen head, crushes Conrad, Manfred's sickly, *fin de race* son. This technique evokes a fantasized, lost naiveté, when things meant what they seemed to mean. At the same time, comic absurdity distances readers from the literary "terror" the tale ostensibly induces. Plots of incest, rape, and mutilation receive little narrative commentary. For example, when Manfred wonders at, walks around, and touches the gigantic "portent," he remains so mesmerized by it that he ignores the mangled body of his son (6). The violation of literary conventions and the monsterization of male ambition, together with this limpid indifference to shocking scenes, liberates readers to enjoy transgressive amusement at society's expense.[34] Walpole establishes literary curiosity as a space in which readers may safely indulge fantasies of power in alternative worlds.

Later Gothics still more openly thematize curiosity as perverse ambition. William Beckford's *The History of the Caliph Vathek* exemplifies a literary rarity created for a mass audience. A collector himself, like Walpole, Beckford threw himself into the acquisition of rarities to decorate his imitation Gothic mansion, Fonthill Abbey. The auction of his belongings after his bankruptcy continued for thirty-seven days.[35] As a materialist, Beckford stands in cultural opposition to the intellectual icon, Samuel Johnson. Whereas Johnson internalizes collecting as a moral activity, Beckford exemplifies collection as the externalization of the self, the loss of self in things, a kind of collection that many people deemed immoral. Johnson's *Rasselas* tames curious tropes to illustrate the uncontrollable power of curiosity itself and to urge a philosophical acceptance of man's nature; Beckford's *Vathek*, written during the period when science and curiosity were both under popular scrutiny, parodies *Rasselas* by means of hyperbole. Curiosity does not merely drive Beckford's characters and readers; it becomes the ritualistically intoned deity justifying all human—even inhuman—endeavors. Under its rubric, all other humanistic values collapse. Curiosity is narrative and thematic excess, the equivalent of tyranny, destruction, perversion, and pleasure.

The History of the Caliph Vathek, with Notes was published first in French, the language of courtly or exotic literature, as befits a work deliberately conceived as a curiosity: something exotic and an example of something tuned for rarefied tastes. It has two titles. The English title, *An Arabian Tale, from an Unpublished Manuscript: with Notes Critical and Explanatory*, emphasizes the need for a mediating professional, a connoisseur to introduce and explain the work, thus again underlining its status as a rarity. The preface underscores this rarity by spinning a tale of the work's exotic provenance from the "East" and the difficulty of its translation, a difficulty underscored by the apparatus of footnotes.[36] Since it is a very simple tale, the notes actually serve to represent the text as a rarity. Details are detached from the narrative and treated as separate literary, historical, or cultural items. The gloss for the phrase "One of his eyes became so terrible," for example, reads, "The Author of Nighiaristan hath preserved a fact, that supports this account; and there is no history of Vathek, in which his *terrible eye* is not mentioned" (213 n. 2). While the text portrays Faustian obsession, these notes parody antiquarian obsession. The critical apparatus makes the text a subject for connoisseurship.

Beckford parodies the quest for forbidden knowledge—of death, heaven, generation, magic. Rife with grotesque extremes of violence, proportion, and quantity, the novel depicts the passion to consume rarities and search for secrets beyond the human sphere as the Arabian ethos, while it simultaneously ridicules through excess the supposed injunction to punish impious seekers:

> Such was, and such should be, the punishment of unrestrained
> passions, and atrocious actions! Such is, and such should be, the

chastisement of blind ambition, that would transgress those
bounds which the Creator hath prescribed to human knowledge;
and, by aiming at discoveries reserved for pure Intelligence,
acquire that infatuated pride, which perceives not the condition
appointed to man, is, TO BE IGNORANT AND HUMBLE. (210)

This rhetoric partakes of the hyperbole that marks every aspect of the
novel, making it an incarnation of the anti-neoclassical. Instead of indicting curiosity as tyrannical exploitation, the book represents it as a
transgressive pleasure appreciated by the refined.

Fantasy literature thus provided inexpensive and safe curiosity for a
public educated to consider themselves experts who read for aesthetic, not
social, rewards. Publishers, as well as authors, leapt at the opportunity to
issue "curious" texts that would convince consumers they were connoisseurs. Whereas many early collections, like John Cowell's *Curious and
Profitable Gardener* (1730), taught readers to improve their land and their
status by growing exotic fruits and flowers, other collections, no longer
practical handbooks of curious artifice, contain art that makes their owners
patrons. One of the most influential of such volumes was Thomas Hearne's
A Collection of Curious Discourses (1720). Learned, meticulous, and comprehensive, it virtually defined the subjects of inquiry and objects of *virtu* for
the bourgeois collector of the period: ancient English law, money, geography, etymology, politics, ranks, duties, and professions, linguistic usages,
epitaphs, wills, bells, and letters—one concerning a collection itself.[37]
Hearne, himself a renowned virtuoso, collected "discourses" on these topics, making the language in which curiosities are discussed itself curious.
One fine example of this fusion of object and subject is Hearne's inclusion
of Ley's discourse "*Of Motts*," which illustrates the term thus: "when the
simple cannot understand it, and yet the wise cannot but understand it"
(204). Such examples make form and content the same, turning language
itself into a collectible item. Moreover, Hearne advocated an individualistic and nonauthoritative approach to collecting that sanctioned argument
yet applauded the social utility of such activities as collecting coins: "Such
as collect Coyns deserve great praise; especially if it be with a design to
benefit the Public" (204). By valuing "discourse," the exchange of information, and the historical process of ratiocination, Hearne is the first to make
intellection itself—man's distinguishing mark, his curiosity—a matter for
collection.

Many other collections present art directly, making bourgeois buyers
art experts. These documents induct buyers into an elite society of collect-

ing travelers—experts in art, history, and, by extension, human nature: a commercially manufactured imitation of the Royal Society. Printed reproductions of foreign art thus symbolized both acquisition and understanding. *A Curious Collection of Ancient Paintings, Accurately Engraved from Excellent Drawings* (1741), an early example, supplements its meticulous engravings of Roman art with "an Account" of "where and when they were found, and where they now are," as well as "several Critical, Historical, and Mythological Observations upon them." The book features learned cultural commentary, and, since it depicts paintings now held in the private collection of the king's physician, it opens the cabinet of curiosities to the wealthy and tasteful buyer. Such a buyer symbolically travels on a Grand Tour and refines his taste by witnessing fine art—significantly, from Italy, where the curious discoveries of priapic mysteries in Pompeii (where Pliny's curiosity led to his death) stood in strange counterpoint to the civic grandeur of Rome.[38] Other books for less educated audiences provided guides for sights that readers would never encounter. Richard Burton's *Extraordinary Adventures, Discoveries and Events* combines historical information and occult wonders, leaving the distinction between the two for the reader to determine.[39]

This empirical perspective by which objects accrue value by virtue of artful observation creates curiosities from familiar objects and subjects. Advertisements for marvelous nature began early in the century and lasted well into its sentimental final quarter, when nostalgia for the pastoral past moved to the center of high literature. Examples from the midcentury return mystery and life to the deserted countryside by staging the bucolic as the occult. For instance:

> A REAL APPLE! *Just arrived from Glocestershire.* . . . It is allowed by the
> Curious, to be the greatest Curiositie ever presented to the Public
> View. This Wonderful and Astonishing Apple is a representation
> of a Head of a new born Infant;—Forehead, Eye-brows, Lids,
> Eyes, Nose, Cheeks of a beautiful colour, Lips, Mouth, Chin &c.
> &c.—Beauty we may justly infer without Paint, because beautified
> by the great Creator of Nature.[40]

This advertisement recasts Eve's bane as a natural beauty surpassing the dissolute charms of painted putti. As a fruit whose value lies in its appearance, not its nutrition, this apple purifies appetite, turning the carnal into the aesthetic. Observers demonstrate both piety and artful spectatorship by simultaneously differentiating and blending nature and humanity.

As a wonderful hybrid of art and nature, animal and vegetable, the apple dramatizes a rusticity lost to alienated urbanites as the occult recedes under the cold light of empiricism.[41] This rustic wonder, however, lies in the observer's powerful eye, rather than in any magic of nature itself. This apple defamiliarizes nature as art constructed by the gaze. Similarly, traditional rural marvels advertise the countryside as a collection of curiosities exhibiting England's past. Recording one of the most famous of these marvels, *The Hampshire Wonder; or the Groaning Tree* (1742) tells of an ancient tree in the New Forest near "new Livingston, in Hampshire" that signals distress by moaning when men approach.[42] Authenticated by a Fellow of the Royal Society and contemporaneous with the Cock Lane Ghost, this animistic oak embodies the memory of past injuries. More directly, the ballad *The Wonder of Surry!* (1756) records "the Genuine Speech of an old British oak" to the Duke of Newcastle, while in response the *Wonder upon Wonder, or the Cocoa Tree's answer to the Surry Oak* satirizes the Newcastle administration (1756). Such wonders locate the occult in the countryside.

By politicizing the landscape, these stories, just as Gothic fictions do, update a long tradition of wonder tales that in earlier decades dramatized the closeness to God that is purportedly available in the country. Like seventeenth-century wonder tales that depict aerial battles and divine apparitions, these wonder tales locate the occult in empirical reality, albeit a reality more strictly earthbound than that of the visionary literature of the late Renaissance. For example, the *Uxbridge Wonder* (1738) chronicles a supernatural hail storm, while *A Wonder in Staffordshire* (1661) records "a strange and horrible Apparition." Tales of spiritual possession, divine revelation, and repentance that are titled and precisely located advertise the blessedness of a particular part of the country or city to potential travelers. *The Guilford Ghost* of Christopher Slaughterford, which still haunts Marchelsea Prison, remedies injustice by appearing "in several dreadful and frightful Shapes . . . crying *Vengeance, Vengeance*" to accuse the comurderers of Jane Young.[43] Published several years before Defoe's account of the vision of Mrs. Veal, *The Buckinghamshire* MIRACLE tells of the conversion of the atheist Edward Barton by the apparition of John Wells, concluding by recording that "the news of this strange thing was soon spread, and many country people came flocking to see him."[44] *The Somersetshire Wonder* (1700) relays the divine punishment of the wicked Mr. Pope and his family; over a century later, *The undutiful daughter; or The Hampshire Wonder* (1811) recounts a countrywoman's correction of her citified daughter. The country can cure other carnal appetites, as well. Darbyshire's *Wonder of Wonders* boasts of Martha Taylor who fasted for over forty weeks (1668); the following year's edition counted it at fifty-two (1669); *The*

Hartfordshire Wonder narrates the tale of Jane Stretton, whose "extraordinary fits" and hauntings by imps have kept her from "sustenance" for nine months (1669).[45] Other ballads record the traditional sexual freedom of the countryside.[46] Exploited by such entrepreneurs as Nathaniel Crouch, in the *Admirable Curiosities of England*, these narratives both turn the countryside into a sentimental site of lost beliefs, and become curiosities themselves that the traveler or reader may collect.

Journalism, literary collections, wonder tales, and Gothic fictions reveal the power of the ambitious literary elite to confine and control public curiosity by diverting it into new forms that nonetheless belonged in the legitimized sphere of highbrow literature. Inspired by the popularity of collecting and fashionable tourism, these new genres redefined curiosity as an aesthetic enterprise. This redefinition was exemplified no less by self-conscious literary rarities like *Vathek* than by the Grand Tour or by less grand tourism in both the countryside and in literature. These genres reoriented curiosity to aesthetic rather than public affairs, presenting it as a means of visual pleasure not social discontent. Nourished by the contemporary loss of faith in professionals' expertise, imaginative literature became the new arena for the exploration of forbidden areas and the testing of truth. The new scientist was the literary connoisseur with a method for defining human nature by aesthetic rules.

COLLECTING CULTURE IN THE PRINTED MUSEUM

The struggle between early modern science and literature to represent the authoritative procedures of inquiry intensified because of the fluidity of genres and modes in the eighteenth century. As fellow writers, scientists and literary authors and critics shared techniques, terms, and ideas. Chief among these was collecting. Collecting in midcentury literature represented intangible value, the accumulation of culture for self-improvement in direct opposition to the scientistic accumulation of things. This ideal was epitomized by Samuel Johnson's proposition that the mind itself is a personal museum of recollections. Such an ideal, however, derived directly from the newly widespread passion for quite tangible collecting epitomized by the British Museum. While it colored many genres, particularly the novel, imaginative collecting peaked in the periodical, the library of the common reader.

The changing reputation of Sir Hans Sloane (1660–1735) strikingly charts the renovation and reinvention of collecting in the mid-eighteenth century. Although revered for benevolence, Sloane had been broadly ridiculed for lack of discrimination in the seventeenth and early eighteenth centuries. In 1700, William King's Virtuoso describes Sloane as the emblem of excess, "so Curious that nothing almost has pass'd him."[47] This conventional charge shapes the literary figuration of the habit of curiosity as the failure to differentiate or hierarchize value.[48] One poem, for example, pinpoints the virtuoso's confusion of kinds of value when the speaker promises Sloane, among other mythic rarities, a tightly corked "Thumb Vial" holding "Drops of Honesty."[49] By conflating materiality and idealism, the poem characterizes scientistic collecting as an exercise that locates values in things. Moreover, Sloane's idiosyncratic sense of value was graphically illustrated by his well-publicized will, which micromanaged his collection's disposal and contained multiple codicils heaped upon each other in a way that bespoke an obsessive possessiveness.[50] Often reprinted, once by "John Virtuoso," this will became itself a curiosity. As a narrative of patriotic generosity that served, like Caesar's touted will in Shakespeare's *Julius Caesar*, to refute the charge of personal ambition, it nonetheless confirmed the defective character of the virtuoso.

By the midcentury, however, as Sloane's reputation soared, museums came to represent a new system of value: the British freedom of inquiry. In making the museum into a national gift, Sloane relocated scientific knowledge outside the universities and academies.[51] Rather that epitomizing bourgeois hoarding and private ambition, Sloane comes to incarnate a national ideal of the curious Englishman. Travelogues and museum guidebooks disseminate this ideal to the British population by a format that artfully designs the tourist's experience as a symphony of art and information. The author of the first guidebook of the British Museum equates the king, Sloane, and the Parliament; praises the "universal . . . Curiosity" of the public; and traces national progress from ignorance to enlightenment to the learning ensconced in the museum (fig. 14). Collecting as enacted by the museum becomes a "public-spirited" activity.[52] George Bickham's *Deliciae Britannicae; or, the Curiosities of Kensington, Hampton Court, and Windsor Castle Delineated* (1755) leads the reader gently from room to room, pointing out rarefied physical sites, explaining the history of the buildings, and describing the painters and paintings observed there. It includes copperplate engravings that function as souvenirs linking readers into the history they observe by "giving each person a purchase on what would otherwise be bewildering experiences."[53] This format, also used by *The Universal Magazine* to describe the British Museum, represents the experience of watching objects as narrative, and so makes the narrative the principle for ordering—indeed, for collecting—personal impressions.

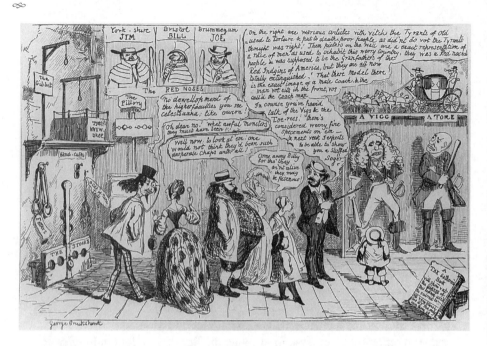

Figure 14. George Cruikshank, "British Museum: Curiosities of Ancient Times." (Colored etching, n.d.) This nineteenth-century satire portrays Cockney tourists, led by a docent, surveying British history in the museum's collection of torture instruments and political factions. It ironically indicts the ideal of social and self-improvement through the mere spectatorship of the past. Courtesy of the Art Collection, the Harry Ransom Humanities Research Center, University of Texas at Austin

By attributing each minor collection to its original owner, the museum guidebook represents Sloane's collection of collections as a historical narrative of British possession. Similarly, the account of the museum in *The Royal Magazine*, noting the "orderly and well-designed" match of the building and its contents, meticulously numbers the contents to impress tourists with the museum's vast scale.[54] A similar "companion" to Sir Ashton Lever's Museum characterizes museuming as elite worship and represents the experience for purchasers with historical accounts of the museum's content.[55] These descriptions organize collecting as the symbolic acquisition and recollection of experience.

This new definition of virtuosoship democratized collecting, which had been ridiculed as an elite activity for over a quarter of a century. The many societies of antiquaries, virtuosi, and connoisseurs continued to attract satire for delusion, snobbery, hedonism, and credulity. Ridiculed by James Gillray, Thomas Rowlandson, and other caricaturists, these new connoisseurs exhibited virtuosi's traditional flaws: they sought immortality, valued frivolities, patronized fraud, and revered ugliness (fig. 15). Most importantly, by paying vast sums for rarities and then removing them from public circulation, they usurped cultural power. *The Connoisseur* (1735), a satire against "modern Men of Taste," excoriates upstart collectors who "'cause they've large Estates will Critics be."[56] Conolly's *The Connoisseur: or, Every Man in his Folly* (1736), dedicated "to the Connoisseurs," reincarnates Shadwell's and Gay's virtuoso heroes in the vain, greedy, envious, and gullible Sir Godfrey Trinket, who collects maps, mosses, books, animals, and fossils; purchases *"Paintings, Busts, old China, and a Fly-trap"*; and ends cheated and humiliated.[57] In contrast to this materialistic accumulation, writers use connoisseurship as the trope to reify experience. They suggest that connoisseurs no longer need be rich; any discriminating observer, properly tutored, could collect rarities in a society replete with social art and human curiosities. Printed "museums" offered readers this tutoring, but periodicals offered even more: the power to make the mind itself a museum of recollected, personal curiosities.

This power to transcend identity and oversee culture itself through imagination becomes the trademark of mid-eighteenth century writers. Samuel Johnson, as a self-made, professional critic whose ambition pulled him up the social ladder, epitomizes the connoisseur; and as a frequent feature in books of biographical curiosities, he also epitomizes a curiosity.[58] At once physically grotesque—excessive and malformed—yet mentally refined, Johnson literally embodies the contradictions of the curious man, simultaneously the monstrous object and omnivorous subject of curiosity. His critical method, by blending humanistic values with the moderns' methodological expertise, expansiveness, and interest in the new and odd, shifts classificatory and evaluative natural knowledge from science to moral observation. At the same time, grimly sensitive to man's capacity for delusion, Johnson recognizes curiosity's dual character as something that both traps one in and liberates one from the world—and that is thus an essential characteristic of humanity. He sketches a blueprint of how any thoughtful reader may turn the mind into a museum by honing perception into a system of moral and aesthetic evaluation.

Johnson's periodical defines the reader as cultural collector. The title, *The Rambler*, alludes to Ned Ward's footloose wanderer, but Johnson's persona wanders in the mental realm. He forges the ruminations that stock his mind from the observation of external nature. Curiosity, as an outward-

Figure 15. George Dance, "The Collector." (10⅛ in. × 8⁹⁄₁₆ in.) This late eighteenth-
century inkwash drawing portrays a collector bowing over old coins while his
grotesque statues laugh at him and his animalistic servant combs his thinning
hair. The text above reads, "Man's Superiority and dignity affected in his efforts
to rescue from the depradations [sic] of time his own head and those of Ancient
Emperors Heroes Oracles Gods & Goddesses &c." Courtesy of the Yale Center
for British Art, Paul Mellon Collection

directed, "perpetual motion," remedies idle daydreaming; it is "in great and
generous minds, the first passion and the last," and "one of the permanent
and certain characteristicks of a vigorous intellect."[59] Inquisitive observation of God's marvels, Johnson maintains, will preserve the curious from
their besetting sin—envy—for "a man that has formed this habit of turn-

ing every new object to his entertainment, finds in the productions of nature an inexhaustible stock of materials upon which he can employ himself."[60] Thus, curiosity cures idleness, rather than promoting it.[61] Both insatiable appetite and internal quality, curiosity defines the natural connoisseur who makes his own art from nature by perception and collects—or recollects—it in his memory.

Even as it propels us forward, however, curiosity is desire itself: Johnson notes, "Curiosity is the thirst of the soul; it inflames and torments us."[62] Like Hobbes and Nabokov, he finds in curiosity the essence of insubordination, the overthrow of the hierarchy of causes and effects, means and ends:

> The desire of knowledge . . . seems on many occasions to operate
> without subordination to any other principle; we are eager to see
> and hear, without intention of referring our observations to a
> farther end. . . . We range from city to city, though we profess
> neither architecture nor fortification; we cross seas only to view
> nature in nakedness, or magnificence in ruins; we are equally
> allured by novelty of every kind . . . by every thing rude, and every
> thing polished, every thing great and every thing little; we do not
> see a thicket but with some temptation to enter it, nor remark an
> insect flying before us but with an inclination to pursue it.[63]

This potential of curiosity to throw off social restraints deeply concerns Johnson. In the first issue of *The Rambler*, he acknowledges that his own enterprise itself implies social ambition. As cultural recorder, the Rambler admits his "expectations," "ambition," and artful or artificial self-"display," but throughout the enterprise he carefully distinguishes his own inquiries into human affairs from vulgar gossip.[64]

Johnson's solution is to differentiate curiosity with a public function from private curiosity, that is, curiosity without social application. Noble curiosity explores the real, whereas ignoble curiosity explores the rumored, marvelous, or fantastic. In his dedication to *A Voyage to Abyssinia* (1735), Johnson applauds cultural exploration: "A generous and elevated mind is distinguish'd by nothing more certainly than an eminent degree of curiosity, nor is curiosity ever more agreeably or usefully employ'd, than in examining the laws and customs of foreign nations." However, in contradistinction to the traditional travel tale that stirs up wonder, he celebrates curiosity into foreignness as mental nobility only when universal human nature is documented by verified observations.[65] In one *Rambler* essay on the joys of curiosity, he remarks, "There is no snare more dangerous to busy and excursive minds, than the cobwebs of petty inquisitiveness, which entangle them in trivial employments and minute studies."[66] Another essay reproves the musing man, shut up in his study like Jane Austen's Mr. Bennet, for failing to fix his wishes "upon external things; he must adopt the joys and pains of others, and excite in his mind the want of social pleasures and amicable communication."[67] In the last *Rambler*, Johnson justifies his endeavor by purging curiosity of topicality, claiming, "I have never complied with temporary curiosity, nor enabled my readers to discuss the topick of the day."[68] Detached from low wonder mongering, Johnson advocates an elite curiosity that concerns high matters of learning and beauty.

This distinction between wonder mongering and elite curiosity relies on technique as much as topic. Johnson's method of avoiding iniquitous gossip resembles that of the natural scientist: he, like the London Spy, and in theory like Pope, identifies types, not individuals. Johnson's types, however, exist universally within all human beings, so his classification extends to the common nature of all members of the species. While many of his essays praise curiosity, his fiction often portrays it as a snare that traps the unwary imagist. Johnson's ambivalence about curiosity is revealed in his portraits of curious men whose mental powers outstrip their public usefulness. One portrait describes Polyphilus (i.e., many loves) as "a man whom all his acquaintances . . . feared for the quickness of his discernment" but whose rapid curiosity leads him merely to tumble from medicine to law to soldiering, without satisfaction, until he resorts to the self-pleasuring of "decyphering the Chinese language, making a farce, collecting a vocabulary of the obsolete terms of the English law, writing an inquiry concerning the ancient Corinthian brass, and forming a new scheme of the variations of the needle [i.e., gravitation]."[69] Johnson deplores the loss of the fruits of Polyphilus's talent to "the world"—and to the man himself.[70] Another portrait of curiosity as a waste of private and public resources is the social anatomist Nugaculus, whose excessive knowledge of people but lack of discrimination turns him into a useless, "perpetual spy."[71] Johnson implies that studying only the particular fritters away true knowledge.

In *Rasselas*, Samuel Johnson illustrates the restlessness of undisciplined curiosity by portraying vignettes of human discontent drawn from a range of places and social ranks. Many of these vignettes evoke the traditional tropes of curiosity: the Happy Valley which the prince's "original curiosity" drives him to leave resembles the Garden of Eden from which Eve's curiosity expelled mankind.[72] The tale adopts the form of an exotic travelogue, describing through "the work of observation . . . many wonders," and even containing Pekuah's captivity narrative (57, 39). Egypt, the setting, is the place from which revered eighteenth-century curiosities derived, and the wanderers, like epic questers and like Gulliver, visit the houses of the dead. Many of the characters embody curious types or types of curiosity: the royal prince, privileged by birth and wealth to collect the universe, not through items but through representative experiences; Imlac, the poet, differently privileged by profession and talent to contrive representations bridging nature and art; the astrologer who violates mortal limits by foreseeing the future and thus oversteps his own nature into madness. As the reader's guide, Imlac learns from his experience what we can learn from the novel: to accept the insatiability of his "predominent desire . . . the thirst of curiosity" (21).

Curiosity as the elite collection of experience also structures fiction with an overtly narrative thrust. Even an author as engaged in plot as Henry Fielding supplies readers with collectible portraits. *Tom Jones*, on one hand, follows the path of the epic: it is the story of the discovery of identity, both personal identity and the generic identity of human beings. On the other hand, *Tom Jones* is a cabinet of types, a narrativized collection of insets: the Man of the Hill, Partridge, Lady Bellaston, Mrs. Waters. In *Joseph Andrews*, Fielding declares, "here once for all, I describe not Men, but Manners; not an Individual, but a Species."[73] The lawyer whom he describes "is not only alive, but hath been so these 4000 Years." Fielding's scientific anatomy allows readers to furnish their mental cabinets with specimens that represent particular social species: the novel becomes an imaginative museum.

Through his essays, Johnson reproves gossip as a mode of unordered information that parodies the regulated mind's rational ordering of impressions. Indeed, gossip becomes the contemporary symbol of undisciplined curiosity. This symbol inspires the midcentury trope of the rake's progress through a tour of professions. Fielding uses this device to characterize both Mr. Wilson in *Joseph Andrews* (1742) and Tom himself in *Tom Jones* (1749) as souls alienated from society. This device thematizes the criticism of curiosity as social opportunism, the selfish search for fame, and the retreat from commitment. However, whereas the defective Curious Man follows unregulated whim at the expense of public good, the Rambler orders this same whim for the good of society and turns valuable impression into collectible language: the periodical essay. While these two faces of curiosity—its restlessness and its hoarding—are familiar throughout the early modern period, here they take on a particular fictional shape. Like the travelogue, the novel and the serialized periodical accumulate the knowledge of man—

or rather of men—as it pursues a final quest. These forms bridge movement and stockpiling.

Johnson describes happiness precisely in terms of disciplined intellectual collecting. Glossing Bacon's panegyric to the "storehouse of the mind,"
one famous passage opens by observing that humans, haunted "by an in-
cessant call for variety, and restless pursuit of enjoyments, which they value
only because unpossessed," store away sensations in the mind's "repository": "nothing can strongly strike or affect us, but what is rare or sudden.
The most important events, when they become familiar, are no longer considered with wonder or solicitude, and that which at first filled up our
whole attention, and left no place for any other thought, is soon thrust
aside into some remote repository of the mind, and lies among other lum-
ber of the memory, over-looked and neglected."[74] Johnson argues, however,
that whereas we cannot make our bodies feel things by an act of will, we
can control our minds, and therefore we ought to choose thoughts as a
collector does art objects—but a collector with a practical agenda:

> It is therefore the business of wisdom and virtue, to select among
> numberless objects striving for our notice, such as many enable us
> to exalt our reason, extend our views, and secure our happiness.
> But this choice is to be made with very little regard to rareness or
> frequency; for nothing is valuable merely because it is either rare
> or common, but because it is adapted to some useful purpose, and
> enables us to supply some deficiency of our nature.[75]

Refuting the tyranny of the physical world, Johnson lauds the imaginative
capacity to forge a collection of beautiful objects from immaterial experience. Like the virtuoso, the wise man chooses only the best to collect—an
ideal Matthew Arnold later immortalized as the very definition of the
critic, to collect with curiosity and disinterestedness "the best that is
known and thought in the world."[76] Johnson, however, replaces the early
virtuoso's value for rarity with something close to its opposite, common-
ness. His test of value is, like Fielding's, the universality of the trait he
diagnoses; its value rests on its general truth, not its uniqueness.

This systematic rationale moralizes observations and analyses of them
as a collection that leads to self-knowledge. Thus, Johnson attempts to
drain the hazardous ambition out of curiosity—its desire to defeat death,
nature, time, and God—while retaining the power over the external world
that it offers. Possession is redefined as mental—the knowledge, or memory, or sensation of the experience—rather than reified as a thing. Indeed,
at one point Johnson defines curiosity as the knowledge that one has too

few mental possessions: he sneers at "beings in the form of men, who appear satisfied with their intellectual possessions, and seem to live without desire of enlarging their conceptions; before whom the world passes without notice, and who are equally unmoved by nature or by art."[77]

Johnson's restructuring of possession is one response to the depopulation and shifting demographic patterns of the time. This idea of the mind as a cabinet that the will, the collector, can arrange and store himself gives autonomy to the intellectual self. Moreover, Johnson's image of mental connoisseurship combats earlier notions of collecting as indiscriminate accumulation. Instead, the image demonstrates elite control—a control and elitism available in theory even to the poor. Like the hungry imagination, however, curiosity for Johnson restlessly and hazardously creates its own world of values.[78] In a telling essay, Johnson recasts Sloane as Quisquilius, an unrestrained virtuoso whose self-adulating biography and account of his rarities inscribes the difference between self-possession and possession by uncontrolled appetite. Bearing the epigraph "Who buys without discretion, buys to sell," the essay reiterates the charge against collectors as profligate megalomaniacs.[79] This self-proclaimed, "uncommon" virtuoso breaks his toys to see how they work; asks "innumerable questions"; collects stones, mosses, shells, and souvenirs; and laments "that I was not one of that happy generation who demolished the convents and monasteries, and broke windows by law." His obsession starves normal "passions and appetites," including "pleasure in the company of boys and girls, who talked on plays, politicks, fashions, or love" (65–66). Quisquilius's ambitious conviction of "superior genius" leads him to despise his father for desiring him to study physick "in which, said he, you may at once gratify your curiosity after natural history, and encrease your fortune by benefiting mankind." Instead, Quisquilius fritters away his inheritance by patronizing hangers-on and curiosity mongers, gradually expanding his collecting to include everything, although "my ruling passion is patriotism" (67). His list of absurd relics reproduces in narrative the catalogue of Tradescant and other virtuosi; under the rubric of Sloane's "patriotism," the list represents the worship of the materials of the past as humiliating to the country. Despite every attempt to stop collecting when he runs out of money, "the sale of the Harleian collection shook my resolution: I mortgaged my land, and purchased thirty medals, which I could never find before." Quisquilius's acquisitive zeal ransacks the natural, political, and moral world, breeding avarice and depleting butterflies; his activity mirrors his own lack of integrity.

Quisquilius's flaw lies in his lack of discrimination. In another essay,

Johnson defends "that thirst after curiosities, which often draws contempt and ridicule upon itself, but which is perhaps no otherways blameable."[80] He argues:

> Those who lay our time or money in assembling matter for
> contemplation, are doubtless entitled to some degree of respect,
> though in a flight of gaiety it be easy to ridicule their treasure, or
> in a fit of sullenness to despise it. A man who thinks only on the
> particular object before him, goes not away much illuminated
> by having enjoyed the privilege of handling the tooth of a shark,
> or the paw of a white bear; yet there is nothing more worthy
> of admiration to a philosophical eye, than the structure of
> animals. . . . They exhibit evidence of infinite wisdom, bear their
> testimony to the supreme reason, and excite in the mind new
> raptures of gratitude, and new incentives to piety.[81]

Johnson explains mankind's reverence for the relics of famous men as an inborn respect for eminence and as "an incitement to labour and an encouragement to expect the same renown." Collection and curiosity thus promote laudable ambition, although Johnson disapproves of men purchasing eminence by accumulating trinkets instead of working for it by thinking about what such trinkets show and mean: "gratifying his desire of eminence by expence rather than by labour" (75). Johnson differentiates the connoisseur as one who knows the meaning of what he sees; he possesses a museum within his mind that contextualizes the objects of his perception.

George Colman and Bonnell Thornton exploit the overlap between scientific and social analysis in *The Connoisseur* (a title that has remained popular for two hundred years, particularly for antiquarian dealers' trade publications at the beginning of the twentieth century). Their persona, Mr. Town, exercises a scientific judgment about aesthetics and society by means of moralized observation. The first issue in 1754 showcases Mr. Town's ability to make experience into collectibles through the imposition of a moral perspective that separates the valuable from the despicable. This Connoisseur, negotiating high literature and popular culture, assumes "the character of CENSOR GENERAL" who prowls around the haunts of London to "read Hope, Fear, and all the various passions excited by a love of gain, strongly pictured in the faces of those who came to buy."[82] His pictorial perspective, albeit often turned satirically on himself, facilitates Mr. Town's functions of scientific observation, disinterested judgment, and experienced cataloguing, functions that classify humans and rate art.

While the Connoisseur exercises scientific techniques, in both his social subject and his sociable manner, he differentiates himself from natural
philosophers. Mr. Town defines his enterprise as illicit inquiry, a "desire of
penetrating into the most secret springs" of human behavior, and his
method is empirical observation of "the countenances of these Bubble-
Brokers" in order to guess at their "minds." His desire leads him to spying,
as he assumes whatever identity is appropriate: "I am a Scotchman at *For-
rester's*, a Frenchman at *Slaughter's*, and at the *Cocoa-Tree* I am—an EN-
GLISHMAN. At the *Robin Hood* I am a Politician, a Logician, a Geometrician,
a Physician. Or any thing—but an Atheist" (5). Yet his Horatian motto,
which announces him as a connoisseur of mankind not of monuments, purifies his endeavor. By characterizing his essays as conversational shifts
from mere gossip about others' possessions or skills to moral questions,
he recasts journalistic curiosity as public good.[83] This Popean role makes
life into art. When he arrives at a gambling club, he compares it to a
"*memento mori*" picturing death and credulity, particularly represented by
the "harangue" of a man "on the possibility of CANNING's subsisting for a
whole month on a few bits of bread" (2). In contrast to the credulous, Mr.
Town will supply expert guidance in the real arts—of recognizing and
avoiding deception; evaluating plays, paintings, rumors, and scenes; and
judging books. Occupying a triple role as censor, connoisseur, and town
observer, the Connoisseur moralizes curiosity as both observing and collecting.

By midcentury, criticism was a competitive profession dedicated to defining value by determining which items and experiences to collect. *The
Connoisseur* quotes English poets and parodies scientific curiosities, as in
the issues "On the Present TASTE in MONUMENTS," on the "Female Thermometer," and on the proposal to tax fashionable luxuries.[84] One issue consisting of a letter on the pretended discovery of a rare manuscript provides
a gloss on Shakespeare's work while ironically commenting on current culture. Colman thus defines the very function of criticism itself as the application of the literary past to the moral present. As in the case of other
collectors, however, disputes raged over where the immaterial value of
"taste" lay.[85] After reporting that "taste is at present the darling idol of the
polite world, and the world of letters; and, indeed, seems to be considered
as the quintessence of almost all the arts and sciences," Mr. Town rattles
off examples of the current jargon:

> The fine ladies and gentlemen dress with Taste; the architects,
> whether *Gothic* or *Chinese*, build with Taste; the painters paint with

> Taste; the poets write with Taste; critics read with taste; and, in
> short, fidlers, players, singers, dancers, and mechanics themselves,
> are all the sons and daughters of Taste. Yet in this amazing
> superabundancy of Taste, few can say what it really is, or what
> the word itself signifies. (No. 120, 121)

Albeit valuable, the term has no meaning to those who require definitions. Unable to define "taste" by precedent, "in the stile of a *Connoisseur*," Mr. Town designates two kinds of "Men of Taste": the Bon Vivant, a man "with a turn for the polite arts, as well as the lesser elegencies of life," who by study can distinguish good from bad art; and the writer or artist who adds to this graceful execution (123). He further adds the definition that "Taste consists in nice harmony between the Fancy and the Judgment," satirizing "Critics" so dedicated "to the study of *Virtú*" that they slavishly imitate ancient models (124–26). The Connoisseur's primary criterion for value is an indefinable act of judgment that simultaneously embodies individual sensibility and social sensitivity: expert taste determines value.

Mr. Town defends his definition of taste and reflects the powerful antagonism to this nouveau riche acquisitiveness and acquisition with a thoroughgoing satire of collecting in the second issue of *The Connoisseur*: "On the different Branches of VIRTU. Letter, containing a Catalogue of Pictures collected abroad by an eminent *Jew*." Whereas the opening issue defined connoisseurship as moral expertise, this one disputes the popular definition of connoisseurship as virtuosoship. Sneering at curiosities as corroded clutter, its Juvenalian epigram identifies collecting with buying: "Maim'd statues, rusty medals, marbles old, / By *Sloane* collected, or by *Langford* sold."[86] The Connoisseur hints that collecting is merely a form of moneymaking:

> I have already received letters from several *Virtuosi*, expressing
> their astonishment and concern at my disappointing the warm
> hopes they had conceived of my undertaking from the title of my
> paper. They tell me, that by deserting the paths of *Virtù*, I at once
> neglect the public interest and my own; that by supporting the
> character of CONNOISSEUR in its usual sense, I might have obtained
> very considerable salaries from the principle auction-rooms, toy-
> shops, and repositories; and might besides very plausibly have
> recommended myself as the properest person in the world, to be
> keeper of Sir *Hans Sloane's Museum.* (No. 2, Thursday, 7 February
> 1754)

Parodying public enthusiasm for Sloane's benevolence, this passage iron-ically identifies connoisseurship and self-interest. Tongue in cheek, Mr. Town confesses that he "cannot be insensible of the importance of this capital business of Taste," but his real business is to distinguish capital from taste. The true connoisseur, he will explain, invents the value of the phe-nomena he collects.

To differentiate self-sprung taste from profiteering, *The Connoisseur* glosses the Shakespearean trope of the Jew. The cultural construction of this figure keenly resembles that of the gypsy. Jews in early modern myth, fairy and folk tale, and literature characteristically wander, exiled from civil society by the act of Christ's murder yet through travel acquiring wealth and precious objects as well as perfidy, the skill of usury, and cunning. They are marginal figures, moving in and out of nationalities, both part of Lon-don society and apart from it.[87] In popular literature as well as for enlight-enment thinkers like Voltaire, Jews embodied not only sectarianism and superstitious legalism, but an alien "group identity" rivaling the hegemony of the surrounding culture.[88] Seen as poor yet miserly, they presented a threat to merchants and tradespeople. These concerns inspire the furor over the English "Jew Bill" or Jewish Naturalization Act, designed to facili-tate naturalization, both passed and repealed in 1753.[89] Colman and Thornton, as enlightened thinkers, endorse naturalization in the issue of 25 April 1754 as a way to Christianize Jews, and other issues ironically replay the stereotype of Shylock.[90] Like Fielding and Goldsmith, Colman and Thornton seek to rescue the persecuted from benighted prejudice; as connoisseurs, they see the art shaping the portrait of the Jew.

Nonetheless, they are willing to exploit the figure of the Jew. In this early *Connoisseur*, this figure serves to explode the pretense that virtuoso-ship is itself a form of art that exhibits the sensitivity of the collector. Instead, the Jew demonstrates that collecting is clearly a kind of antisocial commerce that aggrandizes the collector in several ways. *The Connoisseur* portrays the Jew as the typical collector who, believing he is entering the world of taste, accumulates reflections of himself even when they portray betrayal, greed, and superstition. In a letter, this Jew explains, "The third and fourth [paintings in my collection] are 'PETER denying his Master,' and 'JUDAS betraying him for thirty pieces of silver'; both which I design as presents to our two worthy friends, the BBs of C and C" (no. 2, Thursday, 7 February 1754). Biblical scenes become collectibles, rather than moral prompts.

Moreover, this character intends his pictures as icons to draw the awe of the superstitious. He asks for particular attention to "'the Prophet of *Nazareth* himself, conjuring the Devil into an herd of Swine'" because "from this piece, when I return to *England,* I intend to have a print engraved; being very proper to be had in all *Jewish* families, as a necessary preservative against Pork and Christianity" (15–16). Trained as a Jew, he misreads the painting, seeing not a biblical parable but an occult tale. When he records that he has "picked up an infamous portrait, by an *English* hand, called SHYLOCK; with the . . . inscription . . . 'They have disgraced me, and hindered me half a million, laught at my losses, mockt at my gains, scorned my nation, thwarted my bargains, cooled my friends, heated mine enemies;—and what's the reason? I am a JEW,'" he attributes the quote to the newspapers (16–17). While satirically indicting current prejudice by this list of portraits, Colman and Thornton also identify collecting with supposedly Jewish avarice, gain-galvanized stockbroking, and gambling— the latter also depicted in Will Hazard's letter at the end of the issue. These portraits all suggest that greed is eviscerating culture. This charge indicts all collectors as frauds who pretend to sensibility but act on percents.

The Jew's collection parodies collecting itself. Including "The Deluge, in water colours—The New Jerusalem, in perspective—Some Ruins of the Temple—and—a SAMSON in miniature," the collection combines banality and bathos: the great flood is thinned to a pretty picture in trickling, pale water paints; the possibility of redemption is rendered insignificantly distant by "perspective"; the destruction of the religion is represented as a quaint example of the picturesque; and even mighty Samson is squashed into a miniature. These are religious values eviscerated by fashionable ones: the pictorial flattens the moral.

Moreover, this collection exposes the typical egoism of the connoisseur. In his final piece, the Jewish writer shows that far from respecting conventional scenes, he aims to enter his own experience into art culture directly:

> Besides these, I have employed an ingenious artist here to execute
> a design of my own. It is a picture of FORTUNE, not standing (as
> in the common stile) upon a kind of cart-wheel, but on the two
> wheels of the lottery, with a representation of a net cast over the
> lesser engrossers of tickets, while a CHIEF MANAGER is breaking his
> way through the meshes.

Not only does this project indict the Jew's taste, it also reflects more largely the hidden obsession of all collectors. Here, the Jew puts his own mundane and mercenary life into heroic narrative: he makes a history painting of himself. Collecting thus indicates self-worship.

The clever, virulent, and repellent anti-Semitism of this letter underscores the social hostility that collecting caused by associating it with what Jews traditionally represent in English culture: avarice, usurpation of customary roles and power relations, and usury—the recycling of value. The actor Charles Macklin capitalized on current fears when, as an innovation, he played Shylock as a genuine threat. So powerful was his performance that audiences confused him with the character he played, deeming him "something like the monster in private life which he was upon the stage."[91] When Colman and Thornton launched their maiden issue, they both mocked and perpetrated this confusion of art and life by reading into real life the new character of the dangerous Jew. They endorsed Macklin's remark to Pope that he had studied his character from life, and that therefore life provided malignant Jews in plenty.[92] At the same time, they ridiculed such a confusion.

The confusion of art and life itself provides a source for the satire of connoisseurs. In the sixteenth issue of *The Connoisseur*, Mr. Town reports in a letter the discovery of an ancient ballad in the Ashmolean Museum that recounts the true story from which Shakespeare borrowed the plot of *The Merchant of Venice*. Part of a more extended parody of university virtuosi, the letter recounts a bet between two merchants, a Christian, Paul Secchi, with foreign interests, and a Jew whose interest was to keep lending money. To protect that interest and to prove false the circulating story that Drake had plundered the merchant's booty, the fiery Jew swears a pound of his flesh that the story is false, and the equally fiery Secchi offers a pound of his that it is true. The Jew is proved wrong and thus compelled by Secchi to extract the flesh. The pope warns him not to take any more or less. Our correspondent, however, claims that Thomas Warton has found the real source of the story, an ancient ballad left to the Ashmolean Museum by Anthony à Wood, and offers *The Connoisseur* the chance for the first time to publish a full transcription of this "hidden treasure," which will bring him "more credit . . . than if you had discovered an *Otho* or a *Niger*" (no. 16, 16 May 1754: 124). By reducing art to history, this parody of antiquarian reasoning condemns collectors' corruption of moral value to meaningless information.

In its aim, formula, and contents, *The Connoisseur* was scarcely unique. Like periodicals before and after it, it combined social commentary, essays, poems, parodies, letters, and narratives. Even the persona of Mr. Town borrows heavily from Mr. Spectator and other periodical spokesmen. Nonetheless, its use of the trope of connoisseurship, prominently discussed in the first two issues, marks it as a significant commentary on contemporary preoccupations; as Lance Bertelsen has shown, the standards of taste form its central concern.[93] In *The Connoisseur*, Colman and Thornton reconcile the two sides in the contemporary contest over the understanding of curiosity as either the materialistic enterprise of collecting, or the intellectual activity of criticism. By defining criticism as the literary enactment of a gentlemanly independence that, in judging the present as the lip of the past, values art from moral not mercenary motives, they clear a space for the professional critic as a collector of immaterial culture. Their *Connoisseur* draws the blueprint for the definition of intellectual elitism that galvanizes literary and cultural analysis for the next hundred years. This conception is most clearly articulated by Matthew Arnold's famous formulation that criticism itself is the mental activity of "curiosity," explained as the "disinterested love of a free play of the mind on all subjects, for its own sake." While Colman and Thornton scarcely share Arnold's high-minded disinterest in practical politics, they do claim a kind of scientific detachment—Arnold calls it "the Indian virtue of detachment"—as the touchstone of their reliability.[94]

The transformation of the elite curiosity cabinet into a vessel of public heritage made collecting, museums, and universality the buzzwords of the period. It also established a meaning for curiosity that solidified in the following century: mental imperialism. While *The Connoisseur* presented professional critics as cultural guides, other publications that followed on its heels broadened the scope of information eligible for expert knowledge and promised to make readers themselves connoisseurs. Most notably, *The Universal Magazine, or Gentleman's and Ladies Polite Magazine of History, Politicks and Literature*, quickly renamed *The Universal Museum*, publicizes collecting as mental accumulation for the reading classes. From their own armchairs, audiences may acquire information from all over the globe to furnish their mental storehouses.

At midcentury, accruing information for curiosity's sake—for private pleasure—was depicted as an English privilege. The information in *The Universal Magazine* is considered "curious" in several ways. It offers information that does not directly comment on the national interest, as in the anthropological accounts "a curious geographical Account of Portugal" (June) and "A curious account of the Indian Chief and his Attendants" (July). Many issues contain anecdotes disconnected from known narratives or larger contexts and therefore severed from public significance: "some very curious Anecdotes of the Russian Revolution" (August). Readers are encouraged to use these tales as general knowledge to enhance their own store of information for their own pleasure. Other "curious" fragments offer skills or show artful nature: "a very curious new Method of preserving Birds with their elegant Plumage unhurt . . . curious Letter to a Lady . . . with many other curious and equally interesting Particulars" (December).[95] "Curious" means both detailed and distinct, disconnected and careful, things or tales that can be absorbed in isolation from other contents. The term is generally used to incite the reader's interest in issues that are conceived to have no intrinsic or immediate pertinence, unlike an account of the current war. Other "curious essays," similarly, constitute ironic commentaries on common issues designed to be perused for leisure rather than to induce or decide on action. But "curious" is also used in a specialized sense to indicate something pertaining to natural or ancient history, as in the British Museum. This overlapping of meanings reciprocally defines the knowledge of the unfamiliar world—physical or cultural—and curiosity as twin objective and subjective sides of the same phenomenon. Such a conception of curiosity as both contemplation and prestige echoes Renaissance definitions of the museum as a liminal space between monastic and social enterprises.[96] Curiosity emerges as the appetite for knowledge that has no apparent use but that demonstrates the acquisitive power of the English reader.

Like *The Connoisseur*, *The Universal Magazine* and similar periodicals fret at the border between subjective and objective curiosity. The exchange between reification and conceptualization remains fluid; just as things can be represented as ideas, so ideas can appear as things. While this reciprocity prompts satire in the early eighteenth century, by the midcentury, on the cusp of sentimentalism, it rather offers readers an enfranchising role as connoisseurs. For example, *The Universal Magazine*'s "*Humorous Catalogue of Curiosities*" recounts "an exhibition of the Cosmetic artists in painting, enamelling, and varnish" who will exhibit in the large dancing room in Carlisle House seven female figures that slip between life and art. Among them are Bayley's "Courtesan full length very fine; the neck and hand all painted with virginal milk"; an anonymously made "Countess and Courtesan kit-cat; the Countess highly coloured, and the pearl power so disposed as to conceal the natural redness of the eyes; the Courtesan's lips best vermillion"; and "A Woman of Quality in the character of a Courtesan, after the English manner. The character finely hit by *Gibson*." The footnote adds, "As most of the performances are for sale, it is hoped some of the Virtù club will become purchasers" ("Of the Love of Novelty," vol. 4, chap. 3, sec. 3, p. 196). This punning catalogue represents sexual and social experience as the collection of types, or of types of experience. It mocks both social and scientific connoisseurs: those who collect sexual experience, and those who collect representations of it. This strange combination of natural and artificial phenomena blends art and nature so intricately that correct knowledge of painting becomes the criterion for sexual success and the means to detect the false exchanges, fraudulence, and identity confusions that victimize credulous virtuosi.

If materialistic virtuosi self-indulgently merge life and art, nevertheless their reciprocity offers moral collectors an imperialistic power analogous to that of England itself. Another essay equates the acquisition of people with the acquisition of art:

> Curiosities are commonly highly estimated amongst us; and the more precious they are in their own nature, so much the more are they valued, and sought after. This may be very justly applied to friends; since there is not any thing so rare as the faithful ones, or so excellent and perfect as those we make choice of, if they be both good and prudent. (*The Universal Magazine*, vol. 4, p. 204)

Whereas Toft, the Conjuror, Canning, and the Cock Lane Ghost embody ontological perversion, friends embody internal rarity. Human curiosities become opportunities for moral growth.

Similarly, rare items can represent history and its correlative virtues. The passage on *"Curious Pieces of Antiquity"* describes the mourning ring that Charles II wore to commemorate his father; it was an enamel picture with a legend engraved inside: "Cha. Rex. Remem—Obiit—ber 30 Jan. 1648." The object is given an interpretative gloss that reconciles its physical rarity and its social meaning: "*Remember* was the last word that King Charles spoke." Moreover, it is linked with similar souvenirs, including "a toothpick case curiously ornamented with silver, made of the piece of the oak which King Charles II cut from the tree" in which he was hiding. This item has its own legend: "His Majesty wore it in his pocket for 20 years" (*Universal Museum*, vol. 4, p. 397). As historical relics that touched the monarch's body, these charms convey loyalty and history. Represented in print, these curiosities, soon to be donated to the University of Cambridge, become symbolic items for the reader's mental cabinet and means for the reader's absorption of history's lessons. Curiosity exercised in the national interest transmutes into moral virtue.

Printed museums presenting curiosities persist well into the nineteenth century. *Kirby's Wonderful and Eccentric Museum; or Magazine of Re-*

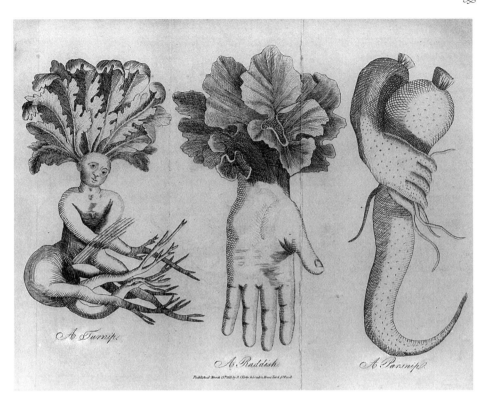

A Turnip.

A Raddish.

A Parsnip.

Published March 15th 1815 by R. Kirby & London Street Yard St Pauls

Figure 16. "A Parsnip resembling a Human Hand." From *Kirby's Wonderful and Eccentric Museum*, vol. 1 (15 March 1815), following p. 148. Courtesy of the Harry Ransom Humanities Research Center Library, University of Texas at Austin

markable Characters. Including all the Curiosities of Nature and Art, from the Remotest period to the present time features creatures and people who transgress categories and embody ontological ambition. The frontispiece portrays Dr. Isaac Gosset, "the greatest Collector of curious Books of his time," as a grotesque: a grim-faced, giant-lipped dwarf in eighteenth-century clothing.[97] As a character and a bibliophile, he represents simultaneously the collector and the collection, the acquisition of curiosity and the exhibition of it. The magazine includes anecdotes, accounts of natural wonders, plates and tales of curious characters, and pseudo-scientific stories, like the description of "A Parsnip resembling a Human Hand"—illustrated beside two other human-like vegetables (fig. 16)—or of the conversion of a human body into a hair (vol. 1, pp. 149, 152). Manningham's account of Mary Toft's delivery, the armless John Valerius, bearded ladies, ghosts, and Miss Beffin all appear. This magazine packages England's marvelous monsters as esoteric history in which ontological transgressions, genuine or fraudulent, make up an English tradition legitimating the responses of inquiry and wonder.

Moreover, like other serial publications featuring remarkable London types or characters, *Kirby's Wonderful and Eccentric Museum* extends this esoteric history to observable life so that the curious consumer, trained by the periodical to recognize the rare, can find living curiosities throughout the city. Notably, the miser Daniel Dancer, whose curious adventures charmed Dickens as a child, earns both a biography and an illustration (vol. 3, pp. 169–75). Indeed, daily life itself is narrativized into a collection of wonderful characters, sights, and events. "Particulars concerning the 'Polite Grocers' of the Strand," for example, celebrates two exemplary grocers whose silence about themselves and expert service has stimulated a "curiosity, ever in quest of food for its own insatiable appetite," that profits their business (vol. 3, p. 305). By including the specifics of the shop's address and stock, and by disparaging Dicky Dart and other shops, the magazine becomes an urban guide for the experienced Londoner. Moreover, the plentiful illustrations provide readers with their own gallery of types. These printed museums cast the readers as connoisseurs.

&

Faced with the widespread questioning of expertise and authority in the mid-eighteenth century and the flurry of curious fraud uncontrolled by the law or the press, cultural leaders sought to channel curiosity into safe forms. The publicly controlled spectatorship of curiosities, exemplified by the British Museum, provided one such form. Politicians and journalists represented the experience of museuming as patriotism; guidebooks equated seeing with owning, and they rhetorically enfranchised visitors as fellow collectors like Sloane. This validation of curiosity as the experience of ownership flourished in the symbolic realm of literature. This literature, like museums, permitted readers to blur the boundaries between public and private experience, between display and memory. Literary museums, prose fictions, and periodicals adopted the rhetoric of collection and narrativized social experience into cabinets of types, while publishers issued literary "cabinets" that mirrored curiosity collections. As *The Connoisseur,* a poetic satire on "the Modern Men of Taste," explains, connoisseurship was the fashionable skill claimed by all would-be social leaders. Collecting was the licensed mode of cultural ambition.

Contemporary journalists, critics, and writers exploited this mode. In transferring this connoisseurship from the material realm of object collection to an aesthetic realm, ambitious literary leaders legitimized literary modes that fused popular and high techniques: Gothic fictions, parodic adventures, sentimental stories. They thus positioned themselves to shape the persistent subversiveness of curiosity: its power to release phenomena from the fretwork of public use and value and to feed forbidden desires. Similar and other alternative literary forms—self-conscious curiosities like *The Castle of Otranto*, travelogues that violated narrative conventions, wonder narratives that resurrected the occult, and "secret" collections of illicit information—spun information into private pleasure. These texts mocked the moral channeling of inquiry into a search for moral principles of behavior, public truth, or even happiness; they resisted rational arguments against unseen truths; they overturned hierarchies of value and meaning. Instead, they refigured curiosity as the urge for personal enjoyment through the exploration of forbidden ideas.

These alternative literary forms confuted most censorship precisely because of the public legitimization of collecting. Johnson's role as moral connoisseur epitomizes this sanctioned curiosity. By devoting inquiry to public and private improvement, he provided a model of cultural ambition that threatened none and that all readers could imaginatively imitate. Indeed, this technique turned readers into agents of their own commodification. As collection became the cultural mode, the culturally ambitious became themselves not merely collectors, but collections, molded into displays of knowledge acquired by storing their minds with information from art and life.[98] This collector of impressions and experience turns his or her imagination into a container stocked with rare memories, social curiosities, and recollected art in quotes and pictures—each item honed by perception, meaningfully ordered, and arranged for public and private use. Such a collector was furnished with method and materials by literary guides who acted as connoisseurs of culture: Goldsmith, Johnson, Colman and Thornton, and many others. Theirs was considered the legitimate use of the empirical pleasure and the moral application of literary defamiliarization. At midcentury, this internalization of collecting made literature the source of cultural connoisseurship and turned curiosity aesthetic. Readers read to collect themselves.

CHAPTER FIVE

Performing Curiosity

Curiosity at the end of the century offered a rich form of resistance to the cultural march toward systematization, classification, and the regulation of morality and social behavior. Among all English people, the practice of collecting as a sign of cultural mastery expanded, but increasingly these collections became specialized along class lines.[1] Whereas poorer people accumulated natural curiosities from the countryside and shore, the wealthy continued to amass fine art, especially antiquities.[2] Such relics, even if publicly valueless, not only make the past material, but, by their ineffable irreplaceability, testify to the authentic uniqueness of the collector's experience.[3] Moreover, when the collected items are fragments of the natural world, they make nature itself, as specifically perceived and experienced at a moment in past time, part of the collector's expanded identity. Both natural and historical collections seek to capture time and invent heritage: to authenticate the past as something valuable to the collector.

This internalization of collecting as a performance of identity in time expands into public exhibitions and high literature in the period from 1780 to 1820. Curiosity matures as a dynamic bridging object and subject: an enactment of transgression that reciprocally defines the exhibit, the exhibitor, and the audience. Fairs and museums negotiate this use of public space and the violation of public taxonomies by justifying the carnivalesque with the didactic.[4] Exhibitions of skill, deformity, or wonder hint at an explanation of the past—a *monstrum* or warning—while exploiting the unique impression of the sublime sold to the spectator. Collecting the past in objects or texts verifies the collector's or reader's identity as owner of that past.

Both elite and popular cabinets and circuses are forms of collecting that co-opt or deploy the systematization of science outside the public organization of value for a variety of personal ends. Rather than becoming a subject of classification in a moral or sociological system, the collector or the spectator of an exhibition systematizes his or her own experience and objectifies time and nature according to individual desire and memory. Instead of emblematizing universal knowledge, as the cabinets of the great Renaissance princes did, these collections are designed specifically to illustrate the eccentric limitations of the owner's tastes. This individualistic approach to collection and display infuses both public and private, material and literary exhibitions. Public fairs, shows, and mechanical and chemical displays fostered this approach by staging science for popular amusement. Although didactic rhetoric abounded, exhibitors depended on visual lures, the spectacle of the rare, to draw customers. Since they advertised each show as a unique experience, they continually altered their shows and dramatized the live or mobile element: spectral appearances, performances, and the personality of the showman or of the show creature.

Contemporary literary texts exploit this fascination with authentication through uniqueness and with romantic individuality as decontextualized identity. Gothic fictions, sentimental tales, and miscellanies of literary "curiosities" play on the traditional, dual heritage accorded curiosity as at once masturbatory peeping into the forbidden and also farsighted discovery of the unknown. These works feature literary devices, like the shredded or just-discovered manuscript, that emphasize the rarity, secrecy, or obscurity of their texts and that deliberately evoke the occult past, a past that is represented through the tropes of religion, politics, or time as Catholic superstition, medieval brutality, or Renaissance tyranny.

Simultaneously, many of these texts construe curiosity as the noble collection of impressions and information about others, garnered in the course of traveling abroad or at home. Such texts imply a moral rationale or application that endorses gossip and prurience as the acquisition of enlightenment. This enlightenment can entail either self-improvement or benevolence. Even before the French Revolution, many travelogues laced tourism with a satire as much class directed as nationalistic. *The Gentleman's Guide in his Tour through France*, for example, is "wrote by an Officer who lately travelled on a Principle which he most sincerely recommends to his Countrymen, viz. Not to spend more Money in the Country of our natural Enemy, than is requisite to support, with Decency, the Character of an Englishman." Noting that "the first thing to attract your admiration, is the curious workmanship of the beautiful gates," the author extensively lists "*Curiosities worth seeing in Paris*," weighting heavily national institutions, collections, and buildings, many of which can be admired from outside.[5] As objective curiosity remains a feature of state art, the viewing of which endows the spectator with status, so subjective curiosity proves the travel-er's capacity for self-improvement: his social ambition.

However, when exercised by women or socially marginalized people, this kind of curiosity is dangerous, both for the curious characters them-selves and for society. Late century writers use curiosity to condemn social injustice. They depict protagonists who resemble private collectors in their use of individualistic procedures of social stratification, classification, and regulation—including the de- and recontextualization of phenomena, in-vented hierarchies and classes of artifacts, and the renaming as well as the revaluing of objects and subjects. Whereas dilettantes redeploy value in their private collections, inquisitive literary characters collect privacies by gossip and questioning. Both activities appear in literature as unregulated reconstructions of the past. Many late century writers use this impertinent curiosity to condemn social injustice; some represent it, whether figured as sentimental, romantic, or material, as an appetite that reenacts England's historical abuse of nature through class and sexual oppression. These texts depict curious men as tyrannical usurpers of others' subjectivity.

Other texts represent curiosity as a benign quality, as a manifestation of utopian rebellion, the desire to find true, generous nature behind false masks and to restore just social relations. Most sophisticated literature, however, represents curiosity as both virtuous and a hazardous social viola-tion, and this period provides the genre that most ably articulates this ambiguity, the Gothic novel. Gothic stories of hazardous penetration into the past are motored by the characters' (and readers') curiosity, yet these stories criticize this motive: the very impulse that drives Gothic protago-nists to uncover the past betrays their suspect affinity with it. Curious read-ers are similarly entangled in a quest for truth that plunges toward mor-tality.

As literature becomes more didactic at the end of the eighteenth cen-tury, authorial personae increasingly insist that the reader make moral choices. Readers become more than witnesses of culture; their reading im-plicates them in its formation. These later Gothic narratives present in-creasingly serious comments on human nature and the human condition. William Godwin's novel *Caleb Williams* exemplifies the thematic explora-tion of curiosity as a rebellion that is simultaneously refreshing and de-structive. The story of a servant's ruination of his master by the pursuit of the master's secret, *Caleb Williams* is a tragic narrative that retells *Bluebeard*, in which curiosity is both feminized weakness and the justified overthrow of tyranny. Ann Radcliffe similarly imbues curiosity with purifying power, but by embodying it in sentimental heroines, she avoids directly implicating her agents of inquiry in the crimes they discover: they are usually female witnesses of male evil. Mary Shelley's Romantic novel of impious inquiry, *Frankenstein*, exemplifies this depiction of curiosity as redemption and doom. The book portrays man's scientific curiosity as a violation of divine nature that makes monsters, yet it renders the monster and the scientist sympathetically.

These novelists express the late century discourse in which moralized curiosity symbolizes man's capacity for progress, while perverse curiosity symbolizes his satanic capacity for corruption. This view differentiates curiosity by class. As before in literary history, one of the most powerful popular tropes or types expressing this hazardous fusion of peeking and seeking, of self-gratification and appropriation, is the virtuoso—the scientific or scientistic collector. This image inspires the creation of Victor Frankenstein, who as an advocate of New Science disinters dead dreams, ideals, and bodies from the benighted graveyard of the past and patches them into a corporate monster of collected culture—all to reflect his own glory. His transgressive act is mirrored in the text by framing narratives that, in retelling his tale, similarly paste together past parts to impart a "hideous progeny." Yet these breaches of nature, order, and decorum release sublimity, the bold leap over ordinary boundaries to the stars. As *Frankenstein* exemplifies, at the turn of the century literary and visual representations present a new, ambiguous ideal of curiosity as transgression itself.

Frankenstein's creation also embodies the debate over the valuation of original creation as opposed to imitated or recycled things and texts. Monstrosity, figured as excess, deformity, or multiplicity of identity, remained a preoccupation of English culture. The questions of whether curiosity is "natural" or perverse, or of what kind or extent of curiosity is tolerable, receive added impetus from the contemporary popularity of the sentimental theory that mankind is born good, possessed of a natural morality that is only distorted by social restraints. The traditional designation of "unnatural" men—be these hypocrites or hermaphrodites—as monsters took a new twist as thinkers like David Hume, Jean-Jacques Rousseau, Francis Hutcheson, and Adam Smith blamed culture, instead of nature, for mankind's ills. Once emblems of mankind's innate deformity, monsters became curiosities of cultural corruption. They exhibited society's abuse of human nature. In contrast, scientific or mechanical innovations like the hot-air balloon offered, if not an escape to a lunar ideal, at least a global perspective from which man seemed nestled within a civilized nature or a naturalized culture. At the end of the century, curiosity is represented as producing both rebellion and redemption.

THE CURIOUS CONTROL OF NATURE

In the period from the 1770s to the 1820s, natural philosophy turned science was staged as popular spectacle. This "science" constituted a knowledge of the natural universe manifest by both mechanical inventions and the dexterous mastery of devices or creatures. For the consuming public and contemporary authors, the question remained whether such science held any benefit for mankind or merely fed and fed on humanity's lust for wonder.[6] Satiric literature often suggested that curious discoveries and skills are merely exhibitions of trickery, performed either with the audience's willing suspension of disbelief or without it, as in the incident of the Bottle Conjuror. Satires hint that rather than advancing knowledge, these demonstrations revive and exploit superstitious credulity. Alternatively, the rhetoric of performers and fans touts their science as a display of cultural progress, natural wonder, and human—notably male—control. Extolling enlightenment, showmen represent their exhibitions as public opportunities to learn the principles of nature, to penetrate the mysteries of elite skill, and to watch history. Both satire and panegyric nonetheless tend to focus on the power of the individual performer over the occult or unseen nature. This contention about the status, function, and effect of public shows reinforces the romantic notion that the uniquely talented man trained in science—be he Napoleon, Mr. Katterfelto, or Victor Frankenstein—possesses a hazardous power over nature and humanity.

The circus supplied a public venue for this display of masculine power. Although fairs had flourished in England for hundreds of years, the circus was a profit-making version of the eighteenth-century riding school built by the nobility for the display of arms and developed by Philip Astley, a retired sergeant-major and son of a cabinetmaker.[7] Astley's amphitheater staged feats of horsemanship and military maneuvers for a lay audience from the 1770s through the Regency. Among other tricks, Astley began to appear with a Little Military Learned Horse that could "turn Conjuror" by counting, destroying, and restoring handkerchiefs and by turning "a Gold Watch to an Orange, and the Orange to a living Bird, which will fly away."[8] The Little Military Learned Horse staged the expansion of expert horsemanship to the mental control of animal intelligence. Astley's rival, Charles Hughes, instantly countered with a Horse of Knowledge that fired a cannon and pistol, along with the usual card conjuring, and he added female riders, including his wife, the touted "Diversion of the Riding School." Although Astley also quickly employed conjuring, tumblers, and a clown, he resisted feminizing his act. Instead, he adopted a stentorian tone of military authority—still evident in circus masters today—to repel "pretenders." He proclaimed that since he was a soldier, only his performance was authentic.

By capitalizing on his own background, Astley represented his act as "manly": the exhibition of masculinity itself. He emphasized his military credentials by publishing vignettes of himself performing on horseback, and his published advertisements linked expert riding with the control of brute creation. His "MANLY EXERCISES, With the Horse, from the Horse, and on the Horse" included dancing and displays of bestial obedience designed to represent him as an equestrian authority.[9] He reinforced his claims to expertise by a series of books on the techniques of riding and training horses, one of which, *Astley's System of Equestrian Education*, was republished throughout the early decades of the century.[10] When his show was closed in July 1774 for breaching the license for music and dancing, Astley published *Natural Magic*, a treatise on riding dedicated to the king that resulted in its reopening.[11] In 1776, he moved into a room at 22 Piccadilly and featured "Fire-Side Amusements," consisting of *Ombres Chinoises* (moving shadows of Chinese figures on a screen), renditions of bird calls by the renowned Signor Rossignol, mathematical calculations by the Little Military Learned Horse, and a series of satirical displays of high society performed by a troop of trained dogs. Increasingly, Astley's "manly" exhibitions featured himself as master manipulating animals to imitate human behavior. He represented himself as the conjurer of natural science.

Astley fed a current fad with his performing animals. Marvelously human-like animals galvanized the public partly because they embodied the conquest over nature and time. Since the seventeenth century, lions and wild animals, examples of captured nature, had constituted the "Wonders" in the Tower of London; throughout the eighteenth century menageries and zoos, stages for witnessing the control of foreign lands, featured exotic animals. Dromedaries, giraffes, and other animals toured Europe as natural curiosities. "Just Arrived from the East, At Mr. Gough's Manegre," for example, along with the Lyon Monster, the grand Cassawary, the Porcupine, and others, came the Stupendious Pelican that metamorphosed myth into science:

> The Stupendious PELICAN, So remarkable in its Nature as to be
> recorded in Sacred History; and was one of the Emblems of
> paternal Affection with the Ancients. It is the inhabitant of great
> Lakes and Rivers of Arabia; and is stiled by the Mahometans, the
> Bird of Mahomet. The History of the present Pelican is no less

remarkable than its Natural History. It was found in the City of
Belgrade, when taken by Marshal Loudhon, and by him sent to
Vienna, as one of the Trophies of Victory.[12]

This symbolic and specific history makes the bird a unique "trophy." On
26 November 1787, a fisherman brought to London "A Sea Monster . . .
with a MOUTH of a most ENORMOUS SIZE, capable of holding the largest Man
in England," a creature from biblical myth who was yet verified by Dr.
Hunter as "the most wonderful Prodigy the Ocean ever produced." Again,
in 1770, the "Rhinoceros or Real Unicorn" brought myth to life. These
creatures offer glimpses of unknown lands, histories, and genealogies by
slipping between ontological categories or corporeally manifesting possible human histories.

Showmen began to match these "monsters" with familiar creatures
made marvelous by man. Knowledgeable animals who performed intellectual feats like humans offered a rival kind of natural curiosity to the public.
These beasts imitated the skills of learned "professors." Notoriously, the
Wonderful Pig was "well versed in all Languages, perfect Arithmatician,
Mathematician, and Composer of Music."[13] He was followed by the Saga-
cious Goose who could perform tricks "upon Cards, Money, and Watches,
telling the Day of the Month, and the Month of the year; as also the value
of any Piece, either English or Foreign," among other talents.[14] Not only
does the goose mimic a human conjurer, she also violates her own obtuse
nature. Thus, she incarnates genuine wonder and, as the advertisement explains, constitutes a spectacle for the learned because she is "the most Stupid and Insensate of the FEATHER'D CREATION." Repeatedly, visitors are
urged *"Vide et Crede,"* since only eyewitnesses can authenticate a marvel.

These intelligent animals characteristically burlesque both intelligence
and wonder. Rather than presenting spectators with the sublime, they trot
out the control of man over brute. These astute animals parody sophisticated science, but they also demonstrate human superiority. Audiences
came to be fooled for fun, as fifty years earlier they had flocked to listen to
the Cock Lane Ghost, and by the ingenious skill of showmen who manipulated audience and animal to create occult illusion they were. Performing
animals, like conjurers, convert the public desire for wonder into admiration for curious skill.

Astley exploited this desire for wonder. Like the collections of Renaissance virtuosi, Astley's living cabinet of curiosities does more than juxta-
pose art and nature. It also blurs the boundaries between *naturalia* and *"ar-
tefacta*, the products of man," by giving prominent place to phenomena that

demonstrate "man's ability to overcome the difficulties arising from the raw materials."¹⁵ With the bird-calling Signor Rossignol, dancing dogs, tumblers, dancers, feats of horsemanship, and a lunar spectacle called "HARLEQUIN EMPEROR of the MOON," featuring "a grand Procession of the Inhabitants of the MOON" (1784), Astley completes what is virtually a register of popular topics of curiosity. By skill and the manipulation of the audience's vision, his museum in movement turns the live into the static, and vice versa, and transforms bodies into sculptures. These slippages between art and nature, life and death, flesh and representation make curiosity the fantasy of escape from conventional restrictions, whether social or physical. Astley's amphitheater becomes a cabinet of live curiosities or curiosity in action, extending across the borders of art, nature, and time.¹⁶

Persistently, however, Astley reminds audiences that he controls the illusion. His touting rhetoric balances the wonder of his creatures against the wonder of his skill in training them, while his increasingly baroque exhibitions themselves expand to a range of curiosities that blend art and nature. One show boasts "the amazing Phaenomenon, The Musical Child," who, although "only Thirty Months old, has the Judgment of the most professed Theorist in Music, and is allowed by all Ranks of Persons, to be the most astonishing natural Production that ever made the Appearance in the known World."¹⁷ Astley joins his own performances with those of a "natural" phenomenon, an infant prodigy whose "unnatural" talent, whose monstrosity, is made benign as art. Such combinations collapse the distinctions between curiosity as a contrived skill and as a freak of nature. Indeed, this performance also features "the Astonishing MONKEY, GENERAL JACKOO," tumblers, fireworks, a clown and "THE SIEGE OF PORTOBELLO," a dramatic representation of gunfire, canon shot, and burning ships "displayed in allegorical Fire-Works." By featuring the exotic ape Jackoo, represented as a human, and war, represented in the traditional idiom of wonder as an allegorical vision in the sky, Astley's show blends apocalyptic omens, freak fairs, and curiosity cabinets with didactic displays of human phylogeny and military history. His match of beauty and skill turns aristocratic exercises into the traditional popular entertainment of viewing physical curiosities that bridge ontological categories. Astley's amphitheater makes national power frivolous spectacle.

By popularizing military exercises, Astley demystified elite expertise. The skills of horsemanship that he performed had previously been restricted to the military, preserved for the specialized uses of battle, and kept out of the public eye. Astley made this privileged science public spectacle. Moreover, by staging an ancient aristocratic art in the same arena with a bevy of dancing dogs dressed as *raffiné* gentry performing the rituals of Regency high society, he parodied class pretensions. Like traditional monsters, these creatures revealed the concealed bestiality in civilized society and the mechanical repetitiveness and degradation (or dogradation) of social customs, not only at present but through history. These dogs stimulated a burst of prints that meticulously reproduce the animals' flexibility, variety, and human-like postures. In one example, a double plate (designed to allow buyers to separate the two pictures) of "An Exact Representation of the Dancing Dogs at Sadlers Wells" and of a balloon ascension transforms Astley's ostensibly serious feat of training into satire by depicting vignettes of "Ladies on a Visit" and so on (fig. 17). Astley's dogs showed the animal in the elite. In ironic juxtaposition, the companion print shows spectators awed at the balloon's transcendence. As animals act like humans, so humans act like gods. Astley's animals, however, provided blunt satire of society and a crude example of social mobility. By training and controlling these horses and dogs, the sergeant-major took the place of the master. Astley's amphitheater literally and figuratively rendered some of the most solemn and guarded aspects of class society as a circus. It was curiosity turned charivari.

For a hundred and fifty years, scientists had in various ways offered the public an escape from nature, but Astley's device of endowing spectators with the feeling of class superiority or sublimity by rendering the occult, the monstrous, and the transgressive as spectacular experience proved wildly popular at the end of the century. In the 1780s another performer who spectacularized science rose to prominence: Mr. Gustavus Katterfelto. Performing nightly at Cox's Museum, Katterfelto blended the roles of conjurer and lecturer, magician and natural philosopher. As his advertisements declare, "Mr. KATTERFELTO's Lectures are [in] Philosophical, Mathematical, Optical, Magnetical, Electrical, Physical, Chymical, Pneumatic, Hydraulic, Hydrostatic, Styangraphic, Palenchic, and Caprimantic Art." After this daunting didactic display, however, he would "shew various uncommon experiments" with an "apparatus . . . very numerous and elegantly finished . . . on the newest construction." This enabled him to "discover various arts, by which many persons lose their fortunes by Dice, Cards, Billiards, and E. O. tables."[18] Both performer and professor, he is the "cunning man" turned people's defender who reveals others' occult fraud.[19]

Katterfelto energetically distinguishes himself from other performers as a benevolist. On Good Friday, he distributed the takings from his lecture to the poor as a sign of his piety and social responsibility, declaring, "Our maker says, 'Those who relieve the poor shall be rewarded, and live in

Figure 17. "An Exact Representation of the Dancing Dogs" and "The Duke D'Chartres & M. Robert ascending in an Air Balloon from the Park of St. Cloud." 4 September 1784. (Published by E. Fringham, 76 Hosier Lane, West Smithfield.) By permission of the British Library

glory in the kingdom of Heaven for ever and ever.'"[20] Moreover, like Astley, he also represents himself as a professional, indeed a "Professor," an expert scientist or "knower." His mission to save the credulous from trusting cardsharps and tricksters entails adopting a heritage and experience that will guarantee his reliability. By announcing in the newspapers that his father is a general, and by citing the nobles before whom he has lectured and who urge him to further performances, he declares his allegiance to order and his gentility. In his advertisements, he refers to himself repeatedly, always in the third person, and invariably capitalizes his name, paying to have the script set off from the rest of the text as a visual litany. In the tradition of other self-advertising performers, "monsters," and "freaks," he claims rarity and thus prestige by being observed and respected by the prominent. He further authenticates his scientific expertise by proclaiming the admiration of other scientists, particularly Benjamin Franklin.[21] When Captain Baterson dropped a silk purse holding three golden guineas and a note of hand for two thousand pounds in his exhibition room, Mr. Katterfelto advertised in the papers for its owner—objecting later, however, that "Katterfelto is very happy that Capt. Patterson has had his purse with the money and 2000*l*. Note again. The gentleman was very polite to leave 1*l*. 7*s*. but the different advertisements cost Katterfelt 2*l*."[22] Later advertisements contain thanks to the nobility and gentry who visit his rooms.[23]

Although like Astley, he emphasizes the science of his enterprise, Katterfelto underscores its marvelous visual aspects. Through his "Solar Microscope" he magnifies (in the same room as Astley's exhibition of optical marvels) for "all LOVERS of NATURE, and to the Nobility and Public in general . . . those most astonishing Insects, which have been advertised in the different papers, and which have threatened this kingdom with a plague," each appearing "as large as an ox." He further displays curiosities "collected in his travels," including "some Water where there are above 5000 insects in one drop."[24] By exhibiting natural wonders through scientific instruments, Mr. Katterfelto attempts to sew together conjuring and visual magic with the instrument-aided discoveries of the New Science. His performance turns live scientific wonders into popular spectacle.

After 90,000 persons had witnessed his act, however, Mr. Katterfelto was compelled to discover or invent wonders that drew him away from empirical science and allied him more closely with the tricksters he had originally exposed.[25] His advertisements suddenly represent him "as a DIVINE and MORAL PHILOSOPHER" who discloses "WONDERS! WONDERS! WONDERS! and WONDERS!" and "NEW OCCULT SECRETS," coupled with his lectures to and "on those who are NOT BLIND BUT WONT SEE." With the help of a black cat whose tail he could conjure away, he began to parody his own rhetoric, declaring, "We are informed that *Katterfelto* is not only the greatest philosopher that ever lived, but that a most bloody war is likely to take place between the King of France and Prussia, contending for the honour of having the said philosopher at Versailles or Berlin," and asseverating that his absence "is the very business which retards the forming [of] a new Administration." He particularly underscores the growing notoriety of his feline companion, who serves as an alter ego, turning him from an entrepreneur of curiosities into a curiosity himself:

> Mr. Katterfelto and his *black cat* are regarded as two of the greatest
> *natural* curiosities ever imported into this kingdom. They say it is
> the very cat which *Own Glendower* used to exercise the patience of
> *Harry Hotspur!* . . . [Franklin reports that] all Paris were wild for his
> arrival, and that the Queen and some Ladies of the first Quality
> were anxiously waiting to see the Philosopher's black cat. Why the
> Queen of France should be so anxious to see Col. Katterfelto's
> black cat, is not easily accounted for, as it wants its *queue;* a
> circumstance which her Majesty, perhaps, is not acquainted with!
> We are informed by the Paris Gazette, that the Queen of France
> has a gold snuff box ready, set with diamonds, to present that great
> philosopher Katterfelto.[26]

With an increasingly ambiguous self-promotion that jokes with deference, Mr. Katterfelto becomes both the exhibitor and the exhibit.

Katterfelto's identification with his cat, however, almost turned him into a monster. In his frenzy to preserve an audience, he exploited this feline fame by encouraging sporting gentlemen to lay bets on whether Katterfelto's cat had a tail. Whether deliberately or not, this notoriety began to erode the distinction between entertainer and witch. The *General Advertiser* for 5 April 1783 reports that some people believe that "his Black Cat was Devil, for one minute she had a tail, and the next minute she had none; and many would have it that he himself was Devil, otherwise it was impossible that he could shew such dexterity of hand." Instantly, Katterfelto published a refutation, vowing, "May the BLACK CAT have nine Times nine Lives!" and denying the charge that he and the cat are devils as printshop cartoons depicted them: "On the contrary, KATTERFELTO professes himself to be nothing more than Moral and Divine Philosopher, Teacher in Mathematics and Natural Philosophy."[27] For weeks he reasserted his innocence, thereby further exploiting the charge itself.[28] Finally on 14 May 1783, Katterfelto announced that the cat had delivered 9 kittens (7 black,

2 white), which proved her to be a natural creature. The conjurer of imperceptible skill became the conjurer of unseen powers, until reproduction confirmed natural distinctions between female animal and man. Reduced to the sentimental, Mr. Katterfelto's fame subsided, rearing only briefly when, immediately after the first balloon ascension, he claimed to have made "The Grand Air Balloon" sixteen years earlier in St. Petersburg and volunteered to scoop pretentious aeronauts by showing people how to make and fill one "at small expense."[29]

Despite his repeated asseverations of piety and elite superiority to money, reinforced by his particular act of exposing cardsharping tricks, Mr. Katterfelto offered the public the frisson of ambitious transgression. Was he providing an exhibition, a performance, or a didactic lecture? One panegyric—"On Seeing Mr. KATTERFELTO's Grand exhibition"—celebrates his act for channeling curiosity into public education.[30] Possibly authored by Katterfelto himself, it depicts him as an agent of enlightenment who will save the profligate, ignorant, and deceived from trickery. As a professional, his curious science penetrates popular deception; it is the art of seeing into mystery. Like the Renaissance *Wonder of the World*, curiosity is represented as human beings' natural device for self-protection.

At the same time, Mr. Katterfelto evoked wonder by visual illusions. Throughout London, people flocked to see exhibitions of mechanical marvels that bordered but evaded the occult. Mr. Bologna's poster, for example, enclosing its text with a sketch of a ghost rising from a bubbling cauldron, advertises to the nobility, gentry, and connoisseurs of fine art:

> MORE NOVELTY. PANTASCOPIA. AUTOMATRON FIGURES,
> PHANTASMAGORIA, And HYDRAULICS . . . This NOVEL, CURIOUS, *and*
> *INTERESTING EXHIBITION*, has been enriched by the addition of
> some surprising Optical Effects which have *never before been shewn*
> *in this or any other Country*, called FAIRY GAMBOLS, Which with the
> EIDOTHAUMATA, OPTICAL AUTOMATA, PHANTASMAGORIA, and other
> VISIONARY SPECTRES.[31]

Adding fireworks, a mechanical "MARVELOUS SWAN," and a "TURKISH CONJURER" who reveals cards and numbers, this display is authenticated by the announcement that

> a considerable Part of the Apparatus employed, has been prepared
> by M. Dumutier, under the Direction of Professor ROBERTSON,
> of Paris; and, the whole, it is hoped, instead of being like many
> Exhibitions, calculated only to divert Children, will be found to

furnish a Variety of Rational Amusement, even to the most
Refined and Classical Taste. *Beware of Imposters.*

While visual pleasures were sanctioned as science, they operated as spectacle. Artists like Mr. Katterfelto had to distinguish themselves from "imposters" by scientific authority and elite rhetoric. In these advertisements,
publications, and licensing battles, performers like Astley and Mr. Katterfelto struggle to retain the identity of a scientist or expert while appealing
to the popular hoard in search of entertainment. Their struggle delineates
the ambiguity in the status of science and curiosity during this period.
While expertise and intricate artistry still win the performer applause, his
use of these curious skills to incite the curious appetite for novelty and
sensation in the public condemns him as a fraud, a trickster, or even a
devil.[32]

Visual pleasures appeared plentifully in connection with print. Caricature, allegorical engravings, and broadside illustration, like Mr. Bologna's
ghost, that had served as propaganda for the last two hundred years flourished at the end of the eighteenth century. Partly thanks to Thomas Bewick's invention of woodcut engraving, an inexpensive method to reproduce paintings and engravings finely, publishers embellished all kinds of
literary texts with vignettes; print shops selling a range of kinds of illustrations simultaneously burgeoned. This visual tradition was enriched by the
contemporary obsession with monstrosity as a trope to indict others.

During this period of social and international unrest, threatening others were figured by their sex, race, class, nationality, and violation of these
neat categories. Mr. Katterfelto skillfully exploited his ambiguous nationality to enhance his status as both a conjurer of curiosities and a curiosity
himself. Like Matthew Buchinger, Miss Sarah Beffin, and a host of other
human curiosities who exhibited their bodies as art, he embodied the ambiguity of art and nature. Count Boruwlaski, a blue-blooded midget living
on the respectful charity of visitors who admired curious royalty, embodied
Lilliputian power by challenging a giant to a duel in 1782 at a masquerade
where all humanity is both masked and unmasked.[33]

At the end of the century, Napoleon epitomized the monstrous appetite for blood and bestial appetites. "*A True Relation* from Rome of a bloody
and cruel Monster, That for many Years hath destroyed an infinite Number of Men, Women, and Children; devoured the Growth of that Country,
and reduced other Nations to want: With a Description of its prodigious
Shape, terrifying Aspect, and Fox-like Craftiness . . ." describes him with
conscious archaism as an allegorical hybrid image of Satan with leopard's

spots, bear's feet, and a lion's mouth: "He is Letcherous as a *Bore*, as full of Poison as a *Toade*, Cunning as a *Fox*, Surly as a *Lyon*, Bloody minded as a *shee Bear*, Deceitful as a *Leopard*, Wise as a *Serpent*, and as Proud as the *Devil*. . . . And although he is of the Nature of a *Wolfe*, yet he always goes in *Sheeps Cloathing*, the better to deceive the multitude."[34] Displaying the monstrous traits of ingratitude, excessive greed, bloodthirstiness, and duplicity, Napoleon appears as both metaphorically and literally a monster.

In the seventeenth and eighteenth centuries, monstrosity shifted between being a satirical and a scientific, an allegorical and an empirical, category. To the observing eye, it revealed concealed continuity and expressed the ambiguity of an age in which identity shifted between being a social and a physical construction. Monstrosity distinguished normal appetite from grotesque excess and documented historical progress or cultural regress. As it had done for the previous two centuries, monstrosity at the end of the eighteenth century still uneasily straddled science, superstition, satire, and religion. Whereas medieval and Renaissance popular culture had woven these categories together, the natural philosophers of early modern England sought to differentiate them. Once monstrosity had proven God's power and man's sin by corporealizing, in violation of nature's rules, vices like lust, gluttony, and bestiality.[35] Now, it was used to explain physical development. Still, the earlier penumbra of metaphorical significance persisted, especially in printed popular culture, and no aspect persisted more powerfully than the notion that monsters were a warning.[36] Monsters revealed either the hidden condition or the destiny of mankind, biologically and/or morally. While Dudley Wilson and others distinguish scientific analysis from wonder and use this distinction to argue that the end of the eighteenth century marks the shift from "curiosity" to "science," wonder remained a vital impulse in an English culture searching for clues to its future.[37] Indeed, wonder directed the topics and terms of analysis and continued to inform the press's approach to social problems.[38] At the height of the English reaction to the French Revolution, when anxiety induced the regulation of political, social, moral, intellectual, and religious life, the traditional trope of monstrosity surfaced.[39] Challenging scientific explanations of deviation, it was deployed to define the animal part of humanity itself.

The notorious Monster of 1790 provides a cogent example of the way monstrosity came to denote social dissent. He focused political, social, and sexual anxiety on what made a man.[40] This forerunner of Jack the Ripper snaked through London, evading police and vigilantes, uttering obscenities to women and stabbing them in the thighs. Highly publicized by the press, the Monster's exploits terrified London and prompted paranoid rumors about gangs, banditti, and noblemen gone wild. When a suspect was finally arrested—Renwick Williams, a mild-mannered maker of artificial flowers—he embodied the effeminate opposite of monstrous violence. As a working-class gigolo or homosexual whose phalanx of female friends testified in his favor, however, he represented other forms of social threat: excessive sexual prowess or sexual ambiguity—both interpreted as social ambition. As a result, despite his alibis, he was condemned to Newgate. His trial drew a frenzy of attention; noblemen, workers, and journalists flocked to watch sex on display, laughing at the testimony of his gallantry from working-class women and pitying the injuries of the gentle victims. Caricaturists depicted the stabbed women as sexual curiosities, wearing copper undergarments to protect themselves. Some broadsides portrayed the Monster with a gigantic mouth, signifying monstrous appetite—the embodiment of Napoleonic ambition at home. Other prints showed the obdurate members of the court who leered at the salacious particulars as the true monsters.

The Monster embodied the slippage between inquiry and prurience, humanity and inhumanity, the natural and the unnatural. Although he looked "normal," and thus did not fit into teratological categories, he seemed to have acted in a fashion, at once human and inhuman, that resembled monstrosity or animality. Politically, legally, and psychologically, the Monster's motive remained as elusive as Elizabeth Canning's. What did he want? Whereas teratology located monstrosity corporeally, this Monster displayed a social bestiality. His sexual attacks hinted at a private identity beyond social conditioning, an identity whose publicity threatened harmonious relations between the classes and genders; this secret identity in turn seemed to warn of the collapse of civilized humanity into something either beyond nature, or so close to nature that it lay beyond culture. The public's fascination with the Monster suggested that perverse sexuality and sexual violence were broadly appealing: the case revealed a sympathetic bond between curious spectators and monstrosity.

This public appetite for spectacular performance, and the cultural representation of it as a curiosity that monsterizes spectators, characterizes many contemporary performances of scientific endeavor, but none more powerfully than hot-air ballooning. As ballooning swept through England and France from the 1780s to the 1820s, artists depicted, and print-sellers disseminated, colorful prints and cartoons of balloons that reveal them as a powerful contemporary image of the conversion of scientific progress into popular curiosity. Amateur scientists, wallpaper merchants, caricaturists, nationalists, chemical engineers, aerial performers, and satirists used the emblem of the balloon to advance themselves and their causes, and the result was a cacophony of competing discourses about the purpose, merits, and revelations of mechanical advancements and human ambitions. These discourses rework the issues of the previous century to define curiosity at the beginning of the next.

Balloons occupied several cultural spaces. The launching of the first Montgolfier hot-air balloon in the summer of 1783 also launched an ecstatic faith in a new "age of wonders" replicating the age of Newton, Cavendish (who discovered "inflammable air"), Priestley, and Boyle.[41] *The Balloon, or Aerostatic Spy*, lauding Lunardi, Blanchard, Sheldon, Jeffries, and Sadler, promises that once balloons are perfected and become cheaper, "By their means Intelligence may be conveyed to Cities besieged; inaccessible Mountains and trackless Wastes may be explored; and, in short, scarcely any Place on the Surface of the terraquous Globe will be impervious to the AERONAUTS."[42] In this period of deepening political tensions between England and France, balloons supplied a new field for international competition that illustrates the colonization of science as a part of national identity.[43] The English rivaled the French with a hydrogen balloon invented by the English Professor J. A. C. Charles in the same year as the hot-air "Montgolfière" ascended.[44] Since Englishmen had discovered both oxygen and inflammable air, some felt the balloon was rightfully their own invention.[45] Promoters revived the ideal of science as a symbol of the progress of peace by envisioning ballooning as the most recent example of the heroic quest for a new frontier. Prints typically depicted "the GALLANT LUNARDI" as a lone captain, waving a flag and staring solemnly into the skies from his lonely vessel (fig. 18).

Ballooning peaked as the modern manifestation of mass scientific culture: a re-evocation of the broadly hospitable science of the Renaissance that would bridge the divisions of learning and class and draw specialized and popular audiences together to embrace an invention at once scientific and aesthetic, technical and popular. Using the idiom of the Royal Society, balloonists portrayed their enterprises as scientific experiments and recorded every mathematical detail of their expeditions, along with the thrilling descriptions of the traditional travelogue. Like Katterfelto, they adopted an altruistic rhetoric to whip up public sympathy and respect, releasing ballooning from the narrow realm of mechanical engineering into an enterprise as a public good. As balloonists experimented with useless

Figure 18. "An Exact Representation of Mr. Lunardi's *New Balloon as it ascended with Himself 13 May 1785.*" (Printed and sold by Carington Bowles, no. 69 in St. Paul's Church Yard, London.) By permission of the British Library

devices like revolving fans or moulinets, as well as oars and sails, which de Lana had first suggested in 1670, the market brimmed with narratives, diagrams, and sketches of balloons being made, filled, and released, many drawn in the same technical fashion as illustrations of other inventions. Advertisements for ascensions invariably recorded the "Dimensions of the Globe" and the weight of air, globe, net, gondola, ornaments, and even oars, wings, fans, and people.[46]

Several books promote ballooning as popular science. George Kearsley, a prominent publisher of children's literature and popular miscellanies, issued an adaptation of *Considèrations sur Le Globe Aèrostatique* (1783) called *The Air Balloon: Or a Treatise on The Aerostatic Globe* (1783). It hails the invention as a belated resumption of the experimental concerns of the *Philosophical Transactions*, which, the author argues, has recently been preoccupied with "Moral Philosophy" at the expense of "Natural Philosophy."[47] To "satisfy the wishes of unlettered curiosity," Kearsley explains the properties of air and barometers, various methods of making air to inflate balloons, and how to construct an air balloon itself from household goods (6–7). The balloonist James Sadler's narrative concludes with the publisher's defense of ballooning as scientific progress. Quoting Bacon, "the great parent of inductive science," on the accidental nature of the discovery of truth, W. H. Tyrell excuses the creeping rate of aeronautic discovery by pointing out that the new-born enterprise requires great time, scientific expertise, repetitions, and skill to discover truths themselves "delicate."[48] The publisher's final protest—that "to reject the Art as useless because it has not rewarded our desultory efforts, would be of all conclusions the most unphilosophical"—is supported by the assertion that "AERO-STATION is too intimately connected with the entire range of Science, its Exhibitions are too brilliant and interesting not to deserve [public] patronage" (23).

Ballooning also promised fulfillment of the fantasy of a relentless advance of national power. Even before Napoleon used it for military surveillance in 1794, publicists saw it as a weapon. One 1784 broadside portrays four balloons in fighting order with a caption predicting "such Fights will be common (as Dunce to feel Rod) / In the Year of One Thousand eight Hundred and odd."[49] The balloon did become a symbol of Napoleonic ambition. The fourth in the satirical print series entitled *Constructing of Air Balloons for the Grand Monarque* depicts "Montgolfier in the Clouds," exclaiming: "O by gar! Dis be de grande invention—Dis will immortalize my King, my Country, and myself; We will declare de War against our ennemi; we will make des English quake, by gar."[50] Blowing bubbles from a long pipe, Montgolfier embodies the delusions of grandeur traditionally identified as a weakness of curious men. Significantly, his vanity takes the form of the desire for conquest—a contemporary manifestation of the derogation of curiosity as the restless desire to rise above others. Subsequently, a striped Regency balloon was prepared for James Sadler's ascent for the "Grand Jubilee in Celebration of Peace" between France and England after Waterloo on 1 August 1814, and tiny tickets stamped with balloons were printed as souvenirs of the Jubilee Fair in Hyde Park.[51] Balloons had failed as weapons of war, but they took off as symbols of national celebration. Centrally, the balloon represented not merely scientific "progress," but the popular staging of it. As a universal spectacle, an ascension drew all classes together in awe: an ascent in the early 1780s was a *"Moment d'Hilarité Universelle."*[52]

Balloons bordered art and performance. Because of their visual appeal and simple (if dangerous) mechanics, they symbolized adventure. Prints advertised ascensions, costing as much as five shillings a ticket, as popular amusement, while balloonists began to turn acrobats, one even ascending astride a white horse.[53] Balloon sculptures were displayed on tethers for poorer spectators. Crowds, at least at first, flocked to watch balloons, and printed representations of both the device itself and the popular experience of watching it ballooned themselves. These representations often focus on the sublime contrast between the miniature throngs and the lone floating machine. *"Expérience de la Machine Aréostatique* de Mrs. [i.e., Monsieur] Montgolfier, d'Anonai en Vivarais,"* for example, depicts a colored sphere floating at the very top of the print, a great expanse of empty air, and a minute palace, countryside, and mass of chattering, gaping people far below, and it rapidly appeared in an English version.[54] Such representations play with the oppositions between the rotund balloon and the spiky shapes of the people, between empty air and cluttered land, and between the near and far distance in order to emphasize the balloon ascent's violation of familiar perspective and experience. These prints present ballooning as an experiential rarity that breaks out of the order of the known: visually and conceptually, it is therefore curious.

The intense popular interest in the phenomenon of ballooning, however, aroused the concern of social watchdogs. As *The Balloon*, a miniature narrative issued by the Religious Tract Society in 1799, describes, "thousands of people . . . assembled" to watch ascensions: "Men, women, and children were crowded around," and as it floated beyond the city over a country village, the two tiny figures seated in its car waving flags, "the whole place was soon in a hubbub."[55] According to this narrative, children shout at the sight, shopkeepers rush to their doors, while their customers lean from the windows to see it, and villagers gaze mesmerized at the vanishing bubble in the sky. All normal business is suspended to watch the wonder. In contrast to the dazzled admiration of the townspeople, the servants of the farmers who help the crashed balloonists from their vessel laugh at the balloonists' folly, but even their traditional skepticism disrupts their duties: "One wondered if they had been up to the moon, and another wondered what they had brought down with them from the clouds, so that it was some time before the men set to work again as heartily as they had worked before" (5). This tract depicts ballooning as a distraction that draws people away from their proper tasks and social obligations. "*Symposia; or Table Talk* . . . Being a rhapsodical Hodge-podge, containing . . . BALLOON INTELLIGENCE for the Years 1785, 1786, and 1787" records "that all ranks of men seem to have forgot all other avocations, and that their attention is now collected like the *radii* of a circle, to one common *focus*, namely the *Pantheon*, where is exhibited Mr. *Lunardi*, his Balloon, his Dog, and his Cat."[56] Despite Lunardi's apparent popularity, the author of *Symposia* registers the contemporary distrust of ballooning as idleness, for he feels the need to defend Lunardi as "a wonderful man" and to recite a long list of those whom ballooning benefits, comprising mathematicians, metaphysicians, physicians, lawyers, politicians, naval and military gentlemen, merchants, manufacturers, mechanics, and farmers (xxiii). Indeed, the author claims that the thirst for novelty increases in proportion to the "refinement" of a civilization: "the roving imagination of a cultured and enlightened mind is seeking every where for new improvements, new enjoyments, and . . . new gratifications of his corporeal and mental sensations" (xxxiv). For this author, balloons represent progress and open up possibilities, from discovery to plunder and innovation to crime (23–24). Balloons are the vehicle of a popular curiosity threatening social disruption.

The accounts written by voyagers themselves scrupulously address all these concerns, methodically moving from a defense of the enterprise, through sentimental records of the crowds' compassion, to sublime description and technical detail. By the early nineteenth century, balloon events were carefully supervised to satisfy the tastes of all classes and to preserve the panache of scientific heroism. In the case of Sadler's ascent on 1 October 1812, physical separation enforced the class distinctions that ballooning tended to overlook, as military guards separated the crowds from the assembled spectators, themselves divided by lawn and platform. This physical separation of the performer and the watchers is reinforced by the rhetoric that valorizes Sadler's exploit as dangerous, romantically high-minded, and independent. In most popular posters and discourse, however, ballooning served as an emblem of commercialized leisure; reactive caricatures, many by George Cruikshank, reflect the fear that crowds with leisure to wonder have leisure to wander, like Godwin's character Caleb Williams, and possibly even to wander into revolutionary France.

As repeated failures accustomed spectators to disappointment, however, the balloon descended from being an emblem of scientific progress to a form of circus entertainment. It provided a forum to restage the conventional attack on the virtuoso for credulity, hypocrisy, the abuse of power, impotence, and fraud. One print, depicting Lunardi born on the shoulders of the cheering crowd in Tottenham Court Road, bears the superscription:

> An adventurous stripling so sweet Ovid sings
> Had the boldness to soar once on two mighty wings.
> Unguided by Judgment, and wandring too high
> He met his just Fate and was plungd from the Sky.[57]

Similarly, balloonists engaged in profiteering: Lunardi became a quasi-inventor, experimenting with a submersible "water balloon" or tiny lifeboat, and was portrayed as something between a scientist, a conjurer, and a hero.[58]

Elizabeth Inchbald capitalizes on this criticism of balloonists' trickery and ineptitude in *The Mogul Tale; or The Descent of the Balloon* (1788), a dramatic farce that mercilessly mocks scientific pretension. Inchbald's tale was no doubt stimulated by the balloon voyage of a Persian physician and two officers of the Royal Harem from Constantinople; they sailed across the sea to the courtyard of the Castle of Bursia, where a testimonial balloon was suspended from the Mosque of St. Sophia.[59] *The Mogul Tale* recounts the adventures of Johny, the cobbler, and his wife, Fanny, from Wapping who are blown off course from their month-long outing (or upping) and descend on the Seraglio of the Mogul. The play is dominated by the portrait of the fraudulent but feeble Doctor who acts as their balloon guide. Pedantic and idealistic in his speech, he embodies hypocrisy—the monstrous rift between body and mind that is seen as especially characteristic of Puritans like Malvolio and Tartuffe, and also of Puritan-infused natural science. While he pontificates on "the pure air we breath'd while so many degrees above the earth, [that] supplied every want," his companions remark satirically on his heavy consumption of ham, chicken, and wine.[60] Defensively, he replies, "That was only by way of experiment, I had no wants I assure you," whereupon Fanny bluntly counters with, "Why yes, you had, you know you wanted to kiss me when you thought Johny was asleep" (act 1, p. 4).

The Doctor, however, whatever his desires, is as deflated as his collapsed globe. Johny remarks that the Mogul need not fear the Doctor's depredations on his harem because "he has no longer any inflammable air about him, either in his balloon or in himself" (act 1, p. 4). When challenged by the pagan Mogul later in the play, he confesses, "I am a Doctor—I am a Doctor of music universally known, and acknowledged—master of legerdemain, adept in philosophy, giver of health, prolonger of life, child of the sun, interpreter of the stars, and privy councellor to the moon" (act 2, p. 18). While he attempts to dazzle the superstitious oriental, he reveals his own culture's slippage between fantasy, science, entertainment, and illusion. Indeed, he defines the balloon as the emblem of English philosophic vacancy: it is "a Machine of French invention, founded on English Philosophy, an experiment by air—lighter than air—a method of navigation in the Clouds with winds, wanting only another discovery, still in Nubibus" (act 2, p. 19). Since it was this "English Philosophy" of inflammable air that grounded the hot-air invention in the Mogul's land, this remark is simultaneously scientific and satirical: the balloon is vacation indeed.

Inchbald reinforces her equation of science and superstition by mirroring the Doctor in the Grand Mogul. Whereas the astonished women of the harem believe the party to be Gods, the Grand Mogul knows precisely who they are. Himself a kind of scientific tyrant, he decides to indulge himself by tormenting them before releasing them because "in the hour of reflection I love to contemplate that greatest work of heaven, the mind of man" (act 1, p. 7). His unchristian ethic echoes scientific indifference, but his human motives closely resemble those of the Doctor, who asks Johny to "contrive if you can to bring one of the females with you, as I want to try an experiment, which can live longest in the air, the women of this Country, or our own—N. B. Let her have black eyes, neither too large or too small, lest my experiment should fail" (act 2, p. 12). Experimentation becomes a code word for the male tool used for sexual exploitation—not practiced by but on women. Indeed, Inchbald emphasizes the misogynistic side of science when Johny, masquerading as the pope, becomes embroiled in a fight with the Mogul's eunuch over the ownership of Fanny, whom he dubs his "property" (act 2, p. 17). Science is also inhuman: the Doctor himself fears that "they are going to try some experiment on me, to broil me—to implame, perhaps to anatomize me"—images that identify appetite and experiment while evoking Hogarth's portrait of surgical dissection (act 2, p. 18).

As middle-class entertainment, ballooning could represent the sublime. Rumor traced its origin to Montgolfier's epiphanic sight of an orphan blowing soap bubbles or of billowing lingerie, but Anna Letitia Barbauld and Mrs. Sage, "The first English Female Aerial Traveller," saw ballooning as an emblem of transcendence.[61] Sage records, "We arose in a slow and majestic manner, forming a most beautiful object, amidst the acclamations of thousands, whose hearts at that moment appeared to feel but one sentiment, and that for the safety of the two adventurers. . . . The objects of my affection or esteem were . . . so very distant from me, and so perfectly unacquainted with my situation . . . that I seemed to exist but for myself."[62] Like the Romantic explorers Frankenstein and Walton, Sage desires escape from human complication for the contemplation of God in nature, and this contemplation essentializes her as a human beyond humanity.

One sentimental author uses the conceit of sublime transcendence via balloon to structure a picaresque in the tradition of adventure satires. His *Adventures of an Air Balloon* naughtily features a false imprint claiming it to be the fifth edition of 1780—three years before the first flight. This text personifies the balloon as a spectator on society who—like Eliza Haywood's invisible spy, Explorabilis—can see without being seen and, as a travelogue, follows the lead of spa culture in discovering corruption in the city and virtue and health in rural nature.[63] Another text written in the manner of Delariviére Manley uses balloon travel for satire: "*The Modern Atalantis: or, the* DEVIL *in an* AIR BALLOON, containing the characters and secret Memoirs of the most conspicuous Persons of High Quality, of Both Sexes, in the Island of Libertusia" (1784) fantasizes that demons, envious of the "vast machine" created by man's "restless ingenuity," fly with the hero Urgando and point out the follies of ground-bound sparks and belles in the cities below.[64] The novel entitled *The Balloon, or Aerostatic Spy* recounts the story of a Robinson Crusoe-like inventor stranded on a West Indian island who constructs a balloon from hide (45–47). These texts represent the balloon, like other inventions, as the means for unfettered observation into others' affairs.

Other writers, reviving traditional charges against curiosity, used the balloon to parody sublime disinterest. Since the balloon proffered the future inhabitation of the sphere above the earth, a sphere conceived as physical rather than metaphysical, it suggested escape, fantasy, ambition, delusion, even lunacy. One illustration, entitled "Chevalier Humgruffier and the Marquis de Gull making an excursion to the Moon in their new Aerial Vehicle," depicts Jean-Pierre Blanchard and Dr. John Jeffries in the tradition of utopian voyagers, rising aloft in a boat harnessed to a starry globe.[65] A watercolor by P. Sandby shows an enormous, grinning, long-eared head, anchored on both sides by fashionable spectators of a similarly balloon-like shape who admire it with reflective grins. Religious enthusiasts glossed this material version of spiritual ascent in several ways. "We are all too fond of this trade of ballooning," pronounces Margaret Hill, the pious old woman in *The Balloon* who knits while others rush to watch the floating bubble, "and the pride of our hearts is always persuading us to get above the heads of our neighbours; but what says the bible? 'Pride goeth before destruction, and haughty spirit before a fall.' Now my advice is not to give over sending balloons up into the air, but only to let them be of a different kind ... prayers and praises" (7). Caricatures appeared of balloons festooned with instruments, entertainments, and decorations, like Etienne Gaspard Robertson's "'*La Minerve,' Vaisseau Aërien Destiné aux Découvertes, 1803*," which sported, among many other features, a full orchestra, a birdcage bordello with two floors, a gigantic barrel-shaped cellar accessed by a long ladder, and, slung on the far right, an outhouse toilet. Such images modernize a traditional complaint against scientific inventions as merely expensive new toys facilitating pride, conquest, vice, and other abuses of power.

Many satirists used the balloon and the practice of ballooning to lambaste hubris, naiveté, the vanity of mankind's dreams, and a range of social vices and flaws, from credulity to overpopulation.[66] A political broadside uses the balloon to condemn Morret by categorizing him and it as simply further examples of traditional frauds perpetrated on the public by mercenary tricksters (fig. 19). In "The Air Balloon; or, Flying Mortal," Mary Alcock humorously mocks the dreams of transcendent power implied by the promises of ambitious aeronauts and weekend balloon voyagers.[67] Composed "for the benefit of those, who wishing to become AERIAL BEINGS, may have too much spirit and ambition to continue a day longer to creep on the earth, like the brute beasts which perish," a note hints, "The *Air Balloon* will be found to be of the greatest importance to those who wish TO EVADE THE LAWS OF THEIR KING OR COUNTRY." With increasing arrogance, the speaker rises above the "enquiring" multitude (18); moreover, she mocks scientific ambition by pitying Newton and commemorating "greater *Newtons*" who fly aloft "and leave the stupid multitude below" (st. 6, 33, 36, p. 4). After triumphing over distance, party politics, law, poetry, and geography, the poem ends with a paean to dizzying superiority:

Figure 19. "English Credulity, or the Chevalere Morret taking a French Leave." 17 August
1784. (Published by W. Wells, no. 132 Fleet Street.) This satire portrays the
French Chevalier clutching a bag of guineas and escaping atop an "Areostatic
Diligence" to Ostend; he is surrounded by emblems of popular frauds deceiving
the credulous learned, including Mary Toft; the Stokewell Wonder, a
poltergeist; the Bottle Conjuror; and the Cock Lane Ghost. Two overfed
gentlemen enviously wish him well. By permission of the British Library

How few the worldly evils now I dread,
No more confin'd this narrow earth to tread:
Should fire, or water, spread destruction drear;
Or earth-quake shake this sublunary sphere,
In Air balloon to distant realms I'd fly,
And leave the creeping world, to sink and dye.
     (St. 12, lines 67–72, p. 7)

Like Dr. Frankenstein, the aeronaut ignores conventional science to rein-
flate exploded ideas and find new truths. Both kinds of science, however,
result only in the elevation of the scientist, not in the benefit of mankind.
Balloons appear as mankind's newest invention to escape the human coil
and fulfill the ambition for immortality—not, in this case, by creating a
monster but by rising above the monstrous mob and seeing the world from
a divine perspective.[68]

Ballooning supplied the occasion for the first public recognition of a
new, mass audience for curious spectacle. All England, it seemed, had the
leisure to watch these ascensions from rooftops, trees, balconies, and
parks—and, presumably, to dream of themselves rising above the very curious mob they composed. This tension between satirical and worshipful
depictions placed ballooning on the margin of entertainment and science,
art and nature—like museums. Like popular curiosity itself, ballooning
shifts from being regarded as an aspect of social progress to being casti-
gated as a sign of cultural corruption, fed by the laboring classes' misuse of
their overabundant leisure. As disasters grew and improvements declined,
balloon performers increasingly occupied the status of circus performers.
No longer scientists, they now portrayed themselves as magicians who
performed marvelous acts of derring-do above the earth. Curiosity shifts
from the elite enterprise of amateur gentlemen to a sign of the abuse of
mental resources by decadent and undisciplined masses. It remains, however, the sign of social ambition.

CURIOSITY AS SOCIAL REFORM

As law courts and popular broadsides isolate and ridicule aberrant Others
as curiosities and curiosity itself as aberration, many late century novels
valorize curiosity as revolution and curious people as reformers. These dis-
parate views of curiosity and the curious reflect the struggle in contemporary culture between competing ideals and classes. The difference between
laudable and impious inquiry lies in who conducts such inquiry, on what

topics, and how. While popular curiosity signifies credulity and conformity—the appetite for sensational spectacle—learned inquiry denotes
precisely the opposite: skepticism and individuality. It is tautologically this
individuality that marks the gentility of the learned inquirer and his inquiry; a parallel individuality in the unlearned shows inappropriate ambition to transcend his or her social place.

Fundamental to this distinction between laudable and impious inquiry
is the ambiguity of definitions demarcating the natural and either the unnatural or the supernatural. This ambiguity filtered into every area of English public life at the end of the eighteenth century. Just as the legal question of the existence and activities of witches touched on the margins of
superstition, religion, and empirical philosophy, so the representation of
crime itself partook of both superstitious and literalistic language in the
courts and, especially, in the literary arena.[69] Unnatural men driven by natural urges—or natural men driven by unnatural urges—form the subjects
of many Romantic and Gothic novels from the period. Indeed, the question of the naturalness of curiosity is one of the primary philosophical
questions behind all Gothic fictions. None shows this more clearly than
Caleb Williams, a Romantic reworking of the Prometheus myth and of the
early modern adjurations against illegitimate prying, and this novel itself
is indebted to another fictional tour de force of curiosity: Ann Radcliffe's
The Mysteries of Udolpho.

In 1794, three years after Renwick Williams was publicly condemned
as the Monster and refused a retrial, William Godwin was reading Ann
Radcliffe's *The Mysteries of Udolpho* while writing *Caleb Williams*.[70] From
Radcliffe, Godwin borrowed not only the archetypal struggle between
youth and authority, and the Gothic mood of brooding oppression, but
also Radcliffe's central trope: curiosity. Both books are plotted around the
consequences of unregulated inquiry, and notwithstanding their enlightened philosophies, both portray curiosity as a cultural ambition that dangerously sexualizes identity and threatens the very integrity of the self.[71]

Representing curiosity alternately as a threat to established institutions
and as a promise of progress, fin de siècle discourse both lauds the Aristotelian urge to know and denigrates the impertinent desire to inquire. For the
writers of 1794, the familiar issue took on added significance, for they were
living in a period of postempirical disillusion, when it seemed that the
methods of science could not answer the problems of society.[72] Under the
pressure of contemporary debates, these novels transform a traditional exploration of the limits of curiosity into a political drama about what happens to identity in an environment rent by tyranny and oppression. The

topical issue of the conflict between interpretations of mankind's nature as nobly free or as perilously wild is thus dramatized through reworking a traditional discourse that tests the limits, consequences, and rewards of curiosity. Curiosity expresses the struggle to define the self for oneself, as well as the correlative fear of a disintegration of identity in a postrevolutionary period.[73]

On several fictional levels—plot, characterization, and metaphor—both Radcliffe and Godwin explore the way curiosity demarcates and dismantles identity. As a variety of passion, the opponent of enlightened reason, curiosity is a fundamental motive in both novels. Both plots center on the discovery by a disenfranchised seeker—young woman or young servant—of a concealed past that liberates their identity. In *The Mysteries of Udolpho*, Radcliffe's heroine, Emily St. Aubert, orphaned and stripped of her rightful estate, is given over to the care of a tyrannical guardian, Signor Montoni, ambitious, restless, mercenary, a perpetrator both of civil wars and domestic discord. Through observation and inquiry, Emily discovers that he is a robber and a murderer and that she herself is by birth the legal owner of his estates. After a series of sensational adventures and rational decisions, including relinquishing her claim to preserve her life, Emily wins not only her own estate but that of her father: law conquers violence. Subplots dramatize the alternative to her self-disciplined submission through the figure of Signora Laurentini di Udolpho, who commits murder for sexual passion and becomes insane. While Emily triumphs through her rational virtue, her superstitious curiosity torments her throughout the novel. Her trials arise as much from the transgressive probings of her mind as from the tyranny of her guardian.

Caleb Williams similarly recounts the exposure of murder, the madness murder produces, and the (belated) restoration of social justice through curiosity.[74] Caleb, observing the melancholy of his master Falkland, inquires persistently into his past, finally to discover him to be a murderer thrice over; this knowledge eventually frees Caleb from his role as dependent and enables him to stand equal with his master. Falkland, however, is a murderer obsessed by his secret, and as Caleb himself realizes, equality with a murderer makes Caleb into a murderer himself. Caleb's curiosity liberates him from servitude and dooms him to wandering without a social identity. In the traditional characterology of seventeenth-century satire, the types of the credulous and the curious man are linked; both are believers in a unsubstantiated world.[75] Both Emily and Caleb suffer from this mental debility: both reject the apparent for the invisible, the accepted for the unacceptable. Such debility subjects them both to mental instability.

Indeed, it is on the level of character conveyed through the psychological texture of the narrative that the ambiguity of curiosity is dramatized. These heroes are flawed by their very virtue. Their curiosity, the same impulse that drives them to seek the truth and see justice done, marks them as discontented, possessed by irrational, antisocial urges, even as superstitious: motivated by impulses antagonistic to neoclassical ideals of control and self-possession. Caleb and Emily also demonstrate modern youths' inability to use their leisure for self-improvement; instead, they fret at the margins of reality, brooding on their identities or on the nature of the natural. Both Emily's exemplary father, St. Aubert, and the plot reprove Emily for indulging emotions that spur her imagination. However, whereas Emily learns to discipline desire to control her curiosity, Caleb's curiosity overwhelms him. Self-cultivated, Emily resists the identities of wife, servant, lover, nun, and madwoman thrust upon her by Montoni, Count Morano, her aunt, Agnes, Dupont, and others. Caleb, on the other hand, indulging his passionate curiosity, pursues information and in the end destroys his master's mastery—and thus his own identity: Caleb's desire to own the other consumes him. As a moral example, Emily inherits; she possesses culture where Caleb is possessed by it: "I have now no character," he admits at the end of his chronicle.

When Ann Radcliffe was writing, the shadow of the French Revolution and the Terror had chilled the Romantic fervor for free inquiry and political and social justice—at least for some. Mary Wollstonecraft, Hester Chapone, Hannah More, Lady Pennington, and many other women moralists were proposing a new rational ideal for women, albeit one channeled by contemporary anxieties about the disintegration of society. Such cultural forces sharpened the traditional tensions over curiosity by pitting the desire for a feminine ideal of duty and rationality against the fear of women's inquiry and penetration into the public sphere. These women moralists suggest that the right use for women's minds for the public good is to speculate only on the empirically perceptible and the socially categorized: the roles of daughter, wife, mother. They are not to question the unknown: the motives of murderers, the occult, fairies, ghosts, and sexual impulses.

Radcliffe's novels thematize female curiosity by portraying it as both social revolution and personal danger. Many critics have remarked on the sexual undercurrents in Radcliffe's fiction, but it is the larger issue of inquiry that is Radcliffe's central concern.[76] Indeed, Radcliffe's narrator neither entirely endorses nor entirely condemns her heroines' curiosity; moreover, while tracing an empirical narrative, her novels offer readers a pleasure that is distinctly not rational.[77] Even while she condemns her heroines' sensitivity to nature as a weak feminization of science as much as an admirable aesthetic capacity, the focus of her novels is women's probing into the hidden secrets of the past, secrets concerning both domestic and political power, religion, inheritance, and wealth: all the substantial institutions of society. The heroines' curiosity shakes the status quo; in so doing, however, it also threatens their own identity. Through a narrative style that emphasizes uncertainty by its multiple qualifiers and shifting point of view, and through a repetitive structure that reintroduces the moral and social consequences of decisions already made, Radcliffe underscores the dangers of female inquiry. Questioning and questing hazard virginity and purity, of mind as well as body. Her novels, indeed, pit the threat of irremediable corruption of the woman against the exposure and destruction of the state. Indeed, partly because Radcliffe's heroines do not know their genealogies, they are apparently (but not really) free from social bonds. This freedom licenses their unrestricted inquiry into the bases of society.

Radcliffe's redefinition of the novel as the dynamic of female curiosity provides a structure for Jane Austen's work. When, in *Northanger Abbey* (1806/1818), Austen ridicules her heroine for interpreting Radcliffe's *The Mysteries of Udolpho* literally, she is partly commenting on the way in which female curiosity is culturally categorized.[78] Catherine Morland, fascinated by the mystery of what lies behind the black veil, is unable to concentrate on the social life around her. Like Radcliffe herself, Austen indicates both applause and disapproval of Catherine's condition. Contemporary critics of women's reading claim that Catherine is wasting the social resource of her mind by dwelling on fiction when her duty lies in responding to the public scene, a perspective Austen, as a novelist, refutes in her defense of novels in chapter five. Indeed, Catherine's desire to tear back the veil comments ironically on the social masquerade in front of her, epitomized by her affected and vain companion, Isabella Thorpe. Which is the greater fiction? Although untutored—indeed, *because* untutored—Catherine's curiosity exposes the superficiality of the social posturing she sees before her. But, like Radcliffe's heroines, Catherine pays for her preoccupation: her socially illegitimate curiosity earns her Henry's reproof and bitter regrets. If Catherine sees the truth behind the veil—the General's monstrous avarice and violence; the injustice of birth, inheritance, and appearance; the hypocrisy of friends and brothers (and it is questionable whether she permits herself really to know these things)—she cannot remedy it: there is no dramatic escape in Austen's world.

Austen's irony results from a postrevolutionary perspective that neither Radcliffe nor Godwin had yet experienced. Sexualized oppression galvanizes Radcliffe's and Godwin's most significant similarity: their ambiguous treatment of their propelling motive, curiosity.[79] Curiosity establishes fresh identity by deconstructing conventional roles. Emily's and Caleb's inquiry enacts their liberation from repressive custom and opens their way to social equality. By questioning Montoni's behavior and motives, Emily challenges his usurped authority, exposes his wickedness, and asserts her probity. Caleb's probing eventually reveals Falkland's crimes and the corresponding flaws in the social structure that supports him. This portrayal of free inquiry—the individual challenge to the status quo—marks the two novels as postrevolutionary rejections of political oppression.

Nonetheless, both authors also depict inquiry as a desire that compromises not only society, but also the virtue and integrity of heroines and heroes themselves. Although Emily and Caleb display courageous independence in interrogating Montoni and Falkland, their questions reveal morally suspect desire that mirrors that of their oppressors—the desire for power, for domination, for superiority, for property.[80] Because Montoni repeatedly ignores, attacks, or evades Emily's curiosity and because she must take recourse in silence, she is restored to her integrity as submissive sufferer, but Caleb's success transforms him into his own enemy. Releasing yet imprisoning, this heroic curiosity is at once the sign of the freeborn mind and of irrational, undisciplined appetite. This paradoxical quality expresses the contemporary tension between enlightenment and traditional ideals.

This trait of intellectual ambition, like desire, is predicated on lack, on the absence of the desired thing: knowledge. Thus, in these novels, the bold confrontation with the status quo implies an impious quest for spiritual freedom in a fallen world—the Gothic quest itself. This quest rejects the material reality revealed through empirical science for its negative, the world of wonder, idealism, irrationality—all available to the popular imagination through folk tradition. Indeed, both Radcliffe's and Godwin's novels dramatize the limitations of empiricism in a world always partly inexplicable. As Terry Castle has argued, Radcliffe spectralizes her others.[81] Representing the irrepressible, irrational shadows of the mind, these spirits threaten to possess Emily, Radcliffe's heroine; she must use empirical observation and reason to combat them. Although she triumphs, this triumph remains ambiguous. Even at her wedding, a ceremonial tapestry celebrating "necromantic feats" symbolizes her partial inhabitation in unseen spheres. Similarly, Godwin infuses Caleb's curiosity with a mesmerizing, antirational power: it is a "demon" that "possesse[s]" him at the expense of his life and sanity, rather than a tool that he can use.[82] By depicting curiosity as a trap and an escape, these novels articulate the tension between the contemporary ideal of transparency—the conviction that if everything were revealed by clear questions and honest answers, all would be reasonable and controllable—and a traditional, pessimistic conviction that what is hidden is wisely hidden, a philosophical fear of hidden evil growing as the century drew to a close.[83]

The double view of curiosity in these fictions reflects their mediating function as bridges between philosophical treatises and entertainment for middle-class and servant audiences familiar with biblical indictments against undisciplined curiosity.[84] Godwin refers explicitly to this function when he defines his novel as aimed at "persons whom books of philosophy and science are never likely to reach."[85] Indeed, he alludes to the popular tradition in his preface to the 1832 edition when he records playing with the resemblance between his idea and Bluebeard: "Caleb Williams was the wife, who in spite of warning, persisted in his attempts to discover the forbidden secret."[86] Radcliffe not only wrote for readers of her class and gender, but simultaneously published verse in periodicals bought by the same audiences.[87] The tales inserted in both novels, Radcliffe's romance of Lady Blanche De Villefort and Godwin's story of Emily Melvile, resemble in their typical characterology, self-enclosed narratives, and sentimental motifs the republished vignettes culled from Sterne, Mackenzie, Goldsmith, and other sentimental writers littering the popular market at the end of the century.[88] Moreover, just as both writers mix indictments and endorsements of sentimentalism, both move between narrative modes: Radcliffe employs poetry, meditation, description, and narrative, while Godwin, less heterogeneously, merges reportage and fictional autobiography. Their medley of forms permits a medley of messages characteristic of the genre of the novel, which was founded on the audience's multiple desires for novelty, sensation, and revelation.[89] Like Shelley's *Frankenstein*, these are novels written for sale: they are commodities purveying instruction through delight to an audience accustomed to buying culture. The fluidity of genre is mirrored by the instability of the Gothic heroes, who move between idealized exempla and cautionary protagonists. Accordingly, both novels—and *Frankenstein* too—participate in a class-colored ambivalence about curiosity as the misuse of leisure. Both Emily and Caleb abuse their mental and occupational freedom.

In *The Mysteries of Udolpho*, curiosity slips between the central poles of value. Positioned between empiricism and superstition, reason and imagination, it represents the distinction between mental masculinity and femininity, and between supervisory, elite mastery and instinctive, uncontrolled subordination. In St. Aubert, Emily's father and tutor in self-command—the control of sensibility and imagination—curiosity is the disciplined examination of nature. He and M. Barreaux botanize rather than rhapsodize over nature, exercising an amateur science that replaces Romantic enthusiasm and testifies to a pious, enlightened reason. Upon seeing a mysterious light in the woods, he identifies the "glow worm," where Emily sees fanciful fairies.[90] His "science, rather than the eye, enable[s] him to describe" scenes beyond his vision, such as Emily can describe only through unreliable imagination. Her ignorance of such science induces her to believe that the pictorial image of death, inadequately observed, is a murdered body.

Emily's curiosity, moreover, like Eve's original curiosity, is transgressive with specifically sexual implications. Despite serving as her avenue to self-discovery and as the principle that drives the truth from the shadows, her curiosity torments her with irrational fears throughout the novel. When she peeps at St. Aubert grieving over the miniature of his sister, she understands the scene as illicit love (26); Radcliffe enables her to reassert her innocence by burning his papers *without examining them*," a task almost beyond her power (78; original italics). As she begins the task by pulling papers and money from their secret cavity, her "excellent understanding" suffers from a "temporary failure" manifested by "superstition" in the form of visions of the ghost of her father watching her perform his command (102–3). She struggles between "Returning reason" and a curiosity that leads her to "transgressing her father's strict injunction" (103). But her "re-animated . . . sense of duty" brings about "the triumph of integrity over temptation" (103). Emily's obedience cures her of Pandora's crime and Eve's sin and returns her to patriarchy, possession, and domination.[91] This obedience is portrayed as equivalent to "reason" and opposed to "inflaming" imagination, superstition, and curiosity.

Even while overtly reproving it, however, Radcliffe identifies this curiosity as the female sublime. Predicated on ignorance and awe, it produces the sensation of terror and humility that Burke identified as the pious apprehension of mortality. Whereas St. Aubert experiences sublimity through the scientific understanding of nature, Emily feels it through inquiry into human affairs. When she determines to examine the veiled picture "which had attracted her curiosity," she experiences "a faint degree of terror" from its "mystery," a terror the narrator condones: "But a terror of this nature, as it occupies and expands the mind, and elevates it to high expectation, is purely sublime, and leads us, by a kind of fascination, to seek even the object, from which we appear to shrink" (248). Later, sensing movement on the ramparts, "a thrilling curiosity" draws Emily to stay

(356). Even as this curiosity reveals Emily's own mortality to her and fills her with religious awe, it seeps into superstition, the enemy of reason. Like superstition, female curiosity refutes empirical fact and privileges unsubstantiated rumor and traditional mythic wisdom. Most of Emily's misobservations, including that of the veiled memento mori, are conditioned by her practice of gossiping with her serving maid, Annette. Indeed, Annette scoffs at Emily's decorum by declaring that the servants "had all a little more *curiousness* than you had," and the narrator identifies "surprise and curiosity" as "natural" to Annette (279, original italics; 297). Emily's curiosity threatens her class status.

Similarly, Caleb's "ruling passion" is curiosity (118). Since it is a "principle stronger in [his] bosom than even the love of independence," it serves as the tyrant over his mind: it is his owner, the element of his identity that possesses the rest.[92] Thus, it is equivalent to Falkland's love of fame or reputation, the "ruling passion" that tyrannizes over his benevolence (122). Caleb admits that "curiosity is a restless propensity" that brings on its own danger (113), childish and "unreasonable" (144), yet this is the trait that defines Caleb as socially ambitious, a threat to the established order. His curiosity lifts Caleb above his birth. Although a peasant, Caleb explains, "I had an inquisitive mind, and neglected no means of information," and he claims that in prompting him to high tales rather than low gossip, his "curiosity . . . was not entirely ignoble" (3–4). Caleb's curiosity protects him from tyranny by redeeming him from degradation in prison: asking, "Have I not been employed from my infancy in gratifying an insatiable curiosity?" he employs his imagination to remain "insensible to the disorder" surrounding him (184). Moreover, Caleb's curiosity dispels the mystification of social rituals and prejudices, bringing reason and logic to replace superstition. Although Caleb notes that "Mr. Falkland had always been to [his] imagination an object of wonder" and remarks that "that which excites our wonder we scarcely suppose ourselves competent to analyze," nonetheless, Caleb penetrates this "marvel" to find the murderer (297). After his initial wonder at Collins's recital of Falkland's history, Caleb "turn[s]" the tale "a thousand ways" to extract its mystery, explaining that "to do what is forbidden always has its charms, because we have an indistinct apprehension of something arbitrary and tyrannical in the prohibition" (107). In his account of the composition of the novel, Godwin writes that his vision of a Gothic pursuit tale "could best be effected by a secret murder, to the investigation of which the innocent victim should be impelled by an unconquerable spirit of curiosity."[93] Curiosity thus designates the individual quest to defeat despotism.

Caleb's curiosity, however, transgresses the limits of reason and becomes tyrannical: he not longer possesses curiosity; it, as an irrational impulse, possesses him. He blames his curiosity for his fate, asserting, "My offence had merely been a mistaken thirst of knowledge . . . ungoverned curiosity" (133). While this certainly suggests irony on Godwin's part, it also points to the pollution in curiosity itself. If this trait permits Caleb to excel, it also drives his downfall. This ambiguity arises from the double nature of curiosity as an intellectual appetite, the product of reason turned into passion. Godwin blatantly locates his narrator-hero within a Christian tradition that records the history of the chosen people after the Fall.[94] As Robert Kiely notes, Caleb's curiosity leads to the loss of innocence, a biblical parallel to the contemporary political condition of surveillance.[95] Caleb confesses that his adventurousness stems from "the gratification of an infantine and unreasonable curiosity." This venturesome curiosity drives him to open Falkland's "trunk," releasing like Pandora all evils but Hope (143–44).

In this regard, Caleb's Eve-like curiosity resembles sexual passion, bringing to the fore the ominously erotic quality of his relationship with the sentimentally feminine Falkland. This sexualized sense of self compromises identity by making it vulnerable and antirational. Caleb and Falkland love each other because, in the postlapsarian world, they create each other. Falkland's crime creates Caleb's identity—curiosity—and Falkland's crime is the result of commodifying his own identity. He is "the fool of honour and fame" (102, 135). He makes reputation, the public shadow of himself, his "idol," his "jewel" (102). It is in defending this property—this sexualized, objectified self—that he commits every one of his crimes. Both Caleb and Falkland act as pursuer and pursued, attempting to possess rather than be possessed by the other. This power struggle has sexual overtones that underscore the biblical context of curiosity as forbidden knowledge, carnal knowledge, the knowledge of human origins. When he has convinced himself of Falkland's crime by watching Falkland's guilty response to a parallel case brought to him as a justice of the peace to try, Caleb rushes into the garden, ecstatic with knowledge:

> While I thus proceeded with hasty steps along the most secret
> paths of the garden, and from time to time gave vent to the tumult
> of my thoughts in involuntary exclamations, I felt as if my animal
> system had undergone a total revolution. My blood boiled within
> me. I was conscious of a kind of rapture for which I could not
> account. I was solemn, yet full of rapid emotion, burning with

indignation and energy. In the very tempest and hurricane of the
passions, I seem to enjoy the most soul-ravishing calm. I cannot
better express the then state of my mind, than by saying, I was
never so perfectly alive as at that moment. (129–30)

In the garden, released from the house, Caleb experiences a kind of or-
gasm, a sexualized penetration of Falkland's secret that sows the seeds for
and eventually gives birth to an alternative, albeit negative, identity as
someone who is not a servant.

In both *Caleb Williams* and *The Mysteries of Udolpho*, the tendency of
curiosity to fragment identity, to overtake or possess the possessor, colors
curiosity as a dangerous virtue. The works both prohibit and permit transgression, re-inscribe the necessity of traditional limits and the necessity
of violating them, advocate restraint and yet license excess.[96] This radical
deconstruction of curiosity informs many Romantic texts, most notably
the novel that has come to represent the Romantic challenge to scientific
progress, Mary Shelley's *Frankenstein* (1818).[97] *Frankenstein* has spawned a
legion of interpretations. The misshapen monster that the idealistic Doctor Frankenstein creates can be interpreted as a symbol of a huge range of
abuses and problems: of scientific or industrial hubris, the masculine attempt to reproduce without the feminine principle; of the revenge of nature for mankind's abuses; of the separation of poetry from science; of the
Oedipal instinct; of the alienated proletariat; even of language itself.[98]
Working off the argument that "the metaphor of monster turns into the
monstrosity of metaphor," Fred Botting underscores the destabilizations of
authority and order that the monstrous excesses in and of the book and
even of the book's own progeny in film and literature engender.[99] More
recently, James A. Heffernan has suggested that the *monstrum* reveals desire itself, a desire created and repressed by the Victorians.[100] All of these
possibilities, however, really reflect the fundamental and simple fact that
Dr. Frankenstein's acts of inquiry, invention, and rejection are a series of
repeated violations of nature by impious investigation. In the context of a
commonly known, literary discourse already over a hundred years old and
contemporaneously sharpened by revolution, Frankenstein's monster is the
impulse that separates, both ontologically and psychologically, men from
beasts and Gods: curiosity itself.

Shelley deliberately presents her story as a mythic, rather than a realistic, narrative. The narrative places Dr. Frankenstein's central story in a
quadruple frame. Frankenstein, discovered in pursuit of his monster in the

remote North Pole, relates his tale to Walton, his adventuring doppel-gänger, who writes it to his sister Margaret: this letter is what Shelley's readers encounter. Moreover, Frankenstein's own account subsumes Eliza-beth's letters and the monster's autobiography. Readers thus encounter Frankenstein's tale through frames that reinforce the traditional indictment of curiosity. Readerly curiosity is incited by Walton's and Frankenstein's promises to tell tales of wild adventure into unknown and forbidden areas, and it is titillated by reading private conversations and letters. The struc-ture of the novel thus implicates us in the story and makes reading itself an ambitious act of transgression.

Curiosity as adventure earns an ambiguous condemnation that yet allows room for envious wonder. Walton's admiring ambition or ambitious admiration of the wretched Frankenstein foreshadows his own plight should he continue to chase dreams across the polar wilds; exploration is condemned as a soul-searing loneliness that Walton articulates in every letter. This loneliness is one of the main costs of curiosity: it is the mon-ster's plight as he lives without love, and correspondingly it is Franken-stein's plight, as his lovelessly created monster murders all the people Frank-enstein loved, leaving him, too, alone with hatred. The monster's own experience of social rejection serves to satirize a society based hypocriti-cally on superficial values even while it reinforces the necessity of human interaction for happiness and mental health.

Frankenstein's monster shares the trait of curiosity. By enduing him with subjectivity, the monster's autobiography proves his humanity. In-formed by Locke's and Hume's theories of the growth of human under-standing, the autobiography is itself a chronicle of the discovery of the world that parodies earlier literature. The monster's naive encounters with nature evoke *Robinson Crusoe*, while the awakening of his intellect and sen-sitivity through the discovery of literature echoes the autobiographies of Gibbon and Rousseau. His natural inquisitiveness here appears as the very trait that marks him as human. At the same time, he suffers socially for his curiosity. When he learns "that the possessions most esteemed by your fellow-creatures were, high and unsullied descent united with riches," he discovers the shallowness of a Yahoo-like creature that neglects divine rea-son for glittering dross (69). Similarly, despite learning to love the virtues of the De Lacey family, he exposes their hypocrisy when even this family of ideal rural cottagers rejects him because of visual and ontological "preju-dice" (77). Such indictments of shallow social values echo the sentimental dicta in travelogues by Sterne and Mackenzie, and they even touch on

Swift's satiric reversal of monsters and men in *Gulliver's Travels*. If the monster's initial discoveries open the world to him, they also make that world intolerable.

The sentimental value of human sociability is, in turn, heavily underscored by repeated accounts of how Frankenstein went astray. First, like Robinson Crusoe, he disobeys his father's injunctions, not by venturing literally on forbidden seas but by reading forbidden material secretly (19). This initial sin is reinforced by his neglect of his proper duties: "partly from curiosity, and partly, from idleness," he dabbles in the discredited sciences (24). Second, he rejects his social role, ignoring friends, lover, and family. Self-taught, he conceives antisocial ambitions. This rejection of social connections distorts his nature. He pursues ugliness instead of beauty, as do all who worship curiosity over symmetry; this pursuit is symbolized in part by his dedication to M. Krempe despite his "repulsive physiognomy and manners" (25). Moreover, Frankenstein believes Krempe's features make him "not on that account the less valuable," an ironic foreshadowing of the social rejection of the monster; his disregard for beauty—equated with harmony and sociability—eventually condemns him to live with ugliness, violence, and isolation.

Frankenstein's curiosity also entails rejecting the golden balance of mental and physical, private and social pursuits that forms the Horatian ideal, in order to concentrate obsessively on a single study: the natural philosophy that he ambitiously hopes will lead him to excel all mankind (25). "I seemed to have lost all soul or sensation but for this one pursuit," he confesses, when trying to explain why he persisted in his horrible enterprise despite a natural repugnance (28). Such self-distortion pits part of man's nature against itself and makes the curious man either a hypocrite or a monster: "My internal being was in a state of insurrection and turmoil," Frankenstein recounts.[101] His curiosity is so excessive that it pulls him away from his human nature and, until Clerval "called forth the better feelings of [his] heart," costs him his human integrity (29, 37). Curiosity thus verges on madness, the sign of humanity alienated from itself.[102] All of Frankenstein's errors evoke traditional indictments of curiosity, and all demonstrate Frankenstein's corrupt ambition to be something other than himself. "Learn from me," he intones to Walton, "if not by my precepts, at least by my example, how dangerous is the acquirement of knowledge, and how much happier that man is who believes his native town to be the world, than he who aspires to become greater than his nature will allow" (27).

Throughout the novel, Shelley employs the term "curiosity" to mean an investigation infected with discreditable ambition, and she explicates it in a range of ways. Early in the narrative, Dr. Frankenstein notes that his inquiries after the monster have "excited [Walton's] curiosity," and he admires Walton's restraint in asking nothing, whereupon Walton replies, "Certainly; it would indeed be very impertinent and inhuman in me to trouble you with any inquisitiveness of mine" (13). Walton's "inhuman impertinence"—his desire to know evil—nonetheless appears in his own narrative, which is explosive with the desire to discover and penetrate both nature in its polar extreme, and man in the form of Frankenstein in extremis. Walton learns, however, to abjure his ambitious journey.

Frankenstein himself deplores his own youthful "lofty ambition" and the pride that had led him to think that his creation of a "sensitive and rational animal" had lifted him above "the herd of common projectors" (123). Yet in a fevered attempt to draw all the ship into death with him, he adjures Walton's men to pursue their "glorious expedition" (125). All glorious enterprises fail, however; the sublime gives way to the beautiful, and Walton returns to human love. Indeed, the book draws to an end with the dying Dr. Frankenstein's injunction to Walton, his questing alter ego, to "seek happiness in tranquillity, and avoid ambition, even if it be only the apparently innocent one of distinguishing yourself in science and discoveries" (127). Shelley revives a traditional castigation of curiosity as an attempt to peer into God's secrets and to become more than man by leaping over the boundaries of life and death. This conventional indictment exploits the now familiar image of the deluded scientist pursuing an eternal life that entails death, and so invokes the popular resistance to elite science. Indeed, a recent study points out the pragmatic and profit-seeking circumstances of the text's composition and sale.[103] Shelley deliberately rehearses a discourse about curiosity that dates back more than 150 years.

Just as in Walton's narrative the reader is implicated in curiosity, so the demonic impulse driving the monster inspires Frankenstein. Shelley underscores the transference of identity between the creator and the creation. Frankenstein himself is so curious that he not only practices but also partakes of the occult. As a youth, he is possessed by the "genius" of "Natural philosophy," a persistent spirit that makes him something of a witch (19). He desires to raise "ghosts" and to find both the philosopher's stone that changes lead to gold, and "the elixir of life" that confers immortality— all traditional enterprises of superstitious alchemy designed to reverse or confute the laws of nature (20). His enterprise is openly ambitious: "Curiosity, earnest research to learn the hidden laws of nature," motivates him. "It was," he says, especially "the secrets of heaven and earth that I desired to learn."[104] The knowledge of these secrets, however, segregates him from humanity. Speaking of what he did after creating the monster, he says, "I wandered like an evil spirit, for I had committed deeds of mischief beyond description horrible" (51).

Self-distorted or self-created like Milton's Satan, Frankenstein in effect becomes his own ghastly creature. To Walton, he is a curiosity, a wreck, a rarity, or a relic of past achievement. His creature, in turn, becomes a "dae-mon" or "monster," possessed by the traditional appetite for blood (19, 56). Like his creator, the monster consumes bodies, but whereas Frankenstein digs up corpses, the monster devours live humans. Walton marvels that the monster's speed is "superhuman," his "stature . . . seemed to exceed that of a man," and his face is disfigured with an "unearthly ugliness that rendered it almost too horrible for human eyes" (56). Frankenstein himself sees the monster as supernatural: "who could attempt to pursue him? It is impos-sible," he asserts; "one might as well try to overtake the winds, or confine a mountain-stream with a straw" (42–43). Both doctor and monster im-pinge on the otherworldly; both become distorted by desire and turn into creatures that slip off the scale of humanity.

As a parodic distortion of the divine form, Frankenstein's monster ex-emplifies curiosity, both subjectively and objectively. Frankenstein first de-scribes him as "a mummy again endued with animation" (30); he incarnates the very emblem of elite curiosity—he is the past revivified, the secret un-buried, the borders of life and death penetrated. Whereas Shadwell and Gay ridicule this enterprise, Shelley, the Romantic writer, gothicizes it. The monster is a spectacle: his grotesque exterior blurs the margins of life and death, man and beast, contained body and excrescence, subject and object. The contemplation of this transgressive body, of the aberrant in-stead of the beautiful, excites spectacular shock and horror. Despite the fact that his exterior conceals a yearning, poetic soul, the curiosity of both the monster himself and the human beings he encounters transforms this soul into a reflection of the body. Even the blind old man, Tiresian emblem of sooth, who listens sympathetically to the monster's tale is turned from him at the insistence of his family, who sees with their eyes (76).

Moreover, just as men cannot see beyond the superficial, so the mon-ster himself suffers from this lust of the eyes that disregards the spiritual: "I had admired the perfect forms of my cottagers," he confesses, "—their grace, beauty, and delicate complexions; but how was I terrified, when I viewed myself in a transparent pool! At first I started back, unable to be-lieve that it was indeed I who was reflected in the mirror. . . . I became fully convinced that I was in reality the monster that I am" (65). Burlesquing Narcissus, the monster betrays his own identity by becoming that which others see him as, not the ideal of perfect symmetry but its opposite. Referring to Lacan's analysis of infantile self-realization, Peter Brooks defines the monster's realization as the discovery of "himself as different, as violation of the law." This discovery, reversing Lacan's formula, renders the monster's subjectivity complete but his body inadequate (206–7). Dr. Frankenstein and the monster are the two faces of impious curiosity: they represent mankind transformed by a curiosity that rejects humanity and turns human beings into curiosities themselves.

While these novels examine curiosity as rebellion and present curious people as rebels, they also contain an endorsement, sometimes veiled, of curiosity as the means to escape social corruptions and confinements. This Romantic justification for inquiry as the yearning for transcendental truth defends the socially disenfranchised, ambitious, and unconventional against a hierarchy rigged against them. Curiosity in Romantic texts simultaneously applauds and condemns the urge to break out of the conventional confinements of society. Like ballooning, the quest for escape denotes both imaginative grandeur and impious ambition: public-minded generosity in the elite, but self-serving desire in everyone else.

&a.

In the period from the 1770s to 1820, shows of human and animal skill flourished. The circus at Astley's amphitheater, Katterfelto's lectures, displays of mathematical calculation by farmyard animals, demonstrations of exotic creatures, and balloon ascensions were all staged in the public arena, and all were demonstrations of the control that these curious men exercised over time, space, and a nature both visible and occult. These scientific spectacles glorified the skilled masters of ceremonies—the animal trainers, the seers, conjurers, magicians, and aeronauts—but at the same time these spectacles dramatized that these masters were themselves subjects to mastery. Such men made reason itself ridiculous even as they trotted it out as mankind's defining power. The Monster of 1790 epitomized this paradox, as his nature, both male and inhuman, mastered him. Such human curiosities represented the ambiguous power of human nature: its slippage between species and its ambition to transcend itself.

All of these explorers and entrepreneurs depended entirely on the public's curiosity for their status, even their survival. Astley, Katterfelto, and hot-air aeronauts, in the furor of competition for the public's attention, produced more and more frivolous appeals to an audience jaded by mere science and skill. Renwick Williams, the man arrested as the Monster, was condemned through pressure from the press. Like Williams, the overtly curious were objectified by spectatorship and became curiosities themselves. In their textual representations—prints, advertisements, treatises, and narratives—these curious performers struggle to project themselves as professionals, explorers, and scientists, yet they all survive in literary culture as examples of foolish or deceptive virtuosity. If they were seeking ambitiously to control nature, the audience nevertheless controlled them. While the public luxuriated in this dramatization of curiosity, the literary elite linked the ambitious attempts of curious performers to the public's own burgeoning curiosity. This elite feared that the true monstrosity brought about by these scientific spectacles sprang from the unregulated public curiosity that had the power to raise and destroy fortunes.[105] The real tyrant was the force of unseen political and social power.

Literary writers of this period address the question of the political and social uses of curiosity through a similarly ambiguous indictment of tyrannical curiosity or curious tyranny. Like Mr. Katterfelto, Victor Frankenstein and Caleb Williams possess a curiosity that drives them to transgress conventional boundaries. They, however, like the Monster of 1790, remain isolated in their obsessions, never subject to public approval or disdain. These protagonists thus become tyrants of Romantic solipsism like Radcliffe's Montoni. Godwin, Radcliffe, and Shelley indict the isolated mastery of nature represented by private curiosity. By soliciting a broadly popular audience for their works, all three authors seek to reproduce the dynamic of public exhibitions in which excessive curiosity and individually curious monsters are regulated or balanced by the reflective curiosity of the audience. At the same time, Radcliffe's questing heroines, Shelley's yearning heroes, and Godwin's rebellious narrator all demonstrate that curiosity has the power to reveal and redress past injustices. As a monster whose transgressive form breaks sublimely out of the mold of social convention, curiosity re-forms society. Many writers in the Romantic and Regency period of English culture may have fallen in love with revolution, social equality, and the imagination, but they did not lose the traditional fear of the dangers of curiosity. Inquirers in English culture pay a high price for the knowledge they seek.

Transgression and Ambition

Curiosity, said Nabokov, is the purest form of insubordination. Particularly in the early modern period, when curiosity garners a new legitimacy as the mode of cultural progress, it offers a threat to established economies of value. Mutating from a sign of Eve's sin and a mark of mankind's skill to an internal power to reassemble culture through idiosyncratic impressions, curiosity nonetheless retains its menace as the rebellious confutation of public meanings. Depictions of curious men and women, human curiosities, collections, and investigations represent curiosity as unstructured empiricism, the pursuit and collection of information for unlicensed or unknown purposes. At the same time, it comes to define the modern personality: the upstart. Curiosity betrays the desire to move beyond one's assigned place, through information, art, fraud, transformation, or rebellion. Early modern literature renders curiosity as both an impious urge and its reverse: a self-protective impulse to confute exploitation.

The relationship between curiosity and curiosities, between object and subject, is mediated by representation. "Curious" books perpetuate the experience of transgression by themselves transgressing genres or taboos, by documenting examples of such transgression, or both.[1] I have examined the ways literary and visual texts perform this mediation under the rubric of curiosity, but this book is, of course, also such a mediation. It does not recover the subjective experience of human curiosities, although it registers the hostility and alienation that cultural ideas of curiosity enforce. Nor, as I hope is clear, does it endorse the transformation of people into objects of inquiry, even while it does examine the liberation of repressed desires that such a transformation can enable. Rather, it explores how English culture negotiates the subversiveness of asking and the lawlessness of the intellectual ambition to know more. Early modern writers contest both the nature and the value of inquiry by depicting curious characters as social upstarts and curiosities, from science to conjuring, as impious spectacle.

Curiosity indicates strangeness, desire, and rejection: the longing to know something that has already been identified as other, the loss or transformation of self in a projection outward toward another identity. Throughout this period, English culture wavers between applauding and demonizing this self-escape. Curiosity as elaborateness flows into curiosity as inquiry. An intricacy or skillfulness in objects of art and nature so great that it erases their taxonomic signature makes them cultural trophies, yet admiration of such intricacy marks owners as suspiciously entranced by transgression. People who bridge genders, species, or ontologies—from witches to dwarfs—not only embody such transgression, but undermine the identity of spectators and the authority of taxonomies. These objects and subjects have the power to elicit understandings of the relationships between art and nature that challenge enlightened logic and conjure the uncanny sense of repressed familiarity. Because of that power, such objects and subjects become a rich resource for a consumer culture specializing in providing private pleasure. Any genre or topic that strains the borders of nature and culture, that releases the fantasy of an identity untutored and unrestrained by society, is curious: monstrosity, advertisement, pornography, travelogue, ethnographic analysis, witchcraft, spectral displays. Curiosity still denotes the overstepping of boundaries.

In the early modern period, curiosities, material embodiments of elite inquiry and acquisition, were vessels of social power. Made valuable by the prestige of their collector, they mirrored back that prestige. The explosion of rarities, many from overseas, for the consumption of the nonaristocratic public transformed possession into a middle-class display of status, coded as taste.[2] This desire for possession of novelty fed publications dedicated to the exploration of all matters. These publications were hospitable to all forms of curious query.[3] Under the proclamation of empirical purity, they intermixed empiricism and superstition, folktales and discoveries, traditional and fresh questions. Whereas Restoration inquirers were socially identified by their exercise of a newly sanctioned curiosity, the curious of the early eighteenth century were playing an already conventional, fashionable role. In a world in which curiosity itself was being commodified through print and the collection of rare items, and in which social identity could be artfully fashioned by the exercise of taste, human identity itself was vulnerable to objectification. As John R. Clark says, for Swift and similar "ancients," "the Modern is . . . distracted from self-knowledge by his curiosity, his interest in tales, theories concerning vapors, and scientific anatomies."[4] The self-contrived curious consumer commodified himself and thus simultaneously became a curious commodity.

During the eighteenth century, England developed means to exploit this transgression of identity through print. Many genres and texts negotiate both distrust of and admiration for the materialistic, secular, and individualistic exploration of the world. These genres and texts stimulate yet channel curiosity; they reproduce the physical trophies of travel, science, and discovery in the symbolic sphere of literature, shaping the reader into an explorer, investigator, conqueror, owner. This process begins in the Restoration; by the 1720s, pornographic literature provides the opportunity for unlicensed investigation—peeping—while ostensibly reasserting public values of morality. Rather than either prurient inquiry or the rarefied studies of the virtuosi, some literature of the early eighteenth century endorses a version of the alternative, "confident, unintellectual, common-sensical scepticism" that had opposed the religiously conservative New Science in the previous century.[5] The three most widely sold works during this decade, Jonathan Swift's *Gulliver's Travels*, Daniel Defoe's *Robinson Crusoe*, and Elizabeth Haywood's *Love in Excess; or, The Fatal Enquiry* all play with the border between legitimate and illegitimate curiosity.[6] As the moral ambiguity of most texts concerning curiosity shows, English literature in the eighteenth century was working out how to order the inquiring impulse.

Advertisements and public announcements of novelties, either objects or events, vitally shape the redefinition of curiosity as modernity. Throughout the century, journalism—in news reports, travelogues, and biographies—explores the capacity of prose to inquire beyond the physical. In prose as in poetry, writers explore the ambiguity of language, which at once reveals and yet only represents, defines and still remains symbolic. Many texts thematize the duality of language through narratives about the occult: the unseen made somehow visible by writing. Ghost and miracle narratives, news reports, periodical essays, and adventure and amatory fictions use the ideological signature of prose as the tool of empiricism in order to exploit the audience's thirst for investigations into a reality unperceived by the senses, particularly by the eyes. This prose vaunts empirical opacity, sight beyond sight, not through poetic artistry but through narratives of wonder that relegitimize the desire to be astonished as piety.

In the second half of the eighteenth century and the beginning of the nineteenth, English culture portrays curiosity as the willful penetration of the borders of belief and as the deliberate disruption of established distinctions of nature and culture. This theme flows into the development of curiosity as a subjective habit. As collecting flooded England, it extended to nonmaterial aspects of culture and began to denote connoisseurship: the mental accumulation of curiosities, including people. Even Charles Dickens's *Old Curiosity Shop*, despite its late date, portrays the world as a collection of human curiosities: performers, cheats, waxworks, giants, dwarfs, and misfits whom the narrator, a spectator, delivers in narrative.

Just as curiosity cabinets exemplify the habit, seen as either powerful or greedy, of sequestering objects from social use, revaluing them, and reordering them in the collector's private space, so literary curiosity revives marginalized topics and describes them in an objectifying, cataloguing style that threatens emerging ideals of moral narrative. Human curiosity becomes a performance rather than a condition, the enactment of ontological transgression—through display, self-display, acquisition, or reading. Collecting and spectacularization control strangeness; while they may enact a psychological desire for containment and self-possession, they serve state purposes in demarcating gender and property lines.

Throughout the early modern period, but especially during episodes of social anxiety, people who partake of two natures challenge social economies of identity and are thus stigmatized as curious, monstrous, or useless. This monstrous curiosity has particular application in matters that border nature and culture, notably gender and sexuality. For example, cross-dressers like the late eighteenth-century German bookseller Chevalier John Theodora de Verdion appear as "curious characters" in literary "museums" because, like other women who act in the public sphere or men who dress as women, they commit what Robin Ikegami terms gender treason.[7] Katharine Eisaman Maus analyses this issue in terms of the probative language used to penetrate others' interiority in the Renaissance, language that represented the discovery of crime as the unveiling of monstrosity. As she observes, "The language of monstrosity is characteristically vague, equally applicable to murder, theft, treason, witchcraft, sodomy, or whatever, so that an accusation of one particular crime tends to slide easily into an accusation of generalized criminality."[8] The association of witchcraft and monstrosity with the invisibility of subjective identity, a concealed interiority, reappears throughout the history of curiosity, especially, although not exclusively, in respect to women. As chapter 3 explains, female curiosity is persistently associated with the exposure of a fatal interior that destroys the beauty of the surface. The curiousness of unconventional identity also informs the metaphor of the closet, which, like the cabinet, preserves for private use what is conceived as public property, the body and its properties of reproduction. Queer characters, therefore, are curious both in their monstrous doubleness, whereby they play the roles of oppo-site genders, and in their suspect interiority.[9]

I end this examination of literary representations of curiosity at about 1820. While the topic certainly does not slide to an abrupt halt at this moment, subsequent literary treatments of curiosity tend to rework the themes and genres of the formative period from 1660 to 1820. As the dan-gerous Romantic ethic of unfettered feeling was gradually channeled into the more repressive Victorian age, science was perceived as finally begin-ning to fulfill its promise to cure humanity's ills and to open the natural world to profitable exploration.[10] Publishing and public culture similarly became more regularized and closely monitored. The cultural differences between kinds of curiosity became more easily classifiable as either profes-sional or prurient, even while their interplay remained a constant literary theme. Basic tropes emerged from the caldron of the previous two hundred years. Despite shifting cultural attitudes—Joseph Conrad scarcely shares Wilkie Collins's view of exploration—these tropes are identifiable in En-glish imaginative works from the nineteenth century to today.

Nineteenth-century treatments of early texts about curiosity reveal the growing association of the term with a despised popular culture that en-courages fantasy, in contrast to serious science or the disinterested curios-ity of Arnold's ideal critic. For example, *Gulliver's Travels*, like *Bluebeard*, not only thematizes curiosity but escapes generic fixity by inciting both wonder and satire through visual as well as conceptual jokes.[11] In the early nineteenth century, a period as skeptical about scientific inquiry as the early eighteenth century, two adaptations of *Gulliver's Travels* appear that differently illustrate its power as an allegory of curiosity. In 1807, Peter Vandergoose published *Gulliver and Munchaussen Outdone*, subtitled "*A Truth to Try the Patience of* A Stoick" and bearing the epigraph "O wonder-ful, wonderful, and most wonderful, and again wonderful!" The farce de-scribes a seemingly endless series of bloody encounters with savage animals and thus condemns a ruthlessly mercenary society.[12] Ten years later, the pantomime *Harlequin Gulliver; or, the Flying Island* (1817) fashions the text as spectacle, lacing the denuded story with conventional other-worldly topics of curiosity: astrology, lunar voyages, physical transformations, and spectacular visual effects.[13] This version exaggerates elements of fantasy, whereas Vandergoose's version exaggerates Swift's satire of exploitation. Both, however, use the text as a cultural topos to signal curiosity gone amok.

As a spectacle indulging an illegitimate taste for curiosity, *Blue-Beard* flourished in the nineteenth century. Increasingly, in the face of sentimen-

talism, it shed its gender-specific emphasis and came to represent a new
kind of odd Other or cultural curiosity: the orient. As a refutation of neoclassical aesthetics, it became a cult classic that tested critics' flexibility.
Defenses of the play both as a cultural phenomenon and as a triumph of
stage spectacle identify it with sensual pleasure, the lust of the eyes (and
ears); it became a byword for theatrical special effects.[14] One critic explains
its popularity by noting the contemporary success of "Monk" Lewis's
Castle Spectre.[15] The history he supplies documents its increasing campi-
ness: on the Paris stage in 1746 it was "Barbe Bleu"; in 1791 it was dramatized for Lord Barrymore's Wargrave Theater, which was directed at children, as well as used in Covent Garden as a pantomime; its revival in
Covent Garden in 1811 even used real horses.[16] This version concentrates
so much on sensational visuals that it deletes the subtitle "Female Curiosity!"[17] Henry James Byron's *Blue Beard: From a New Point of Hue* burlesques
the tale with high-camp lyrics, lavish printing that exhibits comically ex-
aggerated Turkish horrors, and a final dance billed as a "Grand Oriental
Kickup."[18] It interprets sister Anne's motive as envy and reverses the ending
so that when Abomelique dies, accidentally run through by Selim's sword,
Fatima mourns him; he revives, rewives, and Selim is cast off. The very
story that valorizes female curiosity in the eighteenth century devolves in
the nineteenth into a parody of the wonderful as infantile taste.

Eighteenth-century denigrations of women's inquiry into forbidden
areas receive parallel treatment in nineteenth-century literature. Victorian
poems and novels usually condemn female curiosity as sexual appetite.
Christina Rossetti's haunting *Goblin Market* (1862), for example, exemplifies the equation of female experience with the Fall. It recounts the tale of
two sisters who are tempted by goblins to taste their fatal fruit; Laura sub-
mits and pines away, agonizingly deaf to the goblins' cries, while Lizzie
resists, to be still tormented by their songs, until she finally saves her sister
by allowing the goblins to crush their fruits on her body and by letting
Laura sate her hunger by sucking the untasted juices. Like Henry Brooke's
curious maid, Laura loses her integrity, even her identity, when she succumbs to appetite, and she can recover it only through the sacrifice of others. Whereas the eighteenth-century poet figures this appetite as the social
search for novelty and sensation, however, the Victorian pre-Raphaelite
sees it as personal gratification. Nonetheless, both poems testify to the
prevalence of a new symbolic figure of female curiosity: the fallen woman
in need of redemption.

These Christian parables reflect a shift in the culture's sense of the role
of women's inquiry. Whereas in the Restoration and early eighteenth cen-

tury, questing women endangered the status quo, by the later eighteenth century, they endanger mainly themselves. The fallen woman whose curiosity served as the agent of evil, or at least of its exposure, becomes herself the curiosity. At the same time, sentimental conventions commodify and infantilize female curiosity in order to keep it innocent: Little Nell, the live curio in Dickens's *Old Curiosity Shop* who is encased in a cabinet, first at the shop and then at the grave, emblematizes the safe reduction of female inquiry to commodified sexuality. Nonetheless, she serves to criticize the world by her suffering and her artless inquiries.

From the Renaissance, curiosity has connoted the exploration of unknown lands. During the eighteenth and nineteenth centuries, it increasingly comes to serve as a code word for ethnographic investigation, represented as knowledge or global education. While the analysis of curiosity as a legitimization for imperialism falls beyond the scope of this book, it should be noted here that at the beginning of the nineteenth century, curiosity serves as the rubric to discipline—both classify and restrict—foreign customs according to English categories of understanding and power. Several Jacobin manuals, confident that observation and reflection would correct prejudices, urge youth to exercise their curiosity in order to explode the "curious" customs of the unenlightened. The Benthamite John Bowring's *Minor Morals for Young People* converts the ostensibly useless exploration of the exotic and occult into moral education. Strongly liberal, Bowring discusses the derisive "Curiosity" of racist Americans, comparing it with the Catholic oppression of the Jews and condemning it as the response of the persecutor to the persecuted.[19] At the same time, in essays on "Ancient Times," travel and habits in the Orient, witches, and vampires, he explodes exotic customs as fraud. "Affection for Inanimate Objects," however, earns praise as the love of "objects which are the sources of pleasure and subjects of sympathy" (chap. 2, p. 197). While suggesting that "to inquire" may be indecorous, he maintains that "*to observe* was always right and proper . . . as was the communication of what had been observed" (chap. 2, p. 14–15). Socialized through "communication," scientific curiosity, distinct from intrusive gossip, becomes legitimate.

As curious "histories," novels and biographies continue even today to worry at the relationship between nature and culture, normality and abnormality. While the stereotype of the curious character—the "queer," the Oriental, the secretive or marginal Other who violates sexual, racial, or social categories—appears in an enormous number of novels, many other texts continue to anatomize the defective detective. John Fowles's *The Collector* (1963) portrays collecting as a sexual aberration correlated with degraded, mechanistic culture in opposition to free art, beauty, and humanistic values. Norman Mailer's journalistic account of Gary Gilmore, *The Executioner's Song* (1979), attempts to rationalize violation by finding motive in personal history, but most fictional accounts treat the relationship of inquisitor to inquiry with more irony. Margaret Drabble's *A Natural Curiosity* (1989) recounts the relationship between a female investigator, Alix Bowen, and "her" murderer, whom she visits regularly in order, she tells herself, to find a satisfactory motive for his actions. "Attractive danger. Natural curiosity. Unnatural curiosity," muses the narrator, interrogating the oxymoronic relationship between nature and culture.[20]

Some texts play with the permeable border between the object and agent of curiosity. Allen Kurzweil's *A Case of Curiosities* (1992) puns on the quest of the collector and the container of the collection. At an auction, the novel's narrator, an amateur antique hound, acquires a *memento hominem*: a biography made material, a compilation of items assembled in a curiosity cabinet, each a souvenir representing "a decisive moment or relationship in the personal history of the compositor."[21] By reconstructing the history of a late eighteenth-century picaro, maker of watches and books, the novel examines the relationship of narrative to memory. Further, Kurzweil suggests that ownership itself forms a way of inventing identity by the construction of a logic connecting causes and effects, objects and meanings: at auction, "a single tap of the mallet declared the union of object and collector" (viii). This exposure of the economy of making meaning links collecting with conjuring, the occult, and the postmodern identity as an assemblage of traces of a fluid, shifting self.[22] Paul Auster takes this theme to its limit in his existential detective tales in which surveillance eviscerates the detective's personality, dissolving the border between curious object and subject.

The budding of detective fiction from the branches of journalism and from the Gothic strikingly shows the persistence of one of the main motifs in the history of literary curiosity: the incompatibility of scientific and social study. In this genre, the investigator is essentially flawed as a human being. The more expert his scientific eye, the blinder he is to his own nature and to social relations, even if these form the material for his scientific study. Conan Doyle's detective, Sherlock Holmes, albeit derived from French and American models, exemplifies the inquirer who cannot belong to his society: his cocaine habit and hostility to women are symptoms of the humoral imbalance of the curious man. Jerry Lewis parodies the cliché as the scientist ignorant of his own sexuality in his film comedies. Much television fiction of the last twenty years replays this trope by depicting defective detectives: the blind Longstreet; Ironside, trapped in a wheel-chair; Cannon, almost too fat to walk. These human curiosities revisit the historical charge that scientific investigators must have something wrong with them, some vital masculine impulse diverted, some inadequacy. More specifically, this figure of the investigator cannot love women, for he has peered into the secrets of generation and seen the obverse face of Eve, death in birth, the corruption of mankind. Unlike the members of a team in police dramas showing the power of the state, these individuals stand alone, against (and often in trouble with) the law: their allegiance is to a socially hazardous truth. The penalty for the curious man's impious peering is social exile.

In contrast, women detectives, like the gossipy Jessica Fletcher, exhibit a curiosity only too human. In 1822, Joan de Luce's circulating novel *Curiosity*, recounting the heroine's sufferings from gossip, bears an epigraph excoriating curiosity as an "elfish fiend! / Who comes ... To scan thy neighbour's works, and steal his thoughts, / Then scatter them abroad ... And call it pastime."[23] A series of twentieth-century books glossing the maxim "curiosity killed the cat" work the discourse associating investigation with a dangerous prying usually gendered as female. The child's tale *A Cat Called Curiosity* (1989) recounts the story of a cat frightened out of his nature by a snake. In *Curiosity Killed a Cat* (1941), after the murders have been solved, Inspector Pettengill pronounces of an inquisitive neighbor endangered by the killer, "If he *had* murdered her, it would have been a Bluebeard case of 'Curiosity killed the cat.'"[24] The cat hides a vital clue in M. K. Wren's revisionist murder mystery *Curiosity Didn't Kill the Cat* (1975). Alan Steward trumps this with *Curiosity Killed the Cop* (1980), detailing the murder of an inquisitive young woman, although two years later J. M. O'Donnell reverses the paradigm in *Curiosity Won't Kill You* (1982), his examination of ghosts, the Bermuda Triangle, and ancient mysteries. Nonetheless, the distinctions between female and male curiosity continue to blur in popular culture as in literature. This fuzziness of distinction appears in the riotously popular cult series *The X-Files*, which melds the occult and the empirical with its epigraph, "The Truth is Out There." Its rebellious hero believes in life beyond the borders of scientific knowledge; its skeptical heroine believes in him, the individual man, and practical science. They dramatize the uneasy relationship between areas and methods of investigation.

Curiosity is the expression of the contest between individual and public truth. Cultural representations of inquiry explore boundaries between individual and state desires, popular and enlightened methodologies, gossip and legislated information, art and nature. As subjects and objects, curious people and things overstep or dismantle these boundaries. Curious viewers and readers are invited to come along, thus entering the world of the curious themselves. The thirst for information, the quest to penetrate forbidden areas, the insistence on personal witnessing throughout early modern culture thus signals the ambition to escape public categories or established truths. It is represented as ontological transgression, the violation of role, of species, of a public self; it is an invitation to elude identity. Curiosity is the ambition to go beyond.

NOTES

Introduction

1. Verna Virginia Gehring, "The Role of Curiosity in Hobbes's Philosophy" (Ph.D. diss., Columbia University, 1993), 12; David Hume, *A Treatise of Human Nature*, 2d ed., with analytical index by L. A. Selby-Bigge (Oxford: Clarendon Press, 1978), pt. 3, bk. 2, sec. 10, pp. 448–49.

2. Roger Shattuck's *Forbidden Knowledge: From Prometheus to Pornography* (New York: St. Martin's Press, 1996), despite its humanity, stands in a long tradition of arguments against the impious seeking out of the unknown.

3. Lorraine Daston and Katharine Park, *Wonders and the Order of Nature* (New York: Zone Books, 1998), 122.

4. Samuel Johnson, *A Dictionary of the English Language* (1755; reprint, London: Time Books, 1979). *Oxford English Dictionary* (Oxford: Oxford University Press, 1985). For a discussion of the earlier distinction between divine and human kinds of inquiry and knowledge, see Christian K. Zacher, *Curiosity and Pilgrimage: The Literature of Discovery in Fourteenth-Century England* (Baltimore: Johns Hopkins University Press, 1976), 19.

5. Stephen Greenblatt, *Marvelous Possessions: The Wonder of the New World* (Chicago: University of Chicago Press, 1991), 75; see also 17–19.

6. Daston and Park, *Wonders*, 306–29.

7. *The Penguin Dictionary of Historical Slang*, ed. Eric Partridge (Harmondsworth, Middlesex: Penguin, 1972), 588. In "Private Interests: The Portrait and the Novel in Eighteenth-Century England," Alison Conway demonstrates the affinity between aesthetic values used to evaluate portrait painting and the novel, particularly that of uniqueness and private sensibility; see *Eighteenth-Century Life*, n.s., 21, no. 3 (November 1997): 1–15.

8. In "Perfectly Inhuman: Moral Monstrosity in Eighteenth-Century Discourse," James A. Steintrager argues that enlightenment philosophers conceived of monstrosity as a pleasure in or indifference to others' pain that was absolutely opposed to humanity, "not an aberration from a norm of behavior . . . [or] an exaggeration of certain self-centered drives"; see *Eighteenth-Century Life*, n.s. 21, no. 2 (May 1997): 114–32, esp. 115. While Steintrager seeks to trace the ways in which the construction of monstrosity served social ends, I suggest that the curious subsumes it for empirical pleasure.

9. Barbara Maria Stafford, *Body Criticism: Imaging the Unseen in Enlightenment Art and Medicine* (Cambridge, Mass. and London: MIT Press, 1991), 234–66; Ronald Paulson points out that this ideal changes during the eighteenth century as deistic and heterodox notions of beauty defeat the symmetrical ideal; see *The Beautiful, Novel, and Strange: Aesthetics and Heterodoxy* (Baltimore and London: Johns Hopkins University Press, 1996), 66–69.

10. Charlton T. Lewis and Charles Short, *A Latin Dictionary* (Oxford: Clarendon Press, 1975), 1163; C. J. S. Thompson, *The Mystery and Lore of Monsters: With Accounts of Some Giants, Dwarfs, and Prodigies* (London: Williams and Norgate Ltd., 1930), 23–24. Frederick John Stopp traces the term "monster" to a combination of *moneo* and *ostentum* or *ostendo*, "to make manifest" or "display"; see *Monsters and Hieroglyphs: Broadsheets and Emblem Books in Sixteenth-Century Germany* (Cambridge: The Sandars Lectures, 1972), 2, 7.

11. See Barbara M. Benedict, "European Monsters through English Eyes: Eighteenth-Century Cultural Icons," *Symbolism* (forthcoming); Marie-Hélène Huet, *Monstrous Imagination* (Cambridge, Mass. and London: Harvard University Press, 1993), 6, 272 n. 9; Evelleen Richards, "A Political Anatomy of Monsters, Hopeful and Otherwise: Teratology, Transcendentalism, and Evolutionary Theorizing," *Isis* 85, no. 3 (September 1994): 377–411. In *Science and the Shape of Orthodoxy: Studies of Intellectual Change in Late Seventeenth-Century Britain* (Woodbridge, Suffolk: Boydell Press, 1995), Michael Hunter notes that scientific texts intended for a popular audience featured allegorical plates (160).

12. See Lorraine Daston, "Marvelous Facts and Miraculous Evidence in Early Modern Europe," *Critical Inquiry* 18 (autumn 1991): 93–124. For an account of the secularization of science, see Robert Wokler, "Anthropology and Conjectural History," in *Inventing Human Science: Eighteenth-Century Domains*, ed. Christopher Fox, Roy Porter, and Robert Wokler (Berkeley and Los Angeles: University of California Press, 1995), 31–52, esp. 33.

13. Barbara Maria Stafford, *Body Criticism: Imagining the Unseen in Enlightenment Art and Medicine* (Cambridge, Mass. and London: MIT Press, 1991), 259.

14. "The Nobility, Ladies and Gentlemen, are respectfully informed that the astonishing Curiosity Miss Beffin Intends exhibiting her wonderful Powers, In a commodius Booth. During these Present Fairs . . ." (London: T. Romney, 1820); also see Henry Morley, *Memoirs of Bartholomew Fair* (London: Chapman and Hall, 1859).

15. Michel Foucault, *The Order of Things* (New York: Vintage, 1973), 303–43, 312; Tony Bennett, *The Birth of the Museum: History, Theory, Politics* (London and New York: Routledge, 1995), 7.

16. *The Birth of a Consumer Society: The Commercialization of Eighteenth-Century England*, ed. Neil McKendrick, John Brewer, and J. H. Plumb (Bloomington: Indiana University Press, 1982).

17. Jürgen Habermas, *The Structural Transformation of the Public Sphere: An Inquiry into a Category of Bourgeois Society* (Cambridge, Mass.: MIT Press, 1989).

18. Tony Bennett, *The Birth of the Museum: History, Theory, Politics* (London and New York: Routledge, 1995), 25.

19. Laura Seelig, "The Munich Kunstkammer, 1565–1807," in *The Origins of Museums: The Cabinet of Curiosities in Sixteenth-and Seventeenth-Century Europe*, ed. Oliver Impey and Arthur MacGregor (Oxford: Clarendon Press, 1985), 76–89.

20. This process through which collecting shifts between functioning as expert work and as a frivolous hobby is analogous to the transferal of chivalric warlike activities to the realm of leisure sports as new social and economic conditions

changed the aspects of life that courtiers deemed serious. See "Debate: The Invention of Leisure in Early Modern Europe," comment by Joan-Lluís Marfany, and reply by Peter Burke, in *Past and Present* 156 (August 1997): 174–91, 192–97.

21. Dean MacCannell describes tourist souvenirs similarly as idiosyncratic identity markers in *The Tourist: A New Theory of the Leisure Class* (New York: Schocken Books, 1989), 147–51.

22. Bogdan differentiates between two modes of presenting "monsters": the exotic, which emphasizes their difference from spectators in geographical terms, and the "aggrandized": "With the aggrandized mode the presentation emphasized how, with the exception of the particular physical, mental, or behavioral condition, the freak was an upstanding, high-status person with talents of a conventional and socially prestigious nature." Bogdan specifies that in the aggrandized mode, the presentation included such things as the invention of titles, skills, cultivated habits, and interviews with prestigious people or royalty, as well as the adoption of fancy clothes, families, and children. See Robert Bogdan, *Freak Show: Presenting Human Oddities for Amusement and Profit* (Chicago: University of Chicago Press, 1988), 108, 95–96, 110.

23. George Cruikshank contributes to a late eighteenth-century tradition of depicting distressed artists; see M. Dorothy George, *Hogarth to Cruikshank: Social Change in Graphic Satire* (1967; reprint, London: Viking, 1987), 121.

24. On the historical uses of distancing and estrangement to re-perceive reality, see Carlo Ginzburg, "Making Things Strange: The Pre-history of a Literary Device," *Representations* 56 (fall 1996): 8–28. Ginzburg discusses the fragmentation of the familiar that liberates impressions to be recombined as art, perhaps in the manner that Coleridge intended; curiosity, on the other hand, as a cultural category, fragments or decontextualizes impressions and observations without recombining them into a meaningful shape.

25. Henry Iliff, *A Tear of Sympathy!!! or, Striking Objects of Travel, Antient and Modern! In Italy, Prussia, Spain, France, Russia, Etc. With Reflections Critical, Moral, and Biographical* (London: Allen and West, 1796), 10.

26. See for example "*An Exact Relation* of the Entertainment of His Most Sacred Majesty WILLIAM III. King of England, Scotland, France, and Ireland . . . By an English Gentleman," which describes customs and commodities like "a Book of the Rarities" of the Anatomy School (London, 1691), 11.

27. Daston, "Marvelous Facts," 94–95.

28. Mary Poovey explores the early modern separation of description from interpretation in *A History of the Modern Fact: Problems of Knowledge in the Sciences of Wealth and Society* (Chicago: University of Chicago Press, 1998). Also see Percy Adams, *Travelers and Travel Liars, 1660–1800* (Berkeley, Los Angeles, and London: University of California Press, 1962).

29. In *Marvelous Possessions*, Stephen Greenblatt contrasts this kind of "theoretical curiosity" with genuine cultural tolerance; see also his examination of Hans Blumenberg's analysis of curiosity as heterodox in the fourteenth century (46).

30. Peter Brooks, "What Is a Monster? (according to *Frankenstein*)" in *Body*

Work: Objects of Desire in Modern Narrative (Cambridge: Cambridge University Press, 1993), 199–220.

31. Andrew Curran and Patrick Graille, introduction to *Faces of Monstrosity*, special issue of *Eighteenth-Century Life*, n.s., 21, no. 2 (May 1997), 4, 3; see also 8–9, 12.

32. See Michel Foucault's analysis of the early modern development of the human sciences that treat mankind as an object of empirical inquiry, in *The Order of Things: An Archaeology of the Human Sciences* (New York: Vintage Books, 1970).

33. See Leslie Fiedler's Freudian argument that spectators respond with fascinated fear to "freaks" because they embody our repressed desires and fears about our own, especially sexual, identities, in *Freaks: Myths and Images of the Secret Self* (Middlesex: Penguin Books, 1978).

34. *A Collection of Curious Advertisements [1682–1836]*, 28 October 1799. British Library, 1889.b.8. See also Robert Bogdan, *Freak Show: Presenting Human Oddities for Amusement and Profit* (Chicago: University of Chicago Press, 1988), esp. 262.

35. Gerald R. Cragg, *Reason and Authority in the Eighteenth Century* (Cambridge: Cambridge University Press, 1964), 5–8.

36. Oliver A. Johnson, *The Mind of David Hume: A Companion to Book I of "A Treatise of Human Nature"* (Urbana and Chicago: University of Illinois Press, 1995), 40–41.

37. See the database for the Harry Ransom Center; see also the catalogue of *Belles Écritures*, which shows a delightful variety of seventeenth-century representational engraving (Librarie Paul Jammes, 1992). My thanks to Professor Bob Dawson for showing me the catalogue.

38. By the end of the eighteenth century, polygraphy meant the artistic duplication of a visual phenomenon, something between a souvenir and a copy, like the postcard, designed to provide a mass audience with fine art. Ironically, the modern term indicates the cipher-like scribblings of a machine that records pulse and other physical changes over time and is used to detect "truth" in criminal investigations. See *Woodfall's Register*, no. 88 (London: Pall Mall, 10 December 1792).

39. See Susan Stewart, *On Longing: Narratives of the Miniature, the Gigantic, the Souvenir, the Collection* (Baltimore and London: Johns Hopkins University Press, 1984).

40. Douglas and Elizabeth Rigby, *Lock, Stock, and Barrel: The Story of Collecting* (Philadelphia, New York, London: J. B. Lippincott, Co., 1944), 224–25.

41. See Barbara M. Benedict, "The Curious Attitude in Eighteenth-Century Britain: Observing and Owning," *Eighteenth-Century Life*, n.s., 14, no.3 (November 1990): 59–98.

42. "To the Curious. The word Scissars appears capable of more variations in the spelling than any other . . ." (Enfield: T. T. Barrow, [1829]). British Library, Tab. 597.7.

43. Francis Bacon, *The Advancement of Learning*, ed. G. W. Kitchin, intro. Arthur Johnston (London: Dent, 1973): bk. 1, p. 3. All citations to this text refer to this edition. In *Science, Faith, and Politics: Francis Bacon and the Utopian Roots of the*

Modern Age: A Commentary on Bacon's Advancement of Learning, Jerry Weinberger emphasizes Bacon's debt to utopianism and his political purpose in writing the book, which was to combat current corruption (Ithaca: Cornell University Press, 1985).

44. See N. A. Keeble, *The Literary Culture of Nonconformity in Late Seventeenth-Century England* (Athens: University of Georgia Press, 1987), and George DeForest Lord, *Classical Presences in Seventeenth-Century English Poetry* (New Haven and London: New Haven Press, 1987).

45. Samuel Johnson, *The Rambler,* no. 103 (12 March 1751), a translation from a passage in Boethius's *De Consolatione Philosophiae.* See Samuel Johnson, *The Rambler,* vols. 3, 4, 5 of the Yale edition of the *Works of Samuel Johnson,* 9 vols., ed. W. J. Bate and Albrecht B. Strauss (New Haven and London: Yale University Press, 1969), 4:184.

CHAPTER ONE

1. Cesare Ripa, *Iconologia* (Padua: Pietro Paolo Tozzi, 1611), 113–14. My thanks to Piero Garofalo for translating the text. Ripa's narrative explains that frogs symbolized curiosity to the Egyptians; see Hans-Joachim Zimmermann, "English Translations and Adaptations of Cesare Ripa's *Iconologia*: From the Seventeenth to the Nineteenth Century," *De Zeventiende eeuw* 11, no. 1 (1995): 12–26, esp. 18. Zimmermann notes that Benjamin Motte's 1709 edition of *Iconologia* omits Ripa's Catholic allegories (22).

2. Several scholars have noted that English literature had already begun to distrust any truth that was not demonstrable; see Thomas L. Hankins, *Science and Enlightenment* (Cambridge, London, New York: Cambridge University Press, 1985), esp. 3–9.

3. Marie Boas Hall observes that although the *Philosophical Transactions* was not the official organ of the Royal Society but rather Oldenburg's "private venture," it became associated with the Society, while disseminating Oldenburg's particular balance of science and technology. See "Oldenburg, the *Philosophical Transactions,* and Technology" in *The Uses of Science in the Age of Newton,* ed. John G. Burke (Berkeley, Los Angeles, London: University of California Press, 1983), 21–47.

4. See, for example, John Wynne, *An Abridgement of Mr. Locke's Essay Concerning Humane Understanding* (London: A. and J. Churchill, 1696), with a dedication "To the Much Esteemed Mr. John Locke."

5. Peter Dear, *Discipline and Experience: The Mathematical Way in the Scientific Revolution* (Chicago: University of Chicago Press, 1995), 32–62, esp. 44, 61.

6. See Michael Hunter's analysis of the fractures and shifts in the early development of the scientific method, in *Science and the Shape of Orthodoxy: Intellectual Change in Late Seventeenth-Century Britain* (Woodbridge, England: The Boydell Press, 1995).

7. See Tim Harris, "What's New about the Restoration?" *Albion* 29, no. 2 (summer 1997): 187–222.

8. See Mario Biagioli's analysis of the differences between the relatively independent Royal Society and the European academies that relied on monarchical
support, in "Etiquette, Interdependence, and Sociability in Seventeenth-Century
Science," *Critical Inquiry* 22 (winter 1996): 193–238.

9. Barbara Shapiro points out the overlap in methodologies and topics of antiquarians, scientists, and other men of learning, in "History and Natural History
in Sixteenth- and Seventeenth-Century England: An Essay on the Relationship
between Humanism and Science," in *English Scientific Virtuosi in the Sixteenth and
Seventeenth Centuries: Papers Read at a Clark Library Seminar, 5 February 1977* (Los
Angeles: University of California, William Andrews Clark Memorial Library,
1979), 38.

10. Peter Burke, *Popular Culture in Early Modern Europe* (New York: Harper
and Rowe, 1978), esp. 65–77; Margaret Spufford, *Small Books and Pleasant Histories: Popular Fiction and Its Readership in Seventeenth-Century England* (Athens: University of Georgia Press, 1981), esp. 45–82; Tessa Watt, *Cheap Print and Popular
Piety, 1550–1640* (Cambridge: Cambridge University Press, 1991).

11. See Joseph M. Levine's study of the origin of this archetype, Dr. John
Woodward, in *Dr. Woodward's Shield: History, Science, and Satire in Augustan England* (Ithaca and London: Cornell University Press, 1991), esp. 124–25.

12. Stephen Greenblatt, *Marvelous Possessions: The Wonder of the New World*
(Chicago: University of Chicago Press, 1991), 22–23, passim.

13. See Stephen Greenblatt's seminal study of the malleability of a middle
class endowed with a freshly self-conscious subjectivity, in *Renaissance Self-
Fashioning: From More to Shakespeare* (Chicago: University of Chicago Press,
1980).

14. See Percy Adams, *Travelers and Travel Liars, 1660–1800* (Berkeley and
Los Angeles: University of California Press, 1962); also see Philip Edwards, *Sea-
Narratives in Eighteenth-Century England* (Cambridge: Cambridge University
Press, 1994), esp. the analysis of William Dampier's voyages, 17–43.

15. "The Translator to the Reader," in *"A World of Wonders: or, An Introduction
to a Treatise touching the Conformitie of ancient and moderne wonders*: or A Prepara-
tive Treatise to the Apologie for HERODOTUS," by Henri Etienne (1531–1598)
(London: John Norton, 1607).

16. John R. Clark, *Form and Frenzy in Swift's 'Tale of a Tub'* (Ithaca: Cornell
University Press, 1970), 26–27.

17. Michel Eyquem de Montaigne, "Apology for Raymond Sebond," in *The
Complete Essays of Montaigne*, trans. Donald M. Frame (Stanford: Stanford University Press, 1965), 330. Montaigne's association of curiosity with pride and reason
indicates its potential to corrupt man's divine nature; the opposing faces of curiosity in the Renaissance are epitomized by the conflict between Augustine's idea
that curiosity is presumptuous and distracting, and the contrary idea of Aquinas,
indebted to Aristotle's sanctification of knowledge, that it shows man's attempt to
approach God, only becoming perverse when immoderate. See Jennifer Ann May,
"*Curiositas*: Varying Views of Curiosity in the 'Apologie de Raymond Sebond'
and the Essais of *Montaigne*," (master's thesis, Vanderbilt University, May 1993),

6–9, 15, 42; Lorraine Daston and Katharine Park, *Wonders and the Order of Nature* (New York: Zone Books, 1998), 122.

18. Evelleen Richards, "A Political Anatomy of Monsters, Hopeful and Otherwise: Teratology, Transcendentalism, and Evolutionary Theorizing," *Isis* 85, no. 3 (September 1994): 411.

19. See Jeffrey Jerome Cohen's argument that monsters are the inscription of cultural ideas of difference, disrupting categories and facilitating the expression of subversive desires, in "Monster Culture (Seven Theses)," in *Monster Theory: Reading Culture* (Minneapolis and London: University of Minnesota Press, 1996), 3–25.

20. William Shakespeare, *King Lear*, ed. Russell Fraser (Signet, 1987). Future references of this sort will use abbreviated citations, such as 1.5.40.

21. William Ian Miller, in *The Anatomy of Disgust* (Cambridge, Mass. and London: Harvard University Press, 1997), observes the similarity of hypocrisy and betrayal, analyzing both as morally disgusting (180–205).

22. *A Character of a Turn-Coat: Or, The True Picture of an English Monster* (London?: 1707), lines 65–70.

23. This concept of the essential doubleness of the monster appears in the frenzy of attention given to the "Bohemian sisters" Helena-Judith, joined with common flesh like the nineteenth-century Siamese twins. See Maja-Lisa von Sneidern, "Joined at the Hip: A Monster, Colonialism, and the Scriblerian Project," *Eighteenth-Century Life* 30, no. 3 (spring 1997): 213–31. Barbara Stafford and Richard Altick also discuss these twins; see Barbara Maria Stafford, *Body Criticism: Imaging the Unseen in Enlightenment Art and Medicine* (Cambridge, Mass.: MIT Press, 1991); Richard D. Altick, *The Shows of London* (Cambridge, Mass.: Belknap Press, 1978). See also "The Double Mistress," chap. 14 of the Scriblerus Club's satire *The Memoirs of the Extraordinary Life, Works, and Discoveries of Martinus Scriblerus*, ed. Charles Kerby-Miller (New York: Oxford University Press, 1988), in which Martin marries one of the Bohemian sisters renamed Lindamira-Indamora: "For how much soever our Martin was enamour'd on her as a beautiful Woman, he was infinitely more ravish'd with her as a charming Monster" (146–47).

24. Christopher Marlowe, *Doctor Faustus*, ed. Sylvan Barnet (Penguin, 1969): 1.1.71–74.

25. Sebastian Brant, *The Ship of Fools*, 2 vols., trans. Alexander Barclay (Edinburgh: William Paterson, 1509; reprint, London: Henry Sotherton, 1874), pp. 129–32, st. 3, 4.

26. Marlowe, *Doctor Faustus*, 3.2.134; 3.2.152–53. In *Popular Culture in Early Modern Europe*, Peter Burke examines the festivals during which power symbolically was reversed (London: Temple Smith, 1978); for the literary reenactment of this dynamic, see M. M. Bakhtin's *Rabelais and His World*, trans. Hélène Iswolsky (Cambridge, Mass.: MIT Press, 1968).

27. In the 1611 edition, the stage direction for act 1, scene 3 reads, "Enter Faustus to coniure," suggesting that he was directed to act as a conjurer, as much as a scholar; Christopher Marlowe, *The Tragicall History of the horrible Life and Death of Doctor Faustus* (London: John Wright, 1611).

28. Daston and Park, *Wonders and the Order of Nature*, 328.

29. In *Masquerade and Civilization: The Carnivalesque in Eighteenth-Century English Culture and Fiction* (Stanford: Stanford University Press, 1986), Terry Castle argues that eighteenth-century fiction depicts the masquerade as a privileged place for broaching gender restrictions, but I think that the commercial exploitation of fashion mediates this transgression. Jeffreys' collection of dresses exhibits masquerade as cultural consumption: see Aileen Ribeiro, *The Dress Worn at Masquerades in England, 1730–1790, and Its Relation to Fancy Dress in Portraiture* (New York and London: Garland Publishing Inc., 1984); Daniel Roche, *The Culture of Clothing: Dress and Fashion in the 'Ancien Regime'* (Cambridge: Cambridge University Press, 1994); and Iris Brooke, *Dress and Undress: The Restoration and the Eighteenth Century* (Westport, Conn.: Greenwood Press, 1958). At the turn of the seventeenth century, one beautician "hath most curious *Masks* and *Forehead-cloths*, which take out all Spots, Pits or Scars caused by the Small-Pox" (*Medical Advertisements* [1675–1715], British Library, 551.a.32, no. 230). The uses of "curious" masks may have been several. All citations to medical advertisements refer to this collection, unless otherwise specified.

30. Thomas Jeffreys, *A Collection of the Dresses of Different Nations*, vol. 4 (London: Thomas Jeffreys, 1772), no. 235, p. 37.

31. Karl-Luwig Selig observes that the numerous subscribers to George Richardson's lavish 1779 edition of Ripa's *Iconologia* included eighteen painters, twenty-four architects, twelve engravers, the royal librarian, eighteen booksellers from all over the country, and other print-sellers, sculptors, builders, cabinetmakers, a porcelain manufacturer, and other laborers, as well as Reynolds, Romney, and Chippendale; see "George Richardson and the 'fame' of Ripa's *Iconologia*," in *De Zeventiende eeuw* 11, no. 1 (1995): 27–28.

32. See for example Dunton's *"The Young Students' Library*: Containing Extracts and Abridgements of the Most Valuable Books Printed in *England*, and in the Forreign Journals, from the Year Sixty Five, to this Time. To which is Added, A New Essay upon all sorts of Learning; wherein The Use of the Sciences is Distinctly Treated on. By the Athenian Society" (London: John Dunton, 1692). The *Philosophical Transactions* was published and extracted throughout the eighteenth century.

33. "Strange and Wonderfull News from Cornwall, being an Account of a Miraculous Accident that Lately happen'd neer the Town of *Bodmyn*, at a Place called *Park* (London: J. Wallis, 1687). British Library, 719.m.17 (fol. 11).

34. This claim of printed authenticity becomes part of the trappings of novelistic verisimilitude; see Ian Watt, *The Rise of the Novel: Studies in Defoe, Richardson, and Fielding* (Berkeley and Los Angeles: University of California Press, 1957); in *Factual Fictions: The Origins of the English Novel*, Lennard J. Davis emphasizes the similarity of news discourse to the novel genre, particularly in respect to "recentness" and factuality, although he denies them distinct generic shapes (New York: Columbia University Press, 1983), esp. 67. For an extended analysis of the interrelationship of journalism and novels, see J. Paul Hunter, *Before Novels: The*

Cultural Contexts of Eighteenth-Century English Fiction (New York: W. W. Norton and Co., 1990), esp. chap. 5.

35. "*The* WONDER OF WONDERS, *or Strange* NEWS *From Newton in York-shire*, Being a True and Perfect Relation of a Gentleman turn'd into a statue of Stone, which Statue stands now in the Garden of Goodman *Wilford* . . . Together With the occasion of the Fright upon Himself, Wife and Maid, by four Persons upon the 12th of May, 1675" (London?: 1675), 3.

36. *Medical Advertisements* [1675–1715], British Library, 551.a.32, no. 50.

37. See John Aubrey, *Aubrey's Brief Lives*, ed. with intro. Oliver Lawson Dick (Harmondsworth, Middlesex: Penguin, 1982), 6, 17; Samuel Pepys, *The Shorter Pepys*, ed. Robert Latham (Berkeley and Los Angeles: University of California Press, 1985), xxxv.

38. John Aubrey, "Venetia Digby," in *Brief Lives*, ed. Richard Barber (Woodbridge, Suffolk: The Boydell Press, 1982), 106.

39. Douglas and Elizabeth Rigby characterize Pepys as the exemplar of "the collector who carries 'system' and classification to extremes, the ambitious man using collecting as a tool," in *Lock, Stock, and Barrel: The Story of Collecting* (Philadelphia, New York, London: J. B. Lippincott, Co., 1944), 239.

40. Robert Bogdan, *Freak Show: Presenting Human Oddities for Amusement and Profit* (Chicago and London: University of Chicago Press, 1988), 95–96.

41. "The *Wonder of Wonders*: or the Dumb MAID of WAPPING Restor'd to her Speech again" (London: Tho. Milbourn, 1694). British Library, 719.m.17 (fol. 17).

42. "*The* ENGLISH HERMITE, *or Wonder of this* AGE. Being a relation of the life of ROGER CRAB" (London, 1655). This text was reprinted throughout the eighteenth century.

43. Joy Kenseth, in *The Age of the Marvelous* (Hanover, N.H.: Hood Museum of Art, Dartmouth College, 1991), points out that "it should be emphasized that the growth of interest in the marvelous was directly linked to the spread of printing. By means of various printed materials, information about miracles, prodigious events, natural and artificial wonders was transmitted to a wide, and increasingly literate, public" (30).

44. Charles Gildon, "*The History of the Athenian Society*, For the Resolving all *nice* and *Curious* QUESTIONS. By a GENTLEMAN who got Secret Intelligence of the Whole Proceedings" (London: James Dowley, [1691]).

45. Thomas Sprat, *The History of the Royal-Society of London, For the Improving of Natural Knowledge* (London: J. Martyn, 1667), 67.

46. See Steven Shapin, *A Social History of Truth: Civility and Science in Seventeenth-Century England* (Chicago: University of Chicago Press, 1985); Steven Shapin and Simon Schaffer, *Leviathan and the Air Pump: Hobbes, Boyle, and the Experimental Life* (Princeton, N.J.: Princeton University Press, 1985); Mary Poovey, *A History of the Modern Fact: Problems of Knowledge in the Sciences of Wealth and Society* (Chicago: University of Chicago Press, 1998); Biagioli, "Etiquette, Interdependence, and Sociability."

47. Verna Virginia Gehring, "The Role of Curiosity in Hobbes's Philosophy," (Ph.D. dissertation, Columbia University, 1993), esp. 3–5.

48. M. Hunter, *Science and the Shape of Orthodoxy*, 110–11, 171; Shapin, *A Social History of Truth*, 199, 122–23.

49. I. Bernard Cohen identifies scientific invention with revolutionary individualism in "Scientific Revolution and Creativity in the Enlightenment," *Eighteenth-Century Life*, n.s., 7, no. 2 (January 1982): 46–47.

50. See n. 46, esp. Shapin, *A Social History of Truth*.

51. John Wallis, *"A Defence of the Royal Society, And the Philosophical Transactions, Particularly those of July 1670. In Answer to the Cavils of Dr. William Holder"* (London: Thomas Moore, 1678), 32. See the *Philosophical Transactions*, no. 61 (18 July 1670), vols. 4–6:1087.

52. See *Propositions For the carrying on a Philosophical Correspondence, Already begun, in the County of* SOMMERSET, *Upon incouragement given from the Royal Society* (London: James Collins, 1670), 3.

53. Robert Boyle, *The Works of Robert Boyle*, 5 vols., To Which is prefixed The Life of the Author (London: A. Millar, 1744), 1:6.

54. In "The Birth of the Modern Scientific Instrument, 1550–1700," Albert Van Helden traces the history of instrument and theory, emphasizing the importance of tools in the development of science in the later seventeenth century. See *The Uses of Science in the Age of Newton*, ed. John G. Burke (Berkeley, Los Angeles, London: University of California Press, 1983), 49–84.

55. Boyle, "That the Goods of Mankind maybe much increase by the Naturalist's Insight into TRADES," in *Works*, 3:167.

56. Thomas Shadwell, *"The Virtuoso*. A Comedy. Acted at the Dukes Theatre," licensed 31 May 1676 (London: Henry Herringman, 1676), dedication. In future citations, I note the act and page number only, since the lines are not numbered; all citations refer to this edition, copies of which I have consulted at the British Library and the Harry Ransom Humanities Research Center at the University of Texas at Austin.

57. William van Lennep, Emmett L. Avery, Arthur H. Scouten, George Winchester Stone, and Charles Beecher Hogan, *The London Stage, 1600–1800*, 2 vols. (Carbondale: Southern Illinois University Press, 1965), 1:cxxx. *The Alcymist*, as it was then spelled, was performed at least once in each season from 1660 to 1664, twice in 1668–69, and a month after *Doctor Faustus* in 1675; in 1668–69, the King's Company was given permission to perform it, along with a great number of plays by Jonson and others previously acted at Blackfriars, but apparently it remained unacted from 1680 to 1700; see van Lennep et al., *The London Stage*, 1:21, 29, 31, 35, 44, 47, 55, 79, 151, 160, 224, 239, 523. The play was reprinted in several editions in the first decades of the eighteenth century with typical prologues hinting at the play's contemporary pertinence; see Ben Jonson, *The Alchemist* (London: Jacob Tonson, 1709).

58. "To the Reader," in *The Alchemist*, by Ben Jonson (London: Walter Burre, 1612).

59. Patrick Curry argues that astrology was regarded as irrational, heretical,

and dangerously associated with rising professional classes, in "Saving Astrology in Restoration England: 'Whig' and 'Tory' Reforms," in *Astrology, Science, and Society: Historical Essays*, ed. Patrick Curry (Woodbridge, Suffolk: Boydell Press, 1987), 245–59. See also Patrick Curry, *Prophecy and Power: Astrology in Early Modern England* (Cambridge: Polity Press, 1989), 109–10.

60. See the introduction to "Thomas Shadwell, *The Virtuoso*," ed. Marjorie Hope Nicholson and David Stuart Rodes (London: Edward Arnold Ltd., 1966), esp. xix–xxv; also Claude Lloyd, "Shadwell and the Virtuosi," *Proceedings of the Modern Language Association* 17 (1928): 472–94. The play premiered with George Etherege's *The Man of Mode* and William Wycherley's *The Plain Dealer*, and it proved quite popular during the season; see *The Complete Works of Thomas Shadwell*, 5 vols., ed. Montague Summers (London: Fortune Press, 1927), 3:99. It played three times, and was reprinted and possibly performed in 1691: see van Lennep, et al., *The London Stage*, 1:233, 244, 245, 388. As John Dryden observed in his satire *MacFlecknoe, or A Satyr upon the True-Blew-Protestant Poet, T. S.* (1682), Shadwell had a habit of revising works, including *The Hypocrite* from Moliére's *Tartuffe* and a translation of *The Miser*.

61. J. S. Peters identifies this desire with the search for novelty that becomes meaningless repetition, in "The Novelty; or, Print, Money, Fashion, Getting, Spending, and Glut," in *Cultural Readings of Restoration and Eighteenth-Century English Theater*, ed. J. Douglas Canfield and Deborah C. Payne (Athens and London: University of Georgia Press, 1995), 169–94.

62. Nicholson and Rodes, *The Virtuoso*, xxv. See Harold Love's argument that amateurism in writing composed a tradition rivaling professionalism, in "Shadwell, Rochester, and the Crisis of Amateurism," in *Thomas Shadwell Reconsider'd: Essays in Criticism*, ed. Judith Bailey Slagle, special issue of *Restoration: Studies in English Literary Culture, 1660–1700* 20, no. 2 (fall 1996): 122.

63. Etienne claims that neither sodomy nor the impersonation of men by women is traditionally so considered, although he discusses all in the same chapter and calls a sodomitic rapist a "monster" (pt. 1, chap. 13, p. 69).

64. Giuseppi Olmi, "Science-Honour-Metaphor: Italian Cabinets of the Sixteenth and Seventeenth Centuries," in *The Origins of Museums: The Cabinet of Curiosities in Sixteenth-and Seventeenth-Century Europe*, ed. Oliver Impey and Arthur MacGregor (Oxford: Clarendon Press, 1985), 12.

65. Earl Miner stresses the difference between poetic *sapientia* and the increasingly specialized knowledge that "science" required, in "The Poets and Science in Seventeenth-Century England," in *The Uses of Science in the Age of Newton*, ed. John G. Burke (Berkeley, Los Angeles, London: University of California Press, 1983), 1–19.

66. Clark, *Form and Frenzy*, 26–27.

67. *Oxford English Dictionary* (Oxford: Oxford University Press, 1971).

68. "*The* TRYAL *of Richard Hathaway, Upon* INFORMATION *For being a Cheat and Imposter, For endeavouring to take away The Life of* SARAH MORDUCK, *For being a* WITCH *at Surrey* ASSIZES, *Begun and held in the Burrough of Southwark, March the 24th, 1702.* In which Is discovered the malicious Designs of the said Impostor,

with an Account of his pretended Inchantments and Witchcraft. Before the Right Honourable the Lord Chief Justice Holt and Mr. Baron Hatsell" (London: Isaac Cleave, 1702), 4.

69. *"A Full and True Relation* of the Discovering, Apprehending, and taking of a Notorious *Witch* who was carried before Justice *Bateman* in *Well-Close*, on *Sunday July* the 23rd. Together with her Examination and Commitment to *Bridewell, Clerkenwel*" (London: H. Hills, 24 July 1704); the pages are not numbered.

70. Susan M. Pearce has correlated the contemporary passion for collecting with the decline of religious narratives and physical depositories of relics, in *Museums, Objects, and Collections: A Cultural Study* (Leicester and London: Leicester University Press, 1992), 92. Tales of the supernatural, particularly when assembled into collections, bridge these phenomena by functioning as symbolic cabinets for relics of the unseen.

71. Barbara Shapiro, *Probability and Certainty in Seventeenth-Century England* (Princeton, N.J.: Princeton University Press, 1983). Brian Easlea points out that witch hunting ended only in the middle of the eighteenth century, in *Witch Hunting, Magic, and the New Philosophy: An Introduction to Debates of the Scientific Revolution, 1450–1750* (Sussex England: The Harvester Press; Atlantic Highlands, N.J.: Humanities Press, 1980), 4, passim. Michael Hunter argues that this skepticism led not to a general disbelief in witchcraft, but only to a suspicion of the evidence in specific cases, in *Science and the Shape of Orthodoxy*, 288.

72. *The Spectator,* ed. Donald F. Bond, 5 vols. (Oxford: Clarendon Press, 1965), 1:480.

73. Michael Hunter suggests that most skepticism was "orally expressed" rather than printed; see *Science and the Shape of Orthodoxy*, 289.

74. "Notes Conferr'd: Or, A Dialogue betwixt The Groaning Board and a Jesuite: Demonstrating the Ambiguous Humour of the one, and Curiosity of the other" (London: R. Shuter, 1682).

75. Elaine Hobby notes Cavendish's "overwhelming desire to be an originator," in *Virtue of Necessity: English Women's Writing, 1649–88* (Ann Arbor: University of Michigan Press, 1988), 90.

76. Fifth dedication to *Poems and Fancies*, by Lady Newcastle (London: J. Martin and J. Allestrye, 1653). All citations refer to this edition.

77. In "A Nature of 'Infinite Sense and Reason': Margaret Cavendish's Natural Philosophy and the 'Noise' of a Feminized Nature," *Women's Studies* 25, no. 5 (1996), Rebecca Merrens argues that Cavendish functioned to consolidate the Royal Society by representing an external challenge, but that she also "figures herself as an agent and instigator of communication" (421–38, esp. 426). Marjorie Hope Nichols recounts contemporary sneers at Cavendish's enterprise and her visit to the Royal Society, although Pepys typically found her "comely," in *Pepys' Diary and the New Science* (Charlottesville: University Press of Virginia, 1965), 105–9.

78. Judith Kegan Gardiner argues that Cavendish "eroticizes knowledge" for its own sake, like the virtuosi, rather than for power, but this distinction ignores the reality of the virtuosi's social influence and the personal power knowledge pro-

vides; see "'Singularity of Self': Cavendish's *True Relation*, Narcissism, and the Gendering of Individualism," *Restoration: Studies in English Literary Culture, 1660–1700* 21, no. 2 (fall 1997), 61.

79. Mary Baine Campbell, "Impossible Voyages: Seventeenth-Century Space Travel and the Impulse of Ethnology," *Literature and History*, 3d series, 6, no. 2 (autumn 1997), 1–17, esp. 4–7.

80. Aphra Behn, *"The Emperor of the Moon*, As it is Acted by Their Majesties Servants, at the Queens Theatre" (London: Joseph Knight and Francis Saunders, 1687), stage direction: act 1, scene 2, line 7 (original italics). In the dedication, Behn explains the outdated topicality by confessing that she intended the play for Charles II.

81. Aphra Behn, *The Emperor of the Moon*, in *Plays Written by the late Ingenious Mrs. Behn*, 4 vols. (London: Mary Poulson, A. Bettesworth, 1724), 4:act 1, scene 2, p. 199. This purports to be the authoritative edition for the eighteenth century.

82. Samuel Butler, *The Elephant in the Moon* (London: British Library edition, n.d.). All citations refer to this edition and will be abbreviated so that, for example, 1.1 refers to canto 1, line 1. Alexander C. Spence argues that Butler aims only to attack the extravagances and dishonesty of some members of the Royal Society, rather than to undermine the entire enterprise, and that he "seems to be less concerned with the deceitfulness of telescopes than with the readiness of scientists to be deceived by them"; but specific satires have a notorious tendency to spill into general ones, and Butler's critique engages traditional, as well as topical, plaints against various kinds of cunning men. See *Samuel Butler: Three Poems*, selected with an intro. Alexander C. Spence (Los Angeles: William Andrews Clark Memorial Library, 1961), iii–iv.

83. Like *Hudibras*, *The Elephant in the Moon* satirizes pointless disputations and self-indulgent argumentation; see lines 205–14.

84. Samuel Butler, *Samuel Butler, 1612–1680: Characters*, ed. with intro. and notes Charles W. Daves (Cleveland and London: Case Western Reserve University Press, 1970), 122–22.

85. Shapin and Schaffer, *Leviathan and the Air Pump*, 18.

86. In *Possessing Nature: Museums, Collecting, and Scientific Culture in Early Modern Italy*, Paula Findlen observes that microscopes, increasing in popularity from the 1620s, had become staples of scientific investigation by the 1660s (Berkeley, Los Angeles, London: University of California Press, 1994), 216.

87. *"The Philosophical Transactions of Two Years*, 1665 and 1666, beginning March 6, 1665. and ending with February 1666; abbreviated in an Alphabetical Table: And also afterwards Digested into a more Natural Method" (London: John Martyn, 1668), 401.

88. Ibid. And see Robert Westfall, *Science and Religion in Seventeenth-Century England* (New Haven: Yale University Press, 1958), 135.

89. *The Philosophical Transactions of Two Years*, 403. And see particularly Helvetius's competition with "Hugens" (Christiaan Huygens), *Philosophical Transactions*, vol. 1 (6 November 1665): 98, in *Philosophical Transactions*, ed. Henry Oldenburg (Savoy, London: John Martyn and James Allestry, 1666). See also "An Alphabeti-

cal Table for the Third Volume of the *Philosophical Transactions* In the Year 1668" (London: John Martyn, 1668) under "O": "*Optical Improvements;* by Mr. Smethwick, in a Figure not-Spherical, 33, 631, *Glasses,* how turned at *Paris* by a Turnlath, 40, 795. A way to turn convex *Spherical Glasses* on a Plain, represented here in Cuts, 42, 837. A *Microscope* of a new fashion, taking in large Objects, and discovering more minute Bodies, than formerly discover'd, 42, 842. An *Optical* Contrivance for strange visions, or Apparitions, 38, 471. The *Optick* Nerve and Vision by a New Experiment, examin'd, 35, 668." Also see *Philosophical Transactions,* no. 7 (4 December 1665), discussing lunar changes, glasses, and telescopes; no. 8 (8 January 1665/6) on optical glasses and observations of Jupiter, continued in the debate over "the Permanent *Spott* in *Jupiter*" in no. 10 (12 March 1665/6), 209; and persistent accounts of the barometer, notably no. 13 (4 June 1666).

90. *Curious Advertisements*: British Library, 1889.b.8 (fol. 25).

91. Joseph Glanvill, "*Plus Ultra: or, The Progress and Advancement of Knowledge Since the Days of Aristotle.* In an Account of some of the Most Remarkable Late Improvement of *Practical, Useful* Learning: To Encourage Philosophical Endeavours. Occasioned By a Conference with one of the Notional Way" (London: James Collines, 1668), chap. 9, pp. 65–66. All citations refer to this edition.

92. Biagioli, "Etiquette, Interdependence, and Sociability," 233. See Boyle's autobiography in *Works* 1, esp. 9–10.

93. Margaret C. Jacob notes that the pragmatism, caution, and materialism of the Royal Society were a continuation of Puritan practices, in *The Cultural Meaning of the Scientific Revolution* (New York: Knopf, 1988), 84.

94. An exception might be Dr. John Woodward, who is examined in chapter 2.

95. Michael Hunter and Simon Schaffer, eds., *Robert Hooke: New Studies* (Woodbridge, Suffolk: Boydell Press, 1989).

96. R. T. Gunther, *Early Science in Oxford,* vol. 10, *The Life and Work of Robert Hooke,* pt. 4 (Oxford: for the author, 1935), v.

97. See the introduction to *The Diary of Robert Hooke, 1672–1680,* ed. Henry W. Robinson and Walter Adams (London: Taylor and Francis, 1935).

98. Robinson and Adams, *The Diary of Robert Hooke,* 335.

99. Glanvill, *Plus Ultra,* 75, 9–10; see also 78.

100. Hunter, *Before Novels,* 41–47, 201–5; see also "'News and New Things': Contemporaneity and the Early English Novel," *Critical Inquiry* 15 (spring 1988): 493–515.

101. Lorraine Daston differentiates Baconian, "modern" scientific method from the Aristotelian exemplary scientific method, in "Marvelous Facts and Miraculous Evidence in Early Modern Europe," *Critical Inquiry* 18 (autumn 1991): 93–124, esp. 110.

102. *Curious Advertisements*: British Library, 1889.b.8 (fol. 1); reprinted from a handbill (temp. W. III) in the British Museum, among the Harley Papers, 5931 (fol. 15). See also advertisements for shows of the military camp on Hounslow Heath (fol. 27) and "Paris in London," an eighteen-foot table adorned with 50,000 wooden and pasteboard buildings and 20,000 green silk trees (fol. 31).

103. Butler, *Characters,* 105–6.

CHAPTER TWO

1. John Sitter has argued that poetry claimed a new status as a form of 'truth' rather than metaphor, but I am arguing that the relationship between these modes remained contested at this time; see "Severe Pleasures: The Eighteenth-Century Defense of Poetry," *Johnson Society News Letter* (October 1998): 4. Changes in licensing, censorship, and book trade practices defined new audiences; see John Feather, *A History of British Publishing* (London and New York: Routledge, 1988), esp. 73–74; and *The Provincial Book Trade in Eighteenth-Century England* (Cambridge: Cambridge University Press, 1988).

2. See particularly the multilingual Neapolitan child covered with hairy scales in *A Collection of Advertisements* [1680s], no. 75; and *"The Wonder of our Times*: Being A True and exact Relation of the Body of a mighty Giant dig'd up at Brockford Bridge . . . his height 10 foot, his Head as big as half a bushell; with a description of the severall parts of his body, and manner of his interring" (London: Printed by R. Austin, for W. Ley, 1651), 1. See also the description of John Tates in John Ray, *Travels through the Low Countries, Germany, Italy and France* (London: J. Walthoe et al., 1738), 5; and also in Philip Skippon's *An Account of a Journey Made Thro' Part of the Low-Countries, Germany, Italy, and France* [1732], in *A Collection of Voyages and Travels* (London: John Walthoe, 1732), which, after observing that Skippon could stand under Tates's armpit "with my hat on," records that "He spoke *English*" (365).

3. In the chapter on "The Identity of a Man" in *An Essay concerning Humane Understanding* (1690), Locke explicates the relationship between bodily form and reason in defining human identity by implying that the apparently rational responses of a parrot were actually contrived by human tricks of translation. See John Locke, *An Essay Concerning Human Understanding*, 2 vols., edited, collated, and annotated by Alexander Campbell Fraser (New York: Dover Publications, 1959): bk. 2, chap. 27, sec. 9–10: Christopher Fox refers to Gulliver as a "little speaking animal" in the introduction to *Inventing Human Science: Eighteenth-Century Domains*, ed. Christopher Fox, Roy Porter, and Robert Wokler (Berkeley, Los Angeles, London: University of California Press), 6, 23–24, n. 38. See also Fox's analysis of Augustan concepts of identity in *Locke and the Scriblerians: Identity and Consciousness in Early Eighteenth-Century Britain* (Berkeley, Los Angeles, and London: University of California Press, 1988).

4. *A Collection of Curious Advertisements* [1682–1836], British Library, 1889.b.8.

5. ca. 1700. Harry Ransom Humanities Research Center, AG 241 T6 1700z HRC-TA.

6. Thomas Adams, *Workes* (London, 1629), 471–73. Adams suggests as a remedy passages from the Bible, especially Deut. 29:29: "Secret things belong unto the Lord our God, but those things which are revealed belong unto us."

7. Thomas Griffith, *Evils arising from Misapply'd Curiosity* (Oxford: J. Parker, 1760); William Newton, *Essay against Unnecessary Curiosity in Matters of Religion* (London: S. Billingsley, 1725).

8. See Carol Houlihan Flynn's argument that the unexplained body, particularly bodies amassed in crowded cities, obtruded on current philosophical systematizations of materiality, challenging writers to manage it through language, in *The Body in Swift and Defoe* (Cambridge: Cambridge University Press, 1990).

9. Pat Rogers, observing in particular the reverence for collecting *virtu*, argues that popular entertainments aped those of the gentry, in *Literature and Popular Culture in the Eighteenth Century* (Sussex: The Harvester Press; and N.J.: Barnes and Noble Books, 1985), esp. 9–10.

10. Newton, *Essay*, 17–18; Griffith, *Evils*, 42–43.

11. Dennis Todd, *Imagining Monsters: Miscreations of the Self in Eighteenth-Century England* (Chicago: University of Chicago Press, 1995).

12. Helen Deutsch, *Alexander Pope and the Deformation of Culture* (Cambridge, Mass.: Harvard University Press, 1996), esp. 33–38, 138–41.

13. William King, in the preface to *The Transactioneer* (London: For the Booksellers of London and Westminster, 1700).

14. "*The Country Spy; or a Ramble thro' London.* Containing Many curious Remarks, diverting Tales, and merry Joaks," 2d ed. (London: R. Walker, for the author, n.d.), 46.

15. Alexander Pope, *The Rape of the Lock*, in *Miscellaneous Poems and Translations By Several Hands* (London: Bernard Lintot, 1712), canto 2, line 15 (original italics). In the 1714 edition, revised, expanded from two to five cantos, and produced for an elite audience, these lines have been softened; see Alexander Pope, *The Rape of the Lock* (London: Bernard Lintot, 1714), canto 4, line 98. My citations will refer to the 1714 edition unless the 1712 edition differs; also I will abbreviate canto and line citations, so, for example, "canto 2, line 15" will appear as 2.15.

16. Beth Kowaleski-Wallace explores Belinda's place as consumable and consumer, and women as shifting between objects and subjects of consumption, in "Women, China, and Consumer Culture in Eighteenth-Century England," *Eighteenth-Century Studies* 29, no. 2 (winter 1995–96), 153–67. See also Laura Brown, *Ends of Empire: Women and Ideology in Early Eighteenth-Century English Literature* (Ithaca and London: Cornell University Press, 1993), 113–14.

17. Frederic V. Bogel, *Literature and Insubstantiality in Later Eighteenth-Century England* (Princeton: Princeton University Press, 1984).

18. Ernest B. Gilman, *Literary and Pictorial Wit in the Seventeenth Century* (New Haven and London: Yale University Press, 1978), 50.

19. In "*The Rape of the Lock" and Its Illustrations, 1714–1896* (Oxford: Clarendon Press, 1980), Robert Halsband deduces from Foxon's catalogue that in the previous decade only 7 out of 1,100 poems were illustrated before the 1714 version of *The Rape of the Lock* (4, 13–14).

20. Halsband, "*The Rape of the Lock" and Its Illustrations*, 18.

21. Giles Jacob, *The Rape of the Smock: An Heroi-Comical Poem* (London: R. Burleigh, 1717).

22. Interestingly, the engraving of the rape scene centers on the most usual of courtly curiosities, a richly clad dwarf; see the facsimile edition, Alexander

Pope, *The Rape of the Lock, Illustrated by Aubrey Beardsley* (New York: Dover Publications, 1968), 20–21. Most notoriously, in 1896, Aubrey Beardsley illustrated Pope's text with a spiraling baroque delicacy very close to the polygraphy of the seventeenth century.

23. Felicity A. Nussbaum, *The Brink of All We Hate: English Satires on Women, 1660–1750* (Lexington: University Press of Kentucky, 1984), 105.

24. *The Curious Maid* (London: A. Dodd and T. Edlin, 1720), putatively by Hildebrand Jacob, possibly by Matthew Prior, appeared in broadside and in literary miscellanies. See also David F. Foxon, *English Verse, 1701–1750*, 2 vols. (Cambridge: Cambridge University Press, 1975), 1:156. The 1720 ballad "Sylvia a May Rolling" opens, "Curiosity made Sylvia Seek" and ends with her defloration, in *Merry Songs and Ballads Prior to the Year A.D. 1800*, ed. John S. Farmer (Privately printed, 1897), vol. 3, p. 226, st. 1, line 1.

25. See also [Matthew Prior?], *The members to their Soveraign*, attributed to "the Author of the Curious Maid," using metaphorical language derived from Rochester (London, 1726).

26. *The Curious Maid* (London: A. Dodd and T. Edlin, 1720), st. 1, p. 3. All citations refer to this, probably the first, edition, although another edition appeared in the same year, and the poem is included in *The Works of Hildebrand Jacob, Esq.* (London: W. Lewis, 1735), 74–77, which italicizes key words and phrases, including "*Sign*," "*hidden*," "*curious Maid*," and "*Myst'ries*."

27. "On Caelia's saying she had no secret" (by Matthew Prior?), in *A New Miscellany of Original Poems, Translations and Imitations. By the most Eminent Hands*, ed. Anthony Hammond (London: T. Jauncy, 1720), pp. 226–27, lines 4, 5–12.

28. "The Contest. A Tale," in the Thomas Fisher Rare Book Library, University of Toronto, MS 9263, Item 104 in Todd Gilman's unpublished analysis, lines 20, 51.

29. *The Peeper: being a Sequel To the Curious Maid* (London: Thomas Edlin, 1721). While this has been attributed to Matthew Prior, its style, diction, and genre as a riposte poem suggest another hand.

30. *The Longitude Found out: A Tale* (London: Thomas Edlin, 1721), lines 39–40.

31. See also [John Gay], *An Epistle to the most Learned Doctor Woodward; from a Prude, That was unfortunately Metamorphos'd on Saturday December 29, 1722* (London: J. Roberts, 1723), in which a frustrated female, Prudentia, sprouts a hermaphroditic male member and bewails that "in Petticoats the Monster bolder grows" (8).

32. Claude Rawson, *Order from Confusion Sprung: Studies in Eighteenth-Century Literature from Swift to Cowper* (London: Allen and Unwin, 1985), 160–65.

33. Jonathan Swift, "The Lady's Dressing-Room," in *The Works of J. S., D. D, D. S. P. D.*, vol. 3 (Dublin: George Faulkner, 1735), p. 307, line 7. All parenthetical references are to line numbers.

34. Flynn, *The Body in Swift and Defoe*, 33–35, 92.

35. In *Swift's Anatomy of Misunderstanding: A Study of Swift's Epistemological*

Imagination in 'The Tale of a Tub' and 'Gulliver's Travels,' Frances Deutsch Louis emphasizes Swift's resistance to the modern scientific acceptance of sense perception, "fact," and the Cartesian division between a knower and a thing to be known, between body and soul (London: George Prior Publishers, 1981); see esp. 7–8, 36–37.

36. Jonathan Swift, "A beautiful young Nymph going to Bed," in *The Works of J. S., D. D., D. S. P. D.*, vol. 3 (Dublin: George Faulkner, 1735), 312, line 11.

37. Contemporary audiences considered the work pornographic and libelous, an attack not only on Dr. Woodward but also, through the bombastic character of Sir Tremendous, on the critic John Dennis. The play ran for seven days, but partisan opposition to the Scriblerian anti-Whig stance and possibly the relationship between Woodward and his patient Sir Richard Steele, then governor of Drury Lane, prevented further stagings. See George Sherburn, "The Fortunes and Misfortunes of *Three Hours After Marriage*," *Modern Philology* 24 (August 1926): 91–109.

38. In "'Empiricomany, or an Infatuation in Favour of Empiricism or *Quackery*': The Socio-economics of Eighteenth-Century Quackery," Roger A. Hambridge traces the explosion of satires against medical practices and practitioners to the stagnancy of the profession; see *Literature and Science and Medicine* (Los Angeles: University of California, William Andrews Clark Memorial Library, 1982), 47–102.

39. Warren Chernaik examines this Restoration trope in *Sexual Freedom in Restoration Literature* (Cambridge, New York, Melbourne: Cambridge University Press, 1995), esp. 14.

40. See Joseph M. Levine's analysis of the argument between the "modern" Woodward and his opponent Dr. John Freind, in *Dr. Woodward's Shield: History, Science, and Satire in Augustan England* (Berkeley, Los Angeles, and London: University of California Press, 1977), 9–11, passim.

41. David Price, "John Woodward and a Surviving British Geological Collection from the Early Eighteenth Century," *Journal of the History of Collecting* 1, no. 1 (1989): 79–95.

42. John Gay et al., *Three Hours After Marriage* (London: B. Lintot, 1717), act 2, p. 29; all citations refer to this edition.

43. Lorraine Daston and Katharine Park, *Wonders and the Order of Nature* (New York: Zone Books, 1998), 84–86. The renowned collector Sir William Hamilton acquired two small mummies and fifteen scarabs, which became part of the British Museum collection in 1794. See Stephen Quirke, "Modern Mummies and Ancient Scarabs: The Egyptian Collection of Sir William Hamilton," in *Journal of the History of Collections* 9, no. 2 (1997): 253–62, esp. 254.

44. Helen Whitehouse, "Egyptology and Forgery in the Seventeenth Century: The Case of the Bodleian Shabti," *Journal of the History of Collections* 1, no. 2 (1989): 187–95.

45. Curiosity cabinets and science catalogues document the confusion between natural and artistic objects. Lorraine Daston and Katharine Park further

note the affinity between relics and marvels in *Wonders*, 69–70. See also Adalgisa Lugli, *Naturalia et Mirabilia: Les Cabinets de Curiosités en Europe*, intro. de Roland Recht (Paris: Adam Biro, 1998), 40. Susan Stewart, *On Longing: Narratives of the Miniature, the Gigantic, the Souvenir, the Collection* (Baltimore: Johns Hopkins University Press, 1984), 154–56.

46. Highly desirable china carried sexual innuendoes: Etherege's *The Man of Mode* (1676), itself featuring a Lady Townley, staged a notorious scene in which the fragility of china implies women's sexual vulnerability, while Pope recommends good humor "tho' China fall" (*Of the Characters of Women: An Epistle to a Lady* [London: Lawton Gilliver, 1735], line 268). Charles H. Hinnant, "Pleasure and the Political Economy of Consumption in Restoration Comedy," *Restoration: Studies in English Literary Culture, 1660–1700* 19, no. 2 (fall 1995), 80.

47. Paula Findlen documents early collectors' self-conscious fashioning of their identity, in *Possessing Nature: Museums, Collecting, and Scientific Culture in Early Modern Italy* (Berkeley, Los Angeles, London: University of California Press, 1994), 293–345, esp. 294–95.

48. Leslie Fiedler, identifying collection as a repressed sexuality, in *Freaks: Myths and Images of the Secret Self* (Middlesex: Penguin Books, 1978), suggests that hybrids and monsters show the child the "monstrous discrepancy between his erotic nature and the role expectations of his era," and that seeing the freakish Other dispels the illusion that we differ from the monster (30, 32, 36). Rather, I argue here that contemporary historical tensions lead conservative writers to regard collecting as a cultural ambition that sometimes also implies sexual self-inflation.

49. Alexander Pope, *Of the Use of Riches. An Epistle to the right Honourable Allen Lord Bathurst* (London: Lawton Gilliver, 1732), line 69.

50. Alexander Pope, *Of False Taste: An Epistle to the Right Honourable Richard Earl of Burlington. Occasion'd by his Publishing* PALLADIO's *Designs of the* BATHS, ARCHES, THEATRES, &c. *Of Ancient* ROME, 3d edition (London: L. Gilliver, 1731), lines 1–4. All citations unless otherwise specified refer to this edition.

51. Swift uses this technique of amplification, metanoia, or cataloguing for satirical effect, sometimes to mimic the analogical rhetoric of members of the Royal Society, notably Robert Hooke. See Serge Soupel, "Science and Medicine and the Mid-Eighteenth-Century Novel: Literature and the Language of Science," in *Literature and Medicine* (Los Angeles: William Andrews Clark Memorial Library, University of California, 1982), 19. Swift similarly catalogues abuses in *Gulliver's Travels;* see the King of Brobdingnag's attack on Gulliver's species, and Gulliver's similar attack, parodying Robinson Crusoe's account-keeping, in Houyhnhnmland: "Here were no Gibers, Censurers, Backbiters, Pick-pockets, Highwaymen, Housebreakers, Attorneys, Bawds," or "Virtuoso's"; see Swift, *Gulliver's Travels*, pt. 4, p. 250.

52. Alexander Pope, *Epistle to Burlington*, in *The Poems of Alexander Pope*, ed. John Butt (New Haven: Yale University Press, 1963), p. 588, lines 8, 10.

53. Alexander Pope, *Of the Knowledge and Characters of Men. An Epistle to the*

Right Honourable Lord Viscount Cobham (London, 1734), 11. He opens the *Epistle to . . . Bathurst* by modestly disavowing expertise in a matter "when Doctors disagree" (1).

54. Pat Rogers notes Pope's attraction to Scriblerian and modernist concerns, particularly a passion for moss shared with Dr. Woodward, in "Pope and the Antiquarians," in *Essays on Pope* (Cambridge: Cambridge University Press, 1993), 240–60, esp. 250.

55. Pope, *Of the Characters of Women*, line 170.

56. Alexander Pope, "To the Reader," in *The Dunciad* (Dublin; reprinted, London: A. Dodd, 1728), vii.

57. J. Paul Hunter, *Before Novels: The Cultural Contexts of Eighteenth-Century English Fiction* (New York: W. W. Norton and Co., 1990), 66–67; David Cressy, *Literacy and the Social Order: Reading and Writing in Tudor and Stuart England* (Cambridge: Cambridge University Press, 1980).

58. Margaret J. M. Ezell, "The *Gentleman's Journal* and the Commercialization of Restoration Coterie Literary Practices," *Modern Philology* 89, no. 3 (February 1992), 323–40.

59. Ned Ward, *The London Spy* COMPLEAT. *In Eighteen Parts*, with intro. Ralph Straus (London: The Casanova Society, 1924), preface.

60. Ned Ward, *The London Spy*, ed., with intro. and notes, Kenneth Fenwick (London: The Folio Society, 1955): chap. 1, p. 1.

61. This format was often imitated. See, for example, *The Country Spy*, whose preface attributes agency to "Curiosity, which tempted old Madam *Eve*, whereby a Curse was intail'd upon Mankind"; although the author resists, a lawsuit compels him to come to the metropolis anyway, where he records coarse behavior, including the manic "*Virtuoso*" who abandons his harangues on "*Fossils*, and other Curiosities of Nature, both animate and inanimate" to chase a cricket and is roped as a madman by a miller (pt. 1, p. 43).

62. John Brewer explores the overlap of performer and audience, in "The Most Polite Age and the Most Vicious: Attitudes towards Culture as a Commodity: 1660–1800," in *The Consumption of Culture, 1600–1800: Image, Object, Text*, ed. Ann Bermingham and John Brewer (London and New York: Routledge, 1995), 437.

63. James Grantham Turner, arguing that obscene literature of the late seventeenth century presents "the economic activity of women as a kind of prostitution," locates Bartholomew Fair as a central site of female agency; see "'News from the New Exchange': Commodity, Erotic Fantasy, and the Female Entrepreneur," in *The Consumption of Culture, 1600–1800: Image, Object, Text*, ed. Ann Bermingham and John Brewer (London and New York: Routledge, 1995), 419, 430–32. See also Ronald Paulson's argument in the same volume that the harlot masquerades as gentry, in "Emulative Consumption and Literacy: The Harlot, Moll Flanders, and Mrs. Slipslop," 384–400.

64. In "Modern Prostitution and Gender in *Fanny Hill*: Libertine and Domesticated Fantasy," in *Sexual Worlds of the Enlightenment*, ed. G. S. Rousseau and

Roy Porter (Manchester: Manchester University Press, 1987), Randolph Trumbach says that the gradual reorganization of gender roles, whereby women were no longer all regarded as whores, began in the 1690s (73). Jacqueline Pearson notes, "Published women writers first appear in any numbers, and first exert a real influence on English literature, in the Restoration and early eighteenth century"; Pearson also notes women's new public and political roles, along with men's renewed misogyny, in *The Prostituted Muse: Images of Women and Women Dramatists, 1642–1737* (New York: St. Martin's Press, 1988), 1. See also Christopher Hill's suggestion that the post-Restoration regime was profoundly repressive, in *The World Turned Upside Down: Radical Ideas During the English Revolution* (New York: Viking Books, 1972), 305–6. Michel Foucault develops this idea in *Madness and Civilization: A History of Insanity in the Age of Reason* (New York: Vintage Press, 1973).

65. Benianmin Ionson, *Bartholomew Fayre: A Comedie* (London: Robert Allot, 1631), prologue, lines 4–5.

66. William King, *A Journey to London, In the Year 1698*, 2d ed. (London: A. Baldwin, 1699), 27–28.

67. In her sarcastic *Bart'lemy Fair: Or, An Enquiry after Wit* (London: R. Wilkin, 1709), Mary Astell uses the fair to excoriate her political enemies, the Kit-Cat Club, and their scurrilous publications: in the riot of scandal, "every . . . thing," even wit "may be Purchas'd" for a price (18–19).

68. Richard Altick observes that the undifferentiated mix of scientific invention and grotesque spectacle, particularly as it was encapsulated in the visual "raree show," drew an undifferentiated mix of "quality" and "rabble," in *The Shows of London* (Cambridge, Mass. Belknap Press, 1978), 36. Dennis Todd sees Swift as despising entertainments for indulging "man's bottomless capacity for thoughtlessness," in *Imagining Monsters*, 150.

69. *Reasons Formerly published for the Punctual Limiting of Bartholomew Fair To those* Three Days *to which it is determined by the Royal Grant of it to the City of London. Now Reprinted with Additions, to prevent a* Design *set on Foot to procure an Establishment of the said Fair for Fourteen-Days* (London, 1711), 4.

70. *Bartholomew Fair: An Heroi-Comical Poem* (London: S. Baker, 1717), p. 2, line 11; see also pp. 21–23, lines 280–325.

71. In *Popular Culture in Early Modern Europe* (New York: Harper and Rowe, 1978), Peter Burke lists the traditional themes of carnival: "food, sex, and violence," including the "aggression, destruction, desecration" used to enact popular justice; he further records that during the European Protestant surge to reform popular culture from 1650 to 1800, England notably featured societies whose lay membership sought to reform manners not because they feared witchcraft, but in order to combat irrational "superstition" (186–87, 198, 238–42). See also M. M. Bakhtin's analysis of the literary incarnation of carnival, in *Rabelais and His World*, trans. Hélène Iswolsky (Cambridge, Mass.: Harvard University Press, 1968).

72. See Mary Thomas Crane, *Framing Authority: Sayings, Self, and Society in Sixteenth-Century England* (Princeton, N.J.: Princeton University Press, 1993).

73. Samuel Johnson, *A Dictionary of the English Language* (London: W. Strahan, 1755); the *Oxford English Dictionary* also defines the word oppositionally as "pertaining to matter as opposed to form."

74. *The British Apollo; or, Curious Amusements for the* INGENIOUS. *To which are Added the most Material Occurrences Foreign and Domestick*, ed. Aaron Hill and Marshall Smith, with probable contributions from John Gay, John Arbuthnot, and Samuel Garth, among others (London: Printed for the authors, 1708). Lawrence E. Klein analyzes the adaptive identity and, specifically, politeness of the early eighteenth-century consumer—including the "social voyeur" who reads to enter imaginatively an elite world; see "Politeness for Plebes: Consumption and Social Identity in Early Eighteenth-Century England," in *The Consumption of Culture, 1600–1800: Image, Object, Text*, ed. Ann Bermingham and John Brewer (London and New York: Routledge, 1995), 362–82.

75. William F. Belcher, "The Sale and Distribution of the *British Apollo*," in *Studies in the Early English Periodical*, ed. Richmond P. Bond (Chapel Hill: University of North Carolina Press, 1957), 77, 82 n. 50, 98; see also *The Female Tatler*, no. 21 (24 August 1709).

76. *The British Apollo*, no. 2, (Friday 13 to Wednesday 18 February 1708).

77. See also no. 15. And see Kathryn Shevelow, *Women and Print Culture: The Construction of Femininity in the Early Periodical* (London and New York: Routledge, 1989), 34–35.

78. Daniel Defoe, *A Weekly Review of the Affairs of France* (London: for the booksellers, 1704; facsimile edition, New York: Columbia University Press, 1938), p. 16: no. 2 (26 February 1704).

79. Defoe, *A Weekly Review*, p. 51: no. 9 (4 April 1704).

80. Daniel Defoe, *Defoe's Review*, intro. and notes Arthur Wellesley Secord (New York: Columbia University Press, 1938), xx–xxi.

81. [Sir Richard Steele], *The Tatler*, ed., with intro. and notes, Donald F. Bond (Oxford: Clarendon Press, 1987), p. 15: no. 1 (12 April 1709).

82. Kathryn Shevelow points out that *The Tatler* paradoxically separates public and private realms, while subjecting the latter to "published scrutiny," in *Women and Print Culture*, 93–94.

83. Similarly, Steele's *Town-Talk* and *Chit-Chat* (both 1716) represent current affairs as matter for intimate conversation. In the former, the narrator reports to a country acquaintance about current theater; in the latter he ruminates on the recent execution of Jacobite lords. See [Richard Steele], *Richard Steele's Periodical Journalism, 1714–16*, ed. Rae Blanchard (Oxford: Clarendon Press, 1959), xxi–xxvi. Both publications use the titular advertisement of gossip to draw audiences into public affairs. This device effectually blurs distinctions between public and intimate modes and matters of inquiry. Samuel Johnson's later journal *The Idler* similarly enlists a traditional indictment of curiosity for publicity, and in so doing makes idle curiosity the mark of gentlemanly reflection.

84. Introduction to *The Spectator*, ed. with intro. and notes by Donald F. Bond (Oxford: Clarendon Press, 1965), xviii.

85. *The Spectator*, vol. 4, p. 43: original publication, no. 439, Thursday, 24

July 1712, by Joseph Addison. Addison and Sir Richard Steele collaborated on this periodical, but this issue was written by Addison. All further citations are offered in this form parenthetically in the text.

86. See Hunter, *Before Novels*, esp. 180–81, passim.

87. Ian Watt defines the novel as empirical narrative, in *The Rise of the Novel: Studies in Defoe, Richardson, and Fielding* (Berkeley and Los Angeles: University of California, 1957). While many later critics have disputed Watt's criteria of formal realism, few deny the importance of material detail in the novel; see also Michael McKeon's argument that the novel incorporates progressive individualism; see particularly his examination of the Protestant need for self-documentation and the "extreme skepticism" of early journalism regarding travel documentaries and other chronicles of the individual, in *The Origins of the English Novel, 1600–1740* (Baltimore: Johns Hopkins University Press, 1987), 114–18.

88. Dan Doll notes Swift's "censure of words not properly connected to things," in "The Word and the Thing in Swift's Prose," in *Studies in Eighteenth-Century Culture* 15, ed. O. M. Brack Jr. (Madison: University of Wisconsin Press, 1986), 200. However, Doll ignores Swift's own exploitation of language's imprecisions, inadequacies, and opportunities; see Kevin L. Cope's analysis of the individuality and self-conscious limitations of empiricist didactic rhetoric, in "A 'Roman Commonwealth' of Knowledge: Fragments of Belief and the Disbelieving Power of Didactic," in *Studies in Eighteenth-Century Culture* 20, ed. Leslie Ellen Brown and Patricia B. Craddock (East Lansing, Michigan: Colleagues Press, 1990), esp.17–19.

89. Daniel Defoe, *Journal of the Plague Year*, ed. Anthony Burgess and Christopher Bristow (Middlesex, England; and New York: Penguin, 1986), 21. Citations refer to this edition unless otherwise noted.

90. See John Bender, *Imagining the Penitentiary: Fiction and the Architecture of Mind in Eighteenth-Century England* (Chicago: University of Chicago Press, 1987), esp. 64–84; Peter Stallybrass and Allon White, *The Politics and Poetics of Transgression* (Ithaca: Cornell University Press, 1986); Michel Foucault, *Discipline and Punish: The Birth of the Prison*, trans. Alan Sheridan (New York: Vintage, 1979). Benjamin Moore locates the *Journal*'s tensions in a social conflict "between government and populace," explaining, "the narrator's dual position of observer and observed" as "symptomatic of a deeper opposition between perspectival unity and informational multiplicity, the two elements fundamental to the *Journal*'s realism"; see "Governing Discourses: Problems of Narrative Authority, *A Journal of the Plague Year*," *Eighteenth Century: Theory and Interpretation* 33, no. 2 (summer 1992): 133, 139.

91. Locke, *An Essay Concerning Human Understanding*, sec. 1, "Of Enthusiasm."

92. For the negotiations of these two narrative stances in realism, see Robert Scholes and Robert Kellogg, *The Nature of Narrative* (New York: Oxford University Press, 1966).

93. David Trotter, *Circulation: Defoe, Dickens, and the Economics of the Novel* (London: Macmillan Press, 1988), 19–20; George A. Starr, *Defoe and Spiritual Autobiography* (Princeton, N.J.: Princeton University Press, 1975), 70.

94. In *Before Novels*, Hunter notes that *A Journal of the Plague Year* centers on the question of what constitutes evidence for providence or a metaphorical reading (46; see also 195–224).

95. In *Imagining the Penitentiary*, John Bender points out that the saddler's written memorial demonstrates his "internal restatement of external authority" by representing regulated perception, and so his role as examiner co-opts his lawless appetite for wonder and turns it into scientific, public service (177). George A. Starr argues that Defoe models a balance between rationalism and religion in the saddler, in *Defoe and Casuistry* (Princeton, N.J.: Princeton University Press, 1971), 51–81.

96. Daniel Defoe, *A Journal of the Plague Year: being Observations or Memorials Of the most Remarkable Occurrences, As well Publick as Private* (London: E. Nutt, 1722), 38 (original capital letters).

97. Louis A. Landa remarks that the *Journal* borrows from wonder literature, in his introduction to *A Journal of the Plague Year* (Oxford: Oxford University Press, 1969); reprinted in the Norton edition of the *Journal*, ed. Paula R. Backscheider (New York: W. W. Norton, 1992), 273.

98. Todd, *Imagining Monsters*, 272 n. 13.

99. Jonathan Swift, *The Wonderful Wonder of Wonders; Being an Accurate Description of the Birth, Education, Manner of Living, Religion, Politicks, Learning, &c. Of mine A—se*, 3d ed. (London: T. Bickerton, 1721), vi.

100. Jonathan Swift, *The Blunderful Blunder of Blunders; Being an Answer to the Wonderful Wonder of Wonders*, 2d ed. (London: T. Bickerton, 1721), 6.

101. [Daniel Defoe], *A True Relation of the Apparition of Mrs. Veal, The next Day after Her Death: to one Mrs. Bargrave, at Canterbury, The 8th of September,* 1705 (London: B. Bragg, 1706), preface. P. N. Furbank and W. R. Owens, *Defoe De-Attributions* (London and Rio Grande: Hambledon Press, 1994), 126.

102. In *Daniel Defoe and the Supernatural* (Athens: University of Georgia Press, 1968), Rodney M. Baine argues that the narrator of the tale emphasizes Mrs. Bargrave's cheerfulness in order to counteract any implication that she indulged a morbid imagination (96).

103. Daniel Defoe, *The Secrets of the Invisible World Disclos'd: Or, an Universal History of* APPARITIONS *Sacred and Prophane* (London: J. Clarke et al., 1729), preface.

104. As Keith Hutchison explains, the term itself was ambiguous even in the seventeenth century, designating both unseen effects and unseen causes; see "What Happened to Occult Qualities in the Scientific Revolution?" in *Isis* 73, no. 267 (June 1982): 233–53, esp. 234.

105. Eliza [Fowler] Haywood, *The Dumb Projector: Being a Surprizing* ACCOUNT *of a Trip to Holland Made by Mr. Duncan Campbell* (London: W. Ellis et al., 1725), 6.

106. *Secret Memoirs of the late Mr. Duncan Campbel, the Famous deaf and dumb Gentlemen, written by himself* (London: J. Millani and J. Chrichley, 1732), 77; Baine, *Daniel Defoe and the Supernatural*, 153.

107. Nicholas Steneck illuminates the seventeenth-century debate over the degree to which healers or gifted men were miraculous or natural phenomena in

his account of the struggle between Boyle and Stubbe over the "Stroker," or healer, Valentine Greatrakes, in "Greatrakes the Stroker: The Interpretations of Historians," in *Isis* 73, no. 267 (June 1982): 161–85, esp., 167–69.

108. In "'The Whole Internal World His Own': Locke and Metaphor Reconsidered," *Journal of the History of Ideas* 59, no. 2 (April 1998), 241–65, S. H. Clark argues that Locke uses metaphor in his own prose to enforce the unending mental labor of understanding. John J. Richetti argues that Crusoe acts simultaneously as "masterful economic individual" and as "heroically spiritual slave," acting out a dynamic relativity of helplessness in the context of control and control in the context of helplessness, in *Defoe's Narratives: Situations and Structures* (Oxford: Clarendon Press, 1975), 21–62; reprinted as *"Robinson Crusoe*: The Self as Master," in *Modern Essays on Eighteenth-Century Literature*, ed. Leopold Damrosch Jr. (New York: Oxford University Press, 1988), 201–36, esp. 203.

109. Virginia Ogden Birdsall, *Defoe's Perpetual Seeker: A Study of the Major Fiction* (Lewisburg: Bucknell University Press; London and Toronto: Associated University Press, 1985), 18.

110. Douglas Lane Patey shows the links between Book 3 and Swift's general attack on pride, the travel genre, and the epistemology of fiction, in "Swift's Satire on 'Science' and the Structure of *Gulliver's Travels*," *ELH* 58 (1991): 809–39; reprinted in *Jonathan Swift: A Collection of Critical Essays*, ed. Claude Rawson (Englewood Cliffs, N.J.: Prentice Hall, 1995), 216–40. Charles H. Hinnant sets out the thesis that *Gulliver's Travels*, using the idiom of early anthropology, explores the essentially contextual and relative relationship between the systematic and monstrous anomalies through the fictional realization of the taboos of various societies, in *Purity and Defilement in Gulliver's Travels* (New York: St. Martin's Press, 1987), esp. 2, 15–17.

111. "The Publisher to the Reader," in Jonathan Swift, *Travels into Several Remote Nations of the World. In Four Parts. By Lemuel Gulliver* (London: Benj. Motte, 1726), vii. The original title emphasizes the wonderful travelogue form of the satire.

112. For the contemporary contest over these categories, see Lennard J. Davis, *Factual Fictions: The Origins of the English Novel* (New York: Columbia University Press, 1983).

113. In *Form and Frenzy in Swift's 'Tale of a Tub'* (Ithaca and London: Cornell University Press, 1970), John R. Clark argues that Swift identifies curiosity and credulity as solipsistic attempts to define the world by the observer's terms (18).

114. Jonathan Swift, *Gulliver's Travels*, ed. Christopher Fox (Boston and New York: St. Martin's Press, 1995), pt. 2, p. 98. Unless specified otherwise, all citations refer to this edition.

115. Peter Dear points out that the virtuoso's personal experience lies at the center of the Royal Society's scientific narratives, in *Discipline and Experience: The Mathematical Way in the Scientific Revolution* (Chicago: University of Chicago Press, 1995), 228–30.

116. Claude Rawson, *Gulliver and the Gentle Reader: Studies in Swift and Our Time* (London: Routledge, 1973).

117. "The Publisher to the Reader," in Swift, *Gulliver's Travels*, 31.

118. Aline Mackenzie Taylor, "Sights and Monsters and Gulliver's *Voyage to Brobdingnag*," in *Tulane Studies in English* 7 (New Orleans: Tulane University, 1957), 29–82, esp. 29–57. This essay provides a delightfully thorough map of the uses of curiosity in Book 2 and analyzes Swift's intention to condemn the inhumanity of Gulliver and his society.

119. Aline Mackenzie Taylor draws close linguistic and textual connections between Swift's descriptions of Gulliver's actions and the terms used for shows at Bartholomew Fair, in "Sights and Monsters," 35.

CHAPTER THREE

1. In "Unnatural Conceptions: The Study of Monsters in Sixteenth- and Seventeenth-Century France and England," *Past and Present* 92 (August 1981), Katharine Park and Lorraine Daston trace the "shared culture" of enjoying monsters in enlightenment organs like Dunton's *Athenian Mercury* and in popular contexts (esp. 45–51).

2. Hester Lynch Piozzi, *British Synonymy; or, An Attempt at Regulating the Choice of Words in Familiar Conversation*, 2 vols. (London: G. G. and J. Robinson, 1794), 1:126–27. My thanks to Lisa Berglund for alerting me to this source.

3. Felicity A. Nussbaum connects monstrosity and feminism as violations of patriarchal order, in *On the Brink of All We Hate: English Satires on Women, 1660–1750* (Lexington: The University Press of Kentucky, 1984), 3.

4. Ann Bermingham incisively analyzes the complementarity between connoisseurs, fetishized commodity art, and accomplished (or 'finished') women, in "Elegant Female and Gentlemen Connoisseurs: The Commerce in Culture and Self-Image in Eighteenth-Century England," in *The Consumption of Culture, 1600–1800: Image, Object, Text*, ed. Ann Bermingham and John Brewer (London and New York: Routledge, 1995), 489–513. I am indebted to this essay.

5. William Combe, *Dr. Syntax in Paris; or, A Tour in Search of the Grotesque; A Humorous and Satirical Poem*, 18 plates (London: W. Wright, 1820). See also *Dr. Syntax's Three Tours: In Search of the Picturesque, Consolation, and a Wife*, 80 plates after the originals by Rowlandson (London: John Camden Hotton, 1868), 329.

6. James Clifford, *The Predicament of Culture: Twentieth-Century Ethnography, Literature, and Art* (Cambridge, Mass.: Harvard University Press, 1988), 215–19.

7. Patricia Meyer Spacks, *Gossip* (New York: Knopf, 1985), 3–23.

8. Beth Fowkes Tobin, "Introduction: Feminist Historical Criticism," in *History, Gender, and Eighteenth-Century Literature*, ed. Beth Fowkes Tobin (Athens and London: University of Georgia Press, 1994), 5.

9. Samuel Cobb, *Callipaedia*, in *The Poetical Works of Nicholas Rowe, Esq.* (London: E. Curll, 1715), lines 18, 52.

10. Roger Shattuck discusses the "dark side of curiosity" as presumption, vanity, and doubt encapsulated in biblical tales, in *Forbidden Knowledge: From Prometheus to Pornography* (New York: St. Martin's Press, 1996), 1–47, but he does not

pursue the historical or cultural implications of these myths. In the novel *Lot's Wife* (New York and London: Harper and Brothers, 1942), Max Eastman interprets the wife's death as Lot's revenge: Lot kills her as penance for her single act of rebellion, her moment of real living, in which she sees reality and destruction. The author cites as his "argument" the passages from Genesis 13: 1–13, 18:20–22, and 19.

   11. Mirjam Westen, "The Woman on a Swing and the Sensuous Voyeur," in *From Sappho to De Sade: Moments in the History of Sexuality*, ed. Jan Bremmer (London and New York: Routledge, 1989), 69, 74–75; A. D. Harvey, *Sex in Georgian England: Attitudes and Prejudices from the 1720s to the 1820s* (New York: St. Martin's Press, 1994), 24.

   12. In *Psyche: or Loves Mysterie* (London: George Boddington, 1648), Joseph Beaumont portrays the battle between empiricism and faith as a struggle between Psyche, the soul, and a bullying band of senses, led by the "Sense of Seeing" who claims "Imperiall Direction" over the body (st. 18, lines 4, 6). See, too, Mary Tighe's *Psyche: Or, The legend of Love*, in Mrs. Henry Tighe, *Psyche, with other Poems* (London: Longman, Hurst, Reese, Orme, and Brown, 1811), 102; here Psyche's self-betrayal is blamed on Ambition.

   13. Aphra Behn, *The Lucky Chance, or An Alderman's Bargain* (London: Printed by R. H. for W. Canning, at his shop in Vinecourt, Middle-Temple, 1867).

   14. William Van Lennep notes that one early performance, perhaps the premiere, fell on Friday, 24 February 1671, during Lent; see William van Lennep, Emmett L. Avery, Arthur H. Scouten, George Winchester Stone, and Charles Beecher Hogan, *The London Stage, 1600–1800*, 2 vols. (Carbondale: Southern Illinois University Press, 1965): 1:180–81.

   15. Aphra Behn, *The Amorous Prince, or The Curious Husband. A Comedy.* Duke of York Theatre (London: Thomas Dring, 1671): act 1, scene 4, p. 20.

   16. Richard Kroll argues that empiricism scrutinizes its own ideology, in "Instituting Empiricism: Hobbes's *Leviathan* and Dryden's *Marriage à la Mode*," in *Cultural Readings of Restoration and Eighteenth-Century English Theater*, ed. J. Douglas Canfield and Deborah C. Payne (Athens and London: University of Georgia Press, 1995), 39–66, esp. 42. He points out the interrelationship of romantic and ironic plots in exposing the foundations of empiricism (41).

   17. In "The Novelty; or, Print, Money, Fashion, Getting, Spending, and Glut," J. S. Peters suggests that sexual promiscuity appears in literature as the impulse to repeat specific experience in which the social value for consuming novelty wars with the body's knowledge of sameness; see *Cultural Readings of Restoration and Eighteenth-Century English Theater*, ed. J. Douglas Canfield and Deborah C. Payne (Athens and London: University of Georgia Press, 1995), 184.

   18. John Crowne, *The Married Beau: or, the Curious Impertinent. A Comedy* (London: Richard Bentley, 1694), act 4, p. 54.

   19. "*The Curious Impertinent.* Translated from the *Spanish* Original of Miguel de Cervantes Savedra. Printed in the Year 1720," in *A Select Collection of Novels*, ed. Samuel Croxall (London: pr. for Johns Watts, 1720), vol. 3: p. 139–93. See

the discussion in my article "The Curious Genre: Amatory Fiction and Female Inquiry," *Studies in the Novel* 30, no. 2 (summer 1998): 194–209.

20. This plot was imitated by Stephanie Felicite, comtesse de Genlis (1746–
1830), in *La Curieuse* (n.d.), another text about an impertinent spouse. This text
was translated into English by Francis Latham (1777–1832) as *Curiosity: a Comedy
in three Acts* (London: T. Hurst, [1801?]).

21. Terry Castle, *The Female Thermometer: Eighteenth-Century Culture and the
Invention of the Uncanny* (New York and Oxford: Oxford University Press, 1995),
esp. "'Matters Not Fit to be Mentioned': Fielding's *Female Husband,*" 67–81.

22. *The Female Monster, or the Second Part of The World turn'd Topsy Turvey*
(London: B. Bragg, 1705), st. 1, lines 1–4; st. 7, line 105.

23. Susan Gubar, "The Female Monster in Augustan Satire," *Signs* 3, no. 2
(winter 1977): 381–94.

24. Marina Warner examines Greek monstrous mothers, including Medea,
as examples of "ungovernable female appetite" that perverts its own source of
power by perverting motherhood, in *Six Myths of Our Time: Little Angels, Little
Monsters, Beautiful Beasts, and More* (originally published as *Managing Monsters:
Six Myths of Our Time*; reprint, New York: Vintage Books, 1994), esp. 10–21. See
also Bruce Clarke's discussion of Puritan moralism using Greek myths in which
female erotic misfortune brings about to metamorphosis, in *Allegories of Writing:
The Subject of Metamorphosis* (Albany: State University of New York Press, 1995),
124–25. In *Monstrous Imagination* (Cambridge, Mass. and London: Harvard University Press, 1993), Marie-Hélène Huet observes that the Renaissance combined
"the deformed child and the aberrant mother" (24). Both Elizabeth Eccles in
1843 and Jane Crosby in 1850 were dubbed "female monsters" for presumed in-
fanticide.

25. Dennis Todd, *Imagining Monsters: Miscreations of the Self in Eighteenth-
Century England* (Chicago: University of Chicago Press, 1995), 218.

26. *Pride's Fall:* st. 1, lines 5, 66. British Library Rox. III (806). Citing this
text, Dudley Wilson notes in *Signs and Portents: Monstrous Births from the Middle
Ages to the Renaissance* (London and New York: Routledge, 1993) that Renaissance
texts defined monstrosity as a sign of England's evil (49).

27. See, for example, *The Monster: A Satyr; or, The World turn'd Topsy Turvey*
(London: B. Bragg, 1705), an indictment of libertine irreligion, fashionable corruption, and pride in every rank of life. See also the ambiguous history of the
"monstrous" English hoop-petticoat—prompted by French fashions, exported to
France, but then reimported—explicated in Kimberly Chrisman's "*Unhoop* the
Fair Sex: The Campaign against the Hoop Petticoat in Eighteenth-Century England," *Eighteenth-Century Studies* 30, no. 1 (fall 1996): 5–23.

28. Margaret Cavendish, Duchess of Newcastle, *Poems and Fancies* (London:
J. Martin and J. Allestrye, 1653), esp. 1–45.

29. Kathryn Shevelow documents periodicals' attention to women as readers,
in *Women and Print Culture: The Construction of Femininity in the Early Periodical*
(London and New York: Routledge, 1989), 29–31.

30. See Catherine Ingrassia, "Women Writing/Writing Women: Pope, Dulness, and 'Feminization' in the *Dunciad*," *Eighteenth-Century Life*, n.s., 14, no. 3 (1990): 40–58; and Marilyn Francus, "The Monstrous Mother: Reproductive Anxiety in Swift and Pope," *ELH* 61, no. 4 (1994): 829–51.

31. Edward Thompson, *The Courtesan. By the Author of the Meretriciad* (London: J. Harrison, in Covent Garden, 1765), st. 2: lines 84, 86, 88.

32. Whereas the Restoration tolerated women's inquiry, by the midcentury increasing social anxiety enforced its regulation. David Garrick's 1766–1767 adaptation of *The Country Wife* — *The Country Girl* — demonstrates this change by sentimentalizing sexual curiosity and turning it into the quest for romance fulfillment and town novelties. See also the series of dramatizations of "Female Curiosity." The title first appears in Hayward's *The Masqueraders; or Fatal Curiosity: being the Secret History of a Late Amour* (London: J. Roberts, 1724), a narrative of Philecta's "Curiosity" for a young gallant (16; also 17, 19, 25). Subsequently, George Lillo employs the phrase for his 1736 tragedy about a Cornish peasant who murders his disguised son for the sake of his casket of treasures and then commits suicide. Here, curiosity designates Mother Agnes's Pandoran violation as she opens the casket and covets its contents. In 1784, Henry Mackenzie revises the play as *The Shipwreck: or, Fatal Curiosity* (London: T. Cadell, 1784), adopting a new title "because the word *Curiosity*, does not seem quite applicable to the leading circumstance of the piece," the tragedy of familial murder (6). In 1953, E. O. Knight revises the play as *A Fatal Curiosity: A Thriller*; purportedly based on his research of the incident in Bohethland, Knight reverses the murder: the son kills his father, a ruthless smuggler, in self-defense.

33. Helen Berry argues that women read periodicals and often did so in public spaces, in "'Nice and Curious Questions': Coffee Houses and the Representation of Women in John Dunton's *Athenian Mercury*," *The Seventeenth Century* 12, no. 2 (autumn 1997): 271–72.

34. In *The True Story of the Novel* (London and New York: Routledge, 1996), Margaret A. Doody argues that the novel is a female genre by tracing its love theme to classical sources that valorize women's roles. Many feminist critics have theorized the relationship between women and the novel; see, particularly, John J. Richetti, *Popular Fiction before Richardson: Narrative Patterns, 1700–1739* (Oxford: Clarendon Press, 1969); Laurie Langbauer, *Women and Romance: The Consolations of Gender in the English Novel* (Ithaca and London: Cornell University Press, 1990); Nancy Armstrong, *Desire and Domestic Fiction: A Political History of the Novel* (New York and Oxford: Oxford University Press, 1987).

35. These roles include various kinds of writing, social and political behavior, cross-dressing, and geographical explorations, most of which were the activities of high-class women; for a telling case analysis of gender transgressions, see Jill Campbell's "Lady Mary Wortley Montagu and the Historical Machinery of Female Identity," in *History, Gender, and Eighteenth-Century Literature*, ed. Beth Fowkes Tobin (Athens and London: University of Georgia Press, 1994), 64–85. Thomas Laqueur argues that the period abandons the one-sex model for gender,

by which women are imperfect men, for a two-sex model essentializing gender differences; see *Making Sex: Body and Gender from the Greeks to Freud* (Cambridge, Mass.: Harvard University Press, 1990), esp. 149–54.

36. *Athenian Mercury* (London: J. Dunton, 1690): 17 March 1690; no. 1, p. 1. This periodical was republished by Andrew Bell as *The Athenian Oracle* in three volumes in 1703 and another volume in 1704. *The Athenian Oracle* was revived in 1704 as *Atheniae Rediviae*. See Gilbert D. McEwen, *The Oracle of the Coffee House: John Dunton's Athenian Mercury* (San Marino: Huntington Library, 1972), 223, 227.

37. McEwen, *The Oracle of the Coffee House*, 123. Charles Gildon celebrated Dunton's endeavor by declaring that the reader "is only desired to yield to the force of Reason itself," proved by experiment and observation, not to prior authorities, in *The History of the Athenian Society* (London: James Dowley, 1691): no. 1, p. 4.

38. John Dunton, *Atheniae Rediviae, or the New Athenian Oracle* (London: Geo. Larkin, 1704), preface. Similarly, libels, political scandals, and useless quibbles were edited from the questions. All citations will refer to this edition unless otherwise noted.

39. See McEwen's account of such imitations in *The Oracle of the Coffee House*, 222–28; see also *The Ladies Mercury* (London, 1693), esp. vol. 1, no. 1 (Sunday, 27 February 1693), which discusses problems of sexual satisfaction for women.

40. See the historical analysis of the generation of the category of pornography in *The Invention of Pornography: Obscenity and the Origins of Modernity, 1500–1800*, ed. Lynn Hunt (New York: Zone Books, 1993).

41. In *Licensing Entertainment: The Elevation of Novel Reading in Britain, 1684–1750* (Berkeley: University of California Press, 1998), William B. Warner points out that these novelists' formulaic fiction liberates readers to take selfish pleasure; Warner examines Manley's Charlot scene in particular, although he identifies this education in selfishness with the marketing of print rather than with the marketing of curiosity (92–94, 106–7).

42. Elaine Hobby argues that Behn's stories "map out a world of female possibilities and limits: a bleak world, since the options open to her heroines are shown to be few indeed," but Behn gives fictional life to these roles, albeit she never loses sight of their fictionality; see *Virtue of Necessity: English Women's Writing, 1649–88* (Ann Arbor: University of Michigan Press, 1988), 96.

43. Aphra Behn, *Oroonoko: or, the Royal Slave* (London: Will. Canning, 1688), dedicatory epistle. All citations refer to this edition.

44. Jane Spencer observes perceptively that in adopting the common eighteenth-century posture of both eyewitness and actor, Behn's narrator inscribes a sharp distinction between the writer and the idealized, pure, romantic heroine; see *The Rise of the Woman Novelist: From Aphra Behn to Jane Austen* (Oxford: Basil Blackwell, 1986), 47–52. The connections between the role of narrator and that of scientific observer, of course, are myriad. In "Mrs. A. Behn and the Myth of Oroonoko-Imoinda," *Eighteenth-Century Fiction* 5, no. 4 (July 1993), Robert A. Erickson argues that Behn exculpates her guilt for the deaths of Oroonoko and Imoinda by immortalizing them in literature, but this argument explains only one strain in her narrative voice (201–16).

45. *A Collection of Advertisements* (British Library N. Tab. 2026/25), no. 24 and no. 651.d.10 (fol. 2).

46. Richard Frohock has argued persuasively that Behn endorses colonization and that her novels "aestheticize British imperialism"; certainly her attitude toward individual abuses of violence can work to legitimize government-organized violence. See "Violence and Awe: The Foundations of Government in Aphra Behn's New World Settings," *Eighteenth-Century Fiction* 8, no. 4 (July 1996): 452, 437–52.

47. Janet Todd, *The Sign of Angellica: Women, Writing, and Fiction, 1660–1800* (New York: Columbia University Press, 1989), 88.

48. Delariviére Manley, *Secret Memoirs and Manners Of several Persons of Quality of Both Sexes from the New Atalantis* (London: J. Morphew, 1709), 18. All citations refer to this edition.

49. Dunton, *New Athenian Mercury*, no. 1 (London: J. Dunton, January 1701), preface.

50. Todd, *The Sign of Angellica*, 154.

51. As Jane Spencer notes in *The Rise of the Woman Novelist*, for Manley "chastity, being opposed by nature, is not an innate virtue," possibly not even a virtue at all (114).

52. Toni O'Shaughnessy Bowers, "Sex, Lies, and Invisibility: Amatory Fiction from the Restoration to Mid-Century," in *The Columbia History of the British Novel*, ed. John Richetti (New York: Columbia University Press, 1994), 62.

53. See Thomas Wilson, *"Blue-Beard: A Contribution to History and Folk-Lore. Being the history of Gilles de Retz of Brittany, France, who was executed at Nantes in 1440 A.D. and who was the original of Blue-Beard in the Tales of Mother Goose"* (New York and London: G. P. Putnam's Sons, 1899), esp. 25.

54. See, for example, Arthur Quiller-Couch's remark, "The story of Bluebeard, in essence, is probably nearly as old as the institution of marriage, nearly as old as the curiosity of womankind. There is no evidence that Adam was a brutal husband, but there is all too much evidence that Eve was a nosy wife. But what good is an apple until you eat it?" in Charles Perrault's, *The Whimsical History of* BLUEBEARD, trans. from the French and illustrated by Hans Bendix (New York: The Limited Editions Club, 1952), 5.

55. "The Story of the Third Calendar" recounts a shipwreck adventure; when Agib meets ten young men with blinded right eyes, he is told "be content with what you see, and let not your curiosity extend any farther" (106). Ignoring warnings that satisfying his curiosity will cost him his right eye, he is flown by magic roc to a bejeweled castle on a mountain summit (heaven) where forty perfectly beautiful ladies flatter and welcome him. A year passes in feasting, then the ladies leave for forty days, during which time he is given keys to 100 doors to entertain his curiosity. He is told not to open the golden door whose key they leave, because opening it would be an insult. Each door reveals beauties—"objects of curiosity and value" (114)—that stimulate him to further questing until he opens the forbidden door, mounts the black horse, and is blinded at the end of the flight by its tail. In Arabic, "Agib" means "a wonder," "anything strange or admirable"

(96). *The Arabian Nights* is often printed with visually spectacular bindings and illustrations—Maxfield Parrish does one for Scribner's in 1909. See *The Arabian Nights Entertainments*, 2 vols. (New York: Heritage Press, 1955), 1:374–88.

56. George Colman's father, with Bonnell Thornton, had written other evaluations of women's literary culture in their periodical *The Connoisseur* (1754–1756). Colman the Younger is best known for *Inkle and Yarico* (1787).

57. Colman the Younger, *Blue-Beard; or, Female Curiosity! A Dramatick Romance*, first played at Royal Drury-lane, Tuesday, 16 January 1798 (London: Cadell and Davis, 1798): act 1, scene 1, p. 5. All citations to this text refer to this edition.

58. See *The History of Blue Beard, or The fatal effects of Curiosity and Disobedience* (London: J. Pitts, n.d.); also *Blue Beard; Or, Female Curiosity! A Drama, In Two Acts* (London: Hodgson and Co., [1822]), part of Hodgson's Juvenile Drama Series. *Bluebeard* was very popular and often reprinted: see *Blue-Beard; or Female Curiosity!* (London: Cadell and Davies, [n.d., 1800?]), which is identical to the first edition.

59. In "Locke's Eyes, Swift's Spectacles," Veronica Kelly explores the growing tension between the body and perceptive consciousness, and between internal and external life, in eighteenth-century biography; see *Body and Text in the Eighteenth Century*, ed. Veronica Kelly and Dorothea von Mücke (Stanford, Calif.: Stanford University Press, 1994), 69.

60. Nathaniel Crouch, *Admirable CURIOSITIES, Rarities and Wonders in England, Scotland and Ireland*, 7th ed. (London: Nathaniel Crouch, 1710), 165; 8th ed., 165; 10th ed., 172–73. The eighth edition (London: Crouch, 1718) has no illustration, nor does the tenth edition, published by James Hodges in 1737.

61. Austin Dobson, *Eighteenth-Century Vignettes* (London: Oxford University Press, 1937), vol. 1, p. 121.

62. This process parallels the contemporaneous commodification of women through conduct literature, which turned them into forms of enclosed property who could be blamed for transgressing beyond their sphere; see Kathryn Kirkpatrick, "Sermons and Strictures: Conduct-Book Propriety and Property Relations in late Eighteenth-Century England," in *History, Gender, and Eighteenth-Century Literature*, ed. Beth Fowkes Tobin (Athens and London: University of Georgia Press, 1994), 205–6.

63. The author's preface to the reader in *The Cabinet Open'd, or the Secret History of the AMOURS of Madam de Maintenon, with the French King, Translated from the French* (London: Richard Baldwin, 1690). At a talk given at the American Society for Eighteenth-Century Studies, held in Milwaukee in March 1999, Paul Benhamou recently noted the use of "cabinet" for French subscription libraries in the eighteenth century.

64. Daniel Defoe, *The Fortunes and Misfortunes of the Famous Moll Flanders* (London: W. Chetwood, 1721); *The Fortunate Mistress: Or, A History of the Life and Vast Variety of Fortunes of Mademoiselle de Beleau* (London: T. Warner, 1724).

65. Ronald Paulson, *The Beautiful, Novel, and Strange: Aesthetics and Heterodoxy* (Baltimore: Johns Hopkins University Press, 1996), xi, passim.

66. Jabez Hughes, "*The Rape of Proserpine*, from Claudian" (London: Ferd Burleigh, 1714), lines 355–56. In *Medulla Poetarum Romanorum, Or the Most beautiful and Instructive Passages of the Roman Poets* (London: D. Midwinter et al., 1737), Henry Baker repeats the lines, "With rich Embroidery, the curious maid, / Her native Heav'n, and th'Elements display'd" (lines 5035–36).

67. Tony Tanner, introduction to *Sense and Sensibility*, by Jane Austen (Penguin, 1969), 15–19.

68. See *Elvivre a Rosalie, ou Épitre dur les Courtisannes* (Londres, 1784), an erotic poem discussing prostitution and disease: the propagating "maladie" could be curiosity. Pre-publication censorship existed in France, which helps explain the importance in England of the role of print: Dunton's work could exist simultaneously in both spheres because it avoided prior publication. Thanks to Bob Dawson for this information.

69. Tassie Gwillam, "*Pamela* and the Duplicitous Body of Femininity," *Representations* 34 (spring 1991): 104–33.

70. Karen Hollis argues that Haywood portrays the dangers of women's writing and her awareness of women's double role in print "as a sexualized, circulating object and as producer," in "Eliza Haywood and the Gender of Print," *Eighteenth Century: Theory and Interpretation* 38, no. 1 (spring 1997): 51.

71. See also Richard Payne Knight's analysis of the hazards of sentimental literature, in *An Analytical Inquiry into the Principles of Taste*, 3d. ed. (London: T. Payne, 1806).

72. Jane Austen, *Northanger Abbey*, ed. R. W. Chapman (Oxford: Oxford University Press, 1923), 37–38.

73. Ian Watt, in his influential *Rise of the Novel: Studies in Defoe, Richardson, and Fielding* (Berkeley and Los Angeles: University of California Press, 1957), defines a novelistic tradition that excludes women's literature, an approach echoed in Michael McKeon's *The Origins of the English Novel, 1600–1740* (Baltimore and London: Johns Hopkins University Press, 1987).

74. Catherine Gallagher analyses the relationship of political and feminine personae in the literary marketplace and the commodification of the authorial persona, in *Nobody's Story: The Vanishing Acts of Women Writers in the Marketplace, 1670–1820* (Berkeley and Los Angeles: University of California Press, 1994), esp. 90–107. Especially valuable here is her analysis of the Fortunatus scene as allegory (104). Dustin Griffin points out the exclusion of the novel from political patronage, in *Literary Patronage in England, 1650–1800* (Cambridge: Cambridge University Press, 1996), 10–11.

75. For a provocative exploration of the kinds of arousal offered by narrative, see Susan Stewart, *On Longing: Narratives of the Miniature, the Gigantic, the Souvenir, the Collection* (Baltimore and London: Johns Hopkins Press, 1984); see also Hunt, *The Invention of Pornography*, 36–39.

76. See *Sexuality in Eighteenth-Century Britain*, ed. Paul-Gabriel Boucé (Totowa, N.J.: Barnes and Noble, 1982).

77. Eliza Haywood, *The Invisible Spy* (1755; reprint, London: H. Gardner, 1773), vol. 1, p. 7.

world of women, from which they are rigorously excluded, and thus to enjoy un-fettered intercourse; it nonetheless defines the exposure of the crime in a court of law and the social forgiveness of the incident as ironically redemptive.

97. Walter Kendrick, *The Secret Museum: Pornography in Modern Culture* (New York: Viking Press, 1987), 6, 32–34.

98. See David Foxon, *Libertine Literature in England, 1600–1745* (New York: University Books, 1965).

99. Explorabilis admits deliberately concealing "whether I am even a man or a woman"; see Haywood, *The Invisible Spy*, vol. 1, p. 2.

100. Hal Gladfelder observes that this ambiguity derives from contemporary judicial practices: "the representations and preoccupations of trial reports antici-pated the practice of realism in other kinds of narrative. . . . They embodied a modern sense of epistemological uncertainty and social disharmony while allowing, at least on the surface, for a kind of closure that could repair conflicts and resolve doubts"; see "Criminal Trials and the Dilemmas of Narrative Real-ism, 1650–1750," in *Prose Studies: History, Theory, Criticism* 20, no. 3 (December 1997): 21–48, esp. 24.

101. In several places, Haywood connects virtuosoship and spying: see vol. 1, pp. 11–12, 22, 24, 237.

102. Haywood, *The Invisible Spy*, vol. 1, p. 2.

103. Eliza Haywood, *"A Spy upon the Conjuror,* Or, A Collection of Surprising Stories" (London: Mr. Campbell, 1724), 41.

104. See, among others, the references to "Curiosity" on 9, 20, 64, 70, 80, 87, 95, 98, 120, 126, 133–34, 148, 168, etc. In fact, these references increase in the last third of the book as the formal narrative structure collapses under the weight of repeated instances of correct prediction.

105. Eliza Haywood, *"The Tea-Table: or A Conversation between some Polite Per-sons of both Sexes, at a LADY's VISITING DAY* Wherein are Represented The Various Foibles, and Affectations, which form the character of an Accomplished *Beau,* or Modern *Fine* Lady" (London: J. Roberts, 1725), vol. 2, p. 31.

106. *A Curious Collection of Novels* (London: J. Billingsley, 1731).

107. In "The Other Body: Women's Inscription of Their Physical Images in Sixteenth- and Seventeenth-Century England," *Women's Studies* 26, no. 1 (1997): 27–58, Lynette McGrath, noting especially that women "protected women's lore or secret knowledge about their own health," argues that the slow rewriting of the female body in the sixteenth to the seventeenth centuries expressed resistance to patriarchal coercion (49).

108. See *Unauthorized Sexual Behavior during the Enlightenment,* ed. Robert P. Maccubbin, special issue of *Eighteenth-Century Life,* n.s., 9, no. 3 (May 1985).

109. See Barbara M. Benedict, "'The Curious Attitude' in Eighteenth-Century Britain: Observing and Owning," *Eighteenth-Century Life,* n.s., 14, no. 3 (November 1990): 59–68, esp. 85–92.

110. In "The Chevalier D'Eon and Wilkes: Masculinity and Politics in the Eighteenth Century," *Eighteenth-Century Studies* 32, no. 1 (fall 1998): 19–48,

Anna Clark examines the political and social furor around gender transgression, but she does not address printed representations.

111. Jessica Munns, introduction to *The Clothes That Wear Us: Essays on Dressing and Transgressing in Eighteenth-Century Culture*, ed. Jessica Munns and Penny Richards (Newark: University of Delaware Press, 1999), 11–116. I am deeply grateful for permission to see this book in manuscript.

112. While one biographical sketch derides "Miss Theodora Grahn" for behaving like a man, another claims she concealed her sex in order to teach; both sketches, stressing her passions of anger and appetite, recount that she died of a "tumor in her breast"; see *Lyson's Collectanea*, vol. 1, no. 30, in William Granger's *The Wonderful and Eccentric Museum* (London, 1802–1808), in the Lewis Walpole Library.

113. See Joanne Finkelstein, *The Fashioned Self* (Philadelphia: Temple University Press, 1991), 5.

114. In "The Character of Difference: The Creole Woman as Cultural Mediator in Narratives about Jamaica," in *The Politics of Difference, special issue of Eighteenth-Century Studies*, vol. 23, no. 4 (summer 1990): 406–43, Carol Barash links exploitation and commerce as examples of capitalistic culture subordinating both women and "heathens."

115. The term "queinte" can signify the pudendum—although the word also means "nice" or "careful"—in medieval literature, showing another connection between women's genitals and curiosity. See also Partridge, *The Penguin Dictionary of Historical Slang*. In *Sex and Sensibility: Ideal and Erotic Love from Milton to Mozart* (Chicago: University of Chicago Press, 1980), Jean Hagstrum explains the seventeenth-century view that love of women "feminized" men (37). "The Curious Maid" also indicates impotence by depicting the "bards" at fashionable watering spots straining for clichés.

116. See Sigmund Freud's essay "The Uncanny," in the *Standard Edition of the Complete Psychological Works of Sigmund Freud*, 24 vols., trans. and ed. James Strachey (London: Hogarth Press, 1953–1974), 17:241.

117. "*A Court lady's Curiosity*; or, The VIRGIN Undress'd. Curiously surveying herself in her Glass, with one Leg upon her Toilet. A CHINESE Novel: By a facetious *Florentine*, who accompanied the *Tuscan* Missionaries into *China*, and lived five Years at *Pekin*, the Capital of the Kingdom. Formerly Translated from the ITALIAN; and dedicated to the *Beau Monde;* By a Young English Nobleman. And now adapted to the Taste of the Town, by an Officer of Distinction in the Army. With a Curious FRONTISPIECE, representing the Posture this Beautiful Chinese Lady was surprized in by Her Lover; and the Artifice he made Use of to accomplish his Design upon her" (London: Joseph Pearce, 1741).

118. Hansi Georg Voss and Heidi Keller identify curiosity with infantile masturbation, in *Curiosity and Exploration: Theories and Results* (Wesleyan, Conn.: New York Academic Press, 1983), 3.

119. Caricatures of the Dilettante Society by Thomas Patch and others show gray-headed men bending over a broken chamber pot in order to determine its

cultural significance: the mezzotint of "The Antiquarians Puzzled, or the Chamber Pot Consultation" bears the epigraph: "With a Phiz quite grave and Wig quite big, / Observe each ancient Soloman Prig, / Some think it is a curious Piss Pot, / Whilst others think it really is not" (P. Dawe fecit, 15 May 1770, by W. Humphrey: British Museum 4772.773 5.15). Both Pope and Swift also use "curious" with the innuendo of a sexual insult.

120. Kristina Straub, "Reconstructing the Gaze: Voyeurism in Richardson's *Pamela*," *Studies in Eighteenth-Century Culture* 18 (1988): 419–31.

121. See M. Mercier, *Tableau de Paris*, 4 vols. (Hambourg: Samuel Fauche, 1781), in which Mercier attributes female sexual aggression to the faults of idleness, curiosity, and ambition. This aggression reverses the sexual status quo, imbuing women with the fickleness and power traditionally granted masculine rakes (2:4).William Kennick, *The Whole Duty of Woman* (London: R. Baldwin, 1753).

122. J. E. Svilpis characterized the mad scientist as socially inadequate, barred from both "the personal and biological satisfactions symbolized by the female," and "the public and social ones symbolized by the male," in "The Mad Scientist and Domestic Affections" in *Gothic Fictions: Prohibition/Transgression*, ed. Kenneth W. Graham (New York: AMS Press, 1989), 63–87, esp. 69.

123. Vijay Mishra, *The Gothic Sublime* (New York: State University of New York, 1994), 25; see also Michel Foucault, *The Archeology of Knowledge*, trans. A. M. Sheridan Smith (London: Tavistock Publications, 1978).

124. Steven Marcus, *The Other Victorians: A Study of Sexuality and Pornography in Mid-Nineteenth Century England* (London: Corgi Books, 1966), 73–74, passim.

125. Andrew Ross suggests this may be the form for female sexual pleasure, in "The Popularity of Pornography," in *No Respect: Intellectuals and Popular Culture* (London: Routledge, 1989), but nothing suggests these novels were only (or mainly) women's reading; see D. A. Miller, *Narrative and Its Discontents: Problems of Closure in the Traditional Novel* (Princeton, N.J.: Princeton University Press, 1981). Julie Shaffer suggests that noncanonical novels address responsiveness to others' desires, in "Non-Canonical Women's Novels of the Romantic Era: Romantic Ideologies and the Problematics of Gender and Genre," *Studies in the Novel* 28, no. 4 (winter 1996): 473.

126. Naomi Jacobs notes the "self-defeating" pornographic plot that encourages the sexualizing of the heroine, in "The Seduction of Aphra Behn," *Women's Studies* 18, no. 4 (1991): 400.

CHAPTER FOUR

1. Nicholas Thomas traces the uneasy deployment of curiosity to legitimize travel, in "Licensed Curiosity: Cook's Pacific Voyages," in *The Cultures of Collecting*, ed. John Elsner and Roger Cardinal (Cambridge, Mass.: Harvard University Press, 1994), 118–36.

2. Lance Bertelsen, *The Nonsense Club: Literature and Popular Culture, 1749–1764* (Oxford: Clarendon Press; New York: Oxford University Press, 1986), esp. 34–36, 255–56. Bertelsen distinguishes between the despised and indiscriminate

virtuoso and the ideal connoisseur, "a collector of the highest order," aware of art's moral uses (35). I am indebted to this distinction and this book, although my purpose is to explicate the overlaps between representations of these kinds of curious men.

3. Carol Mavor, "Collecting Loss," *Cultural Studies* 11, no. 1 (January 1997): 111–37.

4. Pierre Bourdieu, *Distinction: A Social Critique of the Judgement of Taste*, trans. Richard Nice (Cambridge, Mass.: Harvard University Press, 1984). Ann Bermingham distinguishes connoisseurship from virtuosoship, in "Culture and Self-Image," in *The Consumption of Culture, 1600–1800: Image, Object, Text*, ed. Ann Bermingham and John Brewer (London and New York: Routledge, 1995), 502–6; but here I intend to stress the way connoisseurship borrowed aspects of virtuosoship, and thus I use the terms interchangeably; see also Jay Tribby, "Body/Building: Living the Museum Life in Early Modern Europe," *Rhetorica* 10, no. 2: 139–63. See also Jay Tribby's dissertation, "Eloquence and Experiment: Essays on the Civil Gestures of Inquiry in Seventeenth-Century France and Italy" (Ph.D. diss., Johns Hopkins, 1991).

5. William King, *The Transactioneer*, intro. Roger D. Lund (1700; reprint, The Augustan Reprint Society, nos. 215–52, Los Angeles: University of California, Andrews Clark Memorial Library, 1988), 54–55.

6. Janet Todd, *Sensibility: An Introduction* (London and New York: Methuen, 1986), 5–6, 14; John Mullan, *Sentiment and Sociability: The Language of Feeling in the Eighteenth Century* (Oxford: Clarendon Press, 1988), 119–20, 123.

7. Eric Rothstein, *Restoration and Eighteenth-Century Poetry, 1660–1780* (Boston, London, and Henley: Routledge and Kegan Paul, 1981), 140–41.

8. Susan M. Pearce, *Museums, Objects, and Collections: A Cultural Study* (Leicester and London: Leicester University Press, 1992), 85.

9. Many popular cabinets contain occult, religious, and sexual secrets possessed by witches. See *The World Turned Upside-Down; or the Folly of Man* (London, n.d. [1750?]), esp. 4–5; Thomas Brooks' *A Cabinet of Choice Jewels or, a Box of precious Ointment*, for example, promises "a plain Discovery of what men are worth for Eternity, and how 'tis like to go with them in another World" (London: John Hancock, 1669). See *"The History of Mother BUNCH of the West* Containing, Many rarities out of her Golden Closet of Curiosities" (London) [Chapbook, 1750].

10. Thomas Hill, *"Natural and Artificial Conclusions*. Compiled in Latin by the worthiest and best Authors, both of the famous University of Padua in Italy, and divers other Places . . . Englished since, and set forth by THOMAS HILL, Londoner, whose own *Experiences* in this kind were held most excellent. And now again published, with a new addition of *Rarities*, for the practice of sundry *Artificers*; as also to recreate Wits at vacant times" (London: Iane Bell, 1649; reprint, London: Edward Brewster, 1670).

11. John Tradescant, "A LETTER FROM DR. DUCAREL, F.R.S. AND F.S.A. to WILLIAM WATSON, M.D. F.R.S. upon The Early Cultivation of Botany in England; and Some Particulars about John Tradescant, A Great Promoter of that Science, as

well as natural History, in the Last Century, and Gardener to King Charles I"
(London: W. Bowyer and J. Nichols, 1773), 6–7.

12. *"Musaeum Tradescantianum: Or, a* COLLECTION OF RARITIES. preserved At
South-Lambeth neer London By John Tradescant" (London: John Grismond,
1656), lines 1–4, 6–10.

13. Douglas Grant, *The Cock Lane Ghost* (London, Melbourne, Toronto: Macmillan; New York: St. Martin's Press, 1965), 91; see *A Modest Apology For the Man
in the Bottle. By Himself* (London: J. Freeman, [1749]): British Library, 641.e.28
(fol. 12).

14. Similarly, Swift portrays class rivalry through sexual gigantism and min-
uteness in books 1 and 2 of *Gulliver's Travels*. Frederick Grose's *Classical Dictionary
of the Vulgar Tongue* (London: S. Hooper, 1788) identifies the slang term "Buck-
inger's Boot" as a reference to the limbless but uxorious dwarf Matthew Buchinger. See Rickey Jay, *Learned Pigs and Fireproof Women* (New York: Villard Books,
1986), 56.

15. In *The Uses of Enchantment: The Meaning and Importance of Fairy Tales*
(New York: A. Knopf, 1976), Bruno Bettelheim, tracing the spirit-in-a-bottle motif to biblical legend, argues that it embodies a fantasy of power reversal of the
son over the father. The Bottle Conjuror, however, embodies a carnivalesque reversal of power relations.

16. See Veronique Dasen's *Dwarfs in Ancient Egypt and Greece* (Oxford:
Clarendon Press, 1993), and Donna J. Hathaway's *Simians, Cyborgs, and Women:
The Reinvention of Nature* (London: Free Association Books, 1991). My thanks to
Judith Hawley for referring me to this text. Richard Altick points out that little
distinction was made in the eighteenth century between midgets and dwarfs, in
The Shows of London (Cambridge, Mass.: Belknap Press, 1978), 42.

17. *The Memoirs of the Extraordinary Life, Works, and Discoveries of Martinus
Scriblerus*, ed. Charles Kerby-Miller (New York: Oxford University Press, 1988),
149–50.

18. Andrew Wilton and Ilaria Bignamini, eds., *Grand Tour: The Lure of Italy
in the Eighteenth Century* (London: Tate Gallery Publishing, 1996), 201.

19. Henry Fielding, *An Enquiry into the Causes of the Late Increase of Robbers
and Related Writings*, ed. Malvin R. Zirker (Middletown: Wesleyan University
Press, 1988), xciv–cxiv; Martin C. Battestin and Ruthe R. Battestin, *Henry Fielding: A Life* (London and New York: Routledge, 1989), 570–76; modern re-
workings include Arthur Machen's *The Canning Wonder* (1926) and Lillian De La
Torre's *Elizabeth Is Missing* (1945). Harvard University mounted an exhibition of
Canning documents entitled *The Virgin and the Witch* from 12 January to 31
March 1987, for which Hugh Amory composed a catalogue (Cambridge, Mass.,
1987).

20. *"The Unfortunate Maid exemplified, In the Story of Elizabeth Canning Vindicated From every Mean Aspersion thrown upon it. To which is added, A full Answer to a certain Pamphlet Intitled Miss Canning and the Gipsy. Together with
Reflections on the Conduct of Sir Crisp Gascoyne . . ."* (London: C. Corbett,
1754), 14, 24; Daniel Cox, M.D., *An Appeal to the Public, in Behalf of Elizabeth Can-*

ning (London: W. Meadows, 1753), 3; see also, Nich. Crisp, J. Payne, James Harriott, Edward Rossiter, Thomas Cox, John Carter, *A Refutation of Sir Crisp Gascoyne's Address to the Liverymen of London* (London: J. Payne, 1754), which also "appeal[s] to REASON" (2).

21. Morris Golden, *Fielding's Moral Psychology* (Amherst: University of Massachusetts Press, 1966), 21; George Sherburn, "Fielding's *Amelia*: An Interpretation," *ELH* 3 (1938): 1–14; Patricia Meyer Spacks, *Imagining a Self: Autobiography and Novel in Eighteenth-Century England* (Cambridge, Mass.: Harvard University Press, 1976), 8; Jo Alyson Parker, *The Author's Inheritance: Henry Fielding, Jane Austen, and the Establishment of the Novel* (DeKalb: Northern Illinois University Press, 1998), 119–24.

22. Henry Fielding, *A Clear State of the Case of Elizabeth Canning* (London: A. Millar, 1753), in Henry Fielding, *An Enquiry into the Causes of the Late Increase of Robbers and Related Writings*, ed. Malvin R. Zirker (Middletown: Wesleyan University Press, 1988), 288; all citations of *A Clear State* and *Enquiry* will refer to this edition; *The Unfortunate Maid*, 9; Dr. John Hill, *The Story of Elizabeth Canning Considered by Dr. Hill* (London: M. Cooper, 1753), 16–17.

23. *Genuine and Impartial Memoirs of Elizabeth Canning* (London: G. Woodfall, 1754), 2.

24. Crisp et al., *A Refutation*, 1.

25. Malvin R. Zirker, introduction to *An Enquiry into the Causes of the Late Increase of Robbers and Related Writings*, by Henry Fielding, ed. Malvin R. Zirker (Middletown: Wesleyan University Press, 1988); Cal Winslow, "Sussex Smugglers," in *Albion's Fatal Tree: Crime and Society in Eighteenth-Century England* (London: Pantheon Books, 1975), 119–66.

26. Fielding, *Enquiry*, 75; Katie Trumpener, "The Time of the Gypsies: A 'People without History' in the Narratives of the West," in *Identities*, ed. Kwame Anthony Appiah and Henry Louis Gates Jr. (Chicago: University of Chicago Press, 1995), 369; Linda Colley, *Britons: Forging the Nation 1707–1837* (New Haven and London: Yale University Press, 1992), 90–100.

27. Henry Fielding, *Joseph Andrews with Shamela and Related Writings*, ed. Homer Goldberg (New York and London: W. W. Norton and Co., 1987), bk. 4, chap. 15. Although fairy tales emerge as a genre only in the nineteenth century, the antiquarian Joseph Ritson, in *Fairy Tales. Now First Collected* (London: Payne and Foss, 1831), includes stories featuring changelings (tale 11, 123–24), fairy feasts (tale 15, 140–41), and kidnapping (tale 18, 146–49). For the popularity of changelings, see Warren W. Wooden's *Children's Literature of the English Renaissance*, ed. and intro. Janie Watson (Lexington: University Press of Kentucky, 1986), 102–3. See also Joseph Ritson's *A Select Collection of English Songs*, 3. vols. (1783; reprint, London: J. Johnson, 1813); and John Goldthwaite, *The Natural History of Make-Believe: A Guide to the Principal Works of Britain, Europe, and America* (New York and Oxford: Oxford University Press, 1996), 19–25.

28. In "On the Repeal of the Witchcraft Act," no. 503 of *The Craftsman* (1735/6), Henry Fielding mocks the passage of the repeal as a sign of superstition; see "*New Essays by Henry Fielding: His Contributions to the 'Craftesman' and*

Other Early Journalism, with a Stylometric Analysis by Michael G. Farringdon," ed. Martin C. Battestin (Charlottesville: University Press of Virginia, 1989), 127–38.

29. *The Trial of Elizabeth Canning, Spinster, for Wilful and Corrupt Perjury* (London: Thomas Rawlinson, 1754), 2.

30. Grant, *The Cock Lane Ghost,* 113–15, 81–83; the verses appear in the *London Chronicle,* 16–18 March 1760, p. 93.

31. [Oliver Goldsmith], *The Mystery Revealed; Containing a Series of* TRANSACTIONS *and* AUTHENTIC TESTIMONIALS, *Respecting the supposed Cock Lane* GHOST; *Which have hitherto been concealed from the* PUBLIC (London: W. Bristow, 1742), 3, 19.

32. Lorraine Daston and Katharine Park, *Wonders and the Order of Nature* (New York: Zone Books, 1998), 345.

33. Horace Walpole, *"The Castle of Otranto, A Story Translated by William Marshall, Gent.* From the Original Italian of Onuphrio Muralto, Canon of the Church of the St. Nicolas at Otranto" (London: Tho. Lownds, 1765), iv–v.

34. For illicit sexual undercurrents in male Gothic fiction, see George E. Haggerty, "Literature and Homosexuality in the Late Eighteenth Century: Walpole, Beckford, and Lewis," *Studies in the Novel* 18, no. 4 (winter 1986), 341–52; Ruth Perry argues that these novels enact a subversive refutation of male power, in "Incest as the Meaning of the Gothic Novel," *The Eighteenth Century: Theory and Interpretation* 39, no. 3 (fall 1998), 261–78, esp. 270.

35. *"The Valuable Library of Books in Fonthill Abbey. A Catalogue of the Magnificent, Rare, and Valuable Library (of 20,000 Volumes)* . . . Also, of the Books of Prints, Galleries of Art, Curious Missals and Manuscripts, the Persian and Chinese Drawings &c. &c." (Tuesday, 9 September 1823). Items include precious objects like "An old and curious sea-green bottle and an inkstand" (p. 127, no. 121), "A curious bronze crab" (p. 196, no. 131), but also linen breakfast napkins (p. 157, no. 632 and others).

36. [William Beckford], *An Arabian Tale, from an Unpublished Manuscript: with Notes Critical and Explanatory,* [1st English ed.] (London: J. Johnson, 1786), iii–iv.

37. Thomas Hearne, *A Collection of Curious Discourses, Written by Eminent Antiquaries Upon several Heads in our English Antiquities* (Oxford: Printed at the Theater, 1720), item 57, pp. 302–4 in first edition.

38. Ian Jenkins, "'Contemporary Minds': Sir William Hamilton's Affair with Antiquity," in *Vases and Volcanoes: Sir William Hamilton and his Collection,* ed. Ian Jenkins and Kim Sloan (London: British Museum Press, 1996), 41.

39. [Richard Burton], *Extraordinary Adventures, Discoveries and Events By R. B.,* 3d ed. (London: Nathaniel Crouch, 1704). The third edition of 1704 omits Columbus's adventures and other Spaniards' discoveries of America because they have been separately published; the edition features instead the scandalous tales of historical figures, accounts of cultural wonders, supernatural warnings of imminent death, and exotic captivity narratives.

40. British Library, L.R. 301.h.3 (fol. 21AA).

41. Raymond Williams, *The Country and the City* (New York: Oxford University Press, 1973), 65, 71; in *When Dreams Came True: Classic Fairy Tales and Their Tradition* (New York and London: Routledge, 1999), Jack Zipes argues that "wonder tales" reward the naive who "have retained their belief in the miraculous condition of nature" (5).

42. *The Hampshire Wonder; or the Groaning Tree . . . By P. Q., M. D., FRS* (London: W. Smith, 1743). This tradition begins in the seventeenth century; see the *Westminster Wonder* (London: James Read, 1695), which celebrates a robin who mourns the death of the queen by perching on her mausoleum.

43. "*The Guilford Ghost. Being an ACCOUNT of the Strange and Amazing Apparition or Ghost of Mr. Christopher Slaughterford . . .*" (London: J. Wyat, 1709), 4, 8.

44. *The Buckinghamshire MIRACLE; or, the World's WONDER* (London, [1700]), 5.

45. *The Yorkshire Wonder* (1698) describes the resurrection of H. W. forty-eight hours after his death, and so does *The Surrey Wonder* (ca. 1700–1800), a chapbook version of the tale transported south. *The Norfolk Wonder; or the Maiden's Trance* tells the same story, embellished with angelic prophesies, about a young girl who "Liv'd and Died an unspotted Virgin . . . being the Wonder and Glory of her Sex, and Miracle of her Age" (London: T. Wells, 1708).

46. The *West-Country Wonder* (1690) hails the marriage of a servant William to an old Lady; the *Lincolnshire Wonder* (1800) recounts the "comical dialogue" between a sixty-year-old bride and her youthful spouse.

47. King, *The Transactioneer*, 14.

48. E. St. John Brooks, *Sir Hans Sloane: The Great Collector and his Circle* (London: The Batchworth Press, 1954), 98–99; Joseph T. Smith, M.D., "A REVIEW OF THE LIFE OF SIR HANS SLOANE, BART., M.D." (paper read before The Johns Hopkins Hospital Historical Club, Monday, 14 April 1913); "A CONCISE NARRATIVE OF THE LIFE, TRAVELS, COLLECTIONS, WORKS, &c. of Sir Hans Sloane, Bart. To which is added an Extract of his Last Will," which emphasizes his "Thirst for Knowledge" (London, [1755]), 49. See also "*An ACCOUNT of a Most Efficacious Medicine for Soreness, Weakness, And several Other Distempers of the Eyes*, By Sir Hans Sloane, Bart. Physician to His Majesty" (London: Dan. Browne, 1745), which opens characteristically, "Through an earnest Desire to be useful in my Profession, the Practice, of Physic, to which I was led by a strong natural Inclination, I was always very attentive to Matters of Fact, and the real Cures that fell under my Observation" (British Library, T. 75 [fol. 8]).

49. *An Epistolary Letter from TCHC to Sir HCS− −e* (Dublin: T. Payne, 1729; London: T. Payne, 1729; reprint, London: E. A. B. Mordaunt: 1904), lines 51–52.

50. *The WILL of Sir Hans Sloane, Bar. Deceased* (London: John Virtuoso, 1753), 2.

51. H. J. Braunholtz argues that Sloane's own small but important collections of "'artificial curiosities' of remote and primitive peoples" led the museum to acquire Captain Cook's collections, thus making ethnography as important as natural history, in *Sir Hans Sloane and Ethnography*, with a note by Sir Gavin de Beer FRS, edited, with a foreword, by William Fagg (London: Trustees of the British Museum, 1970), 19.

52. [Edmund Howlett or Powlett], "*The General Contents of the* british museum: With Remarks. Serving as a directory In viewing that Noble cabinet" (London: R. and J. Dodsley, 1761), v. See Joel J. Orosz, *Curators and Culture: The Museum Movement in America, 1740–1870* (Tuscaloosa and London: University of Alabama Press, 1990), 26–30.

53. George Bickham, "*Deliciae Britannicae; or, the Curiosities of Kensington, Hampton Court, and Windsor Castle Delineated; with Occasional Reflections*; and embellished with Copper-Plates of the Three Palaces . . . " (London: E. Owen, 1755); Pearce, *Museums, Objects, and Collections*, 72.

54. "a tour through the cities of london and westminster, and Places adjacent to these populous Cities. With an Elegant View of the British Museum," *The Royal Magazine*, February 1764, 89.

55. *A Companion to the Museum (Late Sir Ashton Lever's)* (London, 1790), preface.

56. *The Connoisseur. A Satire on the modern Men of Taste* (London: Robert Turbutt, [1735]), line 118.

57. Mr. Conolly, *The Connoisseur: or, Every Man in his Folly* (London: Richard Wellington, 1736), pt. 1, st. 1, line 8.

58. Alvin Kernan argues that Johnson invented the role of professional author, in *Printing Technology, Letters, and Samuel Johnson* (Princeton, N.J.: Princeton University Press, 1987); see for example, the account of Johnson and other luminaries in *Anecdotes, Bon-Mots, and Characteristic Traits* (Dublin, 1789).

59. Samuel Johnson, *The Rambler*, vols. 3, 4, 5, of the Yale edition of the *Works of Samuel Johnson*, 9 vols., ed. W. J. Bate and Albrecht B. Strauss (New Haven and London: Yale University Press, 1969); all citations refer to this edition unless otherwise noted. See specifically: 4:107 (no. 89, Tuesday, 22 January 1751); 5:34 (no. 146, Saturday, 10 August 1751); 4:185 (no. 103, Tuesday, 12 March 1751).

60. Ibid., 3:28–29 (no. 5, Tuesday, 3 April 1750).

61. Bate and Strauss, introduction to *The Rambler*, xxii.

62. *The Rambler*, 4:186 (no. 103, Tuesday, 12 March 1751).

63. Ibid.

64. *The Rambler*, 3:6 (no. 1, Tuesday, 20 March 1750).

65. Samuel Johnson, *A Voyage to Abyssinia*, trans. from the French, ed. Joel J. Gold, vol. 15 of the Yale edition of the *Works of Samuel Johnson* (New Haven and London: Yale University Press, 1985), dedication; esp. 3.

66. *The Rambler*, 4:187 (no. 103, Tuesday, 12 March 1751).

67. Ibid., 4:108 (no. 89, Tuesday, 22 January 1751).

68. Ibid., 5: 316 (no. 208, Saturday, 14 March 1752).

69. Ibid., 3:104 (no. 19, Tuesday, 22 May 1750).

70. Ibid., p. 109.

71. Ibid., 4:189 (no. 103, Tuesday, 12 March 1751).

72. Samuel Johnson, *The History of Rasselas, Prince of Abyssinia* (Oxford and New York: Oxford University Press, 1991), 13.

73. Fielding, *Joseph Andrews*, bk. 3, chap. 1, p. 148.

74. *The Rambler*, 4:46 (no. 78, Saturday, 15 December 1750).

75. Ibid., pp. 25–47.

76. Matthew Arnold, "The Function of Criticism at the Present Time," in *Lectures and Essays in Criticism*, vol. 3 of *The Complete Prose Works of Matthew Arnold*, 11. vols., ed. R. H. Super (Ann Arbor: University of Michigan Press, 1960–1977), 3:283.

77. *The Rambler*, 4:186 (no. 103, Tuesday, 12 March 1751).

78. See *The Rambler*, 3:25 (no. 5, Tuesday, 3 April 1750), which compares spring and the restlessness of the imagination, itself analogous to curiosity.

79. Ibid., 4:65 (no. 82, Saturday, 29 December 1750).

80. Ibid., 4:70 (no. 83, Tuesday, 1 January 1751).

81. Ibid., p. 72. Compare this to Johnson's attack in *The Idler* (no. 56, Saturday, 12 May 1759) on the proliferation of false value in auctions; see *The Idler and the Adventurer*, ed. W. J. Bate, John M. Bullitt, L. F. Powell (New Haven and London: Yale University Press, 1963), vol. 2, p. 175. *The Idler* was published as a column in the newspaper *The Universal Chronicle, or Weekly Gazette* from 15 April 1758 to 5 April 1760, along with intelligence and stock reports, advertisements, and weekly news. Johnson observes, "To those who are accustomed to value every thing by its use, and have no such superfluity of time or money as may prompt them to unnatural wants or capricious emulations, nothing appears more improbable or extravagant than the love of curiosities, or that desire of accumulating trifles, which distinguishes many by whom no other distinction could ever have been obtained" (2:175).

82. George Colman and Bonnell Thornton, *The Connoisseur*, [1st ed.], no. 1 (Thursday, 31 January 1754): 1–2.

83. Horace, *Sermones*, bk. 2, no. 6, lines 71–73. My thanks to A. D. Macro for help in translation and context. "*The Connoisseur*. By Mr. Town, Critic and Censor-General." 4 vols. 6th ed. (Oxford: J. Rivington et al., 1774); all citations refer to this edition unless otherwise specified.

84. For example, in no. 3 (14 February 1754) he adopts words from Dryden's *MacFlecknoe*, "*Sleepless ourselves to give our readers sleep*" (19), and no. 11 (11 April 1754) includes an entire ode humorously adapting Horace (90–91). Also see no. 73 (19 June 1756), no. 85 (11 September 1755), and no. 110 (4 March 1756); see, as well, Terry Castle, *The Female Thermometer: Eighteenth-Century Culture and the Invention of the Uncanny* (New York and Oxford: Oxford University Press, 1995), 21–43.

85. Among many sneers at false taste, Mr. Town reproves the bombastic epitaph of every "obscure grocer or tallow-chandler" whom newspapers eulogize as if he were a Duke (no. 73, 19 June 1756, 17). In no. 15 (5 December 1754), "On News-Papers," Mr. Town, satirizing the passion for gossip as news, reproduces a "Specimen of curious *Advertisements* in the *Daily Papers*," six advertisements for illicit or sexual encounters. No. 120 is indexed merely as "On Taste" in imitation of Pope.

86. *The Connoisseur*, no. 2 (Thursday, 7 February 1754): "On the different Branches of VIRTU. Letter, containing a Catalogue of Pictures collected abroad by

an eminent *Jew*. Letter from a Gamester, advising the Author to undertake a Defence of Gaming" (11).

87. Fielding associates Jews with the criminal underworld in his *Enquiry*, 126; see Zirker, "introduction to *An Enquiry*," lv. Stephen Greenblatt discusses Mandeville's resistance to the Jews' marginal status between the realms of belief and heterodoxy, in *Marvelous Possessions: The Wonder of the New World* (Chicago: University of Chicago Press, 1991), 50–51.

88. Frank Felsenstein, *Anti-Semitic Stereotypes: A Paradigm of Otherness in English Popular Culture, 1660–1830* (Baltimore and London: Johns Hopkins Press, 1995), 7, 191, 202–4; Adam Sutcliffe, "Myth, Origins, Identity: Voltaire, the Jews, and the Enlightenment Notion of Toleration," *The Eighteenth Century: Theory and Interpretation* 39, no. 2 (summer 1998), 109–11.

89. Peter R. Erspamer, *The Elusiveness of Tolerance: The 'Jewish Question' from Lessing to the Napoleonic Wars* (Chapel Hill and London: University of North Carolina Press, 1997), 9, 25.

90. See *The Connoisseur*, no. 100 (25 December 1755).

91. *Memoirs of Charles Macklin Comedian* (anon. 1804), 91, 95. Thanks to John Ripley for alerting me to this source.

92. Philip H. Highfill Jr., Kalman A. Burnim, and Edward A. Langhans, *A Biographical Dictionary of Actors, Actresses, Musicians, Dancers, Managers, and Other Stage Personnel in London, 1660–1800* (Carbondale: Southern Illinois University Press, 1982), 7, 263. Macklin remained interesting to Colman and Thornton in later issues, one of which is largely dedicated to evaluating his school for eloquence, which was open to women, and satirizing the infantile taste for pantomime as theatrical morality. See *The Connoisseur*, no. 47 (19 December 1754); see also no. 65 (5 December 1754), which debates the rival eloquence of "Orator Macklin and Orator Henley" (72).

93. Bertelsen, *The Nonsense Club*.

94. Arnold, "The Function of Criticism," 3:268, 274. See also his definition of "disinterestedness," as the first "rule" of criticism: the steadfast refusal of the mind "to lend itself to any of those ulterior, political, practical considerations about ideas" (3:270).

95. *The Universal Magazine* (London, 1762), vol. 1, p. 2. By 1781, the title expands to "THE UNIVERSAL MAGAZINE FOR KNOWLEDGE AND PLEASURE, CONTAINING NEWS, LETTERS, DEBATES, POETRY, MUSICK, BIOGRAPHY, HISTORY, GEOGRAPHY . . . AND OTHER ARTS AND SCIENCES Which may render it Instructive and Entertaining to Gentry, Merchants, Farmers and Tradesmen . . ."

96. Paula Findlen, "The Museum: Its Classical Etymology and Renaissance Genealogy," *Journal of the History of Collections* 1, no. 1 (1989): 59–78.

97. *Kirby's Wonderful and Eccentric Museum; or Magazine of Remarkable Characters. Including all the Curiosities of Nature and Art, from the Remotest period to the present time, Drawn from every authentic source* (London: R. S. Kirby, 1820), vol. 1, frontispiece.

98. Tribby, "Body/Building."

CHAPTER FIVE

1. See Arthur MacGregor's examination of the encyclopedic ambitions of these collections, in "The Cabinet of Curiosities in Seventeenth-Century Britain," in *The Origins of Museums: The Cabinet of Curiosities in Sixteenth and Seventeenth-Century Europe*, ed. Oliver Impey and Arthur MacGregor (Oxford: Clarendon Press, 1985), 147–58; also see Douglas and Elizabeth Rigby, *Lock, Stock, and Barrel: The Story of Collecting* (Philadelphia, New York, London: J. B. Lippincott, Co., 1944), 252–53.

2. Clive Wainwright, *The Romantic Interior* (London: Victoria and Albert Museum, 1990), 9–10.

3. Susan Stewart, *On Longing: Narratives of the Miniature, the Gigantic, the Souvenir, the Collection* (Baltimore: Johns Hopkins University Press, 1984), 135–36.

4. Tony Bennett notes that the display of power in public exhibitions and the use of culture as a "resource" to regulate and enforce behavior increased in the nineteenth century, in *The Birth of the Museum: History, Theory, Politics* (London and New York: Routledge, 1995), 23.

5. "*The Gentleman's Guide in his Tour through* France. Wrote by an Officer who lately travelled on a Principle which he most sincerely recommends to his Countrymen, viz. Not to spend more Money in the Country of our natural Enemy, than is requisite to support, with Decency, the Character of an Englishman," 4th ed. (London: G. Kearsley, 1770), 47, 53.

6. Edmund Burke speculated on the unnaturalness and impiety of science in the aftermath of the Revolution; see Maurice Crosland's "The Image of Science as a Threat: Burke versus Priestly and the 'Philosophic Revolution,'" in *Studies in the Culture of Science in France and Britain Since the Enlightenment* (Aldershot, Great Britain: Variorum, 1995): 277–307.

7. M. Willson Disher, *Greatest Show on Earth, As Performed for over a Century at* ASTLEY's *(afterwards Sanger's) Royal Amphitheatre of Arts*, intro. D. L. Murray (London: G. Bell and Sons, Ltd. Publishers, 1937), 11–12.

8. The advertisement cites boxes at three shillings, pit seats at two shillings, the gallery at one shilling, and the side gallery at sixpence (London: H. Pace, [1784?]). British Library, L.R. 301.h.3 (fol. AA). These advertisements can be found in this collection compiled by Sarah S. Banks.

9. "First Seats Two Shillings, Second Seats One Shilling. Our stay will be but two or three days" (1 August 1784). British Library, 301.h.3 (fol. 1AA).

10. Philip Astley, *Astley's System of Equestrian Education, Exhibiting the* BEAUTIES *and* DEFECTS *of the* HORSE; *With Serious and Important* OBSERVATIONS *On his General Excellence, Preserving him in Health, Grooming, &c. With Plates*, 6th ed. (London: S. Creed et al., [1804]). See also "*Astley's Projects*, in his management of the HORSE . . . being an Abridgement of his . . . Equestrian Education" (London: T. Borton, 1804), which is intended for the "rising Generation [of] Farmers, Horsedealers, Grooms, Coachmen . . ." and is signed "Philip Astley, Professor of the Art of Riding."

11. This book plagiarizes Henri Decremps's *La Magie Blanche Déviolée*, which had been translated as *The Conjuror Unmasked*.

12. British Library, L.R. 301.h.3 (fol. 14AA), ca. 1790.

13. *General Advertizer*, 13 April 1785; one print by Rowlandson depicts an announcement on a wall reading, "The Surprising PIG . . ." (London: S. W. Fores, no. 3 Piccadilly, 12 April 1785); also see the other prints of "The Wonderful Pig of Knowledge."

14. British Library, L.R. 301.h.3 (fol. 15AA).

15. Elisabeth Scheicher, "The Collection of Archduke Ferdinand II at Schloss Ambras: Its Purpose, Composition, and Evolution," in *The Origins of Museums: The Cabinet of Curiosities in Sixteenth and Seventeenth-Century Europe*, eds. Oliver Impey and Arthur MacGregor (Oxford: Clarendon Press, 1985), 33.

16. Susan Pearce, *Museums, Objects, and Collections: A Cultural Study* (Leicester and London: Leicester University Press, 1992), 67–88, 116.

17. "This Infant is to perform in the Centre of the School, on the Forte Piano, several known Airs . . . With a splendid Display of MACHINERY. ROPE DANCING, by very eminent Performers. The droll Musical Piece, called, NINE TAYLORS at a FOX-HUNT, on Masquerade Horses. The Exhibition of The ORIGINAL DANCING DOGS, And Vigorous ENGLISH BULL DOG." British Library, L.R. 301.h.3 (fol. 2AA).

18. "Front Seats 3s. 2nd Seats 2s. Back Seats 1s. N.B. He will exhibit every day from Twelve to Two o'clock to private Companies. The Room is kept very warm." This advertisement from the *General Advertiser* for 26 March 1782 is very similar to the one in the *Morning Herald* on same date.

19. Keith Thomas, *Religion and the Decline of Magic* (New York: Charles Scribner's Sons, 1971), 212–52.

20. *Morning Herald*, 29 March 1782.

21. *General Advertiser*, 3 June 1782.

22. *General Advertiser*, 10 March 1783. See also *General Advertiser*, 28 March 1783.

23. *General Advertiser*, 28 March 1783.

24. *General Advertiser*, 11 April 1782. See also *Morning Post*, 9 May 1782, as well as Katterfelto's account of recovering from this sinister illness with the help of Dr. Batto's Medicines ("at the low price of Five Shillings the bottle") in the *General Advertiser*, 3 June 1782.

25. See the *General Advertiser*, 12 March and 17 March 1783.

26. *General Advertiser*, 28 March 1783.

27. *General Advertiser*, 7 April 1783; also 14 April 1783.

28. See the *General Advertiser* for 15 April, 24 April, 1 May, 5 May, and 8 May 1783.

29. *General Advertiser*, 14 February 1784.

30. *General Advertiser*, 27 March 1782.

31. Lyceum, Strand's Lower Theatre; boxes 4s. Pit 2s. (Glendinning Printer: [1 February?] 1805). British Library, L.R. 301.h.3 (fol. 13AA).

32. Terry Castle traces the "displaced supernaturalism" that characterizes post-enlightenment culture in its demystification of the occult: see especially

"Phantasmagoria and the Metaphorics of Modern Reverie," in *The Female Thermometer: Eighteenth-Century Culture and the Invention of the Uncanny* (New York and Oxford: Oxford University Press, 1995), 140–67, esp. 143–44.

33. Daniel Lysons's *Collectanea:* vol. 4 (fol. 40): 30 May 1782; Richard Altick, *The Shows of London* (Cambridge, Mass.: Belknap Press, 1978), 44; Terry Castle, *Masquerade and Civilization: The Carnivalesque in Eighteenth-Century English Culture and Fiction* (Stanford: Stanford University Press, 1986).

34. *. A True Relation . . .* (London?: n.d.). British Library, c. 122. I. 5 (fol. 27).

35. See Marie-Hélène Huet, *Monstrous Imagination* (Cambridge, Mass. and London: Harvard University Press, 1993), 6; Evelleen Richards, "A Political Anatomy of Monsters, Hopeful and Otherwise: Teratology, Transcendentalism, and Evolutionary Theorizing," *Isis* 85, no. 3 (September 1994): 377–411; Katharine Park and Lorraine J. Daston, "Unnatural Conceptions: The Study of Monsters in Sixteenth- and Seventeenth-Century France and England," *Past and Present* 92 (1981): 21–54.

36. See *Inventing Human Science: Eighteenth-Century Domains*, ed. Christopher Fox, Roy Porter, and Robert Wokler (Berkeley, Los Angeles, London: University of California Press, 1995), esp. Wokler's "Anthropology and Conjectural History," 31–52. Roger Chartier, among others, has explicated the two-way dissemination of "high" and "low" culture, in *The Order of Books: Readers, Authors, and Libraries in Europe between the Fourteenth and the Eighteenth Centuries*, trans. Lydia G. Cochrane (Cambridge: Polity Press, 1994). I explore the cross-pollination of empirical theory and popular culture in my "Reading Faces: Physiognomy and Epistemology in Late Eighteenth-Century Sentimental Novels," *Studies in Philology* 92, no. 3 (summer 1995): 311–28.

37. Dudley Wilson, *Signs and Portents: Monstrous Births from the Middle Ages to the Renaissance* (London and New York: Routledge, 1993). See Dennis Todd, *Imagining Monsters: Miscreations of the Self in Eighteenth-Century England* (Chicago: University of Chicago Press, 1995); and Thomas, *Religion and the Decline of Magic*.

38. Early periodicals, notably John Dunton's *Athenian Gazette* (1691–1697) and its successors, had used scientific inquiry for social issues; the two areas of analysis had long overlapped in the press. Wonder, then and now, dictates, and indeed can compromise, the analytic impulse itself; see Donna J. Hathaway, *Simians, Cyborgs, and Women: The Reinvention of Nature* (London: Free Association Books, 1991); Robert Bogdan, *Freak Show: Presenting Human Oddities for Amusement and Profit* (Chicago: University of Chicago Press, 1988).

39. See Michel Foucault, *Madness and Civilization: A History of Insanity in the Age of Reason*, trans. Richard Howard (New York: Vintage, 1985); and *Discipline and Punish: The Birth of the Prison*, trans. Alan Sheridan (New York: Random House, 1979). For analyses of fin de siècle anxiety, see Ronald Paulson, *Representations of Revolution, 1789–1820* (New Haven and London: Yale University Press, 1983); and Marilyn Butler, *Romantics, Rebels and Reactionaries: English Literature and Its Background, 1760–1830* (Oxford: Oxford University Press, 1981).

40. See my chapter "Making a Monster: Socializing Sexuality and the Monster of 1790," in *"Defects": Engendering the Modern Body*, eds. Felicity Nussbaum

and Helen Deutsch (Ann Arbor: University of Michigan Press, 2000), 127–53. In "Frekes, Monsters, and the Ladies: Attitudes to Female Sexuality in the 1790s," Darryl Jones mentions this episode in his general analysis of the "intensification of the discourse surrounding sexuality in general, and female sexuality and sexual deviancy in particular," in *Literature and History* 4, no. 2 (autumn 1995): 1–24, esp. 1–3.

41. Elizabeth Kraft, "Anna Letitia Barbauld's 'The Washing-Day' and the Montgolfier Balloon," *Literature and History*, 3d series, 4, no. 2 (autumn 1995): 27 n. 11, quoted from the postscript to *London Magazine*, n.s., 1 (December 1783): 567; and n. 13, quoted from "An Account of the Aerostatical Ball Which has Lately Been Made to Ascend Up into the Air at Paris, and the Principles on which it is Constructed; Together with a Short History of the Discoveries that have led to Them," *The London Magazine*, n.s., 1 (September 1783): 264. See also Robert Beavan, *The History of the Balloon, From Its Discovery to the Present Time* (London: M'Gowan and Co., 1839), esp. 8.

42. *"The Balloon, or Aerostatic Spy.* A Novel, containing a Series of Adventures of an Aerial Traveller; Including a variety of HISTORIES and CHARACTERS IN REAL LIFE," 2 vols. (London: W. Lane, 1786), vi–v.

43. Linda Colley, *Britons: Forging the Nation, 1707–1837* (New Haven and London: Yale University Press, 1992), 284–86.

44. C. H. Gibbs-Smith, *Balloons*, with intro. and notes (London: Ariel Press, 1956), ix.

45. See the anonymous poem *Air-Balloon, or Blanchard's Triumphal Entry in to the Etherial World* (London, 1 shilling), st. 16, lines 236–43. British Library, 11630.ee.6

46. See *Globe Arèostatique que l'on se propose d'enlever* (Paris: M. de Nouvautes [fol. 11]); *Rearque dur le* BALON AREOSTATIQUE DE M. BLANCHARD *comme it etoit pro-jettè* (fol. 12); also *Mr. Lunardi's Aerial Excursion With his* BALOON. *On Sept. 15, 1784,* showing four stages of balloon ascent (printed and sold by C. Fourdrinier, 28 September 1784 [fol. 29T]); also, for one example, *British Balloon,* Count Zambeccari's advertisement, 17 September 1784 (fol. 39). See also *A Professor Filling, & Explaining to an Audience, the Nature of a Baloon* [sic] (London: J. Basire, no. 16 St. John's Lane, Clerkenwell, 29 January 1784 [fol. 46 B]).

47. *The Air Balloon: Or a Treatise on The Aerostatic Globe, Lately invented by The celebrated Mons. Montgolfier of Paris* (London: G. Kearsley, 1783), 3–4. See *Considèrations sur le Globe Aèrostatique, par M. D**** (Paris: Chez Le Jay . . . et chez les Marchands de Nouveautès, 1783).

48. James Sadler, *Balloon: An Authentic Narrative of the Aerial Voyage of Mr. Sadler* (Dublin: W. H. Tyrell, 1812), 20–22.

49. 16 December 1784 (fol. 48c).

50. *Constructing of Air Balloons for the Grand Monarque* (S. Fores, no. 3 Piccadilly, 2 March 1784 [fol. 6]).

51. See "The Tower and Preparation for the Fire Works, with the Balloon, a print published and sold 14 August 1814 by Edward Orme" (J. H. Clark, del.; M. Debourg, sculpt., 14 August 1814); L.R. 301.h.11 (fol. 39); and also the colored

print from 1 August 1814; L.H. 301.h. (fol. 40). See as well "The Fortress (which inclosed the Grand Pavillion,) in the Green Park, with the ascent of the Balloon" (London: Thomas Pulser, Surrey side of West Bridge, 12 August 1814 [fol. 31]); and also the page glued with jubilee souvenirs (fol. 49, etc.).

52. *"Le Moment D'Hilaritè Universelle* ou le Triomphe de Mssrs. Charles and Robert au Jardin des Thuileries le 1 er. Xbre, 1783" (J. HE. invenit et delineavit, H. G. Bertaux, sculpt., 2 November 1783; se vend chez M. le Noir au Louvre, Voyès le Journal du Paris du 2 Xbre [fol. 8]).

53. See *"New Areostatic Machine* Being 65 Feet High and 120 in Circumference, in which M. Le Chev. de Moret will go up the 10th of Augt. 1784" (W. Skelton, no. 29 Portland Street, 1784 [fol. 9]); also the advertisement *Pantheon* (J. P. Coghlan, Duke-street [fol. 22b]); Count Zambeccari's advertisement *Ascends Tomorrow* (3 May 1785 [fol. 63T]). Blanchard, however, charged half guinea tickets as well as five shilling ones (11 October 1784 [fol. 63b]).

54. *"Expérience de la Machine Aréostatique* de Mrs. [i.e., Monsieur] Montgolfier, d'Anonai en Vivarais. Reppeteé à Paris le 27 Aoust 1783, au Champ de Mars, avec un Balon de Taffetas enduit de Gomme, élastique, de 36. Pieds 6 pouces de Circonférence. Ce Balon plein d'air Inflamable a été éxécuté par Mrs., Robert, en vertu d'une Souscription Nationale, sous la direction de Mr. Faujas d Saint Fond" (Se vend à Paris, chez La Noir Mr. d Estampes au Louvre et rue du Coq. Ste. Honorè; n.d. [1783?]; fol. 1). See also "Representation of the Air Baloon of Mr. Montgolfier, in the Field of Mars near Paris," which depicts a more formal but equally diminutive crowd (London: John Wallis, 26 November 1783 [fol. 2]). See also *"A Monsieur de Faujaci*[?] de St. Fond, de Plusieurs Accadémies" (Paris: 19 September 1783), which shows the ascension over a vast mass of people in Versailles and describes the ascension as "majestic"(fol. 4); and *Experience du Globe Aèrostatique de M. M. Charles et Robert* over the Chateau de Tuileries (1 November 1783 [fol. 7]). British Library, L.R. 301.h.3 (fol. 4).

55. *The Balloon* (London: Religious Tract Society, 1799), 1–2. British Library, 863.a.17 (fol. 1).

56. *"Symposia; or Table Talk* In the Month of September, 1784. Being a rhapsodical Hodge-podge, containing, among other Things, BALLOON INTELLIGENCE for the Years 1785, 1786, and 1787" (London: for the author, [1787]), xxii.

57. *The Grand English Air Balloon* (H. Humphreys, 3 Bedford Court, Covent Garden, 20 October 1784 [fol. 27]); "Sig. L-N-RD-'s Grand TRIUMPHANT ENTRY into Tottenham Court Road taken on the spot May 13. 1785, publ. R. Haraden, no. 85 Totten Ct. Road" (fol. 35b).

58. This device was widely advertised in the newspapers; see *The World* 26 and 28 June 1787. See also the idealized portrait of a fair-headed Lunardi rowing selflessly across the river in *Representation of Mr. Lunardi making an Experiment on the Thames, of his Invention to save persons from drowning* (London: I. Acret, no. 44 Wardour St., 4 June 1787 [fol. 36]).

59. Beavan, *The History of the Balloon*, 16–17.

60. Elizabeth Inchbald, *The Mogul Tale; or The Descent of the Balloon*. A Farce. Theatre-Royal, Smocke-Alley (London: for the booksellers, 1788), act 1, p. 3.

61. Kraft, "Anna Letitia," esp. 33–36. "The Lady's Balloon, or, Female Aerial Traveller" records her ascent on Tuesday, 3 May 1785, which was advertised as "British Aerial Female Heroism" (fols. 60A, 63T).

62. Mrs. Sage, *A Letter . . . to a Female Friend* (London: for the writer, [1785]), 14, 20. This account contradicts Angela D. Jones's argument that eighteenth-century women's travelogues show women's immersion in daily experiences and sociability, in "Romantic Women Travel Writers and the Representation of Everyday Experience," in *Women's Studies* 26, no. 5 (1997): 499.

63. *The Adventures of an Air Balloon*, 5th ed. (London: H. Hogge, 1780).

64. "*The Modern Atalantis: or, the* DEVIL *in an* AIR BALLOON, containing the characters and secret Memoirs of the most conspicuous Persons of High Quality, of Both Sexes, in the Island of Libertusia" (London: G. Kearsley, 1784), 3.

65. "Chevalier Humgruffier and the Marquis de Gull making an excursion to the Moon in their new Aerial Vehicle" (London: J. Basire, St. John's Lane, Clerkenwell, 20 February 1784).

66. See Aratus [pseud.], "*A Voyage to the Moon* Strongly Recommended to All Lovers of Real Freedom" (London: for the author and sold by James Ridgway et al., 1793), esp. 3; also *The Grand Air Balloon* (printed and sold for Carington Bowels; no. 69 St. Paul's Church-Yard, 16 October 1784 [fols. 14t, 14b]).

67. Mary Alcock, "The Air Balloon; or, Flying Mortal" (London: E. Macklew, 1784).

68. See also R. S. Medley's ironic "The Air Balloon Spiritualized. In a Poetical Letter to his Son" (London: L. I. Higham, 1823), esp. 2, lines 5–12.

69. See Malcolm Gaskill's account of the use of supernatural narratives in murder trials, in "Reporting Murder: Fiction in the Archives in Early Modern England," *Social History* 23, no. 1 (January 1998): 1–30.

70. Godwin also read other contemporary and older matter, including Horace Walpole's tragedy *The Mysterious Mother;* Swift's *Gulliver's Travels;* Burke's *A Philosophical Enquiry into . . . the Sublime;* and novels by, notably, Smollett and Richardson. See Vijay Mishra, *The Gothic Sublime* (New York: State University of New York Press, 1994), 130.

71. Ronald Paulson differentiates between "Monk" Lewis's depiction of the revolutionary experience itself and Radcliffe's depiction of the spectator of revolution, in *Representations of Revolution*, 227.

72. As Vijay Mishra explains at length, the historical similarity between the 1790s and the 1980s suggests a parallel, postmodern mood; see *The Gothic Sublime*, and also Jean-François Lyotard, *The Postmodern Condition: A Report on Knowledge*, trans. Geoff Bennington and Brian Massumi, foreword by Fredric Jameson (Manchester: Manchester University Press, 1986).

73. Lucy Newlyn, "'Questionable Shape': The Aesthetics of Indeterminacy," in *Questioning Romanticism*, ed. John Beer (Baltimore and London: Johns Hopkins University Press, 1995), 209–33; Gary Kelly, *The English Jacobin Novel, 1780–1805* (Oxford: Clarendon Press, 1976), 189; Paulson, *Representations of Revolution*, 215–47. Also see Chris Jones, *Radical Sensibility: Literature and Ideas in the 1790s* (London and New York: Routledge, 1993), 101–2; Marilyn Butler, *Jane Austen*

and the War of Ideas (Oxford: Clarendon Press, 1975), esp. 57–87; Pamela Clemit, *The Godwinian Novel: The Rational Fictions of Godwin, Brockden Brown, Mary Shelley* (Oxford: Clarendon Press, 1993), 41.

74. In the original ending, Caleb does go mad; Godwin claimed that he wrote this ending before composing the rest of the tale, even though he changed it before publication.

75. Walter E. Houghton Jr., "The English Virtuoso in the Seventeenth Century," pts. 1 and 2, *Journal of the History of Ideas*, vol. 3 (1942): 51–73; vol. 4 (1942): 190–219.

76. Margaret A. Doody likens the enclosed world of Montoni's castle to the repressed sexual world of women in patriarchal society, in the seminal "Deserts, Ruins, and Troubled Waters: Female Dreams in Fiction and the Development of the Gothic Novel," *Genre* 10 (1977): 529–72; see also Robert Miles's argument that Emily is an actively desiring agent whose "secretive quest," aroused by curiosity and terror, is sexuality, in *Ann Radcliffe: The Great Enchantress* (Manchester and New York: Manchester University Press, 1995), 129–48. In *Fictions of Modesty: Women and Courtship in the English Novel* (Chicago: University of Chicago Press, 1984), Ruth Bernard Yeazell analyzes the novel's naturalization of female modesty as a way to negotiate the sex's original immodesty. See also Deborah D. Rogers' introduction to *The Critical Response to Ann Radcliffe* (Westport, Conn. and London: Greenwood Press, 1994), xxiii–iv, xxxvii–xxx. Claudia L. Johnson points out the contemporary crisis in masculinity, in *Equivocal Beings: Politics, Gender, and Sentimentality in the 1790s: Wollstonecraft, Radcliffe, Burney, Austen* (Chicago: University of Chicago Press, 1995), esp. 1–19.

77. See Coral Ann Howells, "The Pleasure of the Woman's Text: Ann Radcliffe's Subtle Transgressions in *The Mysteries of Udolpho* and *The Italian*," in *Gothic Fictions: Prohibition/Transgression*, ed. Kenneth W. Graham (New York: AMS Press, 1989), which argues that Radcliffe counterpoises conventional images of womanhood and transgressive images of women's sexuality, evil, independence, and abandonment (151–62). David H. Richter argues that the Gothic offers readers immersion in a fantasy world, in *The Progress of Romance: Literary Historiography and the Gothic Novel* (Columbus: Ohio State University Press, 1996), 112–18; also see Terry Castle, "The Spectralization of the Other in *The Mysteries of Udolpho*," in *The New Eighteenth Century: Theory, Politics, English Literature*, ed. Felicity Nussbaum and Laura Brown (London: Methuen, 1987): 231–53.

78. Bette B. Roberts suggests that Austen satirizes Radcliffe for violations of generic realism, not for her aesthetic control, in "The Horrid Novels: The Mysteries of Udolpho and *Northanger Abbey*," in *Gothic Fictions: Prohibition/Transgression*, ed. Kenneth W. Graham (New York: AMS Press, 1989), 89–112. Jacqueline Howard has recently argued that in different ways, both novels unsettle patriarchal power and languages representing women as weak and supporting male contempt for female creative authorship, in *Reading Gothic Fiction: A Bakhtinian Approach* (Oxford: Clarendon Press, 1994), 106–82, esp. 179–81.

79. For discussions of this ambiguity, see Clemit, *The Godwinian Novel*, 39, and Rogers, "introduction."

80. In *Ann Radcliffe*, Robert Miles argues that Emily's desire makes her an active subject; see chap. 7, "The Hermeneutics of Reading: *The Mysteries of Udolpho*," 129–48.

81. Castle, "The Spectralization of the Other," 231–53.

82. William Godwin, *Caleb Williams*, ed., with intro., David McCracken (New York and London: Norton, 1977), 119; all citations refer to this edition unless otherwise noted.

83. Jean Starobinski, *L'Invention de la Liberté, 1700–1789* (Geneva: Skira, 1987).

84. See Butler, *Romantics, Rebels, and Reactionaries;* James P. Carson, "Enlightenment, Popular Culture, and Gothic Fiction," in *The Cambridge Companion to the Eighteenth-Century Novel*, ed. John Richetti (Cambridge: Cambridge University Press, 1996), 271.

85. Quoted from Godwin's 1831 preface to *Caleb Williams*, in Clemit, *The Godwinian Novel*, 47.

86. *Caleb Williams*, vol. 2 in Fleetwood's *Standard Novels* (London, 1832), 340.

87. For an account of the female audiences of the 1790s and of the influence of Radcliffe's Gothics, see Stuart Curran, "Women Readers, Women Writers," in *The Cambridge Companion to British Romanticism*, ed. Stuart Curran (Cambridge: Cambridge University Press, 1993), 177–95, esp. 187–88. In *The Progress of Romance*, David H. Richter argues that Radcliffe's novels "presume an identification between the reader and the focalizing character that goes well beyond" earlier fiction (117).

88. See Barbara M. Benedict, "Literary Miscellanies: The Cultural Mediation of Fragmented Feeling," *ELH* 57, no. 2 (summer 1990): 407–30.

89. M. M. Bakhtin, *The Dialogic Imagination*, ed. Michael Holquist; trans. Caryl Emerson and Michael Holquist (Austin: University of Texas Press, 1981); also J. Paul Hunter, *Before Novels: The Cultural Contexts of Eighteenth-Century Fiction* (New York and London: Norton, 1990).

90. Ann Radcliffe, *The Mysteries of Udolpho*, ed., with intro., Bonomy Dobrée (Oxford and New York: Oxford University Press, 1970), 15.

91. See Patricia Yaeger, "Toward a Female Sublime," in *Gender and Theory: Dialogues on Feminist Criticism*, ed. Linda Kauffman (Oxford: Basil Blackwell, 1989), 191–212.

92. Robert Kiely observes that Caleb's curiosity is "more like a physical hunger than a quality of rational intellect," in *The Romantic Novel in England* (Cambridge, Mass.: Harvard University Press, 1972), 90.

93. Godwin, *Caleb Williams*, 337. This account formed part of the preface to Fleetwood's *Standard Novels* edition of 1832 and was therefore written and published well after Mary Shelley's *Frankenstein* (1818), which similarly focuses on the evils of (scientific) curiosity.

94. Godwin himself, a Calvinist clergyman who lost his faith and left his congregation to write in London, must have been well acquainted not only with the biblical account of Caleb, but also with the connotations of the story. For an ac-

count of *Caleb Williams* as a religious allegory, see Kelly, *The English Jacobin Novel*, 208. The "logic of internalized conscience" characteristic of Godwin's novel marks his debt to religious structures of meaning: see Victor Sage, *Horror Fiction in the Protestant Tradition* (New York: St. Martin's Press, 1988), 90.

95. Kiely, *The Romantic Novel in England*, 93; James Thomson, "Surveillance in William Godwin's *Caleb Williams*," in *Gothic Fictions: Prohibition/Transgression*, ed. Kenneth W. Graham (New York: AMS Press, 1989), 173–98.

96. In his introduction to *Gothic Fictions: Prohibition/Transgression*, Kenneth W. Graham allows Gothic novels each only one of these stances (New York: AMS Press, 1989).

97. Mary Shelley, *Frankenstein: The 1818 Text*, ed. J. Paul Hunter, foreword by Jack Stillinger (New York and London: W. W. Norton, 1996), 13. Unless otherwise indicated, all citations refer to this edition.

98. See Anne K. Mellor's argument in *Mary Shelley: Her Life, Her Fiction, Her Monsters* (New York and London: Methuen Press, 1988) that the book condemns all revolution. Also see Mary Poovey's claim that the book attacks masculine egotism, in "My Hideous Progeny: Mary Shelley and the Feminization of Romanticism," *Publications of the Modern Language Associaton* 95 (1980): 332–47; see as well, Chris Baldick, *In Frankenstein's Shadow: Myth, Montrosity, and Nineteenth-Century Writing* (Oxford: Oxford University Press, 1987), 10–29.

99. Fred Botting, "*Frankenstein*'s French Revolutions—The Dangerous Necessity of Monsters," *Literature and Society*, 2d ser., 1, no. 2 (autumn 1990), 22–41, esp. 29. Botting suggests that Shelley is interrogating the contemporary prejudice, articulated most famously by Burke, that France bred monsters, whereas England identified and excluded them.

100. James A. Heffernan, "Looking at the Monster: *Frankenstein* and Film," *Critical Inquiry* 24, no. 1 (autumn 1997): 133–58.

101. This line is omitted from the Norton edition; see Mary Shelley, *Frankenstein*, intro. Diane Johnson (New York: Bantam Books, 1991), 33; also, *Frankenstein*, ed., with intro., Maurice Hindle (Harmondsworth, Middlesex: Penguin Classics, 1985), 96.

102. Foucault, *Madness and Civilization*.

103. Peter Brooks suggests that representation, specifically visual representation, symbolized by the parody of Narcissus, is itself the monster, in "What Is a Monster? (According to *Frankenstein*)," in *Body Work: Objects of Desire in Modern Narrative* (Cambridge, Mass.: Harvard University Press, 1993), 199–220, esp. 199–206. As a psychoanalyst, Brooks interprets Frankenstein's "intense curiosity for forbidden knowledge" as "epistemophilia" fixating on his mother's reproductive body, but this reading ignores the historical specificity of Shelley's scientific narrativization of male curiosity (216). See Regina B. Oost's argument that the Shelleys' opportunistic preface deliberately obscures the text's political and economic motives, in "Marketing *Frankenstein*: The Shelleys' Enigmatic Preface," *English Language Notes* 35, no. 1 (September 1997), 26–35.

104. These words are omitted from the Norton edition: see Shelley, *Frankenstein*, intro. Diane Johnson Books (New York: Bantam Books, 1991), 22, 23.

105. Trent A. Mitchell notes the anxiety surrounding the role of audiences in legitimizing science, in "The Politics of Experiment in the Eighteenth Century: The Pursuit of Audience and the Manipulation of Consensus in the Debate over Lightning Rods," *Eighteenth-Century Studies* 31, no. 3 (spring 1998): 307–31, esp. 325.

CONCLUSION

1. Charles Mackay's *Extraordinary Popular Delusions and the Madness of Crowds* (New York: Farrar, Straus, and Giroux, 1932) is the classic example.

2. John Brewer and Roy Porter, eds., *Consumption and the World of Goods* (New York: Routledge, 1993).

3. Exploring the overlap of "public" and "private" spheres, Helen Berry proves that the periodical engaged a female audience and correspondents and was read in various kinds of reading spaces, in "'Nice and Curious Questions': Coffee Houses and the Representation of Women in John Dunton's *Athenian Mercury*," *The Seventeenth Century* 17, no. 2 (autumn 1997): 257–76.

4. John R. Clark, *Form and Frenzy in Swift's "Tale of a Tub"* (Ithaca: Cornell University Press, 1970), 38.

5. Michael Hunter, *Science and the Shape of Orthodoxy: Studies of Intellectual Change in Late Seventeenth-Century Britain* (Woodbridge: The Boydell Press, 1995), 242–44.

6. Elizabeth Haywood, *Love in Excess*, ed. David Oakleaf (Peterborough, Ontario: Broadview, 1994), 3. The fifth edition appeared in *The Collected Works of Eliza Haywood*; see *A Dictionary of British and American Women Writers, 1660–1800*, ed. Janet Todd (Totowa, N.J.: Rowman and Littlefield, 1987), 157.

7. William Granger, *The New and Original and Complete WONDERFUL MUSEUM and Magazine Extraordinary* (London, 1803); Robin Ikegami, *Femmes-Hommes*, She-Bishops, and Hyenas in Petticoats: Women Reformers and Gender Treason, 1789–1830," *Women's Studies* 26, no. 2 (1997): 223–39.

8. Katharine Eisaman Maus, "Proof and Consequences: Inwardness and Its Exposure in the English Renaissance," *Representations* 32 (spring 1991): 39.

9. See Eve Kosofsky Sedgwick, *The Epistemology of the Closet* (Berkeley: University of California Press, 1990). See also Tzvetan Todorov's *The Fantastic: A Structural Approach to a Literary Genre*, trans. Richard Howard (Cleveland: Case Western Reserve, 1973); and Sigmund Freud, "The Uncanny," in the *Standard Edition of the Complete Psychological Works of Sigmund Freud*, 24 vols., trans. and ed. James Strachey (London: Hogarth Press, 1953–1974), 17:219–56.

10. See Roy Porter, *The Greatest Benefit to Mankind: A Medical History of Humanity* (New York and London: W. W. Norton, 1997), for an account of the nineteenth-century increases in professional specialties and varieties of approach to medical problems

11. These qualities also mark *Alice in Wonderland*, according to John Goldthwaite, who traces the beginning of make-believe to the 1690s: see *The Natural His-*

tory of Make-Believe: A Guide to the Principal Works of Britain, Europe, and America (New York and Oxford: Oxford University Press, 1996), 125–26, 11.

12. Peter Vandergoose, *"Gulliver and Munchaussen Outdone. A Truth to Try the Patience of* A Stoick" (London: Jordan and Maxwell, 1807).

13. *Harlequin Gulliver; or, the Flying Island* (London: John Miller, 1817).

14. George Colman, *"Blue Beard: A Dramatick Romance*; with Prefatory Remarks. The only edition existing which is faithfully marked with the stage business, and stage directions . . . By W. Oxberry, Comedian" (London: W. Simpkin and R. Marshall, 1823), iii.

15. See George Daniel Lewis, *The Castle Spectre: A Dramatic Romance in Five Acts* (London: John Cumberland, [1800?]). The comment I refer to in the text is in a copy of the play that was "Printed from the Acting Copy, With Remarks, Biographical and Critical, by DBG. Embellished with a Fine Wood Engraving by Mr. Bonner, from a Drawing taken in the Theatre by Mr. R. Cruickshank," 4th ed. (London: J. Bell, 1797, first performance, 14 December 1797). The introduction defends interest in the supernatural as human nature, in "Remarks" (5).

16. When Colman used the play for the Christmas Harlequin in 1798 at Drury Lane, many believed that the actor Michael Kelly who played Selim had plagiarized it from the French performance, but Colman's preface denies this.

17. See also the melodramatic New York version: George Colman, *Blue Beard; or, Female Curiosity . . . As Altered for the New York Theatre*, with additional songs by W. Dunlap, Esq. (New York: E. B. Clayton, 1830).

18. Henry James Byron, *Blue Beard: From a New Point of Hue* (London and New York: Samuel French, 1860).

19. John Bowring's *Minor Morals for Young People*, embellished with engravings by George Cruikshank and William Heath, 3 vols. (London: Whittaker and Co., 1834–39): 1:196.

20. Margaret Drabble, *A Natural Curiosity* (New York: Penguin, 1989), 1, 51.

21. Allen Kurzweil, *A Case of Curiosities* (New York: Harcourt Brace Jovanovich Publ., 1992), vii.

22. See Jean-François Lyotard, "Defining the Postmodern," in *Postmodernism ICA Documents*, ed. Lisa Appignanesi (London: Free Association Books, 1989).

23. Joan De Luce, *Curiosity: A Novel*, 3 vols. (London: A. K. Newman and Co., 1822), epigraph.

24. Anne Rowe, *Curiosity Killed a Cat* (London: John Gifford Ltd., 1945), 224.

INDEX

Locators in italics refer to pages with illustrations.

Adams, Thomas, 73
Addison, Joseph, 56, 102–3
Adventures of an Air Balloon (1780), 225
advertising: of ballooning, 219, 221; of marvels, 178–79, 247; of performers, 212, 215; of popular medicine, 40–41; and transgression, 246
alchemy, 47
Alcock, Mary, 226
Altick, Richard, 261n.23, 275n.68, 294n.16
ambition, 109, 115–16, 190, 200, 228; and science, 44–45, 68; and transgression, 245–54; of women, 134
animals: in circus, 22, 206–8, *211*, 213–14
antiquities, 202
Arabian Nights, The, 133, 164
Arbuthnot, John. *See* Scriblerians
archaeology, 143
Arnold, Matthew, 188, 196, 249
art: and collecting, 177–78, 202; and curiosities, 41, 72–73
Ashmole, Elias, 47
Astell, Mary, 275n.67
Astley, Philip, 206–10
atheism, as skepticism, 30, 56
Aubrey, John, 41–42, 46
Augustine, Saint, 3
Austen, Jane: *Northanger Abbey,* 126, 137–38, 232
Auster, Paul, 252
authenticity, and collecting, 202–3
autographs, 17

Bacon, Francis, 19
Baine, Rodney M., 278n.102
Ballaster, Ros, 141
Balloon, The (1799), 221–22, 226
Balloon, or Aerostatic Spy, The (1786), 218, 225
ballooning, 22, 205, *211*, 214, 217, *219*, 227; and class, 222–23; and nationalism, 218, 220; and performance, 221–22; satirized, 223–28; and science, 218, 220,

222–23, 228; as social disruption, 221–22; as spectacle, 221–22, 228; and the sublime, 225–26; and voyeurism, 225

Barbauld, Anna Letitia, 225
Bartholomew Fair, 96–97
Bartholomew Fair (1708/11), 97
Beardsley, Aubrey, 271n.22
Beaumont, Joseph, 281n.12
Beckford, William: *Vathek,* 21, 162, 175–77
Beffin, Sarah, 9, 215
Behn, Aphra, 20–21; *Amorous Prince, or, The Curious Husband,* 122–23; *The Curious Impertinent,* 123–24; *The Emperor of the Moon,* 59–63, 86; *Oroonoko,* 129
Bender, John, 278n.95
Benhamou, Paul, 286n.63
Bennett, Tony, 9–10, 301n.4
Bentley, R., 136
Bermingham, Ann, 280n.4, 293n.4
Bernardo, E. S., 36
Berry, Helen, 283n.33, 310n.3
Bertelsen, Lance, 292n.2
Bettelheim, Bruno, 294n.15
Bewick, Thomas, 215
Bickham, George: *Deliciae Britannicae,* 181
biography, 17; of freaks, 43
birth: and monstrosity, 74, 125
Blair, Robert: *The Grave,* 161
Blanchard, Jean-Pierre, 226
Bluebeard (folk tale), 132–34, 204, 234, 249–50
Blue-Beard; or, Female Curiosity! (Colman), 86, 132–33
body: commodification of, 11, 73–74, 76–77; as curiosity, 81, 85, 165; in dressing room poetry, 81–89
Bogdan, Robert, 11, 257n.22
book trade: and journalism, 92–93, 110; and poetry, 74. *See also* print culture
Boruwlaski, Count, 215
Botting, Fred, 238, 309n.99
Bottle Conjuror, 20, 160, 164–66, 206

value, 4, 28, 181, 189, 245; and classification, 202–3; and connoisseurship, 191;
in consumer society, 77; and usury, 195
Van Helden, Albert, 264n.54
Van Lennep, William, 281n.14
Vandergoose, Peter: *Gulliver and Munchaussen Outdone*, 249
virtuoso: as charlatan, 45–46, 51; collector
as, 41, 95, 182–83; in Gothic novel, 205;
megalomania of, 65; as monstrous, 51;
Pope as, 74–75; satirized, 46–51, 189; as
self-interested, 44; and social class, 50,
205. *See also* connoisseur; male curiosity
Voss, Hansi Georg, 291n.118
voyeurism, 122, 151; and ballooning, 225.
See also seeing

Wallis, John, 45
Walpole, Horace: *The Castle of Otranto*, 21,
162, 173, 175
Ward, Ned: *The London Spy*, 93–96, 183
Warner, Marina, 282n.24
Warner, William B., 284n.41
Watt, Ian, 277n.87, 287n.73
Weinberger, Jerry, 259n.43
Wells, Susannah, 166, 170
Williams, Renwick, 216–17, 229, 243–44
Wilmot, John, Earl of Rochester, 58
Wilson, Dudley, 216
witchcraft: and empiricism, 54, 56; and
transgression, 246, 248; trials, 43, 54–
55. *See also* occult
Wollstonecraft, Mary, 231
women: as collectibles, 123, 142; curiosity

of (*see* female curiosity); education of,
126–27, 231; as mothers, 125–26, 231;
and the novel, 137–39; and the occult,
155, 231; power of, 137; satirized,
121–27; sentimentalized, 136, 152; sexuality of, 124, 126–27, 137, 151–54, 231,
250; as writers, 119, 126, 129, 231
Wonder in Staffordshire, A (1661), 179
*Wonder of Wonders, or Strange News from
Newton in Yorkshire, The* (1675), 38–39,
42, 75
"Wonder of Wonders, or the Dumb Maid
of Wapping Restor'd to her Speech
again, The" (1694), 42–43
Wonder of Surry, The (1756), 179
*Wonder upon Wonder, or Cocoa Tree's answer to
the Surry Oak* (1756), 179
wonders, 5, 29–31, 38–39, 173, 186; in countryside, 178–80, 202; exhibitions of,
202; and science, 206, 212, 216. *See also*
marvels
World of Wonders, The, 29–31, 47, 50, 55
Wren, M. K.: *Curiosity Didn't Kill the Cat*,
253
Wycherley, William: *The Country Wife*,
124–25

X-Files, The, 253

Yearsley, Ann, 288n.81
Yeazell, Ruth Bernard, 307n.76

Zimmerman, Hans-Joachim, 259n.1
Zipes, Jack, 297n.41